VIETNAM UNDER COMMUNISM, 1975–1982

VIETNAM UNDER COMMUNISM, 1975–1982

NGUYEN VAN CANH

with Earle Cooper

Foreword by Robert A. Scalapino

Hoover Institution Press

Stanford University, Stanford, California

Photographs 1–5 courtesy of *Der Spiegel* from "Wir sterben und haben keinen Sarg," August 8, 1981.

Photographs 6, 10, and 11 courtesy of Sophia University, Socio-Economic Institute, Asian Relations Center, *Boat People: Today's "Untouchables"* (Tokyo, 1978).

Photographs 7, 8, and 9 by Maekawa Makoto, courtesy of Sophia University, Socio-Economic Institute, Asian Relations Center, *Refugees: The Cry of the Indochinese* (Tokyo, 1980).

Hoover Press Publication 285

First printing, 1983. First paperback printing, 1985.
Manufactured in the United States of America
88 87 86 85 9 8 7 6 5 4 3

Library of Congress Cataloging in Publication Data
Nguyen, Van Canh, 1936–
Vietnam under Communism, 1975–1982.

Bibliography: p.
Includes index.
1. Vietnam—History—1975– . 2. Communism—Vietnam. I. Cooper, Earle. II. Title.
DS559.912.N39 1983 959.704'4 83-10754
ISBN 0-8179-7851-8
ISBN 0-8179-7852-6 (pbk.)

Design by P. Kelley Baker

To my parents

Contents

Foreword

Nguyen Van Canh first became known to me in the course of a brief visit to Saigon in the late 1960s. He was later to become a professor in the law school of Saigon University. I was interested in his research because he had written his doctorate on the Vietnamese communist movement, a subject in which I was greatly interested as a student of comparative communism.

Spending some time with Canh, I was impressed both with his intellect and his integrity. He and his family lived in very humble circumstances. Indeed, for those of us accustomed to the American way of life, his living conditions fell well below the poverty line. But his interest in books, his manner of speech, and his involvement in the problems of the day marked him as an intellectual, albeit one uprooted and tossed about by the turmoil that had engulfed his society.

There could be no doubt regarding his political commitments. He had long been an active member of the Dai Viet, Vietnam's staunchly anticommunist nationalist movement. Canh, like millions of other Vietnamese, was living proof that communism and nationalism were not synonymous, the views of certain Americans to the contrary. His love of Vietnam and his determination to fight against all forms of external domination, including that of communism (which he believed to be a creed foreign to basic Vietnamese values), have long constituted the core of his politics.

Above all, this work represents the perspective of a Vietnamese who was himself actively engaged in the political and intellectual life of his society. Hence, it stands apart from any book that might be produced by a disengaged foreign scholar. Canh's views quickly become apparent. If his criticism of the Communists is trenchant and sustained, he is also critical of the South Vietnamese governments headed by Diem and Thieu. Herein is reflected one of the supreme problems of those who opposed the Communists: the disunity of South Vietnam's noncommunists, who in actuality constituted the great majority of the citizenry. Canh is also critical of key aspects of American policy, most particularly what he regards as the fraudulent Paris Agreement of January 1973, which he believes paved the way for Hanoi's victory.

Fortunately for them, Canh and his family were able to escape from Vietnam at the time of the collapse. Otherwise, he would have certainly met the fate of many whom he describes in the pages that follow. It is not surprising that, on occasion, the searing emotional tragedies that form a part of Canh's life are reflected in the words that he chooses, the critique that he offers. In many instances, he is writing about the fate of friends and associates and recounting developments in a society of which he was a dedicated part.

Given the paucity of information on some subjects and the dispute regarding the facts on others, certain of Canh's interpretations and data will undoubtedly be subject to future revision, as he would be the first to acknowledge. Nonetheless, in this work, we have a comprehensive account of the structure and character of Vietnamese society under communism. In presenting this account, moreover, Nguyen Van Canh has turned to a variety of sources: official statements and documents from the leading officials and organs of the Democratic Republic of Vietnam; accounts provided by Western journalists allowed to visit the country; interpretations by longtime students of Vietnam; and by no means least, interviews with a variety of refugees.

Many of Canh's central themes are verified by other sources, and they present a grim picture indeed. I found particularly depressing his account of the treatment of the Catholics, Buddhists, Hoa Hao, and Cao Dai leaders. Some of us will remember the thesis that if we Americans would only "stop the killing," South Vietnam could have peace, with the South given a goodly measure of autonomy by the North. The National Liberation Front, we were told, would be allowed to establish a system separate from that being operated in Hanoi. A government of reconciliation would be created in Saigon, a united front into which all but the "diehard reactionaries" would be welcomed.

I am convinced that many Americans who repeatedly voiced these sentiments sincerely believed what they said. It is a tragedy that the skeptics among us were not able to convince a sizable portion of the journalist and intellectual communities otherwise. (In fairness, it should be noted that not a few noncommunist Vietnamese took a similar position.)

The facts can no longer be disputed, even though it is too late to help those tens of thousands who have died in prison cells, jungle camps, or at sea. Canh's detailed recital of what has happened to those who will not accept the new faith (or be accepted by it) should dispel any final doubts among individuals who have searched the heavens for signs of Vietnamese communist "humanism" or "liberalism." In the Democratic Republic of Vietnam, we have a system that employs all the right words and practices, but all the wrong deeds. It is a police state no less than those pioneered by Stalin, Hitler, and Kim Il-song. Indeed, I would suggest that in comparative terms the contemporary Soviet Union is considerably more benign, despite the stringent restrictions on civil liberties prevailing there.

Consider the fate of Thich Thien Minh and Thich Tri Quang, for example. Once, these men—and individuals like them—were heroes in certain American circles. I remember observing Tri Quang seated serenely in the park across from the presidential palace. Scores of Westerners, many of them journalists, gathered around to take his picture or ask him questions. His visage was frequently to be found on the front cover of our national newsmagazines, in our most prominent newspapers and on television.

I have not seen Thich Tri Quang's picture in the American media recently—nor any of his pungent quotes. He has become a nonperson insofar as American journalism is concerned—out of sight, out of mind. Would it not be appropriate for those who featured him so prominently just a few years ago to publish an all-black cover for their journals, with only his name displayed and the caption, "Whereabouts and health status unknown"?

One of the individuals with whom Canh deals briefly was a friend of mine—Tran Van Tuyen. I can recall talking with Tuyen on a number of occasions. Highly intelligent, French-educated, urbane, liberal, he never hesitated to speak his mind. The deficiencies of the Thieu government, incidentally, did not include the type of terrorism and suppression that now exists. Critics charging "dictatorship" never understood—or at least, were never prepared to admit—that in the midst of a brutal war, the Saigon government was vastly more tolerant of its opponents—except those committed to the communist cause—than might have been expected. In the years before 1975, it was never difficult to find vocal critics who were prepared to express their grievances quite openly. One of these was Tran Van Tuyen. He bent his knee to no man. But the Communists bent him, and he died in prison, or so his family was informed.

From the foregoing, it should not be thought that Canh's study deals wholly with personalities, communist or noncommunist, and their fate in the new era. Indeed, one of the admirable qualities of this work is the clarity with which the author sets forth the new political structure, from the national to the local level, and the highly useful materials that he presents on the recruitment and training of cadres. In reading these sections, one is reminded once again that a highly statist system spawns an enormous bureaucracy, which generally means too much paper and too little action. Permits, licenses, ration cards, travel permits—and long lines for food and other necessities—all of this is a familiar story to those who study or live in such systems. Contemporary Vietnam proves to be no exception to the rule.

Nor has corruption, the scourge of an earlier era, been eliminated. In certain respects, indeed, it seems to be even more pervasive, if of smaller monetary dimensions due to the current poverty of the society. On this score, incidentally, Canh's data are supported by the account of a compatriot, Nguyen Long, whose personal experiences between 1975 and 1979 have been set forth in *After Saigon Fell: Daily Life Under the Vietnamese Communists*. Both authors indicate that since cadres cannot live on their legal wages, corruption in one form or another is a necessity. This also applies to almost all urban residents, be they professional, clerical, or manual workers. Thus, a huge gray economic order exists, supplementing the official system and enabling it to survive.

We should not be surprised, moreover, to find that the New Vietnam is far from being a classless society, since writers like George Orwell and Milovan Djilas have previously acquainted us with the manner in which some become more equal than others. It is not merely a question of how one handles old enemies, although in the case of Vietnam that is a massive problem. Tens of thousands of individuals affiliated in one manner or another with the previous order remain in custody or under surveillance. It is also a question of how one handles new enemies, namely, those who were once regarded as friends or "neutrals," but subsequently became disenchanted. And above all, the new elite, namely, those who represent the party, especially at its apex, is no less privileged than the old elite. In material terms, it has first access to the society's scarce goods and to the best positions. Canh also hints at a fascinating factor—the role of nepotism at the highest levels, in part no doubt because one places greatest trust in bloodlines—even over strictly political alliances. In political terms, in any case, the new elite is even more powerful than the old; it has organized the society more thoroughly and hence can wield power more effectively.

I differ somewhat from Canh in assessing the Vietnamese-Soviet relationship at present. From his staunchly nationalist perspective, he believes that Hanoi's leaders have permitted themselves to become mere pawns of the Russians. My own view is that a fierce desire for ultimate independence and a goodly quotient of xenophobia remain keys to Vietnamese Communists' attitudes and behavior.

There can be no question that Hanoi's leaders are presently caught in a trap of their own making. As long as they are dedicated to the control of Cambodia and Laos, they are likely to face the enmity of the People's Republic of China. Beijing sees its interests served in exercising influence upon Indochina, and such interests are not advanced by a Vietnamese empire. Confronting China, Hanoi must turn to the Soviet Union for material and political support. No other meaningful source is available.

I suspect, however, that neither the Russians nor the Vietnamese leaders are entirely happy with the current state of affairs. For the Soviet Union, the economic and military commitments are very sizable, possibly amounting to U.S. $3–5 million daily. Nor is there light at the end of this particular tunnel. The Vietnam economy is in shambles, and improvements are likely to be painfully slow as long as the commitment to empire remains overriding.

It should be remembered that Southeast Asia is of less intrinsic importance strategically to the USSR than many other regions, including Northeast and South Asia. It should also be remembered that the Russian-Vietnamese relationship has never been a truly intimate one, with cultural differences huge and racial prejudices on both sides very substantial.

Many Russians are privately (and rightfully) fearful that Hanoi's gratitude is skin-deep and will ebb and flow with needs. If Soviet assistance remains forthcoming, to be sure, it could continue for some time, given the China problem. But what elements of reciprocity are involved? Moscow pays a heavy price in more than monetary terms. Its aid to Vietnam is one of the central issues perpetuating the Sino-Soviet cleavage. Relations with the five Southeast Asian states constituting the Association of Southeast Asian Nations (ASEAN) are also adversely affected. And what is the benefit? The encirclement of China is furthered, if that be a central objective. Beyond this, Russia has access to certain air and naval bases in Indochina. (The strategic advantage thus accrued, however, is questionable since in the event of any U.S.-USSR conflict, these bases would be prime targets, and U.S. power in the immediate region is likely to be preponderant.) In sum, this Soviet investment may have been natural under the circumstances, but its long-range benefits are questionable. Indeed, there are already small signs of restiveness on both sides.

In my view, Canh is entirely correct in questioning the wisdom of American "normalization" of relations with Vietnam at this time. While such a development might make sense at some point in the future and U.S. policies toward Indochina should be periodically re-examined, the re-establishment of relations between the United States and Vietnam now would split ASEAN, raise a further aggravating issue in U.S.-PRC relations, and contribute nothing except confusion to the scene by appearing to underwrite Vietnamese policies, thereby raising not only issues of principle but also reopening the question of American credibility. That any American president or Congress would sanction aid to Vietnam at this point in an effort to compete with the Russians is inconceivable.

One lesson that we might learn from the past is that some of the greatest U.S. triumphs have ensued from situations where we were totally absent: witness the context in which the Egyptian-Soviet and Sino-Soviet cleavages took place. I am not suggesting this as a universal prescription for success, but its selective application—intentional or not—has clearly been meaningful.

Hopefully, Canh's work will be followed by analyses from many other Vietnamese intellectuals, supplementing the work of foreign scholars, including Americans. As we weave different perspectives together, we shall approach the complexity and accuracy with which Vietnam deserves to be treated.

Robert A. Scalapino
Robson Research Professor of Government
and Director, Institute of East Asian Studies
University of California
Berkeley, California

Acknowledgments

In accomplishing a work of this kind, a great deal of effort is involved. For this reason, this book is a product of a large number of individuals who have lent their time and advice to the author.

A special debt of thanks is owed to Dr. Robert A. Scalapino, director of the Institute of East Asian Studies, University of California at Berkeley, who has given advice and input as to how the project should be accomplished. The author would also like to express his thanks to Mr. Douglas Pike, coordinator of the Indochinese Studies Program at the same institute, for all his expert advice. Sincere thanks are offered to Mr. Earle Cooper, who has spent so much time helping with the language and organization of the book, though the actual research and writing of the manuscript were the author's individual effort.

The author wishes to express his deep appreciation of the support of the Hoover Institution and its director, Dr. W. Glenn Campbell, associate director Richard F. Burress, and senior fellow Dr. Richard F. Staar; it was they who made the present undertaking possible. He is grateful to senior fellow Lewis Gann for advice; to Phyllis M. Cairns, publications manager of the Hoover Institution Press, David W. Heron, head of readers' services at the Hoover Library, and to Hilja Kukk and Linda Ann Wheeler, librarians; to Joyce Frederick and others at the Hoover Institution for special help; and to Jeanne O. Nickerson for her painstaking typing of the manuscript, without which the book could not have been produced.

Finally indebtedness is acknowledged to the author's family and his many Vietnamese friends who have assisted him in many different ways in undertaking this work.

The author is, of course, solely responsible for all opinions expressed herein.

1 From the Tet Offensive to the Communist Takeover

Prelude to Surrender

After having unsuccessfully launched the 1968 Tet general offensive to seize power in South Vietnam, the Vietnamese Communists agreed to enter into negotiations, first with the United States and later with South Vietnam as well, to end the war by diplomatic means. The peace talks began in Paris in May 1968. Early in 1969 the talks were expanded to include delegates from both the Republic of Vietnam (RVN), as South Vietnam was officially known, and the communist-run National Liberation Front of South Vietnam (NLF).

It had taken the delegates nine months to arrive at a decision regarding the shape of the conference table. Not until May 1969 did the NLF set forth a ten-point plan, of which the main points were:

1. The United States should withdraw its troops from South Vietnam and renounce all encroachment on the sovereignty, territory, and security of South Vietnam and the Democratic Republic of Vietnam, DRV (North Vietnam).
2. The United States should respect the Vietnamese people's fundamental national rights.
3. The United States should accept responsibility for the losses

and devastation inflicted on the Vietnamese people in both zones (north as well as south).

Communist Designs

The NLF's peace plan was proposed with four objectives in mind. First, the Communists wanted to separate the United States from South Vietnam in order to make it appear as if the Americans were the aggressors who had sent their troops to Vietnam and encroached on Vietnamese territory, and that the South Vietnamese government was just an American lackey. In addition, these aggressors who had caused damage to the country had to bear full responsibility for the war losses. Once the United States was out of South Vietnam, the Communists would take power by force. (This actually occurred in April 1975.) Second, the Communists wanted to raise the NLF's status to the same level as the South Vietnamese government's. The United States and South Vietnam had hitherto considered the NLF a clandestine, insurgent, illegal organization. This objective was therefore very important. Once the United States and South Vietnam agreed to negotiate with the NLF, it would automatically become a legal entity—recognition that the Vietnamese Communists had long aspired to and indeed fought for. Third, the Communists were seeking authorization for North Vietnam to become a necessary outsider at the conference—an outsider who, however, had a strong interest in solving problems between the NLF on the one side and the United States and South Vietnam on the other. In such a role, North Vietnam would be able to negotiate with the United States on equal footing. Finally, the Communists were determined to consider the United States as the master to be dealt with and to neglect the South Vietnamese government, though the NLF's plan did allude vaguely to the need for national concord between Vietnamese on both sides in South Vietnam.

In June 1971 North Vietnam put forward a peace plan that was essentially the same as the NLF's. However, the plan emphasized that the United States must stop supporting the South Vietnamese government (which it carefully refrained from referring to as a government). In July 1971, the Provisional Revolutionary Government (PRG) of South Vietnam repeated in its new plan the main points of the North Vietnamese one. In a clarification made on February 2, 1972, the PRG proposed to dissolve the South Vietnamese government on the grounds that "Nguyen Van Thieu and his machine of oppression are instruments of the U.S. Vietnamization policy which constitutes the main obstacle to the settlement of the political problem in South Vietnam." Only when Thieu was eliminated would the PRG enter into discussion with the "new administration" in order to form a tripartite Government of National Concord that would be composed of members of (1) the NLF, (2) the so-called Third Force, and (3) the South Vietnamese regime (minus Thieu).

On the U.S. and South Vietnamese sides, there were two proposals:

1. In May 1969, President Nixon proposed that all non–South Vietnamese forces should be withdrawn from South Vietnam. This meant that the North Vietnamese army had to go back to the North just as the U.S. army would return to the United States.
2. In October 1971, an eight-point plan was proposed by the United States and South Vietnam in which the U.S. forces would withdraw from South Vietnam and the remaining problems in Indochina would be solved by all parties on the basis of mutual respect. No further infiltration of outside forces would be accepted, and all outside forces would have to be withdrawn from Indochina.

The second proposal, by stating that "all outside forces" had to be withdrawn, and that there should be no further infiltration of such forces, implicitly required North Vietnam to withdraw its troops to the North and to keep them there. But the proposal also tacitly recognized the PRG as having equal footing with South Vietnam, since all parties were to solve matters "on the basis of mutual respect."

The Paris Agreement

In mid-1972 Hanoi was still maintaining the position that, before there could be an agreement, the Thieu regime would have to be removed. Early in October 1972, however, Hanoi submitted a draft of a peace agreement on the basis of which a mutually agreeable document was developed. Both sides agreed that the document would be signed on October 31, 1972, but the signing was called off when President Nixon announced that the agreement "would not bring a lasting peace" because the language of the draft could not ensure it. Negotiations were resumed in order to modify the language. During the negotiations, Le Duc Tho, Hanoi's chief delegate, asked for a recess in order to consult with Hanoi. On his return Tho presented a totally new set of documents with new provisions. After an extended series of negotiations, during which the U.S. delegation tried without success to convince Hanoi to comply with the original agreement, President Nixon ordered very heavy bombing of North Vietnam starting on December 18, 1972. The bombing continued for twelve days. It destroyed major military installations, electric power plants, and other vital targets, in Hanoi and Haiphong. After sustaining such heavy losses, the North Vietnamese soon had to come back to the Paris conference.

The conference resumed on January 8, 1973; Hanoi signed the peace pact on January 27. It was entitled "Agreement on Ending the War and Restoring the Peace in Vietnam," and is generally known as the Paris Accords or the Paris Agreement. In it the United States was required (1) to stop all its military activities against North Vietnam (article 3); (2) not to continue its military involvement or intervene in the internal affairs of South Vietnam (article 4); (3) to withdraw from South Vietnam all its troops, military advisers, and military personnel within 60 days (article 5); and (4) to dismantle all its military bases in South Vietnam within 60 days (article 6). No provisions in the agreement openly required North Vietnam to withdraw its troops from South Vietnam or to stop infiltrating them into the South. The latter condition, however, was at least implied by article 7, which stated that "the two South Vietnamese parties shall not accept the introduction of troops, military advisers and military personnel . . . including armaments, munitions and war materials into South Vietnam." The agreement also admitted the NLF's status as being equal to the Republic of Vietnam's in articles 2b, 2c, 7, 10, 11, 12, and 13.

Why the Agreement Failed

The U.S. government had yielded far too much to communist demands.

The communist party apparatus in South Vietnam was in fact extremely weak as a result of the defeats it had suffered during the Tet offensive of February 1968. Communist military forces were in no better shape. They were not able to mount a large-scale operation throughout South Vietnam. They did launch some attacks from time to time, but these were intended as mere shows of strength. In summer 1972 they had to concentrate three North Vietnamese army divisions in the demilitarized zone across the Ben Hai River in order to take over Quang Tri. However, these forces were severely beaten. There were no compelling military reasons, then, for the United States to make such concessions.

In addition, the U.S. government had committed serious mistakes in the style of its negotiations with the NLF. It was part of the NLF's strategy that negotiations should be made directly with the U.S. government and that the South Vietnamese government should be treated as a puppet. In the process of proposing negotiations and in the course of the negotiations themselves, the U.S. delegates played key roles. The South Vietnamese government was not even included in the eight-point plan until October 1971. Right up to the signing of the 1973 Paris Agreement, the U.S. government continued to mastermind the peace conference and the South Vietnamese government continued to be just a follower. The difference was a crucial one. By its stance at the Paris conference, the United States had tacitly accepted the communist propaganda line that it was a foreign aggressor waging an unjust war. Under this assumption, the U.S. government incurred the chief responsibility for all the problems before the conference, including all the consequences of its military actions. The NLF, then, cut the South Vietnamese government completely out of the picture—a classic example of divide and conquer.

Upon the signing of the Paris Agreement, the American troops gradually pulled out of South Vietnam. The disengagement was completed within the prescribed 60 days. North Vietnam, on the contrary, starting right in 1973, built a road system for the movement of military supplies on the eastern side of the Truong Son Mountains. The road, over one thousand kilometers long, connected Highway 9 (Quang Tri) with areas east of Saigon. According to Van Tien Dung, the general offensive's North Vietnamese commander, it was "an 8-m-wide, two-way road for heavy trucks and year-round tank traffic, transporting hundreds of thousands tons of war matériel to the battlefields." North Vietnam used "thousands of bulldozers, dozens of thousands of troops, engineers, workers, and laborers to build the road." Along it, east of the Truong Son mountain chain, lay a 500-km fuel pipeline from Quang Tri through the Central Highlands to Loc Ninh [north of Saigon] to supply dozens of thousands of vehicles moving in both directions."[1] According to the same source, "military supplies such as tanks, armored vehicles, missiles, long-range artillery, and anti-aircraft weapons" were sent to the battlefields a few at a time until large stockpiles of them had accumulated. "For the first time," he adds, "our long-range artillery pieces and modern tanks were sent to rubber plantations in South Vietnam."[2] George Nash, in *The Dissolution of the Paris Peace Accords*, says that North Vietnam sent many troops to the South.

> In the first two months after the cease-fire, more than 30,000 NVA [North Vietnamese Army] personnel were infiltrated into Vietnam via Laos and Cambodia. By the late fall of 1973, according to American intelligence reports, about 70,000 NVA troops had illegally entered the South; by early 1975, the figure had reached 170,000 . . . Between January 28 and mid-April 1973 alone, over 7,000 illegal NVA military truck crossings occurred between the DMZ [demilitarized zone] and South Vietnam. During 1973, the North constructed 12 airfields in the South, installed SAM-2 missiles in Khe Sanh . . .[3]

By the time the Paris Agreement was signed, the NVA had about 145,000 troops in South Vietnam. In January 1975 it launched an offensive to take over Phuoc Long, a town located near the Cambodia-Vietnam border, 80 km north of Saigon. In March North Vietnamese troops, increased to over 200,000 regulars, launched a general offensive to conquer South Vietnam. They concentrated five infantry divisions, seven independent regiments (including one artillery, one armored, one antiaircraft, and one sapper), and three regional regiments on the South Vietnamese highlands in order to take over Banmethuot, a town situated near the Cambodian border. The town fell on March 10. The communist forces then moved on Saigon via Tuy Hoa, Nha Trang, and Phan Thiet. By April 30 their victory was complete.

What Was the National Liberation Front?

The Geneva Agreement, concluded in July 1954, prescribed that all nationalist Vietnamese and French forces should move to the South and all the communist Vietnamese forces to the North. The people in each zone had a right to freely move to the other zone. The movement was made within 300 days. The Seventeenth Parallel was a temporary boundary to divide the two zones until the country should be reunified by a general election to be held in 1956.

"Staying Behind Is Glory"

The French and nationalist forces completed the movement to the South in mid-1955. Some 800,000 ordinary northern citizens fled the communist regime and went south. In South Vietnam, the communist forces that had been regrouped in designated areas were sent to the North. Not one ordinary citizen left for the North.

In order to win the general election, the communist party had a scheme to plant its agents as underground workers in South Vietnam. In 1962 the author interviewed defectors from the party who stated that when the Geneva Agreement was signed, South Vietnamese party cadres received orders from the party's higher echelons to pack up and report to centers of regroupment from which they could be transported to North Vietnam. The cadres were so excited that they showed up in public places, boasting of the revolution's accomplishments. In early 1955, however, many of them received contradictory orders requiring them to stay back in the South to work as underground agents. Many of them felt very angry about these orders because their identities had now been revealed to the public; now, if they stayed behind as underground agents, their lives would be endangered. The defectors said that the party Central Committee had to convene a meeting to look for a solution to the problem. As a result, a study program was carried out to motivate those cadres on the basis of the principle "Departing is victory; staying behind, however, is glory."

The number of communist cadres planted in South Vietnam at this time is not known. In 1963, a defector who had been a Viet Cong deputy chief of a district security division told the author in Saigon that in his native village of Thuan Hung, An Xuyen Province, which had a population of over ten thousand people, the Communists left behind numbered over one hundred party members grouped into 30 separate cells. In age the members ranged from youth to over 50 or 60. About one in five was a woman. Such communist "sleepers," the nucleus of what later became known as the Viet Cong, were able from 1956 onward to start and lead political movements, including several that demanded peace for the South Vietnamese people.

Until 1958 these underground agents were able to combine the military struggle with the political one (the political struggle consisted of demands for welfare and democracy by communist-led groups). In that year, however, the agents began large-scale guerrilla warfare, using weapons that had been buried during the 1954–55 period before communist troops were regrouped to the North. Remote villages in Kien Hoa and Kien Phong provinces were actually controlled by the Communists. Over the next few years, communist guerrillas were able to create unstable situations in rural areas. They were a particular threat to the security of communications lines between towns. Early in 1960, during the Vietnamese New Year festival, communist military forces successfully attacked the headquarters of a South Vietnamese division in Tay Ninh, seized trucks, weapons, and ammunition, then withdrew into the jungle. With the development of the military forces, communist political units also grew in size and number.

The Concerted Uprising Campaign

The communist expansion in South Vietnam was merely a scheme of the Vietnamese communist party (then officially named the Vietnam Workers Party, or VWP) to conquer South Vietnam by force. This strategy was reflected in Ho Chi Minh's appeal in May 1959 "to unify the country by appropriate means." He also called openly for the "liberation" of South Vietnam. During this period the party staged a new major effort, the Chien Dich Dong Khoi (Concerted Uprising Campaign), which began in July 1959 and ended in June 1960. Its purpose was to expand the amount of territory under direct communist control. The tactics, which the party called "breaking up the machinery of oppression," were, on the one hand, to disrupt the strategic hamlets set up by the Ngo Dinh Diem government for the purpose of isolating communist underground agents from villagers; and, on the other, to liquidate the South Vietnamese hamlet and village officials on whom real authority rested in the countryside. In other words, the Communists tried to eradicate the South Vietnamese administrative machinery from the villages and hamlets, then place them under their direct control. They planned to continue enlarging the communist-controlled areas in this way until they could seize enough of the countryside from which to besiege the cities and launch a general offensive. The communist apparatus and military forces were greatly enlarged by this campaign. During the 1959–60 period, it was the author's estimate that some 100,000 hamlet and village officials of South Vietnam were eliminated either by assassination or by some form of neutralization.

Hanoi Creates the NLF and COSVN

In September 1960, while addressing the Third Party Congress, Ho Chi Minh expounded on the decision, already taken at the 1959 Party Plenum, to "carry out a national democratic revolution in South Vietnam."[4] In December 1960 the NLF came into existence in order to formally conduct the struggle for power in the South. The NLF's leaders were South Vietnamese, either Communists or pro-Communists selected by the communist party for propaganda purposes. The organization that actually conducted the war, staying behind the scenes, was the Central Office for South Vietnam (COSVN), a newly established body of the VWP. COSVN at that time was headed by Gen. Nguyen Chi Thanh, a member of the party Politburo who ranked fourth in the party leadership. Thanh died in 1967, presumably as a result of bombing by B-52s, and Pham Hung, another member of the Politburo, was promoted to Thanh's rank and sent south to conduct the war.

In order to prepare for the peace negotiations, the VWP created the PRG, which in appearance was an offshoot of the NLF. In official documents published by the Hanoi government, the people struggling in South Vietnam "under the leadership of the NLF" were designated as Viet Cong. The term had become current in the West, where many leaders and opinion makers assumed it referred simply to South Vietnamese who were fighting for the independence of their country. In fact, Viet Cong was a short form of Vietnam Cong San, which means Vietnamese Communists, northern as well as southern. To encourage the notion that it was a wholly southern organization was a communist propaganda trick. The NLF and PRG were just front organizations of the Vietnamese communist party. They were founded to achieve a specific objective for the party. After the military victory in South Vietnam in April 1975, the party put an end to them because there was no longer any reason for their existence.

The Military Conquest of South Vietnam

Infiltration and Escalation

From 1958 on, in order to have manpower to fight in South Vietnam, the communist party sent back to South Vietnam those military and political cadres who had been regrouped to the North from 1954 to 1955. The need for infiltration was so great that the party began to build the so-called Ho Chi Minh Trail; its code name was "Line B-59" ("B" was the code for the battlefield in South Vietnam, while "59" stood for the year 1959, when the trail was built). Down the trail came not only military supplies but North Vietnamese troops in increasing numbers.

1. In 1961, communist military forces in the South comprised 10,000 members of regular forces and 40,000 guerrillas.
2. In 1962, North Vietnamese military cadres infiltrating into the South numbered 12,000, all regulars, while 31,000 guerrillas were recruited locally.

3. In 1963 communist forces in the South included 80,000 troops (after replacement), and in 1964 their number had gone to 92,000 (32,000 NVA troops and 60,000 guerrillas).
4. In 1965, there were 124,000 communist troops in the South and in 1966, 200,000, 60,000 of which were NVA troops.
5. From 1965 onwards an estimated 5,000 to 6,000 NVA troops were sent to the South as replacements and reinforcements every month so that, by 1967, NVA troops in South Vietnam numbered approximately 200,000.[5]

The Tet Offensive: Disaster for the NLF

With such strong military forces, the NLF in February 1968 launched a general assault, the famous Tet offensive, against 32 of South Vietnam's 44 cities. The Communists destroyed a number of targets but did not succeed in their objective of seizing power. Three months later, in May, they attempted a second general assault and failed again. Communist losses from both operations were enormous. In the Tet offensive only, the losses on the battlefield were estimated at 70,000 men. From the Tet offensive to October 31, 1970, it was estimated that the communist forces lost 515,000 men, including 44,000 political cadres at the chapter and village levels and some 90,000 defectors. In interviews with defectors the author learned that, by the end of 1968, there were only some four hundred seriously depleted party chapters left in all South Vietnam. The party was in serious trouble because of its pyramidal organization, in which the chapters form the base that supports the top. Now that the base was weakened, the top was in danger of falling. The NLF agreed to join the Paris peace talks in order to buy time: more NVA troops had to be sent to the South and more party members recruited at the local level.

The Lost Opportunity. After the Tet offensive the NLF was unable to launch any more large-scale actions. In 1972, several NVA divisions were sent across the Seventeenth Parallel against the city of Quang Tri, but they too were heavily defeated. Both the NLF's political apparatus and its military forces remained weak. If the U.S. government had provided further assistance to the South Vietnamese people instead of withdrawing its forces, the NLF would have been militarily defeated. The Vietnamese communist party, according to refugees from North Vietnam, was then in a very difficult situation. If the South Vietnamese army had launched a general attack on

North Vietnam, or if American planes had bombed Hanoi and Haiphong heavily, Hanoi would have had to surrender. Its manpower problem was desperate. In South Vietnam during the so-called liberation days that followed the American withdrawal in April 1975, the city of Saigon was taken by a North Vietnamese army that included boys of fourteen. To rule South Vietnam, the party had to rely on "revolutionaries of April 30," or those people who joined the NLF on that day in 1975, the day the South Vietnamese government collapsed.

The Takeover

Transitional Organizations

Immediately following the fall of Saigon on April 30, 1975, there was no formal government in South Vietnam. After the Communists' victory, all the front organizations that they had created specifically to wage war against the South were either dissolved or merged with North Vietnamese organizations. Thus the so-called People's Revolutionary Party, which had led only a nominal existence during the war, now had no reason to exist. Party organizations in the South were henceforth described as branches of the VWP. The VWP's Central Office for South Vietnam, which had operated under the official leadership of Pham Hung, the fourth-ranking member of the VWP Politburo, was dissolved in December 1976 by the Fourth Party Congress; it, too, had done its job. The National Liberation Front of South Vietnam and the Vietnam Alliance of National Democratic and Peace Forces were integrated immediately with the National United Front. Other ostensibly southern organizations, such as the Youth League, the Federation of Trade Unions, and the Women's Union, were also merged in 1976 with their northern counterparts.

Many of the NLF's southern supporters were aghast at these developments. Truong Nhu Tang, for instance, is a former official in the Diem administration who secretly did propaganda work for the NLF and in 1968 was made minister of justice in the PRG. He escaped from Vietnam in 1980 and had this to say on his arrival in France, where he now lives.

> On May 13, 1975, the North Vietnamese put their hands on the South. This treachery had been in the air from the first days of the liberation. On May 15, at the victory celebration, from the stadium, I saw the civilian masses march with the two flags of the Democratic Republic of Vietnam (North) and of the NLF Provisional Revolu-

> tionary Government (South), but the military parade carried only the North Vietnamese flag, red with a yellow star. I asked [NVA commander-in-chief] General Van Tien Dung, "Where are the famous First, Fifth, Seventh, and Ninth Divisions of the National Liberation Front? He replied coldly, "The army has already been unified."[6]

The PRG, though it had existed since the NLF joined the Paris peace talks, did not take over the task of governing. Instead, on May 3 in Saigon, the victors issued the following communiqué.

> COMMUNIQUÉ ON THE ESTABLISHMENT OF THE
> SAIGON GIA DINH CITY MILITARY MANAGEMENT COMMITTEE
>
> In order to rapidly stabilize order and security in the City, to build a new revolutionary order, to consolidate and develop the people's sovereign right, and to rapidly restore and stabilize the normal life of the different strata of the compatriots in Saigon Gia Dinh, based upon a decision made by the PRGRSV, we wish to make public the following name list of the Saigon Gia Dinh City Military Management Committee:
>
> 1. Col. Gen. Tran Van Tra, chairman
> 2. Vo Van Kiet, deputy
> 3. Mai Chi Tho, deputy
> 4. Maj. Gen. Hoang Cam, commander of the Saigon Gia Dinh Defense Army Corps, deputy chairman
> 5. Maj. Gen. Tran Van Danh, deputy
> 6. Cao Dang Tien, deputy
> 7. Sr. Colonel Bui Thanh Khiet, member
> 8. Dr. Nguyen Van Thu, member
> 9. Vong Ky Thuat, deputy minister of economy, member
> 10. Vo Thanh Van, member
> 11. Phan Minh Thanh, member[7]

The communiqué ended with a call to all segments of society from the PRG to uphold public order in a spirit of national reconciliation. However, it was clear that the PRG was not in charge. It was not even clear that the PRG had established the Military Management Committee. The chairman of the committee was a member of the VWP Central Committee who had been sent to command North Vietnamese troops in the South. His number two man, Vo Van Kiet, was a southerner but also a VWP cadre (in 1980 he was elected an alternate member of the Politburo and in March 1982 a full member). Number three, Mai Chi Tho, was the brother of Le Duc Tho, the second most powerful man in North Vietnam (see Chapter 4). The others were lesser figures; indeed, the last six on the list might fairly have been described as unknowns. However, the evidence clearly indicated that Saigon, formally renamed Ho Chi Minh City by the unified National Assembly at its first session in June 1976, had been liberated only to be placed under the control of VWP cadres, not the NLF.

The Western mass media covered only what was happening in Saigon. Simultaneously, however, military management committees were established throughout South Vietnam. At the lower administrative levels, such as the precincts and wards of Saigon, as well as the districts and villages in every province, so-called people's revolutionary committees were set up. In Saigon, until May 25, 1975, ten out of eleven precincts were governed by such committees.[8]

Legitimizing Reunification

The reunification of Vietnam was a fait accompli from the moment of the North Vietnamese military victory. The idea that the country was reunified by some process of negotiation between northern and southern delegations, followed by the election of April 26, 1976, was just a propaganda stunt. Actually, the Communists set about reunifying the country immediately. For instance, rail communications, after having been completely destroyed by communist saboteurs during the two wars, were restored within a year. Thousands of South Vietnamese civilians and prisoners of war, including former civilian and military officers of the Republic of Vietnam, were employed to lay down or repair some two thousand kilometers of track.

Major changes in the civil administration were also made as soon as possible. The currency issued by the former South Vietnamese government was recalled and changed in September 1975 (it was replaced by the North Vietnamese currency in May 1978). All the policies known as "building socialism" were rushed into effect: abolition of all significant private ownership; eradication of private commerce and trade; establishment of state industries; and introduction of state monopolies over education, broadcasting, the press, and postal facilities. These policies were implemented entirely by North Vietnamese party cadres sent to South Vietnam.

The new regime was not imposed without resistance. Internally, the Communists had to encounter what the North Vietnamese premier described as important and complicated problems.[9] The

PRG, a month after the liberation, reiterated its appeals first "to hunt down the remnants of the enemy troops and diehard lackey reactionaries."[10] As late as December 1975 Pham Hung, the PRG's éminence grise, was demanding that the "counterrevolutionaries" be suppressed.[11] In order to implement the policies of socialist construction in South Vietnam, on the one hand, and to impose strict control over the people, on the other hand, the communist party, according to Le Duc Tho's report to the Fourth Party Congress, transferred "a large force of cadres from North Vietnam to take over the management of municipalities, to establish local governments and manage various economic and cultural sectors and agencies." Two prominent refugees, a medical professor and a government financial expert, who came from Vietnam in 1979 have stated that "all key positions in political, administrative, economic, and security agencies" were assigned to North Vietnamese cadres sent from North Vietnam, and that members of the National Liberation Front were not assigned to such positions. According to these informants, even the South Vietnamese cadres who were regrouped to North Vietnam from 1954 to 1955 under the provisions of the 1954 Geneva Agreement were not well treated.[12] Another refugee, a former South Vietnamese army captain, has confirmed: "Thousands of North Vietnamese cadres are there [in the South]. They are present at the district and provincial levels. They don't hold positions on the village committees. But in Ho Chi Minh City and in other cities, in all state agencies, in cooperatives, hospitals, schools, in some factories, the role of North Vietnamese cadres is very important."[13] Truong Nhu Tang, quoted earlier in this chapter, has also described how, at the end of May 1975, a flood of North Vietnamese political, economic, and administrative cadres invaded South Vietnam, competing with each other for "public buildings, houses, firms, personal property, cars, and even furniture."[14]

Foreign observers, even some who formerly favored an NLF victory, have been appalled by the extent of the northerners' takeover. Thus Nariko Sugano, a procommunist Japanese journalist who had often visited Vietnam, including the "liberated" (NLF-occupied) zone during the war, reported in quite unfavorable terms after a postwar visit in April 1979.

> Though unification has been completed, South Vietnam bears the characteristics of a country dominated by North Vietnam. The South Vietnamese people are so strictly controlled and so oppressed that they cannot rise up against the Hanoi regime . . . I have witnessed

> the excessive impoverishment of the South Vietnamese people. I saw North Vietnamese cadres take bribes and then let innocent people flee the oppressive regime . . .[15]

The communist regime's military policy was not quite so exclusionary as its policy for civilians; for instance, it did use local forces that had been guerrillas during the war to repress the "counterrevolutionaries" and "diehard reactionaries." On the other hand, the so-called main forces, which were actually North Vietnamese armies sent to the South to fight the war, were redistributed in order to cover the whole territory of South Vietnam and were reinforced by other North Vietnamese units coming from the North after the victory. Such forces had never operated under southern direction; whenever they moved into an area, the local NLF units were simply ordered to provide them with logistic and other forms of support. The total number of North Vietnamese forces, including artillery and tank units, in South Vietnam by the end of the war, is not known. It included at least four regular infantry corps (twelve divisions), plus the First Corps, stationed in Ninh Binh, North Vietnam, which was ordered to move south on March 25, 1975, to reinforce the others, probably around Saigon.

During the war, as I learned from defecting communist cadres, resentment of northern military dominance led to occasional clashes between northern and southern forces. After the war, according to refugees, what had been friction turned into prolonged resistance in some areas. In Chau Doc Province an NLF unit is said to have fought with an NVA unit and then withdrawn into the That Son Mountains and continued its resistance. One refugee reports that, early in 1976, an archeology team of the North Vietnam Institute of Social Science Research was sent to do research in Ha Tien, Minh Hai Province, but returned in two days. Asked why they had come back so early, the team leader said: "Our armed units are fighting against an NLF unit, and so a member of the District Committee advised us to come back immediately to Saigon."[16]

Given the attitude of the North Vietnamese government, de facto unification of the country was an inevitable result of the victory. Official unification, however, including unification at the central administrative level, needed to be legitimized by negotiation and mutual agreement, followed by elections. Accordingly, two negotiating teams, one representing the North and the other the South, met for a Consultative Conference on National Reunification at Saigon's Independence Palace from November 15 to 21, 1975.[17]

Although each team consisted of 25 delegates, no real negotiation was on the agenda; it was just a media event. Pham Hung, head of the South Vietnamese delegation, had been in the South but had joined the communist movement as long ago as the 1930s. By 1965 he ranked fifth in the North Vietnamese Politburo. Upon the death of Gen. Nguyen Chi Thanh, Pham Hung was sent south to head COSVN. At that time he was promoted to fourth in the Politburo. After the victory he became a vice-premier in the cabinet of northern premier Pham Van Dong. His opposite number on the North Vietnamese delegation was Truong Chinh, the VWP's leading ideologist and former first secretary. He had lost some influence as a result of his savage conduct from 1953 to 1956, of the northern land reform program, but was still number two in the Politburo and still a major author of ideological works. The unification talks, then, consisted of the communist party negotiating with itself, with its number two man on one side and its number four man on the other.

After a week of such negotiation, the conference, not surprisingly, reached the following agreement.

> The Conference was unanimous on the method of unification of the country . . . : A general election over the entire territory of Vietnam must be held soon to elect a common National Assembly. This National Assembly will be the highest organ of state power of a completely independent and socialist Vietnam and will determine the structure of the state, elect the leading organs of the state, and prescribe the new constitution of a unified Vietnam.[18]

The organ managing the election in the North was to be the Standing Committee of the National Assembly of the DRV, and in the South, the Council of Advisers of the PRG.[19] The election was to be held in the first half of the following year.[20]

The general election was held as scheduled on April 25, 1976. As I have said, it did not pave the way for reunification but merely put the stamp of popular approval on the de facto reunification of the country since April 30, 1975. That the election served this function was no secret; it was affirmed, for instance, by Hoang Tung, editor of the party organ *Nhan Dan*, who pointed out to foreigners in Hanoi that "the elections were not to decide the nature of the regime," for "that has been decided during the struggle."[21] Details of the election are given in Chapter 4. Since only candidates approved by the communist party were allowed to run, there were no rival parties or factions at all, or only such as the Communists permitted to exist. There were, for instance, candidates from various social groups—Catholics, Buddhists, industrial workers, women, youth, and so forth. The communist party clearly intended that such groups should be in some sense represented. But it chose as candidates only "progressive elements" from each group, that is, in the great majority of cases, party members who had infiltrated South Vietnamese society and worked for the NLF. In addition, voters were instructed as to how they should cast their votes (a fact confirmed by Nguyen Cong Hoan, a former SRV legislator whose history is further described in Chapter 6).[22] The result was a massive vote for known government and party leaders; few peasant, worker, or youth candidates were elected because few were allowed to run (Saigon had no candidates of peasant origin at all).

Heading the list of successful candidates, with 97 percent of the vote, was Mme. Nguyen Thi Binh, a southerner who had joined the communist movement in the 1950s and later helped to found the NLF. She was followed by Nguyen Huu Tho, a former chairman of the NLF and also of the PRG; by Gen. Tran Van Danh and Vo Van Kiet, both members of the Military Management Committee; by Nguyen Van Hieu, chairman of its successor, the Ho Chi Minh City Revolutionary Committee, which officially ran the city until January 1976; and by Pham Hung. The Third Force—those who saw it as their duty to reconcile both sides in the war while vigorously opposing its continuance—was also represented, but only by persons whose previous actions had shown (or seemed to show) that they could be trusted to follow the communist line. Among them were:

1. Mme. Ngo Ba Thanh, a former research assistant in the law faculty of Saigon University, who had been educated in Switzerland. On her return to South Vietnam she joined the left-wing Buddhist militants in helping to overthrow President Ngo Dinh Diem. She was subsequently very active in the antiwar movement.
2. Ly Chanh Trung, a southerner and a professor in the faculty of letters of Saigon University. He was associated with Ngo Ba Thanh's group.
3. Huynh Lien, a southerner and a Buddhist nun. She too was associated with Ngo Ba Thanh's group.
4. Huynh Tan Mam, from Central Vietnam, chairman of the student body at Saigon University during the 1960s. He was an antiwar activist.
5. Father Huynh Cong Minh, a southerner and a Roman Catho-

> lic priest. With Father Truong Ba Can he had led the Young Catholic Workers Movement, which actively supported the NLF in the name of the Third Force.

On the other hand the well-known civil rights activist Father Chan Tin, a redemptionist Catholic priest from whose files Amnesty International had compiled its report on political prisoners under the Thieu regime, was not elected. The Communists did not trust him.

According to the 1959 Constitution of the DRV, which now covered all Vietnam, the National Assembly appoints the executive. Accordingly, the national government appointed by the first session of the new assembly in June 1976 replaced the PRG. With it the last vestige of the Republic of South Vietnam was dissolved. Huynh Tan Phat, former premier of the PRG, was appointed vice-premier of the new government, and Nguyen Huu Tho, chairman of the NLF, was appointed its vice-president. Very few persons of South Vietnamese birth were appointed members of the Government Council (see Chapters 3 and 4). In effect, the PRG—always a facade in any case—had been dissolved well before the election day. Truong Nhu Tang, the former PRG minister of justice, has described its end.

> They made us disappear quietly. In the course of a meeting to prepare for the forced reunification of the country, while Truong Chinh was delivering a speech, one of my colleagues whispered to me: "How's this? They are burying us without a eulogy! We will go and ask Nguyen Huu Tho to make one for us." The president of the National Liberation Front had to organize a simple dinner of farewell. All official residences had been requisitioned by the North Vietnamese. The burial of the Provisional Revolutionary Government took place in the Rex Dance Hall. It was sad. The leaders of the communist party carried their ingratitude to the point of not showing up.[23]

Hanoi's Reasons for Haste

Before the fall of Saigon, Hanoi had been planning to annex South Vietnam after some five to ten years.[24] The communist leaders were well aware of the great socioeconomic and cultural differences between North and South. The standard of living in South Vietnam was much higher, and the people there had got used to freedom. Free enterprise was in operation, and there was no system of strict control over the people at large. Nor were the values adopted by the South Vietnamese people compatible with the communist ones. Hanoi therefore looked to a slow and gradual integration of the South Vietnamese society into the northern one, a process that would allow for "certain realities and specific characteristics of the two zones."[25] Truong Nhu Tang has confirmed that this was the party's unanimous policy, and that Ho Chi Minh was the first to endorse it.[26] On May 19, 1975, at a celebration in Hanoi of Ho Chi Minh's birthday, Premier Pham Van Dong stated that, now victory had been won, the party leadership was turning its thoughts to Uncle Ho's ultimate wish for a "peaceful, reunified, independent, democratic, prosperous and powerful Vietnam."[27]

In contrast, the NLF leaders and the PRG were planning to make South Vietnam independent of the North. Nguyen Huu Tho, in an August 1975 interview with Nayan Chanda, declared that "South Vietnam pursues a neutrality policy, recognizes private ownership of Vietnamese national bourgeoisie, businessmen and plantation owners; accepts corporations from foreign countries to exploit oil in the South Vietnam continental shelf."[28] In this he was only repeating a policy that the NLF had made part of its political program in 1960. Moreover, during the first two weeks of September 1975, the first six foreign ambassadors to be accredited in South Vietnam presented their credentials to Tho in his capacity as NLF chairman and president of its Central Committee. The ambassadors in question presented their credentials separately to South and North Vietnam. Four of them were from nonaligned countries—Cuba, Congo (Brazzaville), Mauritania, and Mexico—while the other two were from Sweden and Denmark, neutral Scandinavian countries. These attentions were not unwelcome: South Vietnam, at about this time, was seeking United Nations representation separately from North Vietnam.[29] Meanwhile, Mme. Nguyen Thi Binh, the PRG's minister of foreign affairs, was increasing her activities in Third World countries on the PRG's behalf.

Liberation of the South was causing the North still other anxieties. Internally, transportation and communication were open to people of both zones after the military victory. People traveled back and forth in search of relatives. Northerners were startled to discover that the South Vietnamese standard of living was so high. In addition, South Vietnamese culture was smuggled into North Vietnam in the form of books, poems, and music and was soon being passed from hand to hand among northerners everywhere. The state mass media had to be mobilized to attack the supposedly artificial prosperity of the South Vietnamese economy, which was said to have been pumped full of dollars by American imperialists. Their decadent culture, the northern media repeated, had poisoned the South Vietnamese people—and now this culture was spreading to the North. Conversely, southerners became aware of conditions in the North. The Vietnamese communist leadership became convinced that if the unification of the country could not be carried out soon, they would have a hard time not only in subduing the South Vietnamese people, but also in controlling their own country.

Local Administration and Security

In order to rule the whole country the new Government Council, in a resolution dated March 25, 1977, adopted over four hundred laws from the former northern and southern regimes. These were laws and rules for managing the state, the economy, and the society, that were now made applicable throughout the country.[30]

After the general election in April 1976 the Socialist Republic of Vietnam (SRV), as it was now called, held local elections in May 1977 to elect provincial, district, and village people's councils. This was the last step in completing national unification in the domain of state institutions. After the elections the various revolutionary administrations were replaced by local administrative organs. At the lower levels—wards, villages, factories, hospitals, schools, and so on—executive committees were established from May 1977 onward. Finally, many organizations were formed for peasants, workers, women, students, teenage youth and children, intellectuals, and other social groups. All these new political structures were established with the help of North Vietnamese political cadres. Soon after liberation, a security network had been set up. In all the cities of the South, especially in Ho Chi Minh City, security agencies were organized for every ward. At lower levels such as street blocs (from 20 to 30 street blocs form a city ward) security cells were created. The leaders of the security cells and ward security agencies were northerners; southerners played a secondary role. Newly recruited security agents—the "revolutionaries of April 30" to which I have already referred—were used as informants to denounce the activities of former South Vietnamese government officials and to spy on strangers visiting friends living in the area.[31]

2 Communism and the Vietnamese Economy

The fate of South Vietnam under communism was foreshadowed in the North, where the VWP, despite its victory in a war of national liberation, proceeded to treat its compatriots like conquered enemies. It did so in the name of socialist transformation, a concept with both economic and social connotations. The same concept, with modifications forced on the VWP by popular resistance, is now in the process of being applied to the South. It will be appropriate, then, to briefly examine its northern history.

Building Socialism in the North

By any standards except the Marxist one, the main problem facing the government of North Vietnam from its inception was economic, not social. The problem, as Douglas Pike has emphasized, was hardly a new one.

> The society inherited by the Party in 1954 had an ex-colonial agrarian economy in which 90 percent of the labor force was engaged in feeding the total population, a country with the least area of cultivated land per inhabitant of any nation on earth. From the start, in purely economic terms, planners faced a serious endemic agricultural prob-

lem: overpopulation in a relatively small fertile area. Two-thirds of the DRV's 64,344 square miles was mountainous, and only about 5 percent of that area was arable.[1]

The VWP, however, was not capable of viewing anything "in purely economic terms"; its program of socialist transformation was primarily social. In essence, the program aimed at

1. Eradication of private commerce and trade—what the party called "capitalist merchants and compradors"—and their replacement by state institutions that had to be established from scratch
2. Nationalization of industry—primarily French-owned coal mines and other corporations
3. Abolition of private ownership and exploitation of land and reorganization of agricultural production along collective principles

Of these three the VWP gave top priority to land reform, which it had already launched in some remote areas during 1952, while the war was still in progress. The most crucial stage of the program was begun in late 1953. After its takeover of North Vietnam, the VWP relied heavily on land reform as a means of achieving socialist transformation. All the so-called exploiters were eliminated; their lands were confiscated and distributed among poor peasants and the landless. The first stage of agricultural cooperativization began in 1957 with the so-called work exchange teams, which were collectives in organizational structure but not (on the whole) in their distribution of economic rewards. Four crops and two years later low-level agricultural cooperatives were introduced; in these the members of the cooperative retained control over the means of production. Thus, the cooperatives replaced the teams. Finally, in 1966, high-level or advanced agricultural cooperatives began to show what the regime was aiming for: agricultural workers who were state employees producing crops that also belonged to the state. By 1969 the regime was claiming that almost 90 percent of the total population belonged to such large-scale cooperatives. A similar process of collectivization was used to establish state-run retail and wholesale businesses in urban areas.

Since colonial rule had left North Vietnam almost without heavy industry, the First Five-Year Plan (1955–1960) laid great emphasis on acquiring some. The French-owned mines were confiscated and reopened for production, as were the few large cooperatives. A state management committee was charged with developing textile manufacturing, shipbuilding, and metalworking, as well as primary extractive industries such as iron ore mining. Systems of communication and transportation were improved, while electrical power generation was given high priority at the expense of agriculture.

The Transformation Is Completed

By 1975, as a result of socialist transformation, there was very little left of the North's private economic sector. In urban areas, families who owned more than one house were allowed to keep one as shelter; all the others were confiscated by the state and placed under the management of the Bureau of Housing, which rented them out and returned some 15 to 20 percent of the rental value to the owners. In addition, the owner of a large house could rent out rooms in it directly. Stockholders of corporations with a "mixed" (part private, part public) status were allowed to keep a certain number of shares and draw a very small profit from them. In addition, the corporation's owners had a right to work for it as employees. If, however, a corporation had been nationalized in 1954, its owners lost everything.

In rural areas, all cultivated land had been confiscated and made part of agricultural cooperatives. For dwelling purposes, each family was given a small lot on which to build a home and cultivate a small private garden, the produce of which could be sold for profit. However, peasants during the mid-1960s spent so much time on and stole so much state-owned fertilizer for their private gardens that Ho Chi Minh, in early 1969, issued a decree saying that the lot allocated to each family was only on loan to it, since the real owner was the state. At the same time, peasants were forbidden to spend so much time on their gardens.

The average northerner now owns little more than his clothing, his household furniture and utensils, and the bicycle on which he rides to work. Legally (I will postpone discussion of the omnipresent black market), his opportunities for private enterprise are limited to peddling small articles of his own manufacture or to offering his own garden produce for sale at a makeshift booth in the marketplace. As far as the government is concerned, the socialist transformation of the North has now been completed. State ownership, disguised by such phrases as "the people's collective mastery of society," has been extended to virtually all forms of property. In the official view, this means that man no longer exploits man; in practice, it means that the state exploits everybody.

Despite the socialist transformation, socialist production relations, as the regime takes care to point out, are still evolving and stand in great need of improvement. As the state introduces such large-scale units of production as the high-level agricultural cooperatives, which include hundreds of hectares and employ as many as 100,000 persons, relations between the collectivity and the individual become crucial. According to Le Duan, who reported on economic policy to the Fourth Party Congress in December 1976, the party's postwar goals for production relations were

> (a) To step up socialist industrialization in order to strengthen the material basis of the new relations of production and to rapidly broaden the state sector of the economy.
> (b) On the basis of strengthening the agricultural cooperatives and the gradual completion of hydraulic work and mechanism of agriculture, to push ahead the movement for reorganization of agriculture, along the lines of large-scale socialist production.
> (c) To consolidate and strengthen the handicraft cooperatives in order to enable their production favorably in accordance with the state plan.
> (d) With regard to the remaining individual economy in the various branches and crafts, it is necessary to guide and manage it to help it develop in the right direction.[2]

By such political methods the party hoped to further the desperately urgent economic task of ensuring an adequate food supply. The situation was even more critical than it had been at the end of the war against the French. In 1955 the DRV had imported 170,000 tons of rice from the Soviet Union and 50,000 tons from China.[3] In 1976, despite their capture of South Vietnam's rice fields, the leaders in Hanoi were forced to import a million tons of foodstuffs from the same two countries. During the intervening years, while the battle for collectivization was being won, the battle to feed North Vietnam was being lost. In 1961, rice production there was 282 kg per capita; by 1968 it had declined to 206 kg per capita and by 1973 to 186 kg. Food production in North Vietnam, as in other underdeveloped countries, was in a race against population growth, estimated for the 1960s as at least 2.4 percent a year. Wartime demands on manpower and the disruptive effects of American bombing only hastened the decline that collectivization and population growth had begun. No wonder Le Duan, in the report just quoted, called for a Second Five-Year

Plan that would "ensure the minimum needs of the people" and that would "eventually" make possible a food reserve. In the North, by 1975, the former were not being met and the latter remained a utopian dream.

Socialist Reform in the South

Hanoi's plans for reshaping the southern economy do not appear to have crystallized until after the war was over. Even then they had an improvised quality, no doubt because political reunification of North and South, as I explained in Chapter 1, had been unexpectedly speeded up. The main assumption underlying these plans was that the South, despite its very different social and economic makeup, could be subjected to the same kind of socialist transformation, imposed by the same means, as the North. The South might be the more economically developed section of the country, but in all things that mattered the new leaders considered it merely backward.

In July 1976 Le Duan, secretary-general of the VWP, made a keynote speech to the National Assembly in which he gave an official explanation—the earliest I have been able to find—of how the socialist North and the previously nonsocialist South would march together on the road to socialism. In North Vietnam the party would step up "socialist construction" and would perfect "socialist relations," that is to say, the private sector would be totally eliminated. In South Vietnam, however, there was a need for a "socialist transformation" to make socialist construction possible.

> We must immediately abolish the comprador bourgeoisie and the remnants of the feudal landlord classes, undertake the socialist transformation of private capitalist industry and commerce, agriculture, handicraft and small trade through appropriate measures and steps. We [must] also combine transformation and building in order actively to steer the economy of the South into the orbit of socialism and integrate the economies of both zones in a single system of large-scale socialist production.[4]

"Comprador" bourgeoisie (from the Portuguese word for "buyer") was the approved communist term for almost anyone in Vietnam who had made money through business transactions with noncommunist Westerners (the original compradors had been native business agents acting in behalf of European colonialists in India and China).

What Le Duan did not say in this context was that the national bourgeoisie, consisting of business people whose transactions were made with other Vietnamese nationals, were to be abolished too, as they had been in the North. The comprador bourgeoisie were mentioned first only because they had more money and were therefore to be abolished first, by nationalizing their property without compensation.

Introduction of State Ownership

Western economists may doubt the wisdom of beginning a program of economic reconstruction by abolishing the business classes. To Hanoi's theoreticians, however, nothing could have been more natural. Nguyen Van Linh, then a Politburo member and head of the Central Private Capitalist Industry and Commerce Reform Department, exemplified this spirit in a long explanation of the government's economic policy that he gave in January 1978. The policy, he said, was one of socialist reform—that is, of abolishing "all exploitation and all anarchistic competition and production of the capitalist regime."[5] Capitalism consisted in private capitalist ownership of the means of production, which resulted in the capitalist production relationship. Accordingly, both the ownership and the relationship had to be changed. With state ownership of the means of production there could be no such exploitation because all profits would go to the workers.

However, Linh was careful to distinguish between the bourgeoisie, whom he described as the direct product of capitalist ownership, and the managerial, technical, or production workers who had been their tools, and who were no more capitalist or socialist than the machines they tended. Such workers, he stated firmly, were to be not eliminated but "cultivated and developed."[6] Moreover, capitalist institutions that belonged to the middle and petty bourgeoisie (as opposed to the comprador bourgeoisie and "big dishonest merchants") would be advanced to socialism by easy stages.[7]

Introduction of state ownership by stages—a tactic used to make the socialist transformation more acceptable—did not imply a philosophy of gradualism. Here, as in the North, Hanoi's intention was that the work force, after getting used to producing for a small-scale collectivity such as a factory or a cooperative, would, especially in agriculture, be organized into district-sized production units employing 100,000 or more people. In this way it was hoped that Vietnam would move directly to socialism without any intermediate capitalist stage. Vietnam would thus be spared the problems attendant on a capitalist-style division of labor by industry or region.

Such an outcome was not conceivable without strict party control. The regime accordingly nationalized all heavy industries, key light industries, the whole banking system, foreign trade, capital construction, communication and transportation (including railways, motor roads, and waterways), all important technological resources, the greater part of agricultural production, and industrial consumer goods, as well as almost all wholesale and retail trade. At the same time the regime, through its cooperativization policy, grouped all small traders into cooperatives and switched them to the production sector. The General Confederation of Trade Unions helped form cooperatives for the "purpose of creating strength, developing business and production: hog raising, tailoring, dyeing, vehicle body work, shoemaking, leather making, mat weaving, construction, printing, machine work, etc."[8] All this was done within six months of the military victory.

The Vietnamese Economy, 1975–1981

Even by Asian standards, the economy of the new Vietnam is extremely weak. Annual income per capita in 1977 was in the U.S. $70–$140 range, well below the $219–$2,544 range for the ASEAN countries. The war, of course, had taken a heavy toll, particularly in the North. Much of the North's economic infrastructure—its ports, roads, and bridges—had been damaged or destroyed by bombing, as had its factories and power plants. The new regime is endeavoring to rebuild these facilities and restore industrial production. Such basic items as cotton cloth, soap, and bicycles are now being turned out by northern factories in quantities that, although they fall far short of people's needs, are increasing.

The crucial economic area, however, is agricultural production, to which we now turn.

Food Production and Population Growth

Vietnam's top economic priority is food production for survival. Recognition of this fact was the keynote of the Second Five-Year Plan, which Le Duan, as I have said, introduced at the party congress in December 1976. Intensive efforts were mounted to produce enough rice and subsidiary crops—maize, sweet potatoes, manioc, sorghum—for the whole country. The production goal for 1977 was 16 million tons of cereals, including 13.5 million tons of rice.

The figure officially given at the Fourth Party Congress for the total population of Vietnam in 1976 was 51 million (some unofficial estimates put it as high as 60 million). It was increasing at an annual rate of almost 3 percent—an addition of some 1.5 million persons a year. The government's ambition was to provide each citizen with 200 kg of paddy (threshed, unmilled rice) per year. This amounts to some 17 kg a month, but processing the paddy reduces it to only 9.6 kg.

For a variety of reasons, even this modest goal has not been reached. Production figures for 1977 were not announced. In 1978, however, rice production was officially admitted to have fallen 4.5 million tons short of requirements.[9] Among the reasons were heavy rain and typhoons (the worst in 60 years), which had flooded 2.5 million acres.[10] In the same year imports of food from China were cut off. The production goal for all cereals in 1980—the last year of the Second Five-Year Plan—was 21 million tons, an ambitious figure considering the circumstances.[11] The harvest fell short again, this time by 5 million tons.[12] Lack of fertilizer and insecticides, a growing shortage of competent technicians (many of whom had fled the country), and the peasants' unwillingness to cooperate, especially in the South, had aggravated the harm done by bad weather.

Vietnamese refugees arriving in the United States in 1981 reported that the food situation had worsened. Strict food rationing had been introduced. Ordinary citizens living in Ho Chi Minh City were allowed a quota of only 2 kg of rice and 5 kg of subsidiary crops a month; more was available, but only on the black market. Rice is the staple diet of all Vietnamese. Since 1979, however, they have also been eating sorghum, a grain previously raised only as feed for livestock. The monthly meat ration, during the same period, was down to 500 g per household of six persons or less (700 g for larger households). Such a diet amounts to severe malnutrition. Since the population continues to increase, Vietnam will have to increase its food production even to maintain food quotas at their present inadequate level. Their inadequacy is certainly admitted by the government: the official in charge of the Second Five-Year Plan was replaced in 1980 and in 1982 replaced again.

The Manpower Problem

Vietnam's principal resource as a developing nation is its manpower: it has a work force of some 22 million people. The government intends to exploit this resource to the uttermost. Beside laboring for him- or herself, every working person must contribute 60 working days without compensation a year to build dams or dig irrigation systems. Since 1975 some half-million army officers and civil servants of the former regime have been sent to so-called re-education camps in the jungle and mountainous areas to clear land for cultivation or to tend crops.

Facing enemies on three fronts, with 200,000 troops in Cambodia, 60,000 in Laos, and a correspondingly large number on the Vietnam-China border, Hanoi has also had to draft a million men into the army. The million-strong regular army has been on full alert, draining both skilled and unskilled labor from the civilian economy and undermining its morale. The economy is bound to suffer as a result. In the rice fields production depends on women, children, and the old.

In addition, the regime's oppressive policies have caused a great number of experts and technicians to flee the country. There is, for instance, a great shortage of mine workers in the coal mines of Hongay and Quang Yen, and of dock workers in the ports of Haiphong, Da Nang, Cam Ranh, and Ho Chi Minh City. Many of them left Vietnam because they were ethnic Chinese (see Chapter 6). Technicians from the Soviet Union have been brought in to replace them, but even so, much equipment has broken down for lack of proper care and maintenance. The regime has recognized the problem and has tried to remedy it by releasing certain classes of technicians and administrative specialists from the camps. Usually, though, such people take this opportunity to make good their escape.

Despite the government's large-scale mobilization and direction of manpower, unemployment is becoming a serious problem. One reason is that the government cannot prevent people who have been sent to the New Economic Zones (previously uncultivated areas, now scheduled for development) from drifting back to Ho Chi Minh City. There, since they are now homeless, they sleep on the sidewalks, in marketplaces, and even in the main cemetery (see Chapter 10). As Hoang Tung has remarked, "You can't transfer everyone to the NEZs all at once."[13] Another reason is that the economy is not creating enough jobs for young people entering the work force for the first time. In this, too, Vietnam is the victim of its birthrate.

Capital Investment and Technology

In order to implement the Second Five-Year Plan, Hanoi had planned to invest some 30 billion dong, equivalent to U.S. $10 to 12 billion. Nearly all of it was expected to come from foreign aid, including $3.25 billion from the United States in accordance with Section 21 of the 1973 Paris Peace Agreement (see Chapter 11). But the United States, citing Hanoi's numerous violations of the agreement, did not contribute anything. When China, having fallen out with Vietnam, withheld the $3.1 billion it had promised, the Second Five-Year Plan became a financial disaster. Vietnam did receive some $700 million in aid from Japan and a number of Western countries, but the net effect of these developments was to make it dependent on the Soviet Union, which contributed $2.5 billion. Pham Van Dong has since declared that the goals of the next five-year plan will be "moderate."

Hanoi also needs technological assistance, particularly in oil exploration. It is clear from reports by journalists and people in international business circles that it wants American oil companies to develop its offshore oil resources because they are technological leaders in this field and also have adequate capital for exploration. But Hanoi's chances of attracting these companies appear very slim at present, since its view of economic cooperation is narrowly Marxist. Indeed, the communist leaders' limited outlook and expertise is yet another brake on Vietnam's economic development. Marxism—a very old-fashioned brand of Marxism, quite out of tune with current realities—is all they really know. Inevitably, their thinking has been molded by 30 years of war. Having defeated two major powers, France and the United States, they are overconfident and even arrogant about their capacity to deal with future crises. Meanwhile, the society they have vowed to transform into a model socialist state lacks even the spare parts to keep its machines running.

Will the South Be Collectivized?

The Northern Model

Even before the Viet Minh War ended, communist land-reform cadres were being trained at secret hideouts in the Lang Son jungle. A directive from the VWP Politburo that was issued to these cadres in 1953 made much of the allegation, derived from a French survey of the 1930s, that 95 percent of the land in cultivation in North Vietnam was owned by 5 percent of the total population.[14] These figures, as used by Vietnamese communist leaders to justify the brutal northern land reforms of 1951–1956, are actually quite misleading. Only 2 million ha of rice fields were under cultivation. Because the land was so hilly it was parceled out in very small lots, especially in the provinces east and north of Hanoi. Owning 50 mau (equivalent to 18 ha) of such land made a peasant rich; only the very richest owned as many as 100 mau, or 36 ha (equivalent to some 80 acres). Most of the lots were well under 1.0 mau, or 0.068 ha.

The communist land-reform program was based on principles so remote from this reality that some northern peasants were dispossessed, denounced before so-called people's courts as "rich landlords," and finally murdered because they had owned as little as one-third of a hectare. Of the total North Vietnamese population of 17 million about 5 percent fell victim to this bloodbath. As is well known, the program inspired a full-scale revolt against the regime and had to be abandoned at the end of 1956. Starting in 1959, Hanoi began to set up the small-scale agricultural cooperatives that I mentioned earlier in this chapter. Peasants gradually had to put their lands as well as their implements into the cooperatives. Collective life really started at that point. Peasants were not allowed to produce independently. Members of the cooperatives might earn an income based on a system of points for each day worked and fluctuating with the value of crops harvested after deduction of administrative costs and taxes. Collectivization, as we have seen, was virtually complete by 1969, and by 1975 there were 105 state farms.[15]

Ideology and Reality in the South

The pattern of land use in the South in 1975 was not similar to what it had been in the North before communist rule: the holdings ranged mostly from small to quite large. However, thanks in part to land reforms conducted by the former government of South Vietnam, the "rich landlords" denounced by communist theoreticians were even scarcer here than up north. In fact the communist party's program for southern agriculture was motivated not by considerations, however misguided, of social justice but rather by blind adherence to the principles of collectivism. According to a survey of the Mekong Delta made by the party and released in 1979, poor peasants—households owning an average of 0.6 ha—constituted only 25.4 percent of the total. In the majority by far were middle-class peasants—households with an average of 2.05 ha—who constituted 64.1 percent of the households and owned 62.5 percent of the cropland. A holding of 3.6 ha, or less than 8 acres, was enough to place a Mekong Delta farmer in the upper middle class.[16]

Nevertheless, the Vietnamese Communists' favorite word in expounding their land program for the South has been "exploitation." Their goal is clearly the same one that has been achieved in the North, that is, total collectivization of all agricultural land. The means of collectivization has changed somewhat since the early 1950s, but the goal itself has not. The underlying ideology, which equates private ownership of agricultural land and equipment with exploitation of agricultural workers, remains their official and, it appears, sincere belief. Simply to own the means of production, and to earn profit thereby, is to be a public enemy.

Instead of denunciation followed by judicial murder, the Communists now rely on an educational, carrot-and-stick approach that only gradually escalates into coercion. To Huu, a vice-premier and Politburo member who was deeply involved in the 1956 land-reform program, has described the new way to handle landowners ("exploiters") and the last vestiges of private ownership ("exploitation").

> 1. Educate the people to make them fully aware that exploitation is evil and that they must live by their own work.
> 2. All the laboring people should condemn all modes of exploitation, free themselves from exploitation, and demand that the Administration stamp out all forms of exploitation. They should report to the Administration on how they are exploited and by whom, so that action can be taken to eradicate this evil.
> 3. The best way to deal with exploiters is to talk directly with them without the need for official intervention. This is the way to motivate, persuade and enlighten them.
>
> The measure of confiscatory purchase will be applied only after efforts to persuade and educate them have been unsuccessful.
>
> The land offered by peasants or obtained through confiscatory purchases must be immediately turned over to collectives and be considered public property, after a part of [such land] has been given back to the owners.[17]

As to collectivization of privately owned agricultural machinery, the SRV's Council of Ministers has this to say:

> It is necessary to motivate and persuade them [owners] to sell these machines to agricultural machine groups while allowing them to participate in these organizations.
>
> If the attempt to motivate and persuade them fails, the District People's Committee will issue a decision on requisition-purchase. The confiscated or requisitioned machines may be handed over to agricultural machine groups for management and use; the evaluation on [a] yearly basis will be deducted and paid to the State.

> The State will confiscate agricultural machines and accessories belonging to puppet army officers, puppet administration officials and reactionary party leaders . . .[18]

Will Persuasion Work? Collectivization really started in South Vietnam with the work exchange teams set up immediately after the communist victory. Already in 1976 there was a strongly developed movement for collective work in Hau Giang Province, west of the Mekong River's lower branch. In South Vietnam as a whole, more than 116,000 peasants joined 3,200 work exchange teams, a twofold increase compared with 1975.[19] By the end of 1978, 600 cooperatives had been set up.[20] Cooperativization is now widespread, from Binh Tri Thien Province (the former Quang Binh, Quang Tri, and Thua Thien provinces), to the Mekong Delta.

The program, however, has not been nearly as successful as these figures might suggest. In South Vietnam, under the former government, there had been 250 districts and over 2,000 villages. After setting up the work exchange teams, the Communists tried, as they had done in the North, to push people into cooperatives as quickly as possible. Since there can be only one agricultural cooperative per village, a total of 600 cooperatives by the end of 1978 represents a success rate of less than 30 percent. To Huu, in the article already cited, frankly admits the regime's disappointment with this slow rate of progress and offers a number of reasons for it.

1. *Excessive Caution of Cadres.* "Because of this caution, many units including production solidarity teams and production collectives have been slow, very slow, or even worse, unprepared to progress."
2. *Peasant Opposition.* Rich peasants oppose cooperativization and middle-class peasants have adopted a "wait-and-see" attitude.
3. *Persistence of Traditional Attitudes and Practices.* "There are still many cases of exploitation by rich peasants and bourgeoisie in some areas of the Mekong Delta. Rich peasants and rural bourgeoisie account for only 4 to 5 percent of the families in the countryside, but they own large areas of land and rice fields as well as much medium[-sized] and large machinery. They are more influential in society than even the local grassroots-level administration."
4. *Survival of the Bourgeoisie.* "The bourgeoisie, which is no longer a class, is still controlling an important part of the pri-

vate trading system and is continuing to amass wealth dishonestly. Thanks to their lengthy experience, private traders are very well informed about the peasants' economic bases, including gardens, farms and pigsties. Consequently, they have been able to buy agricultural products from the peasants at cheap prices and have even been able to steal state supplies and put large amounts of currency into circulation so as to disrupt the market."

5. *Poor Quality of VCP Cadres.* "Weaknesses are particularly apparent in activities involving basic party organizations, local administrations and mass organizations."
6. *Popular Apprehension.* The general populace is apprehensive about communist land reform because it knows what happened earlier in North Vietnam.
7. *Failure to Control Private Enterprise.* "The longer we tolerate [private enterprise] and all the ways and means of exploiting peasants and workers, the greater danger there will be to socialism, production, people's lives, national defense and security and the Party and government . . . We must first of all eradicate exploitation, the rich peasants, and the bourgeoisie before establishing cooperatives."[21]
8. *The New Ruling Class.* The southern peasants who supported the communist cause and so received land from the revolution are today rich peasants or members of the rural bourgeoisie. They still comply with party and state policies and therefore cannot be handled as reactionaries or exploiters. To deal with them, pleads To Huu, the party "must nevertheless *persuade* them to renounce exploitation definitively and become new laboring people."[22]
9. *Noncommunist Land Reform.* The land reform program of the former South Vietnamese government is also an important factor. Under that program, landless peasants were given free land. Since they began as poor peasants, these landowners do not hesitate to speak out against expropriation.

To Huu's list of problems is probably accurate and comprehensive, but it does not sufficiently emphasize that the Vietnamese communist party's own cadres are the greatest difficulty of all. It was the cadres who bore the major share of blame for the collapse of northern land reform in 1956. Such lessons are not forgotten, and the cadres in charge of southern land reform are likely to err on the side of caution. Southern peasants, moreover, are just not good material for cooperatives. Most of them are not poor (or were not until the Communists took over) and have no good reason to consider themselves exploited by other classes.

How then will the party succeed in collectivizing southern agriculture? If persuasion fails, as it seems likely to, then the party will have to use force. At present, because it is anxious not to repeat the errors of 1955–1956, it is officially committed to persuasion. No one in the party, especially Truong Chinh and his protégé, Ho Viet Thang, who were largely responsible for those errors, can risk the possible consequences of changing that policy. In any case, the few attempts, made soon after the communist victory, at northern-style judicial lynchings of landowners were notably unsuccessful because the southern peasants could not be made to applaud them. If the party cannot use this kind of social leverage against the so-called rich landowners, how will it expropriate those of the middle or lower-middle class?

The party's original goal was to complete the cooperativization of South Vietnam by 1980. Now, with so many other issues at stake, that goal has been postponed, but there is no question of its being abandoned; collectivism is the official religion. The party is already split into pro-Russian and pro-Chinese factions; Ho Chi Minh's death has left it without an outstanding leader. Indeed, as I shall explain in Chapter 4, the only thing saving it from an open fight over the leadership is an alliance of convenience between the two chief contenders and their entourages. If the South cannot be collectivized by currently approved means, then the issue of persuasion versus violence is bound to reoccur. When it does, the party will be rocked to its very foundations.

The End of Private Commerce

On September 10, 1975, the PRG issued a declaration stating that "the State confiscates all or part of the property of the comprador bourgeoisie," with the amount to be confiscated dependent on "the seriousness of their crimes." Such property, whether factories and storehouses or money and jewels, was "the common property of the entire people," and so would "not be divided up among anyone."[23] Industry, too, was nationalized, the process being completed in 1976.

But the party's main offensive against private property was yet to come. On March 23, 1978, it launched a campaign in which an army of specially trained personnel—nearly 100,000 cadres, party members, and so-called revolutionary masses—simultaneously and suddenly appeared in every private business in the South and in the homes of those who owned those businesses. The stated purpose of these inspectors was to compile comprehensive inventories of every item of stock and equipment owned by the businesses. During the inspection, no family members were allowed to go out or in. Refugees have told me that inspectors even dug floors and opened up walls to look for gold and money. After a store had been inspected, it was closed and seals were placed on its doors. When the lists so obtained were collated, they provided the communist administration with a comprehensive inventory of all commercial and trade assets in South Vietnam.

The administration's real purpose, however, was not to take inventory but to remove the goods, and the wealth these represented, from the possession of private individuals. I say this because, after all items had been recorded, their owners might not dispose of them. They would be called to account for them, the administration warned, and should they be unable to do so, would be arrested. Later, the goods were loaded into trucks and driven away. The only compensation given the owners was a government receipt. These measures, the same as had been applied in the North in 1956, were followed by many suicides in the business community. It was not just the sudden deprivation of their wealth and their livelihood that had driven them to despair; it was also the realization that they would soon be deported to the NEZs.[24]

However, private business was still not officially prohibited. Then, on March 31, 1978, Vice-Premier Do Muoi, acting on behalf of Premier Pham Van Dong, signed an order forbidding private trade and directed all those engaged in it to become producers.

> Bourgeois traders may switch to production in agriculture, industry (including artisan industry and handicraft), fishing and forestry, in conforming with the State lines, policies, programs and plans, and in accordance with the requirements of economic zoning and diversification and the redistribution of production forces and populations throughout the country and in each location . . . the State will not collect back taxes on business assets . . . Bourgeois households having to move to [New Economic Zones] designated by the local authorities to carry out production will be given State assistance in transporting their families and property.[25]

Thus private commerce in South Vietnam was abolished at one stroke. Private transportation—in effect, all common carriers, including taxicabs—was already in the process of being nationalized.

According to a Hanoi radio broadcast of April 22, 1979, sixteen out of the nineteen provinces of South Vietnam had completed the socialist transformation of private transport service, which had started in 1977.[26]

Currency Reform. Another method of depriving people of their wealth and eliminating the private commercial sector is to reform the currency. To this end, Prime Minister's Decree No. 88 CP was drawn up on April 25, 1978. It was then kept secret until May 3, 1978, when it was simultaneously announced in all parts of the country. According to the decree, the old banknotes (one series issued in the North and another in the South) became invalid, but might be exchanged for the new issue at designated places. Urban dwellers were allowed to withdraw a maximum sum of 100 dong for single-person households and 200 dong for two-person households. Any additional member of a household could withdraw 50 dong, but the maximum sum for any one household to withdraw was 500 dong. Rural dwellers were permitted to withdraw only 50 dong each for the first two members of the household and an additional 30 dong for each additional member, to a total not exceeding 300 dong. Money in excess of the amounts necessary to purchase the permitted withdrawable number of new notes was not to be confiscated outright but registered as "withdraw/exchange money." This was to be deposited at the bank, which would later consider transferring it to a savings or other personal account. Owners of these accounts might then apply to withdraw their money for personal or production needs in accordance with the prescribed procedures.

A particularly important point was that those who possessed "surplus money" (that is, money in excess of the amounts permitted to be exchanged) had to prove that they had earned it honestly by their own labor.[27] This was the second time the communist regime in South Vietnam had imposed a currency reform along such lines. The first time had been in September 1975 in order to change banknotes issued by the former government. This second currency reform had the same purpose of pauperizing the general population as it did in the North in 1955.

Expropriation by Taxation

The communist regime's program of currency reform was intended to deprive people of any savings they might have accumulated in the past. Its system of taxation is intended to prevent them from accumulating any savings in future.

Agricultural Taxes. Peasant families are taxed according to the area of the rice fields they cultivate and the number of household members. The taxes vary from 10 percent to 33 percent of the yield at each crop and are collected in kind. If a household has fewer members and more rice fields, it has to pay more taxes, and vice versa. For example, each member of a household is supposed to eat 120 kg of rice a year. This quantity is multiplied by the number of household members. The remainder is used to pay taxes. The amount of rice to be paid as taxes thus depends more or less on the number of rice fields in the household's possession.

Unfortunately—from the taxpayer's standpoint, that is—the production of any given household is assessed by the communist cadres rather than by the householder himself. For example, average production per hectare in 1976 was officially assessed at 2.8 tons of rice. By 1979, production had supposedly gone up to 4.8 tons—an improbable estimate, given the prevailing shortages of fertilizers and insecticides, and the impact of droughts and floods. Nevertheless, producers were expected to pay taxes according to the new assessment. The system admits of no excuses. If a peasant does not meet his full fiscal obligations, he is apt to be sent either to a re-education camp or to an NEZ. As one would expect, the prospect inspires not a few peasants to transfer their rice fields to government ownership. Village party chapters and district party committees are each authorized to deduct a certain percentage of the rice taxes for their own use in paying official salaries. The remaining rice goes directly to the state.

Food Duties. Every household also has an obligation to sell rice to the government, which prescribes the quantity. In theory, the sale is not compulsory. In practice, however, if anyone does not sell the rice, he will not be able to purchase such other necessities as cloth, salt, and fish, because the government has a monopoly on them. Moreover, he will be called to the local security office for questioning and very likely placed under house arrest.

The quantity of rice to be sold to the government is assessed village by village. Suppose, for example, that village *A* has 500 ha and is assessed at 100 tons from a particular rice crop. The village people's committee will require each household to sell a quantity prorated according to the number of hectares it owns. The government also sets an official price. In order to prevent sales on the black market (where the price is usually eight to ten times higher), the regime sets up control posts along rivers, highways, footpaths, and other lines of communication. People's security agents also keep track of peasants until they have paid all their taxes and sold their full quota of rice. Peasants are urged by the security agents to denounce each other for evading the duties.

Other food duties may include the Soldier's Rice Pot, an actual pot into which every household must put a handful of uncooked rice at mealtimes (the rice is collected twice a month by a communist cadre); and the Friendship Rice Pot, used in the same way to collect rice for some other province with which one's own province has officially established friendship.

Compulsory sale of meat is also a form of taxation. Each year, a peasant family must sell 10 kg of pork and 2 kg of chicken or ducks to the government at official prices. If a peasant kills a pig or a chicken and tries to sell it on the free market for a higher price, communist cadres may stop the sale and force him to sell it to the government. A statistical cadre must make a weekly inventory of the pigs, chickens, or ducks raised by each household; this is in addition to the reports on livestock production made by front organizations. A peasant who raises a pig that exceeds 10 kg in weight must sell the whole carcass to the state. On no account may he sell the surplus weight to his friends, nor may he raise extra pigs for that purpose. Somebody, however, must be raising a few extra ones, since I am told that peasants who raise no pigs at all, and therefore cannot deliver the compulsory 10 kg, can always buy that amount and swear it was homegrown.

The Unofficial Economy

Official corruption has become such a serious problem in socialist Vietnam that the Council of Ministers, in June 1979, issued a decree that holds heads of government agencies responsible for their subordinates' "irresponsible and undisciplined acts, misappropriation of public property and lack of the spirit of serving the people."[28] Newspaper cartoons frequently depict officials as corrupt (Figure 1). Still more significantly, the matter has been included in the new constitution, which states: "The law severely punishes all acts of speculation, hoarding, and all other illegal undertakings that upset the market, and undermine state plans, as well as all acts of corruption, theft, bribery, waste, or irresponsible action that seriously damage the interests of the state and the people" (chapter 2, article 35).

FIGURE 1

The chain is completed.

Socialism and Survival

Despite these prohibitions, and the campaign launched to enforce them, the new regime has had very little success in eradicating either official corruption or the black-market activities with which it is often linked. Nobody, of course, should be surprised by the failure of an official inquiry into official corruption. This inquiry, though, since it was spearheaded by senior officials in Hanoi, is an intriguing index of how far up the communist hierarchy such corruption goes. Only drastic action could have solved the problem, and it was not taken. Why not? Three reasons have been suggested.

1. Disciplining the principal culprits would not only have weakened the party and robbed it of some of its most experienced personnel; it would also, through resulting scandal, have severely damaged the party's image.

2. The country's economic situation was already very bad, and the failure of so many recent harvests had brought about chronic food shortages that necessitated large cuts in rations. Whatever their other disadvantages might be, the black markets were at least procuring food from somewhere and selling it to the general public.
3. Opposition to the communist regime in the South was endemic, and the flood of illegal refugees was not only growing but receiving unwelcome publicity overseas. Further harsh pressures on the people of South Vietnam could well have made the situation even more difficult to cope with.[29]

To these three reasons I would add a fourth: the regime's consciousness that collectivization is failing. Its unofficial tolerance of small-scale private enterprise is not just a response to temporary shortages. Even in the North, where the socialist transformation has officially been completed, there are many economic activities that fall outside the socialist system. In the South, such expedients as selling part of one's rice ration on the black market make all the difference between survival and starvation for most urban families. Without the unofficial economy the official economy would not work at all, and the regime would collapse.

Theft of Government Property

Reports of corruption on the part of high-ranking party cadres remain, for obvious reasons, in the realm of hearsay. Low-ranking cadres, however, can be observed making off with what the regime calls "socialist property." The following report from a reader appeared in *Nhan Dan* in 1976.

> Recently, on Highway 19 from Qui Nhon to Kontum [Cong Tum], military convoys, consisting of from four to six trucks, were to be seen returning empty to their original units after delivery of goods. What worried people was that each truck was towing another. How could so many trucks have broken down at once? We made inquiries into the matter and found that this was really an "initiative to save gasoline." The nature of this initiative is very simple: One truck's engine is turned off and another is then used to tow it. The fuel thus saved is sent to the black market.[30]

The incident was not exceptional. A year later *Tin Sang*, an apparently private newspaper that had adopted the communist line, was quoting the party Central Committee to the effect that the theft of socialist property had occurred and was continuing to occur in Ho Chi Minh City and a number of other places. So far from being checked, it was "tending to increase and in some respects [was] serious." Government property ranging from vehicles and machinery to furniture had, it appeared, been "lost" in rather large quantities, only to turn up later as personal property. "State materials, from cement, gasoline, oil and fertilizer to equipment, spare parts . . . have been slipped out to the free market in considerable quantities."[31] It appears that the thefts continue (Figure 2). Actually, since the distribution of all such commodities and of most consumer goods is a state monopoly, there can be no such thing as a free market in them. The black market, however, is an institution with many levels, all formally illegal but some more visible than others. The authorities have generally permitted these latter to flourish in the open because they have learned the futility (and perhaps the unwisdom) of trying to control them.

FIGURE 2

This is my acquaintance.

There is evidence that even textbooks from the state warehouses have been stolen and sold on the black market. For instance, the following poem appeared in *Nhan Dan* in 1978.

From Large to Small: A Ballad of Book Smuggling

Let's hope the Ministry tells us
What subjects it's going to test us in.
Math, Literature, and Physics are sure to be three of them,
But what's the fourth?
There's a rumor that this year
It could be Biology . . .
The students are jittery: Where can you get the textbooks?
You can't use old books for a subject like that.
The storekeeper was asked for new ones. "No longer available," says he.
BUT
Everyone knows you can buy a smuggled book.
It may cost six piasters instead of fifty cents, but it's there
All over the sidewalk, in hundreds of copies,
Displayed quite openly.
What a lot of precious books!
(I wonder, though, where they all come from.)[32]

The author of this poem, Le Giao Vien, is from Ha Nam Ninh, a province in North Vietnam. Another poem, composed in 1977 by Nhu Van Lo of Bac Thai Province in the far north of North Vietnam, describes an illegal flea market.

Flea Market in Thai Nguyen

If you come to Thai Nguyen City
You will see an awful sight,
For the market, morn till night,
Bustles with venality.

Anything you want to buy
On the sidewalk is displayed—
Even what the state forbade.
God may know how, but not I![33]

What the author is hinting at here is that if such government-controlled items as chemical fertilizers, gasoline, and top-quality cigarettes, which can be legally sold only in government stores, are found in the black market, then only illegal sales by high-ranking communist cadres could have put them there. Chemical fertilizers, for instance, can be sold only to cooperatives, not individuals, and only high-ranking cadres may purchase top-quality cigarettes.

Ordinary private citizens are also involved in stealing state property and transporting contraband goods. Bang Vu, a high-ranking cadre of the Railroad General Department, called in 1977 for an end to thefts of coal by railroad workers and people in the neighborhood; he also cited a large number of instances of illegal buying and selling, including partnerships with "dishonest merchants" to transport wood, alcohol, and other contraband goods.[34] State power lines are tapped for cooking (Figure 3).

Graft and Corruption

Everyone who is anyone in socialist Vietnam is "on the take." Jean Thoroval, a Western journalist allowed into North Vietnam in 1975, has noted the universality of this attitude.

> If a customer wants a good cut of meat in a state-run butcher's shop, or to be served quickly in a state-run restaurant, either in Hanoi or in the provinces, he can grease a palm. Certainly he will get nowhere if he asks to see the manager. A person who wants to have a suit made by a tailor in a reasonable time is advised to hand over one kilo [2.2 pounds] of sugar or a few packets of tea to give wings to the sewing needle.[35]

He adds that if a foreign embassy wants a good piece of meat to serve a guest, it tells the *bep* (cook) to hand over a few dong to get favored treatment. Hotel guests, too, are looked after only if they hand out a few dong.

The reason for these very unsocialist practices is not far to seek: wages and salaries are pegged so low that nobody could live on them. According to the official scale for 1978, in Ho Chi Minh City

FIGURE 3

The most comfortable situation in the world.

unskilled factory workers are paid 30 dong a month; beginning high school teachers, 40 dong (which is also top of the scale for factory workers); clerks employed by cooperatives, 40 dong; engineers, 60 dong; doctors and pharmacists, 70 dong; and a few top specialists in various professions, 80 dong. Even a government minister in Hanoi is paid only 215 dong. The official value of the dong in 1976 was 2.75 per U.S. dollar (it is now 9.00), but a more accurate picture of its purchasing power can be gained from a review of black-market prices, which are sometimes as much as ten to fifteen times higher than official prices. For instance, the official price of a kilo of rice in 1978 was 0.45 dong, but the corresponding black-market price, again in Ho Chi Minh City, was 6.00 dong. Other black-market prices there during the same period were 12 to 13 dong for a kilo of pork, 20 dong for a kilo of beef, and 30 dong for a live chicken weighing about two kilos. The opportunities for legally increasing one's income by overtime or moonlighting are virtually nil, since shortages of parts and raw materials keep everyone underemployed. There are, however, plenty of opportunities for unpaid labor on government agricultural and construction projects. Such labor, which comes on top of a six-day work week, is compulsory.

Getting by in the new Vietnam is therefore largely a matter of exploiting one's opportunities for illegal gain. In government agencies the corruption has become quite open. Katsuichi Honda, after a tour of Vietnam in April 1978, reported that virtually any kind of government service was for sale. ("Piaster" is the old southern unit of currency, equivalent to "dong" and now officially replaced by it.)

> I don't know how the higher-ups take their bribes. However, bribes of 100 piasters to ordinary government officials are very normal in this society. They openly and calmly ask for such bribes. For example, there are government restrictions on bank withdrawals. If someone wants to withdraw a sum exceeding the amount fixed by the government, he need only press his case insistently with the proper bank official. The latter, after a while, would usually tell the applicant: "Forgive me for being frank. However, if you insist on completing this transaction, I shall need 100 piasters." After receiving the money, the official would split it with an employee.
>
> Tax officials are equally frank. A visitor to one of the taxation department's offices is likely to be told: "If you want your problem to be solved, I need only 100 piasters." In some cases, an additional 50 piasters is required. If you need a certificate of residence, 100 piasters will be enough to make sure you get it.[36]

Some supervisors, a 1981 cartoon implies, must be bribed to take an interest in those they supervise (Figure 4). Moreover, every kind of official permit and authorization is for sale.

> Cadres vie with each other in stealing, taking bribes, and smuggling prohibited goods. All kinds of written authorizations are up for barter. Local security offices have been known to sell stamped blank forms, that is, forms already bearing the stamp of the concerned authorities, with the date and names of recipients left blank. The buyer is free to fill in those blanks.
>
> The price of a commuter's permit valid for one or two months is 50 piasters; 300 piasters will buy a permit to go and visit a rela-

FIGURE 4a

FIGURE 4b

Xuất khẩu hóa ra... nhập khẩu!
Tranh: Đinh Ba

Nếu có được cái động cơ, tôi còn xuống cơ sở nhiều hơn...
Tranh: Nguyễn Nghiêm

(left) *Exportation turns into importation.*

(right) *"If there is motivation, I will come down more often to this basic production unit."*

tive detained in a re-education camp; 200 piasters a permit to go and visit a relative living in South Vietnam; 300 piasters a permit to get through a railway station gate in order to get a place on a Hanoi-bound train.[37]

RETREAT FROM COLLECTIVISM OR TACTICAL WITHDRAWAL?

The VCP, after 26 years of devotion to collectivism, has just awakened to the fact that depriving people of their property is not the best way to obtain their cooperation. Nguyen Khac Vien, editor of *Vietnam Courier*, confessed in an interview in May 1980:

> We had to start fighting against the tendency to bring all sectors of the economy under state control. As to socialization of agriculture, a number of cadres went too fast and the cooperatives have failed. In the South, where smallholding peasants are numerous, and where well-trained cadres are lacking, this unfortunate situation has brought about negative results. It might take fifteen to twenty years to complete collectivization of agriculture in the Mekong Delta (not, as projected [until] 1980). In the North, some cooperatives are too large and their areas should be reduced from 300 hectares to 150–200 hectares.[38]

He was referring to the decision, in September 1979, of the party Central Committee's Sixth Plenum to permit peasants to dispose freely of part of their crops and cattle, and to liberalize the distribution of rice and farm products. Briefly, except for heavy industry, small-scale free enterprise is now being encouraged. In the words of Tran Phuong, vice-chairman of the State Planning Commission:

> We had taken outmoded and wrong decisions—for instance, in 1975, in prohibiting the circulation of goods between provinces and even between districts. Thus we caused widespread discontent.
>
> We have also erred in forbidding the slaughter of cattle, compulsorily kept for draft except when the beasts were too old and their meat unfit for consumption. There was no incentive at all for cattle or pig raising.[39]

For the regime, this represents not so much an abandonment of principle as a tactical withdrawal. It simply does not dare to use the same kind of violent measures to repress southern landowners as it has already used in the North. Southern peasants would undoubtedly resist such measures, of which they were warned by their northern counterparts as soon as communication with them was re-established after the communist victory.

The regime, then, has bowed temporarily to peasant resistance, but it cannot live with the present situation indefinitely. Its authority will crumble if it is forced to adopt one brand of socialism for the North and another for the South. Moreover, its economic policy is now wholly dependent on its foreign policy. Since its invasion of Cambodia, Vietnam's only source of financial aid is the Soviet Union and its satellites.

However, the Soviet aid though great is not adequate to meet the need. Vietnam is now caught in a dilemma. It is poor and has no capital for investment. But if no capital is available for development, it cannot produce; it must consume its reserves, and consequently becomes poorer. From this cycle of poverty no exit is in sight.

3

The New Leaders

The New Constitution: State Power and Party Power

From DRV to SRV

In its first session after reunification of the country in June 1976, the National Assembly renamed the new regime the Socialist Republic of Vietnam (SRV). In December of the same year, at the Fourth Party Congress, the VWP was officially renamed the Vietnam Communist Party (VCP). Both events signified that the organization of the government and appointment of officials to government positions were being readjusted to meet the requirements of this new stage of the revolution.

The measures taken aimed at increasing the pace of so-called socialist construction, at perfecting socialist relations in North Vietnam (meaning, as we saw in Chapter 2, elimination of the private sector), and, simultaneously, at the "socialist transformation" of and "socialist construction" in the South.[1] In other words, the VCP began immediately in the South to pursue the goal it had almost accomplished in the North, namely, the abolition of private ownership. The VCP's policy in the South was the same as the one it had applied to North Vietnam when first taking it over in 1954–1955: eradication of the middle class, nationalization of large enterprises, and a program of collectivization that effectively abolished the right of the individual to own property. The policy, as I have shown, was not wholly effective, but such was its intent.

The 1959 Constitution. Although a new constitution was contemplated, the South for some years after reunification was technically subject to the constitution of the DRV, which dated from 1959. Under this constitution there was a nominal separation of powers between the legislative, executive, and judicial branches of government. The legislature, or National Assembly, not only made laws but also elected the president, who was head of state, together with the vice-president and the various ministers. These, when elected, formed a Council of Ministers that was subject to supervision by the Standing Committee of the National Assembly. This same committee also supervised the Supreme People's Court, which was the chief organ of the judiciary; it was not an independent body, as in the United States.

The National Assembly was vested with power to decide on national economic plans, examine and approve state budgets, and fix taxes. In foreign affairs, it decided on questions of war and peace. Its Standing Committee appointed or removed plenipotentiary diplomatic representatives of the DRV to foreign states, ratified or abrogated treaties, and decided on general or partial mobilization. The National Assembly was also empowered to grant amnesties. The executive branch consisted of a president, who played chiefly a symbolic role, and a Council of Ministers headed by a prime minister. The council was the highest executive organ of state authority. It was empowered to submit draft laws to the National Assembly and its Standing Committee. Finally, the judicial branch was under the supervision of the National Assembly's Standing Committee. The president of the Supreme People's Court was elected by the assembly.

The 1980 Constitution. The new constitution, known as the Constitution of the Socialist Republic of Vietnam, was adopted on December 18, 1980, by the National Assembly meeting in Hanoi. It, too, provides for a nominal separation of powers. Generally, the functions of the legislature are the same as under the 1959 Constitution. Several functions, however, have been transferred to the executive branch or have been assigned to both branches concurrently. In general, the executive branch has been strengthened. There are now two major executive bodies, the Council of State and the Council of Ministers. The Council of State is the highest functioning body of the National Assembly and also is the collective presidency of the state. The council actually rules; unlike the president under the 1959 Constitution, it does not play a mainly symbolic role.

The Council of State has both legislative and executive functions. Among its legislative functions are:

1. Election of deputies
2. Convening meetings of the National Assembly
3. Interpreting decrees, laws, and the constitution
4. Conducting referendums
5. Supervising the work of the Council of Ministers, Supreme People's Court, and the prosecutor general
6. Deciding, when the National Assembly is not in session, on the formation and dissolution of ministries and other executive bodies
7. Appointing and dismissing the vice-chairman of the Council of Ministers
8. Ratifying and abrogating treaties
9. Granting special amnesties
10. Declaring war
11. Proclaiming mobilization or a state of siege

Still more important are the council's executive functions, particularly in matters of national defense and of "building socialism." Among these functions are:

1. Promulgating laws and issuing decrees
2. Arranging for the SRV to be represented in other countries
3. Conferring orders, medals, and other official honors

The council, which is elected and removed by the National Assembly, constitutes a presidium, or collective presidency. It is composed of a chairman, several vice-chairmen, a secretary general, and members. The assembly decides on the number of vice-chairmen and members.

The Council of Ministers, described in the new constitution as "the highest executive and administrative state body," is charged with the implementation of state policies. It consists of a chairman, several vice-chairmen, the various government ministers, and the heads of state "committees" (that is, commissions). It is assigned numerous duties of a chiefly administrative nature, to which the National Assembly and Council of State may add if they please. It is also charged with drafting state plans and budgets. Members of the Council of State cannot at the same time be members of the Council of Ministers.

The outstanding feature of the 1980 Constitution is its resemblance to the 1977 Constitution of the Soviet Union. Since the Council of State is vested with both legislative and executive powers, power is concentrated in it. The collective leadership that it provides is patterned after the Soviet Presidium and operates according to the principle of "democratic centralism." Despite the impressive-sounding functions assigned to them by the 1980 Constitution, both the Council of Ministers and the National Assembly are becoming progressively less important. The 1959 constitution was instituted while the DRV was under the leadership of Ho Chi Minh. It showed a certain independence of the Soviet model of state organization. In addition, it was drawn up during the war and so had to show that the DRV was a democratic regime, worthy of people's support. The 1980 Constitution, however, was drawn up under quite different circumstances. Vietnam was facing a serious threat from China; there was an internal power struggle between pro-Chinese and pro-Soviet factions in the VCP; both political and economic dependence upon the Soviet Union had greatly increased. In addition, the territory of Vietnam was being used by the Soviet Union as a military base to exercise influence over the whole Pacific region. The pro-Soviet faction of Le Duan, Le Duc Tho, possibly Vo Nguyen Giap, and others had gained the upper hand. Adherence to the Soviet model was one means by which it curried favor with the Soviets and so consolidated its power.

The Role of the VCP

According to the SRV's official ideology, the VCP is "the only force leading the state and society, and the main factor determining all successes of the Vietnamese revolution"[2] (*SRV Constitution*, article 4). The VCP plays the primary role in all state activities. The state, in fact, is just a means to implement the VCP's policies, internal as well as external. The party's major undertakings and policies are translated into state laws and resolutions that affect every citizen's life. In order to carry out its policies effectively, the party plants its core cadres in the key positions in all state agencies. The cadres' duties are to control as well as advise state agencies; to educate other party members and state officers so as to maintain revolutionary virtues; and to comply with state laws, which are party policies.

In addition, the VCP leads the society by building mass organizations. Once such organizations have been established—that is, once all ordinary citizens ("the masses") have been placed in the organizations appropriate to their status or occupation—the party cadres, as leaders of such organizations, educate the members and mobilize them to implement the state laws or policies. Briefly, the state and mass organizations are the party instruments for achieving the Vietnamese revolution. The state manages, the people exercise collective ownership, but the communist party leads. This leadership role is enshrined in the new constitution (article 4), where the party is called "the only force leading the state and society." Nevertheless, "all power" in the SRV is said to belong to the people (article 6), and every aspect of state and society is subject to their "collective mastery" (article 3). The rationale for this discrepancy is that, with the revolution in the production relationship, that is, with the people as collective master of all means of production and all property, man will no longer exploit man. At the same time, the so-called mass organizations are formed entirely by the VCP. Though in theory membership is voluntary, in practice everyone, according to his or her age, occupation, sex, etc., is *required* to join an organization. Each locality has a variety of organizations; there is always an elders' association, a trade union, a farmers' association, a youth union, a women's union, and so on. Cadres help their members understand the VCP policies and urge them to carry the policies out.

Party Organization. The VCP Politburo is the party's supreme body; its powers are virtually unlimited. The resolutions made by the Politburo are sent to the National Assembly where they are translated into laws to be enforced throughout the country. Party resolutions are also transmitted throughout the party hierarchy, down to the lowest party echelon, for study followed by implementation. Thus all decisions made by the party are carried out at state agencies of all levels. Party cadres holding key positions as supervisors in these agencies are there to follow up and ensure that the decisions are properly implemented.

The role of cadres, as this description implies, is a crucial one, and the party does not select them casually. First of all, a cadre must have been admitted to the party as a member, after a long period of challenge or trial and after having acquired a record of accomplishment on the party's behalf. When, after becoming a party member, he shows himself loyal to the party, acquires respect from other members, and has had experience in party work, he is promoted to a leading position in his party chapter. Usually he is elected by the chapter members, which means in practice that he is appointed by the party echelon immediately superior to his, with an election to ratify the appointment. To become a party cadre, a member must hold office at least at chapter level.

The State Manages Society

The doctrine put forward in article 12 of the new constitution is that "the state manages society according to law." A great many important functions, particularly economic and social ones, are attributed directly to the state (see especially chapters 2 and 3 of the constitution). In reality, the power of the state is a facade, erected because there is need of an official authority. Actual power resides with the VCP, which leads or gives directives to state authorities in furtherance of its policies.

Nevertheless, the formal structure of the state, as laid down in the constitution, is what makes it possible for the party to undertake the daily tasks of government. The highest organ of state power is the National Assembly, while the people's councils perform the same functions at the local level. Both the National Assembly and the councils are supposedly elected according to the principle of universal, equal, direct, and secret ballot, and are "responsible to the people." The National Assembly under the leadership of the VCP is charged with resolving the most important questions of state. The people's councils resolve important local issues in keeping with the lines and policies of the central state administration—and, of course, the party. The state is said to follow the law and the constitution, but the constitution ensures that its policies with regard to both will always be party policies.

The executive body of the National Assembly is, as I have said, the Council of Ministers. It has local counterparts that are known as people's committees; they are elected and supervised by the corresponding people's councils. Such formal machinery gives surface plausibility to article 2 of the new constitution, which declares the SRV to be a "state of proletarian dictatorship" devoted to "abolishing human exploitation." The true meaning of these phrases becomes evident when one examines the other basic functions of this "proletarian" state: "to crush all acts of opposition by counterrevolutionary elements in the country and all acts of aggression and sabotage by external enemies; build socialism successfully and advance to communism; and contribute to consolidating peace and accelerating the revolutionary cause of the people throughout the world." In other words, violence when used exclusively by the working class (which in the SRV includes poor peasants) is allowable under the new constitution in order to achieve collectivization or any other goal that can be defined as "building socialism." The same principle applies at the international level.

The VCP: Historical Background and Formal Organization

From VWP to VCP

In December 1976 the VWP convened its Fourth Party Congress in Hanoi. The party could no longer apply the line adopted at the third congress, held in 1960. The line at that time had aimed at socialist construction in the North and the struggle to liberate the South and reunite it with the North. Now, the South was liberated; the country was reunified; and the North had gone so far along the path of socialist construction that the program formulated in 1960 no longer fitted the situation.

The Fourth Party Congress was composed of 1,008 delegates representing 1,553,500 party members. Since the total population of North and South Vietnam in 1976 was about 51 million, party members were a little over 3 percent of that total. The congress adopted new lines for socialist revolution in Vietnam; the Second Five-Year Plan (1976–1980) for economic development and transformation; and various amendments to the party constitution.

The name of Vietnam Workers Party was, as I have said, changed to Vietnam Communist Party, in consideration of "the strengthened proletarian dictatorship, the development of the leadership of the working class and . . . a worker-peasant alliance."[3] The party line was now one of combining domestic strength and international support to build socialism. It proposed to "shift from small-scale production to large-scale socialist production, and to build within twenty years a strong, prosperous socialist country, with modern agriculture and industry, a high culture, advanced scientific standards, and a strong national defense force."[4] In other words, as we saw in Chapter 2, the party's ambition was to advance directly from agricultural backwardness to socialism without passing through the state of capitalist development. It hoped to achieve this by combining the existing advanced-level agricultural cooperatives, with their village-sized territories, into large-scale, district-sized production units of some 100,000 ha with working populations of 200,000–300,000 people.

Structural Organization of the VCP

The VCP, unlike its predecessors, which had five levels, is a four-level party organization. The levels, from highest to lowest, are central, provincial, district, and village. At each level, the organization of the party is similar to that of the central level.

Among the VCP's first acts was to dissolve COSVN, the party apparatus in charge of conducting the war, since it was no longer needed. The regional level of party organization, between the provincial and central levels, was also eliminated in order to provide the Central Committee with more direct lines of communication to the local level. The new system also simplified the party hierarchy and made the party line easier to implement. The provincial committees accordingly became more powerful, since they now began to receive orders and directives straight from the Central Committee.

Figure 5 shows party structure at the central level. Officially, and from the standpoint of formal organization, the National Congress of Delegates is the VCP's highest organ. It sets forth party policies—that is, it adopts them by ratification—at its meetings, and elects a Central Committee composed of 116 full members and 36 alternates to carry out the policies, as it did at the Fifth Party Congress held in March 1982. After fulfilling these duties, however, the congress is dissolved. The Central Committee, which has a term of five years, implements the national congress's policies by laying down, in its Plenum, guidelines and directions for the Politburo to follow. Under the plenum system, the Central Committee does not meet very often; therefore, it is the Politburo, elected by the Central Committee, that makes all the decisions. This is called "democratic centralism." Under the fifth congress, the Politburo is composed of 13 full members and 2 alternates. The functions of the Politburo are:

1. To set forth basic programs and measures pertaining to the various revolutionary lines, with instructions, especially on matters regarding the application of the lines for economic construction and management, the organization of life, consolidation of the national defense systems, maintenance of political security, and diplomatic activities
2. To inspect the "accuracy" of the major resolutions of the party (in other words, to see if they comply with party lines), ensure political and ideological unanimity within the party, and personally select, train, and deploy the corps of high-level cadres of the party and state[5]

Figure 5: VCP Structure at the Central Level

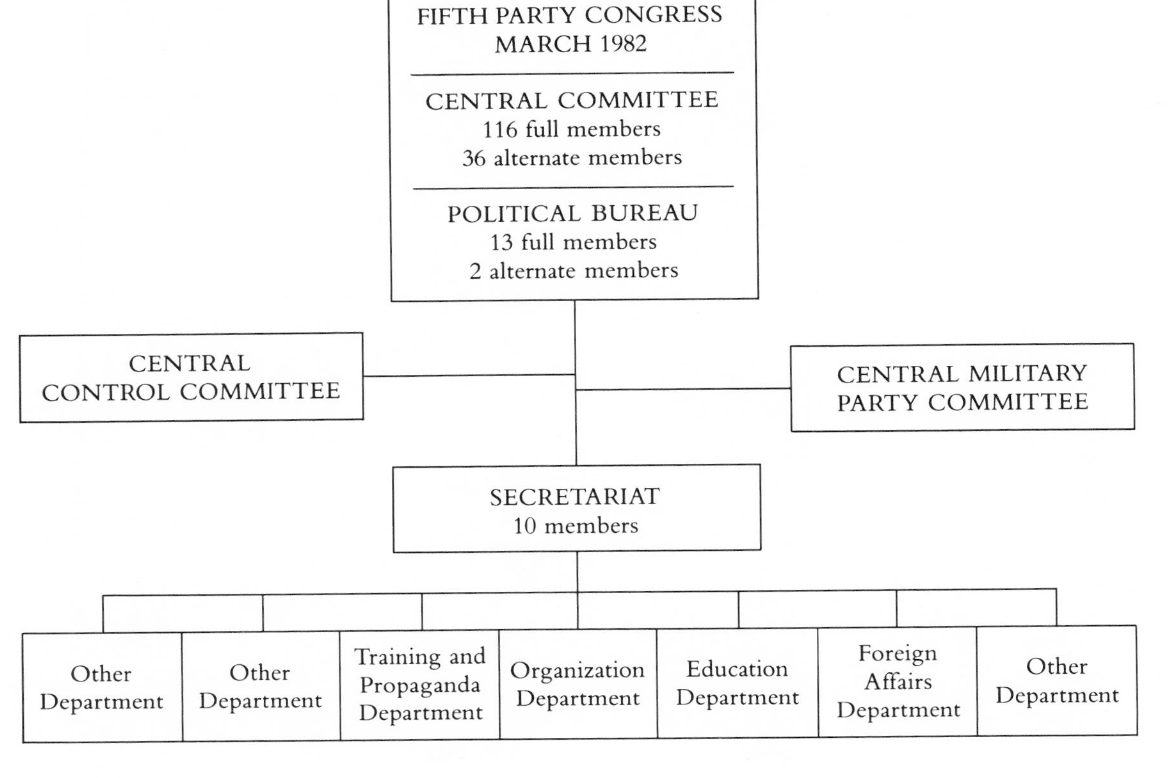

In practice, real power lies in the hands of the Politburo. The Central Committee does not meet very often, and its members are in any case selected in advance; their election by the congress is an empty formality. More important than any electoral procedure is the selection, under Politburo supervision, of candidates for training at the Nguyen Ai Quoc Institute of Marxist-Leninist Studies. This institute, which is headed by a relative of Le Duan himself, exists to train high-ranking party cadres. It plays a most important role in maintaining doctrinal orthodoxy in the party's upper echelons. In order to be able to rise in the party hierarchy, it is very important for a cadre to be selected to go to the institute. Only after a long investigation to see if a party member is loyal to the party (meaning Le Duan and his clique) would that member be selected—not to mention other factors. After graduation, the cadres are deployed throughout the country to hold key positions in the party apparatus.

There is also a party Secretariat composed of ten members and headed by the party secretary-general. It supervises such Central Committee departments as the ones concerned with party organization, propaganda and training, foreign affairs, finance, science and education, and the departments of industry and agriculture. An eleven-member Central Control Commission, appointed by the Central Committee, directs the supervision of party activities.

Finally, the three-member Central Military Party Committee (CMPC) is in charge of the party's military affairs; it, too, is appointed by the Central Committee. "Military affairs" here means, above all, the political indoctrination of military personnel. This involves, in addition to propagandizing such personnel and maintaining their morale, making sure that the military command in each instance is under the control of the appropriate party committee. Here, too, the model is Soviet Russia; thus a military commander cannot launch an attack without permission from his political commissar. Party committees of military men are set up throughout the army at various levels (Figure 6). They are under the supervision of the Directorate-General for Political Affairs of the People's Army of Vietnam (PAVN) and are responsible for maintaining close relations with the local civilian party committees. The Directorate-General is responsible to the CMPC.

VCP Party Caucuses

The new party statute greatly emphasizes the role of party caucuses. These are established in the leadership agencies, that is, in the state apparatus and in the mass organizations. Through party cau-

Figure 6: VCP and the Army

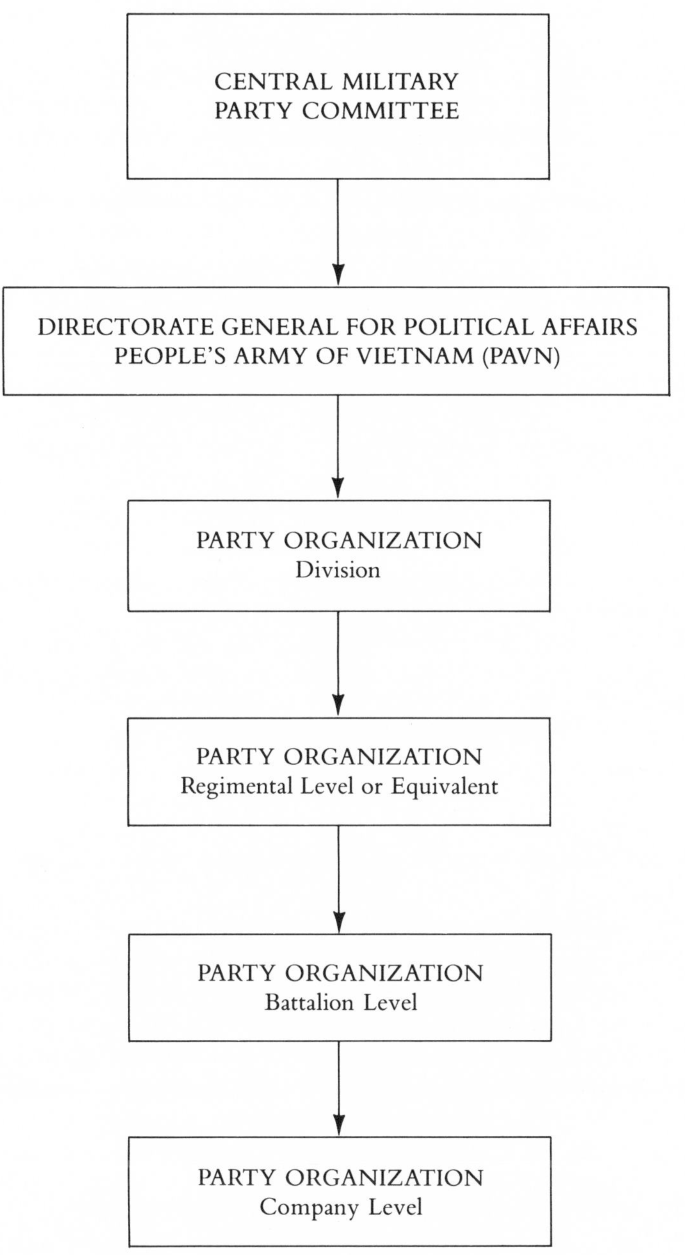

cuses party cadres are appointed to serve as delegates or to hold key positions in state agencies such as the National Assembly; on the people's councils at various levels; in the congresses of delegates of the mass organizations; and in the executive committees of the state and of the mass organizations. According to official statements, the party caucuses have the following important functions to perform:

1. To implement the lines, policies, and resolutions of the party
2. To increase the party's influence and to straighten the unity and close relationship between cadres in and outside the party
3. To research and propose work guidelines and programs for the mass organizations to the corresponding party committee
4. To manage cadres in accordance with the regulations of the Central Committee[6]

The caucuses are supposed to achieve all this through proselyting and persuasion.

However, in state agencies such as ministries, general departments, and commissions, in which the "manager system" is practiced—that is, in which a party cadre has been officially appointed to control the agency—no party caucuses are established. Instead, coordinating and operations committees are set up to ensure that the party lines and policies are thoroughly understood and implemented.

The Party Leadership: Commitment and Conflict

Major Policy Issues

Foreign Affairs. Hanoi's current foreign policy is one of close cooperation with the Soviet Union and of antagonism toward the People's Republic of China. In late December 1978, Vietnamese forces supported by tanks and airplanes were sent to conquer Cambodia. This expedition was paid for by the Soviet Union. Hanoi is now keeping some 180,000 troops in Cambodia to maintain the government of Heng Samrin and 60,000 troops in Laos to suppress the resistance movement against the Pathet Lao. It has also made repeated small-scale military attacks on Thailand and, by using the movement of Vietnamese "boat people" as a cover, has infiltrated its cadres into Thai territory.

Hanoi allows the Soviet Union to use its territory as a military base for expansion of Soviet influence in the region. Cam Ranh Bay has become a Soviet naval base and Cam Ranh airfield is used by Soviet long-range reconnaissance planes to monitor all potential military opposition in the Pacific.

Early in 1979 Hanoi fought a seventeen-day border war with the People's Republic of China. The cease-fire was followed by negotiations, but each side continued to complain of repeated attacks by the other, especially in 1981. Since the war the Chinese government has put heavy military pressure on the China-Vietnam border, pressure that has resulted in a permanent state of emergency throughout Vietnam. Over a million persons have been drafted into the military forces to confront the situation in Cambodia, Laos, and the northern provinces of Vietnam.

Commitment to the Soviet line, especially as evidenced by the conquest of Cambodia, has had a very unfavorable impact on Vietnam's foreign policy. The five nations that make up the Association of Southeast Asian Countries (ASEAN) have become more united than ever. At the same time, Hanoi has become isolated from the Western nations and from Japan—nations that it continues to hope will provide it with economic aid for building socialism. This isolation has deepened since the September 1980 resolution of the U.N. General Assembly requesting Vietnam to withdraw its forces from Cambodia. Hanoi countered with the claim that it could not do so until there was no longer a threat from China. ASEAN's response was to call for a U.N. peacekeeping force to be sent to Cambodia.

Finally, as I shall explain in later chapters, the political situation in Vietnam, combined with the Hanoi government's own human traffic scheme, has led to the exodus of over a million Vietnamese refugees, "land people" as well as "boat people," to countries all over the world. This situation, too, has severely challenged the regime's ability to conduct Vietnam's foreign affairs.

In general, Hanoi persists in the old and backward ideology that has been abandoned by its communist masters.[7] The communist world has changed greatly since the 1960s. The Soviet Union has been forced to adopt revisionist policies; Red China is now importing Western technology and culture. But Hanoi's idea of communism has not changed.

Domestic Affairs. Since 1975 the Vietnamese economy has suffered from natural disasters as well as from lack of capital for agricultural and industrial investment. A drive for greater economic efficiency is needed to develop agriculture and integrate it with industry. There have been serious shortfalls in the current five-year plan. Moreover, the country has been in a continued state of high military preparedness since its border war with China and since it sent 200,000 troops to invade Cambodia.

In 1980, the annual rice shortage was estimated at four million tons. The *International Herald Tribune*, in its issue of April 14, 1981, reported that some six million inhabitants of Vietnam were suffering from malnutrition. The same month Hanoi asked the U.N. Food and Agriculture Organization to send food to Vietnam. At the same time the Hanoi government admitted its errors in implementing the program of cooperativization in the South. In the Mekong Delta the program was halted and peasants were allowed to freely sell their rice and other products and to continue to grow rice in their private fields. Citizens who had been compelled to go to the NEZs were drifting back to Saigon even though many of them, because their houses had been seized by communist cadres at the time of their deportation, were forced to sleep in the streets. Amid so much desperation, robbery and theft soared out of control.

Another major domestic problem was the prevalence of corruption among state and party cadres. In its issue of May 1981, *Tap Chi Cong San* (Communist Review) called on these cadres to "learn from President Ho's ethics and improve their revolutionary qualities." There were, the article continued, "many unhealthy phenomena, such as abuse of authority; arbitrariness; lack of discipline, responsibility, and faithfulness; flattering superiors; oppression of the masses; corruption; making illegal deals; misappropriation of public property; speculation; taking bribes; and leading a debauched life."[8] In *Nhan Dan* on May 20 the same matter was fully discussed and a demand was made to "strictly punish those who practice corruption, bribery and oppression of the masses." A few days later a law was promulgated to punish bribery.[9]

On the ideological front, the party's campaign against "decadent culture" (that is, against any culture influences that seemed inconsistent with communist ideology) was going so badly that it had to be rededicated. In May 1981, in both Hanoi and Ho Chi Minh City, an order was made to stop "the concealment, circulation, and propagation of reactionary and decadent cultural works." Many offenders were tried and sentenced.[10]

There is even armed resistance against the regime. The Front Unifié de la Lutte Pour les Races Opprimées (FULRO) has been actively operating on the Central Plateau. It is a resistance movement led by the Montagnards (the French term for the ethnic minorities who inhabit the region) against communism. The security situation in South Vietnam is not stable. When moving from one city to another, communist military forces must be led by motorized advance teams who open the roads to avoid ambushes by former South Vietnamese troops and other disaffected elements.

The regime's anxiety over its internal security was heightened by the Hoang Van Hoan affair. Hoan had been a communist agent since the 1920s. Ho Chi Minh and he founded the Indochinese Communist Party (ICP) together. He was at one time Hanoi's ambassador to China and was known as pro-Chinese. He was a member of the VWP Politburo and vice-chairman of the National Assembly Standing Committee. At the 1976 Party Congress he was not re-elected to the Central Committee and was therefore dropped from the Politburo. On July 3, 1979, Hoan was being flown to East Germany for treatment of an illness. While waiting for his plane to refuel in Karachi, he complained of acute chest pain and was rushed to hospital. An attendant and a doctor who accompanied him were not allowed to enter the emergency room. When airline officials came to look for him to resume the journey he had disappeared. Hoan had been under house arrest before his escape to China. Several other communist leaders of ethnic Chinese origin, born and raised in provinces close to the China-Vietnam border, were under house arrest at the same time.[11]

The Leaders

At the Fifth National Party Congress in March 1982, the Politburo, which had consisted of seventeen members (fourteen full members and three alternates) under the Fourth Party Congress, was restricted to fifteen members (thirteen full members and two alternates). There are substantial changes in comparison with the Fourth Party Congress.

The Dropouts. Hoang Van Hoan became a political dropout at the Fourth Party Congress in December 1976. At the Fifth Congress six others belonging to the generation of veteran revolutionaries were purged from the central leadership. They were Vo Nguyen Giap, Nguyen Duy Trinh, Le Thanh Nghi, Tran Quoc Hoan, Le Van Luong, and Nguyen Van Linh. The first four had been stripped of other offices before the congress. Vo Nguyen Giap lost his post of minister of defense to Van Tien Dung and his post of secretary of the Military Affairs Committee to Le Duan. There were two main reasons for his replacement: his failure to modernize the Vietnamese armed forces and his incorrect assessment of Chinese capabilities in their invasion of Vietnam in February 1979. Nguyen Duy Trinh was excluded ostensibly for health reasons, but in reality for his failure to anticipate and take effective precautions against the Chinese attack. Le Thanh Nghi was eliminated because the regime's economic plans were failing. Tran Quoc Hoan was accused of having permitted Hoang Van Hoan to escape to China; of failure to collect intelligence on China's intentions; and of tacitly permitting corruption and abuses in the Vietnamese security services, which had led to disintegration of the security system. Le Van Luong and Nguyen Van Linh were found incompetent.

Apparently it is no disgrace for them to have been purged. Rather, it is part of a process of rejuvenating the leadership. The fact is that all six are over 70 and unable to cope with major responsibilities. Besides, they are still full members of the Central Committee with all the privileges of that status. Vo Nguyen Giap still holds a place on the Council of Ministers as its third-ranking vice-chairman. Le Van Luong is secretary of the Hanoi City VCP, while Nguyen Van Linh has been sent south to take over its branch in Ho Chi Minh City. Le Thanh Nghi is a vice-chairman of the Council of State.

The Inner Circle. The real power under the Fifth Party Congress is held by the five oldest Politburo members (ages as of 1982): Le Duan (74), Truong Chinh (75), Pham Van Dong (76), Pham Hung (70), and Le Duc Tho (72). It is they who share power and actually rule Vietnam today. The future of the other ten, who are described in the next subsection, depends on the five mentors in the inner circle.

The average age of the five oldest members of the Politburo is 73.4. Le Duan is said to have been in bad health for a long time. He has been in the Soviet Union very often for treatment during the late 1970s and early 1980s. It is reported that he did not lead the procession of party congress delegates on March 25, 1982, to the Ho Chi Minh Mausoleum, when the late president was honored with a wreath; that he looked old, tired, and weak at the congress and could not finish reading the political report to it; and that he suffered a heart attack immediately after the end of the proceedings and was flown to the Soviet Union for hospitalization (preparations for the congress had been unusually stressful). Pham Van Dong is rumored to have had intestinal surgery from which he has not fully recovered.

All the Politburo members, including the ten younger ones, were educated in the 1920s or 1930s when education in Vietnam was underdeveloped; neither science nor technology was much taught there, and knowledge of the social sciences was rudimentary. All of them spent almost all the earlier part of their lives in jungle and mountainous areas during the war against the French; later, some of them were in the South, involved in fighting the Americans. These circumstances have had great influence on their thinking. In addition, drunk with their victories over those two leading powers of the Free World, France and the United States, they have lost the capacity to blaze new trails. Instead, they have become diligent students of their Soviet masters, doggedly applying the lessons they have learned only too well. Western analysts should have no difficulty in predicting Hanoi's actions; what the Soviet Union says today, Hanoi will do tomorrow. Vietnam's communist leaders have compounded the rigidity of old age with the rigidity of dogmatism and dependence on a foreign power.

The Younger Politburo Members. The future leaders of Vietnam are not much younger than their mentors.

1. Van Tien Dung (b. 1917, Ha Dong) was admitted to full membership before the Fourth Party Congress (1976). He has now been promoted to sixth place in the Politburo. He took Vo Nguyen Giap's rank in the party hierarchy and also the latter's post of minister of defense in February 1980.
2. Vo Chi Cong (b. 1912, Central Vietnam) has been a full member since 1976. Once secretary of the Southern People's Revolutionary Party, which dominated the NLF, he has long been the leader of the communist movement in Zone Five (central South Vietnam). He had been vice-premier until the reshuffle in April 1982. He is also a member of the party Secretariat.
3. Chu Huy Man (b. 1920, possibly in the Central Highlands) is a major general of the PAVN. He has been commander of the Western Highlands region, which borders Laos and Cambodia. In July 1981 he was promoted to vice-chairman of the Council of State.
4. To Huu (b. 1912, Central Vietnam) was an established poet before the war against the French. He later became a leading intellectual and was in charge of propaganda and ideological training as well as active in the land-reform program from 1954 to 1956. He was later promoted to vice-premier and, in March 1982, to full member of the Politburo. To Huu is well remembered in Vietnam for a poem recording his punctilious grief upon the death of Stalin.
5. Vo Van Kiet (b. 1922, South Vietnam) was born into a peas-

ant family. He joined the ICP in the 1930s. Until November 1981, when he was transferred to the North, he had been Ho Chi Minh City party secretary. He was promoted to full membership of the Politburo and, in April 1982, appointed vice-chairman of the Council of Ministers as well as chairman of the State Planning Commission, where he replaced Nguyen Lam.

6. Do Muoi (b. 1917, Hanoi) was a political commissar during the war against the French, but was transferred to the economic sector in 1955. He has been appointed vice-premier in charge of economic activities and promoted to full membership of the Politburo.
7. Le Duc Anh (place and date of birth unavailable) is a colonel general in the PAVN. Promoted to full membership of the Politburo, he replaced Col. Gen. Tran Van Tra as commander and political commissar of the Seventh Military Region bordering Cambodia. He was commander-in-chief of the Vietnamese armed forces in the invasion of Cambodia, working closely with Le Duc Tho.
8. Nguyen Duc Tam (b. 1920, place of birth unavailable) was promoted to full membership of the Politburo in March 1982. Formerly secretary of the Quang Ninh Province Party Committee, he replaced Le Duc Tho as head of the Organization Department before the congress took place. He is also a member of the Secretariat.
9. Nguyen Co Thach (b. 1928, place of birth unavailable) was promoted to alternate membership. Thach was deputy minister to Nguyen Duy Trinh and promoted to minister at the premier's office before becoming minister for foreign affairs. He worked with Le Duc Tho before 1973, during the Paris peace talks with the United States.
10. Dong Si Nguyen (place and date of birth unavailable) was promoted to alternate membership. He is a general in the PAVN and was appointed vice-chairman of the Council of Ministers as well as minister of transportation and communications, a post in which he replaced Dinh Duc Thien, Le Duc Tho's brother.

In the present Politburo four out of fifteen members are military men, while in the previous one the proportion was three out of seventeen.

Changes in the Party Central Committee. One point to note is that 39 of the 133 members of the previous VCP Central Committee have been purged. Among them are Dang Quoc Bao, first secretary of the Ho Chi Minh Communist League (Bao is believed to be Truong Chinh's brother); Dinh Duc Thien, minister of transportation and communications (Thien, as I said, is Le Duc Tho's brother); Phan Van Dang, deputy director of the Organization Department; Tran Nam Trung, former PRG minister of defense and chairman of the Inspectorate; Col. Gen. Tran Van Tra, a legendary military figure in the takeover of the South in 1975, then chairman of the Saigon Gia Dinh Military Management Committee; Le Quoc Than, deputy minister in the Ministry of Interior for almost two decades under Tran Quoc Hoan; Nguyen Thanh Le, director of the Central Committee's Foreign Relations Department and member of the Secretariat of the Council of State; Nguyen Huu Khiem, former ambassador to Moscow; the current ambassador, Nguyen Huu Mai; Duong Quoc Chinh, minister of war invalids and social welfare; Xuan Thuy, a long-time member in charge of foreign relations in the VCP Central Committee, who is not only vice-chairman of the Council of State but also secretary-general of the council and president of the Vietnam-Soviet Friendship Association.

Two former PRG ministers who received promotions to the VCP Central Committee in 1982 were Mme. Nguyen Thi Binh, then minister of education, and Nguyen Van Hieu, an alternate member, then minister of culture.

Government by Resolution. These leaders have not been able to develop realistic policies. Since there is no longer any so-called imperialist intervention to serve as a catalyst for rhetoric and emotion, the leaders fail to inspire.[12] An example is Truong Chinh's appeal to strengthen proletarian dictatorship in the face of the unenthusiastic implementation of party policies by lower-level cadres. The kind of violence that he wreaked on the North during the period from 1953 to 1956 cannot be evoked in the South. Hoang Huu Quynh, a high-ranking VCP member who escaped from Vietnam, said in an interview in France in February 1980:

> The Politburo knows only how to solve problems by means of resolutions. One resolution, though just issued, having not yet gotten through all levels of the party, is already been replaced by another. None of the resolutions truly reflects the realities. On the other hand,

> in sessions of "resolution study" reserved for managers of state agencies (very high-ranking cadres), they also play democratic games such as criticism and self-criticism. In the recapitulation reports, however, they always first write, "We all completely agree with the party Politburo." If there is criticism, then it is merely a farce.[13]

Local leaders do not want to send the true contents of such reports to the Central Committee because by doing so they would waste time and harm themselves.

4
Conflict, Change, and Ideology

How the Leaders Remain in Power

The communist leadership maintains itself in power despite severe internal differences and a system that stifles initiative. There are two main types of internal conflict in Vietnam's communist leadership: between different factions in the Politburo; and between the older and younger generations. Only the former will be dealt with here; the latter, since it is an all-pervasive theme, is discussed in the next section, under "Changes in the Leadership."

Internal Conflict: The Rule of the Two Families

The factions can be roughly described as pro-Soviet, on the one hand, and pro-Chinese, on the other, with a third consisting of middle-of-the-roaders or moderates who try to avoid being drawn into either. Direct evidence is hard to obtain, but the principal figures can be assigned to one or another of the three factions on the strength of their background and connections. They line up as follows:

1. *Pro-Soviet Faction*: Le Duan, Le Duc Tho, To Huu, Vo Nguyen Giap
2. *Pro-Chinese Faction*: Hoang Van Hoan (now in China), Chu Van Tan, Le Quang Ba, Ly Ban (Truong Chinh's ideological sympathies probably place him, too, in this group)
3. *Moderate Faction*: Pham Van Dong

As long as Ho Chi Minh was still alive and—after his death—as long as the war still went on, the VCP could maintain a middle-of-the-road position between Russia and China even though the two had fallen out. After the war ended in 1975, however, this was no longer possible. A struggle ensued between the pro-Soviet and pro-Chinese factions. It was won by the pro-Soviet faction. As a result, those who hold real power in Vietnam today are Le Duan and Le Duc Tho, formerly rivals but now joined in the so-called alliance of the two families. Since 1976, in order to consolidate their power, they have been removing members of the party's old guard, especially those belonging to the pro-Chinese faction, from important party and government positions.

After Hoang Van Hoan, the most important of those removed during this period was Chu Van Tan, a member of the Nung ethnic minority that lives in the mountainous region of North Vietnam near the Chinese border. Born in 1908, Tan began communist party activities in the mid-1930s and led guerrilla forces against the Japanese during World War II. He held important command assignments during the Viet Minh War and was later involved in party work among the military and in ethnic minority affairs. Tan worked closely with Ho Chi Minh during the early days of the Viet Minh War and attained the rank of lieutenant general. As a Nung, however, he fell under suspicion because of this group's close cultural relationship with China (many of them even speak Chinese). He was dropped from the Central Committee and placed under house arrest. Soon after this some 260,000 Vietnamese of Chinese origin were forced to leave for China. Also placed under house arrest in the same coup were Maj. Gen. Le Quang Ba, a founder of the PAVN and former chairman of the Minorities Commission; Ly Ban, former deputy minister of foreign trade; and Tran Dinh Tri, secretary of the National Assembly Standing Committee.

Although the leadership provided by the Politburo is nominally collective, with decisions made by majority vote, Le Duan, by virtue of his position as its secretary-general, has enjoyed superiority over the other members. He could not have done so, however, had he not received support from Le Duc Tho, who is in charge of placing high-ranking party cadres in the party apparatus and state agencies; from former interior minister Tran Quoc Hoan, who was in charge of party and state security matters; and from Vo Nguyen Giap, who was in charge of national defense matters until February 1980. Real power lies in Le Duan's and Le Duc Tho's hands because they control the key appointments to a comparatively small number of important ministries, departments, and other bodies, particularly the following.

1. *Ministry of the Interior.* The ministry is in charge of all security matters, and its minister is therefore a powerful person. Under the current regime, the prime duty of whoever holds this post is to consolidate Le Duan's position. To make sure, Duan has appointed his son, Le Hong, as head of the Secret Police, which he uses to eliminate all opponents, including potential ones. The Secret Police is the most important body under the ministry's control. Tran Quoc Hoan, according to some analysts, was removed from the post of interior minister for failure to deal effectively with the pro-Chinese faction.
2. *Planning Commission.* This commission is in charge of implementing the five-year plan. The head of the commission usually holds the cabinet post of vice-premier. The failure or success of the plan reflects the failure or success of the whole socialist regime.
3. *Ministry of Foreign Affairs.* Since Hanoi desperately needs foreign aid for its five-year plan, the foreign minister is a key member of the ruling elite.
4. *General Political Directorate and General Logistics Department of the PAVN.* Control of these two bodies is vital to control of the state. The PAVN's Political Directorate takes care of the soldiers' morale and sees that they remain loyal to their leader, Le Duan. If there is any opposition or potential opposition to Le Duan in the PAVN, the Political Directorate is supposed to detect and eliminate it. As for the Logistics Directorate, it is clear that all military supplies—food, weapons, ammunition, etc.—must be controlled by someone loyal to Le Duan in order to avoid the possibility of a rebellion.
5. *Ministry of Transportation and Communications.* All activities of the state depend on this ministry, which controls all vehicles, boats, and planes. It also controls transportation arteries and facilities, such as airfields, ports, highways, air lanes, waterways, and roads.

Appointing new members to such sensitive positions has been one means by which the alliance of two families has strengthened its hold on the regime. Thus Phan Trong Tue, minister of transportation and communications, was replaced in February 1980 by Dinh

Duc Thien, who is Le Duc Tho's brother. In April 1982 Dong Sy Nguyen, a newly elected alternate member of the Poltiburo, was appointed minister of transportation and communications; he is presumably a protégé of Le Duan's. Another of Tho's brothers, Mai Chi Tho, was, as of 1982, the chairman of the Ho Chi Minh City People's Committee, a position equivalent to mayor. Le Duan, besides a son who was head of the Secret Police, had a brother-in-law, Tran Lam, who was head of the government-run Propaganda, Radio, and Television Sector, and a son-in-law who controlled the air force. Nor was it any coincidence that Tran Lam's brother, Tran Quynh, was director of the prestigious Nguyen Ai Quoc Institute of Marxist-Leninist Studies. Not all the key people were relatives, of course. Pham Hung, for instance, who replaced Tran Quoc Hoan as minister of the interior in February 1980, was the general who directed Hanoi's final victory in the South. But he was and is also an associate and protégé of Le Duan. The important thing is that Le Duan and Le Duc Tho are in a position to decide who the key people shall be. Le Duan has enhanced his position since 1975, and it is possible that his rivalry with Le Duc Tho continues. It would not, however, be possible to eliminate Tho's influence without also eliminating that of his relatives. One must also remember the advanced age of the parties concerned. Any power struggle between members of the top leadership will of necessity be less significant for the future of Vietnam than the careers of the younger men who are now moving up the party hierarchy.

Changes in the Leadership: The Younger Generation

The communist regime is aware of the need to rejuvenate its aging leadership. There has been wholesale reshuffling of cabinet ministers and other top executives several times since 1975. Seven important ministerial changes were approved by the National Assembly in February 1977; later that year the minister of agriculture was replaced. The changes in February 1980 were the most extensive since the Third Party Congress in 1960. A new Ministry of Foreign Information was created to deal with Vietnam's isolated international position after its invasion of Cambodia. Then, in January and July 1981, there was another major series of changes, particularly in the Council of State, but also in many ministries. In April 1982 fourteen members of the Council of Ministers were replaced. The majority of the new faces were unfamiliar to Western correspondents. Two leading exceptions were Vo Van Kiet and Dong Sy Nguyen, whose ministerial appointments I have already described.

The changes, however, proceeded less from the need for an orderly succession of authority than from the regime's conspicuous lack of competence. The Second Five-Year Plan, from 1976 to 1980, has been a complete failure. Production of rice and subsidiary crops, targeted for 1980 at 21 million metric tons, has fallen short by 5 million metric tons. The population of Vietnam now stands at about 62 million, and some of these crops are used to feed livestock. When allowance is also made for loss of bulk due to processing, this works out at about 7 kg per head per month—a catastrophe. Somebody had to take the responsibility, and that somebody, if Le Duan and the VCP were to be absolved, had to be the head of the Planning Commission. In February 1980 commission chairman Le Thanh Nghi was replaced by 57-year-old Nguyen Lam, a youngster by Vietnamese communist standards.

Another disaster area has been Vietnam's foreign relations. Seven years after the signing of the Paris Agreement, no economic aid had been obtained from the United States, and relations with Western Europe were cooling off. A more aggressive person was needed for the post of foreign minister. Nguyen Duy Trinh, 79, was replaced in February 1980 by the 52-year-old Nguyen Co Thach, a professional diplomat who speaks English and French. Van Tien Dung, comparatively youthful at 62, replaced the ailing General Giap as defense minister.

Overshadowing these changes, however, was the election, in July 1981, of Truong Chinh, the veteran pro-Chinese hardliner, to chairmanship of the Council of State. The re-emergence of Truong Chinh was a distinct setback to those who had theorized that the government of Vietnam was gradually being taken over by younger, apolitical technocrats. Truong Chinh was the ideological mentor of the party's old guard. As the party's secretary-general he was appointed head of the brutal northern land-reform program described in Chapter 2. Having received the communist ideology from China in the late 1920s, he adopted the Chinese approach to land reform, which is based on the concept of proletarian dictatorship. Although Le Duan, Pham Van Dong, and Vo Nguyen Giap often flew to Moscow for consultation, Truong Chinh was hardly ever among them.

If Truong Chinh's background is any indication, then, his election as chief of state, with the power to formulate policy, may well be a political tactic of the VCP for dealing with China. Vietnam's present military situation with regard to China is an extremely difficult one; simply by tieing down so many troops on Vietnam's northern border it threatens the regime's survival. If anyone can effect reconciliation with China, that person is Truong Chinh. In addition, his appointment to such an important position probably represents the emergence of a hard line in solving domestic problems. Truong Chinh has repeatedly and openly called for the application of "proletarian dictatorship" in socialist construction. Since nothing else has worked, this formerly discredited line may be due for a comeback.

Whether or not this is so, the fact that Le Duan, the most powerful figure in Vietnam today, has not followed the example of his mentor Truong Chinh in becoming chief executive is surely some kind of signal to the Chinese. Le Duc Tho, the other main exponent of the Soviet line, though he is still cooperating with Le Duan, was not elected to any official state position in 1981 and has not been mentioned in this connection for quite a while. Other state appointments in 1981 reflected the regime's desire to conciliate ethnic minorities, especially those in the Central Highlands and along the Vietnam-China border, and to appease southerners in general and the former NLF leaders in particular. The March 1982 appointments and promotions in the Politburo apparently reflect the victory of the pro-Soviet line. The issue to watch, when future rounds of appointments are made, is how much conciliation the Soviet Union, which now treats Vietnam as an Asian Cuba, is willing to allow.

The Vietnamese Legislature Since 1975

All Power to the People?

Party leaders are always making statements to the effect that "the people," with their diligence, thrift, productivity, and so on, shall play an active if not indispensable role in building socialism. The list of their duties is comprehensive. They are to care for public welfare, maintain order and security, and readily perform military service and defend the motherland. In return, they are allowed some representation. Indeed, they are encouraged to make their own and their organizations' views known to "the responsible state organs" and to the delegates they ostensibly elect to the National Assembly and people's councils. These institutions, under socialist democracy, are supposed to create a "sense of collective mastery" by and for all workers. The state is regarded as the organization that "materializes," or embodies, the right of workers to this collective mastery—subject, of course, to the leadership of the working class, who have now become the workers par excellence.

On April 25, 1976, a general election was held throughout unified Vietnam to choose representatives for the National Assembly of the SRV. This was the sixth such legislature; the fifth had been elected on April 6, 1975, in North Vietnam, and was composed of 424 representatives. The legislature normally had a longer term—four years under the DRV constitution—but had to be enlarged to include the South. The sixth legislature, then, had 492 seats, of which 243 were allocated to South Vietnam and 249 to North Vietnam. There were 605 candidates.

According to the brief and uninformative official announcement, of the 492 elected, 80 were workers, 100 peasants, 6 craftsmen, 54 military men, 98 so-called democratic intellectuals, 141 political cadres, and 13 religious representatives. Among them, 119 were women, 127 youths, and 29 labor and armed-forces heroes, while 72 came from ethnic minority groups. Of the 243 representatives from South Vietnam, 23 (9.46 percent) were workers, 50 (20.57 percent) peasants, 39 (16.05 percent) democratic intellectuals, 11 (4.53 percent) religious leaders, 39 (16.05 percent) military men, and 80 (32.92 percent) political cadres. There were 58 (23.87 percent) females, 57 (23.45 percent) representatives aged 40 and under, and 29 (11.93 percent) ethnic minorities.[1]

These figures were created for propaganda purposes; insofar as they suggest a genuine electoral process, with all major groups represented, they are misleading. Elections in Communist Vietnam are rigged in advance. Nobody in the South could run for office unless he or she had been selected and recommended by the NLF, the Vietnamese Alliance of National Democratic and Peace Forces (VANDPF), and the mass revolutionary organizations of that person's region. In the words of the official pre-election announcement, "the main revolutionary organization at the grass roots level will nominate patriots who have recorded achievements in fighting the imperialists and their henchmen and who stand for national reunification and Socialism so that the NFLSV [that is, the NLF] and the VANDPF of the region may select and recommend them for candidacy."[2] The names of the candidates, then, were the ones submitted in this way to the appropriate provincial and municipal electoral committees. In the North there was less pretense: the local body of the communist party simply appointed the candidates.

As for the way in which the party decides what proportion of candidates shall come from what social group, very little information is available. Presumably it is related to the tactical needs of the regime. Thus peasants, for instance, have an important role in socialist construction. Because the regime needs their cooperation, it presumably sees that they are more heavily represented in the National Assembly than some other groups. The names given to the southern groups in the sixth legislature were of course tendentious, designed to conceal the fact that all these candidates, unlike the great majority of southerners, were either communist party members or close supporters of the party line during the war. It is impossible on present information to draw a firm line between these two categories because there were many secret members. Some of the latter were probably instructed to go on concealing their membership in order to make the elections seem more representative. I believe that the "democratic intellectuals" included some candidates of this type, but since the official announcement did not say which individuals were counted in which categories, it is impossible to say. The "religious leaders," being either Catholic or Buddhist priests, are of course easily identifiable. All had been involved in antigovernment and anti-American activities, though some had supported the communist line more openly than others (one Buddhist monk actually joined the NLF). About the 80 political cadres—one-third of all the southern representatives—there can be no doubt: they must all have been party members.

How the Assembly Works

The leading role in the National Assembly is played by its Standing Committee and by a variable number of special-purpose committees. All of these committees are elected by the assembly. The Sixth National Assembly (which operated very much like the seventh, elected under the new constitution in 1981) had seven special-purpose committees, one for each of the following fields: planning and budget; drafting laws; nationalities (that is, ethnic minority groups); culture and education; public health and welfare; foreign relations; and the constitution. Since the Constitution Committee, which was chaired by Truong Chinh, was charged with drafting the constitution actually promulgated on December 18, 1980, it has now been dissolved.

The National Assembly, though credited with many formal duties in the 1980 Constitution, serves mainly to furnish the Politburo with a facade of legality. Its function is to turn the Politburo's resolutions into laws and decrees while mobilizing popular support for them. There is no actual debate in the assembly. A subject for legislative action is registered at the office of the Standing Committee and then put on the assembly's agenda. A party member who holds a key position in the committee concerned is assigned to prepare a paper on the subject. He has to receive instructions in advance from the party caucus in the assembly and then read the paper from the floor. After the reading, all the deputies at the assembly meeting clap their hands and then vote. Before the matter is put on the floor, the deputies in each team, under the leadership of a party member, will have held study sessions about it. Their vote is entirely predictable. No deputies become prominent in the National Assembly unless the Politburo wants them to be.

The Election of 1981

Under article 84 of the 1980 Constitution, the term of the National Assembly is five years. Thus, an election for the Seventh National Assembly was held on April 26, 1981. There were 93 electoral districts throughout the country. According to the May 16, 1981, announcement of the Electoral Council, the election took place as follows:

> [1.] The election was held in accordance with the principles of universal, equal, and direct suffrage and *secret balloting*, with the *Socialist spirit* and with the laws [emphasis supplied].
>
> [2.] There were 614 candidates for 496 seats. *All the comrade leaders of the party and state at the central and local levels were elected* with large numbers of votes [emphasis supplied].
>
> [3.] At all electoral units *the percentage of voter turnout was high* [emphasis supplied]. In the country as a whole, the percentage of turnout was 97.96 percent. The province with the highest percentage of turnout was Ha Nam Ninh, with 99.49 percent. The province with the lowest percentage of turnout was Dong Thap with 95.34 percent. Hanoi had a turnout of 99.33 percent and Ho Chi Minh City 97.69 percent. In certain localities, there were a number of city wards and villages, and in some cases even whole districts, which had 100 percent turnout.
>
> [4.] *The Vietnam Fatherland Front committee*[s] did a good job of *holding consultations* and *recommending candidates* for the elections [emphasis supplied].
>
> [5.] The total number of National Assembly deputies elected was 496. Out of the 496 elected, 100 were workers, 98 were col-

> lective peasants, 49 were soldiers, 121 were political cadres, 110 were socialist intellectuals, 15 were democratic notables and representatives of various religious groups, and 9 were cooperative members. Among the elected, there are 108 women, 90 persons in the 21–35 age group, and 73 persons of ethnic minority origin.[3]

On these official claims it is permissible to comment as follows:

1. *Secret Balloting and "Socialist Spirit."* Formally, it is secret. In practice, however, the electorate, enrolled as it is in the various mass organizations, receives advance directives from the party during electoral study sessions as to who should be elected. Not to put too fine a point on it, the voters receive orders to vote according to the party's instructions. In such study sessions, mass organization members are allowed to discuss the candidates and finally a report is made to the party's higher echelons as to the members' compliance with party instructions. This is the "socialist spirit" of the election.
2. *All the Comrade Leaders . . . Were Elected.* Since no one dares to go against the party's instruction, all candidates appointed by the party are elected by large votes.
3. *Good Turnout.* Every citizen has a duty to vote, not a right to vote. At all voting places there is a list of voters for each street and ward of the city. Everyone has to sign the list before going to the polls. At noon on election day, a leading member of the party in charge of the voting place has to check the list to see if anyone has failed to sign his or her name. An agent of the secret police is sent to the missing voter's home to inquire as to why he or she has not voted. The voter is given a choice: Vote, or violate the state law. Under these circumstances voter turnouts of 100 percent at some places are not surprising.
4. *The Vietnam Fatherland Front Committee[s].* The front receives orders from the party to select candidates, then recommends the names of candidates to the election council for registration. There can be no doubt, then, that these are rigged elections. Everybody knows in advance who will be elected.

Proportional Representation. In the 1981 election, the party changed the relative numbers of representatives from the various social categories. The proportion of industrial workers was increased and that of peasants reduced. The absolute number of political cadres was reduced by 20, while that of intellectuals, democratic personages, and religious leaders was increased by 14. Once again, the figures were essentially meaningless.

The Judiciary

The highest court in the SRV is the Supreme People's Court. It is in charge of supervising the proceedings of local courts. At local levels—for instance, the provincial, district, and city levels—there are local people's courts. Appropriate people's organizations are formed at the grass roots to deal with minor breaches of law or private disputes.

The duties of the people's courts are to protect the socialist legal system, the socialist regime, the working people's right to collective mastery, and socialist property. They are also obliged "to ensure respect for the lives, property, freedom, honor, and dignity of citizens" (article 127 of the 1980 Constitution). Judges of the people's courts at all levels are elected, and their terms correspond to those of the bodies that elect them. The constitution also stipulates that "assessors" be elected. The assessors, like jurors in the United States, also participate in the administration of justice.

According to the constitution, defendants have a right to plead their cases, and to be assisted by members of the jurists' organization (who correspond to attorneys in the Western judicial system). Prosecution is the job of the procurator, who has the same role as that of an American district attorney. According to chapter 10 of the 1980 Constitution, all procurators are under the direction of "the People's Organs of Control," a term that refers to the government's prosecuting agencies at all judicial levels, both civil and military. In practice, the party has caucuses in each of the judicial bodies: the people's courts, the people's assessors' organizations, and the so-called people's organs of control. The party caucus gives instructions as to the decision that should be reached in each case. Accordingly, there is no independent judiciary.

Vietnamese Communism and the "Three Revolutions"

The new constitution institutes three revolutions: a "revolution in the relations of production," the ultimate goal of which is to increase productivity under the socialist regime (article 18); an "ideological and cultural revolution," which is designed to mold a new socialist man (article 37); and a "scientific and technological revolution" to develop the forces of production, increase labor efficiency, and henceforth improve living standards and strengthen national defense (article 42). The doctrine, or formula, of the three revolutions, proclaimed at the Fourth Party Congress in December 1976, is the work of Le Duan. It is not new. Its first official appearance was at the eighth session of the VCP Central Committee on May 18, 1963, when Le Duan formulated it in almost identical words. Two years later he published *On the Socialist Revolution in Vietnam*, in which the formula is repeated.[4]

The tragic upheaval in South Vietnam since 1975, in which human lives have been ruined on the same scale, and with the same callous ineptitude, as the Vietnamese economy, is the direct result of applying this formula. It therefore merits the closest study.

The Revolution in Relations of Production

The objective of this revolution is to "abolish the capitalist economy and the system of exploitation of men by men." This is to be done by transforming "the individual economy of the people" into a "collective socialist economy" in which there is "a state-run and collective system of socialist public ownership of production." The revolution is naturally at a stage in the North that is different from the one in the South. In the North, "the VCP continues to perfect socialist production relations." In the South, on the other hand, the party has a crash program for transforming production relations "by means of destruction of the bourgeois ownership; abolition of private ownership [and private] exploitation of land; eradication of private commerce and trade; establishment of agricultural cooperatives, [as well as] production collectives and production teams of state industry and trading; and quickly unifying production relations in both parts of the country on the basis of socialism."[5]

Some of the results obtained by this "transformation" have already been described in Chapter 2. It is important to understand that the program is not necessarily meant to be rational in economic terms; it is above all a political program, aiming at a political result. However, the result is supposed to be a better life for people than before.

The Scientific-Technological Revolution

The revolution in relations of production is the hoped-for result. The scientific-technological revolution is supposed to provide the knowledge and resources for achieving that result and for demonstrating the superiority of socialism.

Scope of the Revolution. A distinctive feature of Vietnamese communism, as I have already remarked, is that it plans to go directly from a peasant society to a modern industrial society, thus bypassing the intermediate stage of "bourgeois revolution." This feature is very noticeable in official accounts of the scientific-technological revolution. The purpose of the revolution is to "build material and technical bases of socialism and increase the production capacity of the economic sectors."[6]

> Agricultural bases to be set up are: irrigation system, mechanization, fertilizers; while industrial bases needed are facilities, equipment, technical personnel, etc. . . .
>
> The ultimate purpose is to develop the economy from small production to large-scale socialist production. Therefore the country becomes one with modern industry and agriculture, [with] firm and strong national defense and advanced culture and science. With such scientific and technological bases, facilities, the "people are able to master not only society but also nature."[7]

The VCP aims at profound changes in all the factors of production, from tools to work sites.

> *Means of Production.* Radical transformation of the tools of production and paying attention to the central links: mechanization and automation.
>
> *Working People.* Overcoming of limitations and habits inherent in age-long small production like individual working style, lack of organization, conservative attitudes, and limited scientific and technical knowledge; acquisition of labor discipline, organizational techniques, management, culture, knowledge of science and technology, a working style akin to that of industry, and mastering the means of production and modern technical methods, thus contributing to [the] molding of the new Vietnamese man.
>
> *Organization of Production.* Reorganization of enterprises in order to achieve a high level of centralization and modernization: state farms, cooperatives, construction sites, small industry and handicraft enterprises, socialist labor work sites of all sizes, especially large ones employing tens of thousands of people in order to

> manufacture large quantities of products for the society; redistribution of the work force and means of production throughout the country.

There must be a revolutionary change in the division of labor in the trade structure of the entire society.

> *Economic Management.* The highest function of management is to control the whole national economy [and] harmoniously coordinate the "creative activities of millions of people to achieve the best results and turn plans into realities."[8]

Red or Expert? Despite all its talk of science and technology, the regime is unable to make effective use of the few genuine experts that it has. The reason is that it values loyalty and conformity, in combination with proletarian class origins, over any kind of specialized knowledge. Hoang Huu Quynh describes a typical instance.

> The VCP Politburo used to look down on the young, regarding them as elements who oppose the party. The party doesn't know how to use [professionals], and therefore wastes their talents, while despising intellectuals in the scientific and technological fields. The Politburo used to declare that "being enthusiastic with the revolution, we are able to move mountains, fill up oceans, and change the whole world." But actually, they could not change anything. Let me give an example.
>
> A Swedish delegation was sent to Vietnam to construct a paper mill. In an agreement between the two countries, it was stipulated that the delegation would cooperate closely with the prime minister's office in implementing the project. At the premier's office, however, no one knew the business. It was then shifted down to a minister who also knew nothing about the matter. Next, it was sent farther down, to a "specialist," but he, too, was unfamiliar with the processing of paper. Finally, a lowest-level state agency was assigned to implement the project, on which Swedish experts worked directly with Vietnamese workers of the lowest rank.
>
> The Swedish delegation asked for bamboo to be planted before constructing the mill. Their Vietnamese counterparts replied: "You should go ahead and construct the mill. Why plant bamboo? Right now we are short of paper. Sweden should give us paper first, bamboo should be planted later."

> Construction of the mill having not yet started, materials and supplies brought in by the Swedish delegation were stolen. The Swedes were angry and protested against the thefts.[9]

The same incompetence of the party's leadership in technical matters is displayed in a second episode that Hoang Huu Quynh personally witnessed.

> Another time, a delegation from the central government visited Nam Dinh Province and found out that a lot of banana trees were grown there. A decision was made to build a factory to produce canned bananas. The factory was built. A year later, it was acknowledged that even all the banana trees grown in the province could not yield enough fruit to keep the factory busy. The authorities then converted the factory into a chicken cannery. But the supply of chicken was not sufficient either, and the factory was closed for good.[10]

The Politburo, he adds, planned at one time to expand the city of Hanoi far beyond its present limits, constructing new buildings with three or four stories. It lacked the technical knowledge, however, and the project was abandoned. New bridge-building plans likewise faltered.

One reason that so few managers are technologically competent is the large number of former military cadres and officers who occupy management positions. After the victory in South Vietnam, a great number of such men, having been released from the army, looked to the VCP for their reward. The VCP could offer them very little. Many of them were angry at having been given unimportant civilian jobs while other party members with war records that did not seem nearly as substantial as theirs had been given lucrative positions. They protested and consequently were placed in better positions, even technical ones, though they were not trained to hold them.

Meanwhile the younger men who might have been trained have been drafted into the army. Under the permanent threat of Chinese intervention in the North, and with over 200,000 troops in Cambodia and Laos, Vietnam has had to declare a general mobilization. The shortage of technical manpower has become serious. Finally, because of conditions in South Vietnam, many technically trained people have fled the country. None of these factors is likely to bring the VCP's technical-scientific revolution any closer.

The Ideological-Cultural Revolution

Carrying out the ideological-cultural revolution includes such tasks as "building a society with elevated culture having a socialist content and a national character," and "molding a new socialist man who nurtures correct thinking, develops noble and beautiful sentiments, and acquires adequate knowledge and abilities as both worker and master of the community, society, nature and himself."[11] The "elevated culture" brought to Vietnam by communism will be discussed in later chapters, where I shall detail the book burnings, thought-reform camps, executions, etc., that are considered necessary for producing the new socialist man.

5

The Party and the People

Local Government

Administrative Levels

Vietnam is divided into 38 provinces and cities. The provinces are subdivided into districts, and these into villages; the cities are divided into precincts. Villages form the lowest level of administration.

At each administrative level—province, district, and village—there is a people's council. It is an organ of government elected by the local population by direct ballot and responsible to them. The council is the most powerful body at its level; it decides all important local questions such as economic plans, budget matters, police and security regulations, and cultural and social affairs. It does not, however, administer directly, but rather elects and supervises a people's committee and a people's court. In other words, the people's committee is the executive body of the corresponding people's council and forms the local administrative organ of the state. The term of the provincial people's councils is three years and that of the lower-level councils two years.

District Governments

Each province of Vietnam is composed of four to twelve districts. Under the communist regime the district has become the basic administrative unit. The Fourth Party Congress has declared:

> Strong Districts must be built; these should become agro-industrial economic units. The District must be the level for reorganizing production, organizing and reassigning the laborer to specific tasks, and uniting industry and agriculture, the economy of all the people and the collective economy, the workers and the peasants. The district-level administration must be built into a state echelon that manages production, communications and life in the district.[1]

The district, in short, is the main administrative unit of the state. It manages political, economic, cultural, social, and national defense matters at the local level and also executes all kinds of plans that affect the lives of all citizens living in the district. It no longer functions at an intermediary level, but is directly involved in production, distribution, and everyday life.[2] Formerly the district merely received directives and transmitted them to the village level. Since reorganization, however, the district has become a virtually autonomous unit, even for defense. Three main reasons are given: (1) "district administration is intended to function as an agency for economic management, planning, and budgeting"; (2) "the District serves as a means of collective planning, as an instrument for building socialism, and for defending the homeland"; and (3) the District is designed to perfect the People's Councils and People's Committees at the base."[3]

The District as an Agro-Industrial Unit. The district is defined as a territorial area consisting of several tens of thousands of hectares of farmland; it comprises some 30 to 50 production units and 15 to 20 production support units. The district

> serves the development of the material-technical basis [of the area] with many machines, agricultural implements and draft power, [an] electricity network, [an] effective water conservancy network, manual tools, water buffaloes . . . The district commands all scientific- and technical-level and management means: the corps of cadres, the manual workers and cooperatives members . . .
>
> Each district encompasses numerous basic production units: a state farm, industrial cooperatives, stations, farms, forestry sites, artisan and handicraft cooperatives, industrial enterprises, many capital construction units, commerce stores, material supply stores, stores purchasing agricultural products and selling industrial products . . .
>
> [With a view to the] defense of the nation, each district with a population of 100,000 to 200,000 will have 40,000 to 80,000 laborers

who become military or self-defense forces in coordination with regular forces.[4]

The District as a Political Unit. Emphasis on the district as the chief political unit of local government has led to the creation of an enormous bureaucracy. Each provincial people's committee in South Vietnam has 36 separate departments, so each district people's committee has to have the same number. Each department is an organ of the local people's committee. It is in charge of carrying out the plans set forth by the local people's council, which in turn implements the policies of the state. However, the department is also an organizational link in the vertical chain of command—a local branch, that is, of the ministry of the central government.

The department with the largest number of employees is the security department. The number is not made public, but can be estimated from the fact that every three families are taken care of by one security agent. For example, Hau Giang Province has about 2 million inhabitants and so more than 200,000 families. As a result, a large proportion of the nation's manpower is set aside for this purpose. Since there is a state monopoly of transportation and communications, the department in charge of these functions is also a very large one.

To get some idea of the numbers involved, let us consider an average-sized department such as the State Bank, which is the government-controlled banking system for the whole of Vietnam. At the local level, the Minh Hai State Bank (that is, the branch in Minh Hai Province), employs about 1,500 persons, about 80 at its provincial office and about 60 at each district office.[5] Under the SRV each new province includes fifteen to twenty districts, so at least 900 to 1,200 persons are employed at district offices. Some of these work at the village level, and all of them—even the bookkeeper—have to do some fieldwork in the villages or on agricultural and industrial projects.

District-level projects, when there are any, occupy a large proportion of the district government's manpower. In 1976, in order to implement the production goals prescribed in the Second Five-Year Plan and in preparation for the move to large-scale production, the VCP started seven model projects of this type in South Vietnam. Seven districts in as many provinces were chosen to take part in testing the concept of the district as the basic unit of production. The provinces in question—with the districts, where I have been able to discover them—are Dac Lac, Phu Khanh, Dong Nai (Long Thanh District), Tien Giang (Cai Lay District), Hau Giang, An Giang, and Minh Hai (Gia Ray District).

City and Precinct Government

There are three cities in Vietnam today. In the North, the capital city of Hanoi has a population of 1.5 million and the port city of Haiphong, located on the coast, has one of over 1 million. In the South, Ho Chi Minh City overshadows them both with a population of 3.5 million.

A city government is composed of a people's council, elected by the people, which in turn elects an executive committee headed by a mayor. Under the executive committee are a dozen departments in charge of specialized activities.

A city is divided into precincts, and these are divided into wards. Each city department gives directives to the precinct executive committees as to how they should implement state policies. The VCP has organized all three cities along the same territorial lines. Each has an "inner city" and an "outer city" as follows:

1. *Hanoi*. The inner city has four areas (equivalent to precincts): Ba Dinh, Hai Ba Trung, Dong Da, and Hoan Kiem. All of these belonged to the old city of Hanoi. The outer city has four districts, two—Gia Lam and Dong Anh—from the former Bac Ninh Province, and two—Tu Liem and Thanh Tri—from the former Ha Dong Province.
2. *Haiphong*. The inner city has three areas: Hong Bang, Ngo Quyen, and Le Chan. The outer city has three districts: Kien An, Thuy Nguyen, and Do Son.
3. *Ho Chi Minh City*. The VCP does not refer to inner and outer cities here, but these in fact are what they are. There are ten precincts (instead of the eleven of the former South Vietnamese regime) from the old city of Saigon. These form the inner city. Ten districts have been taken from Gia Dinh Province: Binh Thanh, Tan Binh, Phu Nhuan, Thu Duc, Nha Be, Go Vap, Hoc Mon, Cu Chi, Quang Xuyen, and Binh Chanh. Together they correspond to the outer city of Hanoi or Haiphong.

The government of the city precinct has less political and administrative importance than the government of a province because the major responsibility for all government functions at the primary level belongs to the ward executive committee. The precinct committee is therefore an intermediary echelon in charge of supervising the ward committees and resolving matters beyond their power. The precinct committee may coordinate all activities in the precinct, but the ward committees see to it that these activities are carried out.

The precinct committee's departments embrace a wide variety of functions—administrative, military, social welfare, security, housing and construction, health, culture and information, education, etc. For the ordinary citizen, everyday life cannot proceed at all without continual application to one or another of these departments. A citizen who wants to go and visit a relative living in a nearby town must go to the security section of the local ward committee for permission, which will be obtained only through the approval of the security officer of the sector where he or she resides. For permission to visit a coastal town, the ward committee security section has to send the applicant's written request to the security department of the precinct committee (the extra precaution is in case the applicant intends to flee the country).

Even a move from one home to another within the same city is difficult and full of risk. A citizen who wants to make such a move must apply to his or her local ward committee and, after getting permission, appear before the precinct committee's security department for approval. If the application is rejected, the citizen has to go to a New Economic Zone. To ensure that this does not happen, he or she must first have offered bribes to the security officer of the precinct committee of the precinct to which the move is planned. Vietnamese traditions, too, are now under the precinct committee's supervision. Someone who wants to compose and offer for sale the fanciful handwritten verses that Vietnamese hang in their homes at Tet to bring them luck in the coming year must go to the cultural and information department of the precinct committee for permission, after having deposited copies of everything he plans to produce. Health care is as carefully regulated as wishes for good health. A person who is sick first has to go and see a nurse working at the ward committee office. If this doesn't help, application must be made to the health department of the precinct committee for permission to go to a hospital. Without the permission, the hospital will not take that person as a patient.

Government at the ward level is extraordinarily complex (Figure 7). In addition to the usual people's council and its executive committee there is a security department whose head is, in effect, the committee's chief of staff. Since this department has vertical connections with the higher-level security apparatus, most of its decisions are kept secret from the chairman of the ward executive committee. Ward government has the same array of departments as state government. Below the ward level is the sector (*khu vuc*), which is usually an area of several streets with some four to six hundred households; there are about ten sectors to a ward. Below the sector is the cell, the basic unit of society, of which there are 28 to 30 per sector. A sector has no formal executive committee, but only a residents' protective committee that takes care of firefighting and organizes against petty crime. There is, however, a sector security officer, with numerous agents and informants working for him, and one of the sector committee's main duties is the suppression of reactionaries.

It is at the subcell (*tieu to*) level that the full extent of communist control becomes apparent. Communism in Vietnam is not just a matter for party members. VCP policies and directives reach the ordinary citizen by two separate routes. One route, as we have seen, is via the party hierarchy, which transmits them to the mass organizations. But they are also transmitted via the central state agencies and their representatives at the ward level (Figure 8). Every head of household must belong to a subcell of only a few families and must report regularly to his neighborhood solidarity cell (*to dan pho*), which comprises some twelve to twenty families. There he must attend study sessions in order to master the party and state lines and be able to implement them. The leader of the neighborhood solidarity cell is some local worthy who (after being screened by the authorities) is chosen by the cell members, but his deputy is generally a security agent, and the leader, too, is drawn into this role, since he or she is bound to report privately on members' activities to the security department. As for heads of households, they have a public and openly acknowledged duty to report on the activities of household members, including any guests or visitors. VCP control of the population, then, is intended to be total, since the administrative structure just described is backed up by the system of food rationing based on registration of household members.

I conclude from these observations that the picture sometimes drawn of the SRV as a people's democracy, in which ordinary citizens take local government into their own hands, is nothing but propaganda. True, one of the official functions of the precinct people's committee is "to manifest the collective rule of the working class." But this function is wholly subordinate to another, which is "to assure that the policies of the party and the laws of the state are thoroughly understood among the people."[6] The precinct people's committee does have a general responsibility for the welfare of all loyal,

Figure 7: A Ward Administration

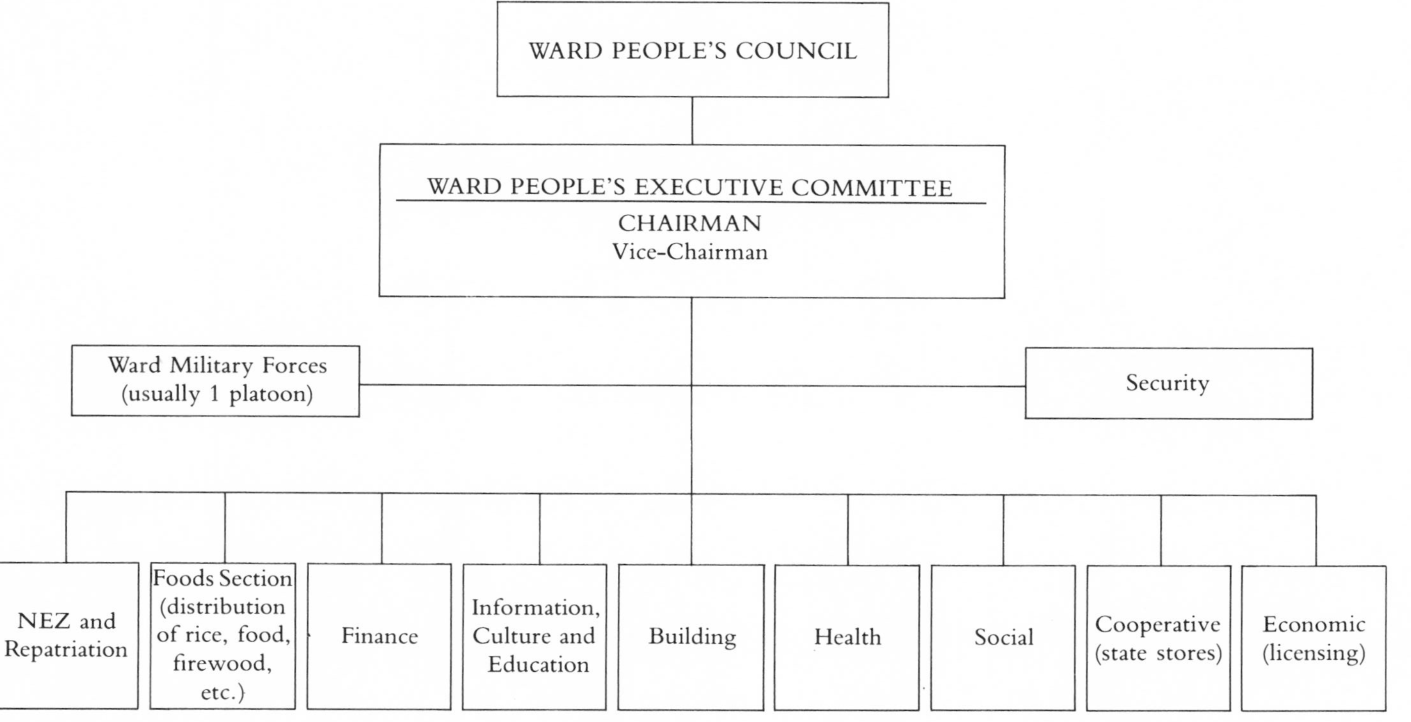

FIGURE 8: LEVELS OF MUNICIPAL ADMINISTRATION

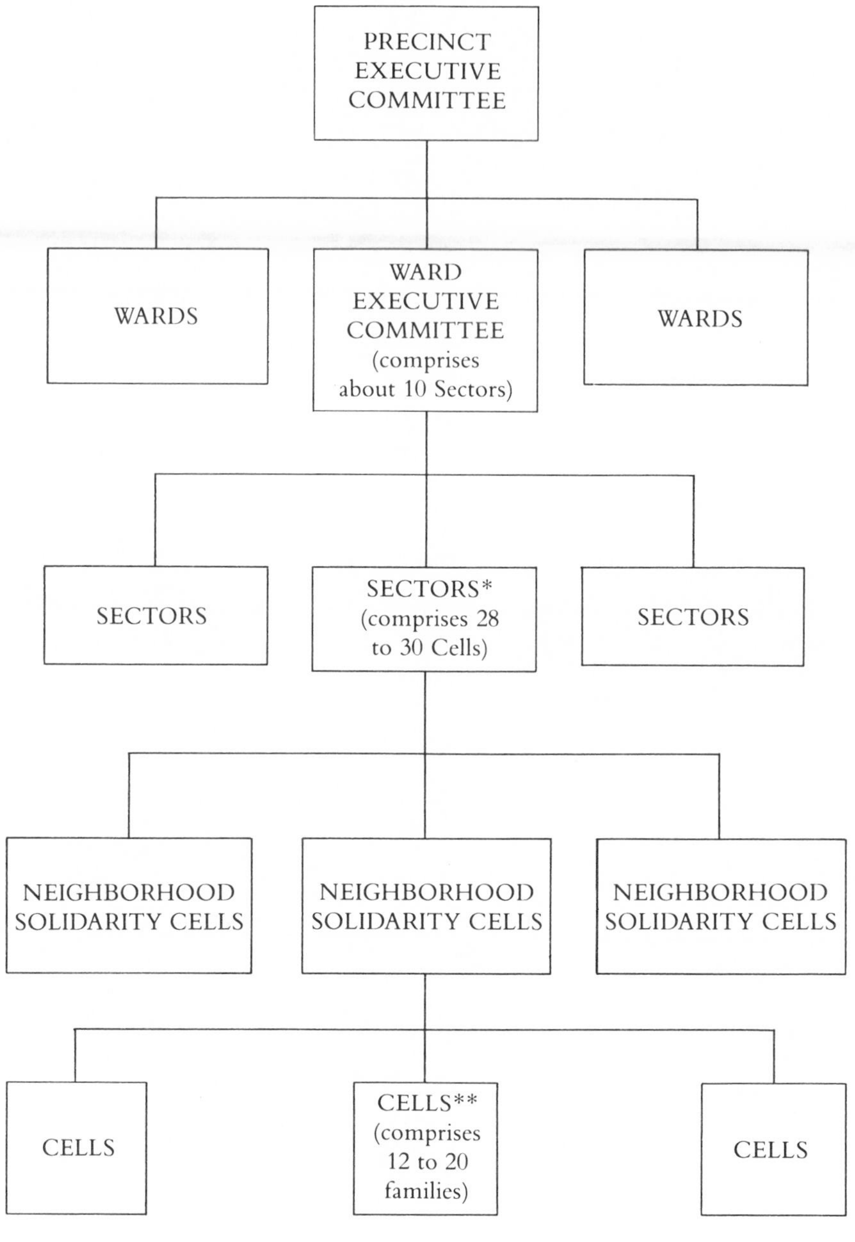

*Actually, local headquarters for Security Services

**Cell leader deputy is usually a security agent

law-abiding citizens who reside in its territory. Its members take charge of local day care, public health, and other such services, and it has special committees on everything from market regulation to benefits for wounded veterans. Ostensibly the role of precinct government is to coordinate the work of government at lower levels—the levels at which the people manifest their collective rule. In reality, however, each precinct-level department must report directly to the state agency set over it. For instance, every precinct security department in Ho Chi Minh City is under the direction and supervision of the city Security Directorate.

The Village

South Vietnam under the republic had about twenty-five hundred villages with populations ranging from three to seven thousand people (a few had populations of over ten thousand). The South Vietnamese village is still an important political and economic unit, though the VCP would like to downgrade and eventually abolish it by organizing groups of villages into so-called Model Districts for the purpose of large-scale production. The cornerstone of party policy in the countryside has been the program of cooperativization, discontinued in December 1980 because of strong peasant opposition.

Village administration corresponds to that of the urban ward. There is a village people's executive committee, with different departments. Of course, there are some departments, such as the departments of agriculture or water conservation, that have no counterpart in the city. The committees are headed by chairmen. All those who were village chiefs under the republic have been killed or put in concentration camps. The VCP has been trying to collectivize the peasants because it sees cooperativization as basic to socialism. This is the same brand of socialism that it has already imposed in the North. From the results there it is clear that, after the peasants of South Vietnam have been herded into agricultural cooperatives, the village will dwindle to a base for a low-level cooperative where peasants are grouped into production teams that work the rice fields according to the plan of the cooperative management board. The teams will be assigned a specific job carrying a specific number of work points per day. Team members will earn work points according to the work they perform on that day. The points will then be recorded in a family book after each evening meeting and the team leader will turn the book in to the management board. There will be high-level cooperatives based on groups of several villages. Village production teams will be formed into production brigades, which will accumulate work points for the glory of the collective.

All these methods of organization have been tried in the South, but the VCP has had little success with them. One could argue that it would have been more successful if it had used the same violent methods as in the northern land reforms of 1954 to 1956. If it does so, however, I believe that unresolved conflict between party hardliners like Truong Chinh and party moderates like To Huu will be brought into the open and cause the regime to collapse. For the time being, the party is choosing to live with a dilemma that it cannot escape. It has therefore called a temporary halt to the policy of cooperativization. Truong Chinh's "proletarian dictatorship"—a term that implies the government will use violence in the implementation of land reform in the South—will continue in the party's ideological repertoire together with To Huu's "persuasion." The party will probably continue to skirt the issue for an extended period, all the while quietly purging or eliminating rich landlords and other rural opponents. It knows that the day for collectivizing the southern peasants is not yet, but that it will come.

Indifferent Comrades

How the Party Rules

In order to rule society as they rule the party faithful, the VCP's leaders rely on two key institutions: party caucuses and the party cadre system.

Party Caucuses. Through proselytizing activities and persuasion, the party caucus is charged with implementing the policies and resolutions of the VCP; with increasing the party's influence; with strengthening the relationship between cadres, whether in or outside the party, and the party organization; with doing research on party organization and proposing work guidelines and programs in that area to the party committee; and with managing cadres in accordance with the regulations of the Central Committee.

State agencies in which the manager system is practiced do not have party caucuses imposed on them. The reason, however, is that the manager is a party member appointed to direct the agency. In order to ensure that the party line is thoroughly understood and implemented in the agency, a coordination and operations committee discusses the manager's suggestions and recommendations with him—for instance, with regard to the annual state plan—before submitting them to the higher party and state echelons. The committee helps the manager thoroughly understand and implement the party line in the agency. However, it does not intervene in the manager's everyday decisions as supervisor.

In contrast, state agencies without the manager system are subject to interference from party caucuses in every area of their operations. But this does not mean that agencies under the manager system are immune from party control at any level. For instance, a state agency such as the Ministry of Education, which has subordinate units at the provincial, district, and village levels, is allowed to manage those units without having a coordination and operations committee imposed on it for each level. At the same time, however, it is subject to control at each level by the appropriate party organ, which has the responsibility of leading and inspecting the unit's operation. The ministry has no policies of its own; only the party can have policies, and it is the party's task to see that they are carried out.

VCP Chapters and the Cadre System. Chapters are the vanguard units of the party. According to the official handbooks, they must be based on party lines and policies, set forth tasks and objectives, and ensure that the lines and policies are fully implemented. They also must uphold the working class's right to collective ownership, coordinate the operations of local government and the mass organizations, and create "the combined strength of the entire dictatorship of the proletariat system" at the lowest level of society. Chapters supply core political leadership for production and combat units, and also serve as schools to indoctrinate party members. They are designed to lead the economy and life of the masses; to provide leadership at meetings; to surpass the targets of the state plan; to improve the relations of socialist production; to carry out reforms in production; and to educate the masses in the fulfillment of their obligations to the state.

Organizationally, VCP chapters should consist of 3 to 30 members according to whether they correspond to a basic production, work, or combat unit. Where the unit is a large one—a factory, cooperative, or ward, for instance—the basic party organizations may be divided into many party chapters. In North Vietnam, in 1960, there were 31,448 party chapters and 16,340 basic party organizations; by 1976 these numbers had grown to 95,486 chapters and 34,545 basic party organizations. Party organization in the South is being developed along the same lines.[7]

Problems of the Cadre System

A cadre is a specially selected party member who occupies a position of leadership and trust in some clearly defined area of party activity. In theory, cadres are perfect Communists—loyal, knowledgeable, well versed in Marxist-Leninist doctrine and the various party lines. Cadres exist at all levels of party organization but are most numerous at the lowest level, where they represent the party directly to the people.

Quality of Party Members. The strength of the cadre system is its potential for mobilizing the people, for controlling and leading them in the furtherance of party goals. The system is well designed for this purpose. However, the individual cadres are vested with unlimited powers to carry out their assignments. If, as often happens, they abuse these powers, they become a menace to the ordinary citizen's life, liberty, and property. No sanctions against them are effective because the higher-echelon cadres have to rely on the lower-echelon ones and therefore shield them from citizens' complaints.

During the war against the United States, the party base in South Vietnam suffered many losses as hundreds of thousands of cadres and party members were killed or imprisoned.[8] As a result, there is today a great shortage of cadres in the South. Le Duc Tho acknowledged in December 1976 that the party had had to parcel out cadres and party members at the local level, and had transferred "a large force" of cadres from North Vietnam in order to take over the South Vietnamese government and economy.[9] Also because of the war, as he further admitted, persons with a "low level of political enlightenment" had been accepted into the party, so that party and state organization in many areas had become "cumbersome," with poorly defined authority and responsibilities; work methods were "bureaucratic, remote from the masses, and divorced from reality." He blamed the situation on parochialism and loose party discipline.[10]

Not only incompetence but actual corruption and abuse of power among party cadres have been the target of Le Duc Tho's criticism. The high-ranking party members who run state affairs have been accused of "misappropriation of public property, bureaucracy, arbitrariness, [manufacture of] prerogatives and lack of loyalty." Such cadres are said to be "violating the laws and intimidating the masses." It is feared their behavior will cause the party to decline.[11]

Statements like these provide a corrective to the mystique of the farsighted, incorruptible cadre who lays down his life for the people.

The mystique is not wholly a creation of VCP propaganda, but such public support as it enjoys can be traced to wartime conditions. Cadres involved in clandestine activities did indeed endure hardships during the war; many, as I have said, were killed. Their prestige rests on what they have been through rather than on any actual display of leadership abilities.

Recruitment of cadres is one of the VCP's most persistent problems. Following agricultural collectivization, the peasant class of North Vietnam has become the class of collective farmers. The party has adopted the policy of selecting cadres and party members from among politically advanced members of cooperatives who had once been working peasants. For the time being in North Vietnam, a class of socialist intellectuals has emerged. It derives primarily from well-indoctrinated persons with a background of manual labor as farmers or factory workers. In South Vietnam, cadres and party members are recruited from among working peasants, primarily poor landholders and the landless laborers—called "exploited" by the VCP—who work for wages.

The party spares no pains to discover these new recruits, of whom it has great expectations. Party committees on the basic organizational level must assign to cadres and party members the task of launching mass movements and building mass organizations, especially the Youth Union; party committees must strongly develop the groups of sympathizers and loyalty teams and, on this basis, discover and train outstanding persons and select the best-qualified persons for admission into the party. All such candidates must have a politically clean personal history. In the past, only landless peasants or peasants whose families had been poor for three generations could be admitted to the party. Today, however, special attention is being given to recruiting people from the industrial working class and to gradually increasing the percentage of party members from a working-class background; this is regarded as a fundamental principle for the period of transition to socialism.

In order to improve the quality of party members, the party plans to do the following:

> 1. Increase . . . teaching [of] the Marxist-Leninist theory and party lines and policies; [make] every effort . . . to cultivate the revolutionary qualities and virtues of the proletariat and struggle against manifestation[s] of individualism, factionalism and . . . bureaucracy.
> 2. An intense study movement must be launched. Every cadre

> and party member must develop a thirst for knowledge and the energy to study; this is very important because the party is . . . running the state; [hence] its cadres must have good general knowledge.[12]

Bureaucracy. During the period of clandestine activities in South Vietnam, the party in fact made a point of recruiting poorly educated people and then promoting them to high-ranking positions in the party hierarchy. Many of these wartime recruits now serve in state agencies, where they display incompetence, stupidity, and ignorance in the eyes of the public. This aspect of communist rule is well documented. Typical is the account by Katsuichi Honda, a procommunist Japanese reporter who visited North Vietnam in 1977, and who gives many details of the state bureaucracy in operation.

> Whenever a person has business with an administrative agency, he must go from one office to another, from one cadre to another, because the one with the authority to make decisions cannot be reached by the public. It must also be said that the majority of the administrative cadres are not competent. Everywhere, long lines of people are waiting—in front of state-operated stores, in front of state agencies.
>
> To protect themselves, lower-level cadres are in the habit of interpreting the higher-level agencies' directives too strictly. In consequence, peasants usually have to pay agricultural taxes so heavy that they have nothing left to eat.
>
> In Vietnam, bureaucracy is a subject of criticism. In a cartoon at an art exhibition in Hanoi, I saw a scene satirizing a village cadre who got water pumps and tractors for plowing after having bribed the communist authorities in charge of distributing them.
>
> Bureaucracy agrees very well with the employees themselves, because the majority of the leaders calling for the elimination of bureaucracy are persons who have been in the very system for ten to fifteen years. I conclude, then, that it is futile for ordinary people to complain.[13]

Honda's account is amply confirmed by the cartoons that appear in *Nhan Dan*. Figures 9–11 are a representative sample. Particularly worthy of note is the pregnant woman on the verge of delivery who is being told to go away and not come back until she has a certificate from her ward health office "and other agencies" (Figure 11).

Figure 9

Bureaucratic red tape.

Figure 10

Medical personnel to mother with sick child: "Have you seen the 'time-off' sign?"

FIGURE 11

"Would you mind going back to get certificates from your local Street Block Administration and the agency with which you are working? Then come back."

Official Privileges. Party members in state government routinely take advantage of their special position to obtain material advantages. In communist South Vietnam, up until 1979, cadres, state employees, and students were allowed every month to buy an additional quantity of foodstuffs (additional, that is, to the normal ration) at official prices through state-operated stores. Thus while an ordinary citizen was allowed to buy 9 kg of foodstuffs (consisting of 2 kg of rice and 7 kg of sweet potatoes, sorghum, or other staples), a cadre might obtain an extra 6 kg of foodstuffs.

There were distinct classes of privilege. Students at schools belonging to one of the industrial ministries (for light or heavy industry) might buy an extra 6 kg of food like a cadre, while students at schools belonging to the Ministry of Education (which dealt only with general education) might buy an extra 3 kg. Really scarce items were reserved for the elite. Each cadre was allowed to buy 550 g of sugar, 30 g of monosodium glutamate, one can of condensed milk (397 g), one bottle of beer, two razor blades, one package of cigarette paper, one toothbrush and one tube of toothpaste every three months, and 2.5 m of cloth per year (not enough to make a shirt and a pair of slacks).

In 1979 growing shortages of basic commodities forced the regime to change its rationing schedules. Citizens in class *A*—in effect, only ministers and vice-ministers—continued to receive about the same amounts as before but rations for other classes were reduced (Table 1). Citizens in classes *A* and *B* are permitted to shop in special state-operated stores where the goods are of first quality and supplies are always adequate. Everybody else must go to stores where the quality ranges from mediocre to poor and whole categories of items are often out of stock. In addition, these stores tend to give short weight.

For ordinary people—the unfortunate majority in class *N*—not even the official ration is guaranteed. Sometimes the state makes up a shortage of rice, for example, by increasing the ration of supplementary crops such as manioc and sweet potatoes. Under these conditions, the black market flourishes. Table 2, based on information from refugees, shows the difference between official and black-market prices for five scarce items in 1979.

TABLE 1. MONTHLY RATIONS IN THE SRV, 1979

Classes	*Meat*	*Fish*	*Sugar*	*Milk (condensed)*	*Butter*	*Cloth*	*Radio/TV*	*Rice*
A	3.0 kg	1.0 kg	1.0 kg	1 can	0.5 kg	—	1 TV 1 Radio	24 kg
B	2.0 kg	1.0 kg	1.0 kg	1 can	—	—	1 TV 1 Radio	15 kg
C	1.5 kg	0.5 kg	0.8 kg	—	—	—	—	15 kg
D	0.5 kg	0.5 kg	0.6 kg	—	—	—	—	15 kg
E	0.3 kg	0.3 kg	2.5 kg	—	—	—	—	15 kg
N	0.1 kg	0.1 kg	0.1 kg	—	—	—	—	13 kg

KEY TO CLASSES (1980 salary scale)
A. Ministers and vice-ministers (215 dong per month).
B. Directors-general (185 dong per month).
C. Directors and managers (125 dong per month).
D. Special workers such as miners and divers (80–100 dong per month).
E. Ordinary workers (30–50 dong per month).
N. Ordinary citizens.

TABLE 2. PRICE DIFFERENTIALS, 1980

Items	*Official Price (State-Operated Stores)*	*Price on Black Market*
Meat	3.50 dong per kg	25 dong
Fish	1.00 dong per kg	15 dong
Sugar	1.30 per kg	25 dong
Milk (condensed)	1.70 per can	3.50 dong
TV sets	700 dong each	3,000–4,000 dong

I almost forget one detail: the state provides each household in class *A* with a personal domestic servant.

Medical care, too, is doled out to state employees on the basis of rank and salary level. Those whose monthly salaries are over 100 dong receive sixteen tablets of some cold medicine if they catch cold, while those whose salaries are from 85 to 100 dong receive fewer. Other cadres and students receive inferior forms of treatment. Patients who are seriously ill may be hospitalized with the approval of the agency's management bureau. However, they are distributed among hospitals by salary, for example in Ho Chi Minh City as follows:

1. Those whose salaries are over 130 piasters are hospitalized at the Thong Nhat Hospital.
2. Those whose salaries are from 100 to 130 piasters are hospitalized at the Grall Hospital.
3. Those whose salaries are from 60 to 100 piasters are sent to Cho Ray Hospital.
4. Students are sent to Trung Vuong Hospital.

A former teacher, I have been told, once raised this matter in a political education class. Why, he asked the discussion leaders, was the regime encouraging this division of classes, perhaps even classes of bacteria? After class the teacher was sent to a re-education camp.

Purging the Party

The VCP is supposedly a party of the working class. The party therefore selects its cadres from among the manual workers who are playing key roles in the socialist industrialization of the country. In rural areas working peasants are recruited into the party for the same reason.

However, the party has had to tailor its recruitment policies to the needs of the moment. During the period of the people's national democratic revolution (that is, before 1953), the party selected cadres and party members from among rich landlords and intellectuals. Such recruits were able to provide not only substantial material support for the war against the French but also a degree of influence among the working classes that the party itself did not have. Then, after the agrarian reform and during the period of agricultural collectivization, all efforts were directed toward recruiting poor and middle-class peasants. Finally, in more recent years, the party has been faced with the task of expelling members who have "degenerated" or "lost their good qualities," persons who have lost their "revolutionary fighting spirit," who have taken advantage of their position or authority to "intimidate the masses," engage in speculation, or misappropriate the property of the socialist state.[14] In addition to members of the Central Committee and Politburo, the party has been purging its lower-level cadres. Since 1978, especially after Hoang Van Hoan's escape to China, this lower-level purge has become obvious. The party, according to its official statements, had always kept a list of its 1.5 million members, but before the purge it had not issued party cards to them. Cards are now being issued to selected cadres and to all recruits and are being denied to members considered pro-Chinese.

Who Will Be Purged? Principal targets of the purge, in addition to suspected Maoists, are well-to-do landowners who joined the party and cadres who have proved incompetent, lazy, or corrupt. The purge of suspected pro-Chinese elements actually began at the Fourth Party Congress, in December 1976, with the elimination of Hoang Van Hoan and others from positions of power. In December 1979 a VCP document released for the party's fiftieth anniversary admitted that the party had recently "carried out an educational drive among its members, helping them clearly to distinguish genuine Marxism from fake Marxism and overcome the noxious influence of the latter."[15] One way the party aims to get rid of Maoism appears to be by reducing the number of peasant members, although peasants had played an important role in the revolution. In contrast, much of the new membership is expected to come from the army or from among the ranks of people with technical expertise. Many of these may not have a working-class background, still less a revolutionary one.

Another major reason for the purge seems to be a serious fall in party morale. In a blunt attack on disaffected cadres, it is remarked in the same document that "wherever public property is available, there is thievery . . . Dishonest officials at various enterprises, shops, and storehouses are gnawing state property away . . . These dangerous rats must be severely punished."[16] More soberly, the *Communist Review* has commented on the many veteran cadres who "contributed to the revolution" but are "no longer capable of providing leadership because of age, or lack of the scientific, technical, or managerial capabilities now required." Such cadres, the article continues, should voluntarily retire, to be replaced by cadres who have youth or expertise to recommend them.[17]

The need to improve party discipline has been a leading theme of VCP propaganda since 1976. At the Fourth Party Congress Le Duc Tho called on the delegates to give full attention to "strengthening the iron discipline of the party and the party's inspection work." Such discipline, he added, permitted neither "liberalism and irresponsibility in the implementation of party resolutions and regulations" nor the voicing and circulating by party members of "opinions contrary to the party line."[18] Earlier the same year, an article in *Hoc Tap* magazine signed by Nguoi Xay Dung ("The Builder," pseudonym for a high-ranking party official) had made quite clear what the party meant by "liberalism and irresponsibility." According to the article, "an unorganized and undisciplined person generally considers himself as having the right to say anything he wants to and do anything he wants to, regardless of the restraints in the organization and discipline of the party, and also regardless of the rules and regulations of the state."[19] The prevalence of such attitudes, the writer implied, was having a great impact on the work of cadres and party members; indeed, it was undermining the party and hindering the struggle to build a new society.

Comrades at Loggerheads. Lack of comradely feelings within the party is another common target of complaint. "In some units and localities," states another Nguoi Xay Dung article, "there have been some comrades who, although working and living together, for one reason or another treat one another with indifference, show only feigned liking for one another and lack of mutual trust and respect." The party, in this view, is overrun with careerists.

> Those comrades remain indifferent and show no concern or sympathy when their fellow party members encounter difficulty[. They]

> are jealous of one another's progress and even seek to deny one another due recognition or to harm one another. Some cadres and party members speak bad of and slander their own comrades. Some gang up against those with whom they do not see eye to eye. Some are utterly localistic, departmentalistic and parochial-minded, and often stir up disputes and cause clashes in party organizations, [in] party committees, and in relationship[s] between the upper and lower level[s].[20]

Among the causes of such disunity are "selfish calculations, coveting of positions, enmity, envy and jealousy," and "claiming merits for oneself while blaming others' shortcomings." Bureaucratism, it appears, is also rampant, since there are leading comrades who "do not respect internal democracy, [and] fail to listen attentively to the views offered by their subordinates and party members."[21]

Party disunity has become so serious that some party organizations have not held a congress in four or five years. Even when a party chapter does hold a meeting, only 40 to 50 percent of its members attend.[22] Such disciplinary action as is taken does not seem particularly effective. According to Nguoi Xay Dung, "there are still more than a few cases of disciplinary action against party members that is not strict and does not conform with the spirit or principles of the party . . . Some cadres who have just been disciplined at one place are transferred to an important position at another place and sometimes promoted and given a raise."[23]

Shortcomings of Cadres and Party Members

Irresponsibility and Incompetence. It is clear from official sources that corruption, irresponsibility, and misappropriation of state property have become increasingly widespread. Le Duan, in his political report before the National Assembly after reunification, thundered against these tendencies.

> We must resolutely oppose loafing, avoidance of work, misappropriation of public property, bribery, corruption and waste. We must severely condemn and resolutely combat such attitudes as irresponsibility, arrogance, authoritarianism, the creation of unnecessary and cumbersome procedures and red tape, indifference and even callousness in face of the difficulties and sufferings of the people, and a perfunctory acceptance of criticism. These manifestations encroach upon the people's right to mastery of society and sometimes even cause political harm to citizens.[24]

From another source we learn of a real lack of responsibility on the part of cadres and party members. They are

> accustomed to the sloppy, haphazard way of working of . . . small-scale production, [and] consider the waste of time [and] waste of manpower to be normal occurrences, to be unavoidable within the society. They waste very much time drinking tea or alcoholic beverages, making idle conversation that is not only useless but frequently harmful, and doing things that are not the least bit productive.[25]

Party members may be so grossly irresponsible that valuable equipment is destroyed. Thus in one factory, nearly three thousand gondola cars were left to rust because, after the cars had been paid for, no arrangements were made for delivery, and nobody inquired what had happened to them.[26]

Incidents like these are commonly blamed on a "habit of selfishness and individualism" inherited from the system of private ownership.[27] It is clear, however, that the inefficiency and incompetence of party members would be sufficient explanation. Many working days are lost through bad management. A writer in the magazine *Hanoi Lao Dong* has painted a devastating picture of this problem as it affected North Vietnam in 1975.

> During the first five months of 1975, work stoppages amounted to 86,131 man-days at the Hon Gai Coal Corp[oration]. During the two months of April and May, 129,136 man-days in overtime work were [called for], the equivalent of 5.1 percent of the total number of required man-days . . .
>
> The number of days taken off by workers at the Railroad Projects Federated Enterprise during the first six months of the year amounted to 22,458 man-days. At the Hon Gai Coal Corporation, the majority of man-days lost to work stoppages were the result of broken equipment, a shortage of materials, and a shortage of fuel. At Railroad Projects, the result came from design problems; lack of estimates; failure to receive a full supply of materials ([the] supply of materials only meets about 40 to 50 percent of requirements); [and] the practice of workers taking time off whenever they want. It is the result of poorly organized management and education.
>
> The upper echelon said that there was no shortage of materials. [So,] why did the situation mentioned above develop? This can only be explained by poor organization and management on our part. Al-

> though the upper echelon said that there would be no shortage of materials, practically all enterprises have complained about a shortage of materials. Moreover, the [person in charge of supervising] the implementation of plans has been neither thorough nor concrete. Upper-level management agencies have not taken positive steps to act upon the proposals of the lower echelon concerning production and living conditions.
>
> In addition, material and financial allocation procedures are complicated and restrict production (at some places, workers have to be paid late or paid only 70 percent of their wages, because much time is taken off, much overtime must be worked; [emergency work] exhausts the energies of the worker and does not yield much by way of returns). If this situation is not studied and improved, the workers will ultimately have to bear each consequence of it and it also will harm the enterprise and the state.[28]

The VCP has brought its flair for bad management to the South. A typical example recounted to me by refugees is the irrigation program of the Cai Lay Agricultural Cooperative, Tien Giang Province. The southern branch of the SRV's Central State Bank, in Ho Chi Minh City, loaned the cooperative 300,000 dong (about U.S. $120,000 by 1976 rates) so that it could buy water pumps for irrigating the district's rice fields. The cooperative's manager, a North Vietnamese with some 30 years' experience of running agricultural cooperatives in the North, bought only old water pumps that had belonged to local peasants. The irrigation system was installed—and failed dismally.

Other schemes fail not only through poor judgment or inept planning but because economic incentives are not present. For instance, in 1976 the VCP ordered twelve plants from Japan for processing and freezing seafood; they cost between 2 and 2.5 million dong each (U.S. $800,000 to $1,000,000), and came complete with installations and equipment. The VCP had the plants set up in several coastal provinces, near their source of supply. What the VCP had overlooked, however, was that the supply of fish and shrimp was inadequate even for the plants built under the previous regime. The new plants, then, remained idle. The party responded with an incentive program: local fishermen were required to sell all the catch at the end of each day to the new plants at official prices. They were to receive a liter of oil for every 3 kg of seafood delivered. The fishermen pleaded in turn that they could not possibly catch fish and shrimp in the quantities that the party required. Privately, though, they were selling the best and freshest portion of their catch on the black market, where they received good prices. The portion they delivered to the plants was already rotting.

The organization of Vietnamese industry under the VCP is so cumbersome that it encourages management incompetence and buck-passing. Figure 12 shows the organization of a typical government corporation in Ho Chi Minh City. In addition to the manager, each deputy manager is a high-ranking party cadre with a superior at a higher party echelon who protects him. It is therefore impossible to make any member of the top management accountable for his errors. The worst punishment he might undergo, if the error is a fairly serious one, is compulsory self-criticism. If the error is catastrophic, he will merely be transferred to another position. Any severer punishment would reflect on the party, which must always appear to be right. In general, a manager who earnestly follows the party line, however absurd it may be, will always avoid real trouble.

The spirit in which the true party hack approaches his responsibilities is well illustrated by a story told of Chin Danh, wartime head of the Financial and Economic Bureau of COSVN, who became head of the State Bank in South Vietnam after the communist victory. When asked if he was ready and prepared for negotiations with representatives of the Asian Development Bank (they were in Ho Chi Minh City with proposals for economic aid), he replied: "I certainly am! I've gone over all the party resolutions, party lines, and party directives. I can handle those people now."

Lack of Education and Technical Knowledge. Thuy Mai, a teacher at Ho Chi Minh City Comprehensive University who escaped from Vietnam in 1979, has spoken of the VCP members' technical qualifications.

> In 1976 we were taken to visit the Electric Lamp Vikyno Company, which produced tubes for fluorescent lighting, in the Bien Hoa Industrial Area. The company had formerly acquired a license to manufacture a product patented by the Toshiba Company, in Japan. When we were at the Vikyno Company, imports of materials were suspended; hence the corporation had to be self-sufficient. The glass production department was moved and merged with another glass production company, while Vikyno had to buy dead tubes for reuse. The zinc sulfide, however, was produced by the Optics Department of the Comprehensive University. A Vikyno engineer stated that if we used the quality criteria set up by the company before April 30,

Figure 12: Organizational Chart of a Typical Ho Chi Minh City Corporation

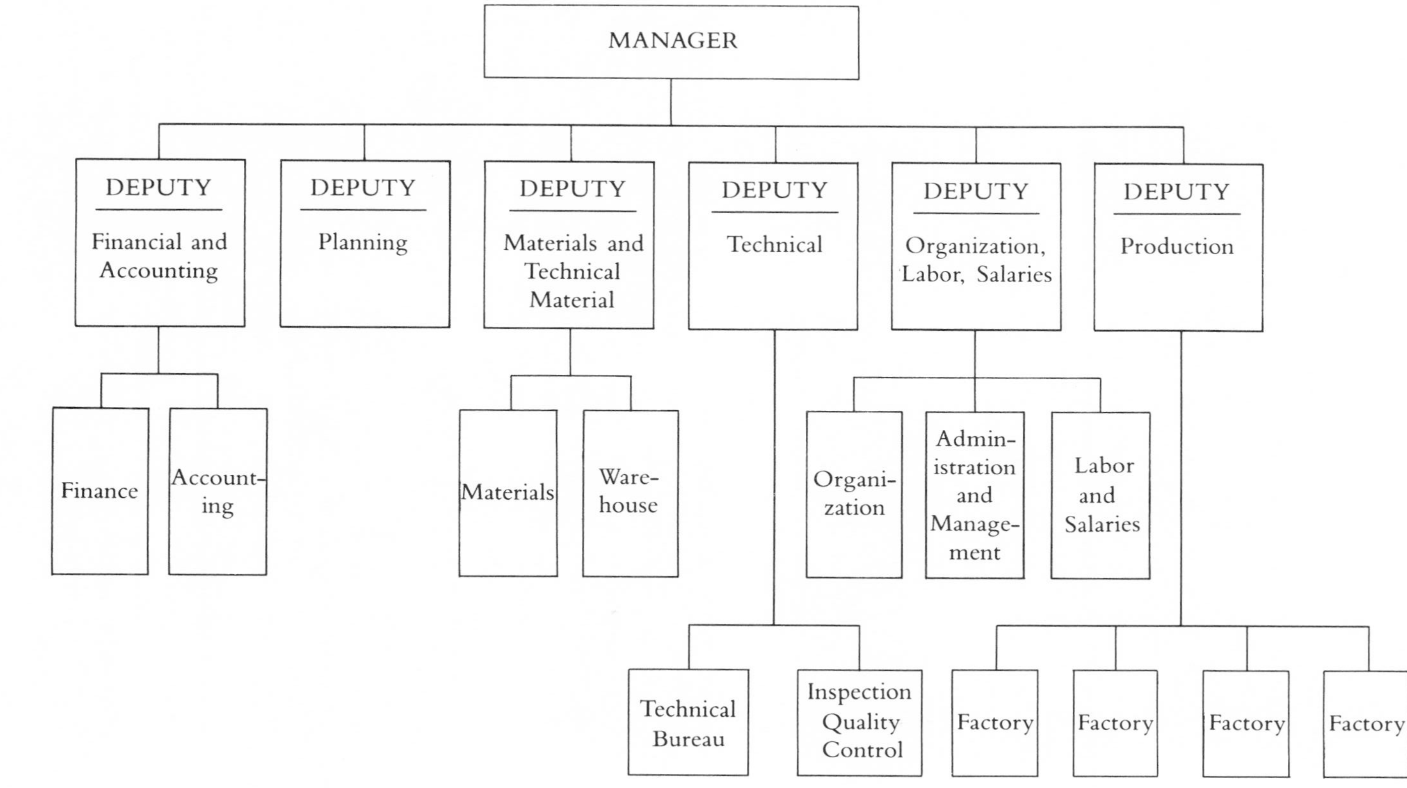

> 1975, only 6 out of 100 tubes would pass. However, the company [now a state corporation] was trying to achieve the objectives set up by the Ho Chi Minh City Party Committee. At the corporation we were presented with a detailed analysis of production before and after April 30, 1975.
>
> The director was a southerner who had been regrouped to North Vietnam in 1954. The technical manager was an engineer of the former South Vietnamese government, a graduate from a university in Canada. After an introduction made by the director, the technical manager showed us round the corporation. He showed us different types of tractors made from local materials. Then he introduced the Lotus tractor made in Hanoi . . . The tractor had been brought to South Vietnam for trial in the Mekong Delta. He said that the peasants did not like the tractor, did not use it because it was so huge, so cumbersome. The cooling system worked through a radiator situated directly in front of the driver, who naturally got rather hot. The City Party Committee had assigned Vikyno to remedy the "heavy weight and heat."
>
> After that, the visitors were split up into small groups for visits to workers. When a party member in my team asked a worker how many wheels were produced a day by each person, he replied that before April 30, 1975, he made one wheel and a half, but now he made only one-third of a wheel. Why, asked the party member, had his efficiency fallen? The worker pointed to his belly and answered: "However much I work, I only get the same level of pay. If I work harder, I'll die sooner. Of course, it's also true that my main food is now sorghum, so I'm just not up to working." The technical manager also told us that North Vietnam has sent the corporation two engineers, to give technical assistance. One visitor asked about their field of experience. The manager explained with a straight face that one of them was in charge of purchasing necessities for workers and the other in charge of financial transactions—collection of money from equipment sales, purchase of materials, and so forth. A few months later, we learned that both the technical manager and the two North Vietnamese engineers had fled Vietnam.[29]

The tea plantations in Bao Loc District, according to the same source, had been ruined by inept North Vietnamese management. Before the communist takeover an expert trained in Taiwan had attended to all the plantations, which produced tea of many types. After the takeover a team of 60 northern engineers was able to grow only two types, while the quality declined drastically and production fell.

I have heard many such stories from refugees. For instance, Dr. Tran Xuan Ninh, a professor at the Faculty of Medicine in Saigon before 1975, spent over two years in a re-education camp and was then released to work at a hospital in the same city. He found that his supervisor, a Communist who had received his medical degree in the North, was ignorant of pharmacology, lacked diagnostic skills, and nearly always prescribed the wrong treatment. People soon discovered this, and began asking for the "puppet" doctor, as the Communists called Dr. Ninh. The communist supervisor, finding himself outclassed and unwanted, assigned Dr. Ninh to do all the medical work.

Dr. Ninh told me of a revealing incident in the same hospital. A communist doctor asked one of the janitors how long he had been on the job. "Twenty years," the man replied. The Communist's eyes widened. "Too bad," he said. "The American imperialists and their puppet government obviously conspired to keep you down. Under the socialist system, you would have been an M.D."

Discrimination Against Southerners. The so-called reunification of Vietnam was in fact a conquest of the South by the North.

> The northerners put their own people in all key positions, hinting that they would not give any jobs to South Vietnamese . . . They trusted only those southerners who had a long record of activities within the northern communist party. Southern resistance leaders such as Nguyen Huu Tho, [acting president of the SRV], Huynh Tan Phat [vice-premier], Mrs. Nguyen Thi Binh [minister of education], and others fell in line with the new arrivals but did not get any advantage out of that.[30]

Even at the lower administrative levels, northerners were appointed to almost all positions of power and influence, while southern appointees "were so few and untypical that they served merely to underline the northern monopoly of political power."[31]

These accounts have been confirmed by refugees and other eyewitnesses. Thus Katsuichi Honda, who visited both North and South Vietnam during the war, wrote in 1977 upon his return from Vietnam:

> After the unification of the country, former members of the National Front for the Liberation of South Vietnam are not allowed to hold appropriate positions and probably are coldly treated . . . appropriate positions after the end of the war are being given to persons

> whose accomplishments reflect the whole period of struggle under the leadership of the VCP.
>
> I met with acquaintances who had lived in the [communist] liberated area [in 1968]. I found that each had cadres as bodyguards. Therefore, she or he could not talk with me freely, especially when I learned that the "bodyguards" were northerners from Hanoi.[32]

These so-called bodyguards are of course northern security agents. The former NLF leaders who have them are virtually under house arrest.

I can illustrate this aspect of VCP rule with a story told me by a refugee who is also a colleague. Professor Bui Tuong Chieu, who turned 78 in 1982, received his Ph.D. in Paris in 1935; he was my professor at the Saigon Faculty of Law. In 1972 I became his deputy when he was dean of the faculty. He could not get out in 1975, but in January 1977 the VCP released him to France. In October 1980 he came to the United States and visited me at my home. His story was as follows.

One of his oldest friends, an attorney named Nguyen Huu Tho, came back to Saigon a few days after it had been liberated. Tho had someone look for Professor Chieu. Finally, Tho contacted Professor Chieu by phone and made an appointment for the professor to come and see him another day at 11:00 A.M. The day having come, Professor Chieu and his wife arrived at Tho's residence at the appointed hour. They found a guard at the gate and told him that they had an appointment with Tho. The guard took them to an office beyond the gate. Here they were presented to an NVA lieutenant who said, on being told of their appointment, "Why didn't I know about that?" He then had the Chieus sit and wait. Around noon Mrs. Chieu asked the lieutenant whether Tho would receive them. Should they go home? The lieutenant said nothing but "Wait." They waited until 12:30, then left.

Professor Chieu proceeded to call Tho on the phone. Tho apologized, saying that he hadn't known what was going on. He gave the Chieus another appointment for the following day. At the time of the appointment, he came out and waited for the Chieus outside the house, then took them to a reception room.

In the reception room, Professor Chieu continued, was a North Vietnamese in civilian clothing who sat on a chair in a corner, while the visitors and their host exchanged greetings. There was one moment when the man left the room and at that time Tho was able to remark: "Those people have been assigned to protect me, but they're really keeping me under surveillance. It's a kind of harassment. I have to go along with it."

Ordinary southerners with no political connections are as much distrusted by the VCP as southerners who are or have been members of the government. Relations between southerners and the northerners who have come south have continued to be so bad that To Huu, by then a vice-premier and member of the Politburo, saw fit, when he addressed a conference of cadres in November 1978, to rebuke the northerners for "mistaken prejudices" against the southern populace.[33] His concern was for the effect these prejudices were having on the growth of southern front organizations, to which we now turn.

Mobilizing the People

The Role of Front Organizations

Grouping people into organizations is another of the VCP's major tasks as it extends its power over the South. These organizations are intended to have two main functions: political mobilization and party recruitment.

Political Mobilization. Everybody in South Vietnam must be grouped into different organizations under the leadership and control of the party. According to official party directives, party lines and policies will reach every individual member of each organization through study sessions. For the time being the doctrine of the three revolutions is paramount. All front organizations have to play an active role in implementing these revolutions.

The local chapters of each organization keep track of members' activities concurrently and together with the local security agents. They also indoctrinate the members, force them to go to evening meetings, and—in cooperation with other agencies, including cooperatives—incite them to work harder to meet the party's production goals. The chapters are supporting agencies of the party and of the state.

All individuals must be grouped into mass organizations according to sex, creed, national origin, age, profession, and any other traits the party considers relevant. The groups are held to constitute a source of strength for the Vietnamese revolution because they are (supposedly) well disciplined, always obedient to the party's orders, and efficient in achieving its goals. The mass organizations, like the chapters, are a link between the party leadership and administration, on the one hand, and the people, on the other.

Party Recruitment. The front organizations screen people, identify "politically clean and enthusiastic elements," and recruit them for the party. Most of the recruiting effort, however, devolves on two organizations: the Red Scarf Teenagers Organization (Doan Thieu Nhi Quang Khan Do) and the Ho Chi Minh Communist Youth League. Members of these organizations can be tested or challenged, and the successful ones can be promoted to be party members. The organizations are schools for training the so-called collective owners of society in political activities, in organizing and leading the masses to act as masters of the economy, of politics, culture, and social affairs.[34] The true function of front organizations is to expand the powers of the party into the whole population (Figure 13).

The Vietnam National United Front

The most important front organization, and one that groups many satellite associations under its aegis, is the Vietnam Fatherland Front (VFF). The purpose of the VFF is to unify all front organizations as part of the process of unifying the country. "This is to demonstrate the VCP's power of self-support and self-strengthening and [to] continue to foster the tradition of great national unity and [to] build as well as defend the independent, unified and socialist Vietnamese fatherland."[35]

The VFF was founded in Hanoi in 1955, when it replaced a similar mass organization created by the ICP to fight the French. On January 31, 1977, the first unified congress of the Fatherland Front opened in Ho Chi Minh City. It was attended by about five hundred delegates of political parties, mass organizations, the PAVN, and religious communities, as well as by private citizens. All national fronts—including, as we have seen, the NLF—were officially merged into the VFF.

The VFF political program now includes the following points:

1. Build the system of socialist collective mastery.
2. Develop large-scale socialist production.
3. Foster a new culture and new, socialist men.
4. Care for the material and cultural life of the people.
5. Strengthen national defense, maintain political security and social order.

FIGURE 13: VCP AND FRONT ORGANIZATIONS

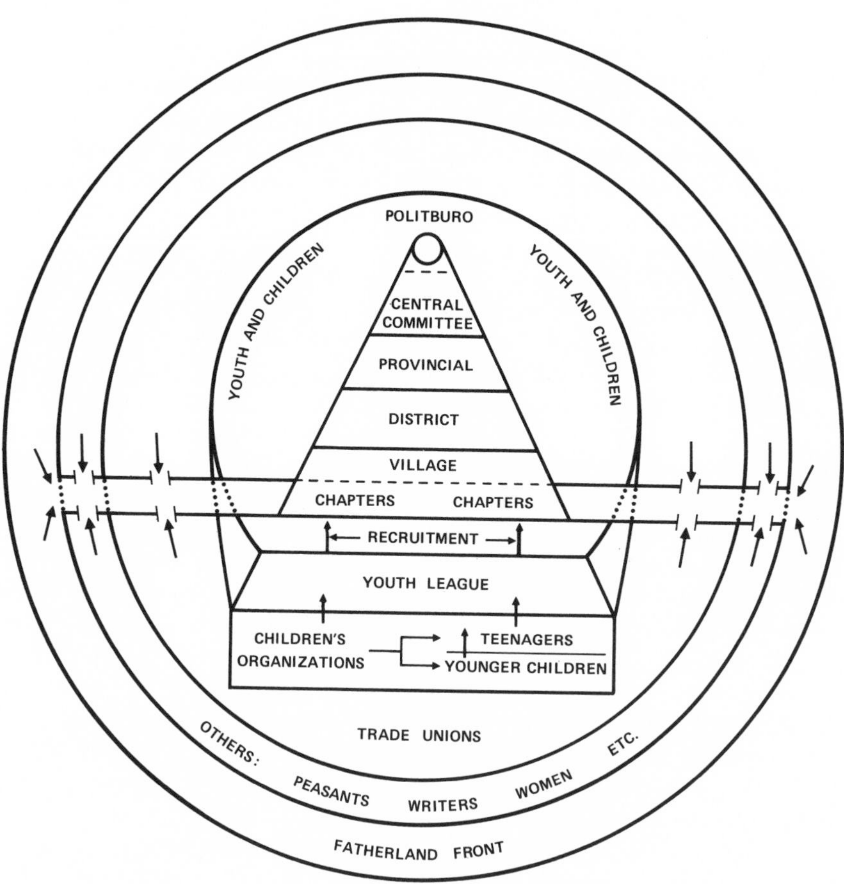

6. Achieve equality between various nationalities, between man and woman, and respect the freedom of belief.
7. Promote international relations of friendship and cooperation.
8. Achieve broad unity of patriotic forces and those that love socialism.[36]

The Vietnam General Confederation of Trade Unions (VGFTV)

The confederation is the "broadest mass organization of the working class, a school of communism and school for management of the economy and the state." The trade unions have the duty to "take part in state affairs, control the work of the state and take part in managing the factories." They educate workers in "socialist labor," constantly raise their "political, cultural, technical and professional standards," and "encourage a large-scale industry method of thinking and working." They also train workers to be qualified technical and management cadres, launch labor emulation movements, and—together with state bodies—overcome problems concerning the living and working conditions, welfare, study, and recreation of workers.[37]

Article 67 of the 1980 Constitution stipulates that citizens enjoy "freedom to demonstrate in accordance with the interests of socialism and of the people." It goes on to say, however, that "no one may misuse democratic freedoms to violate the interests of the state and the people." Although the constitution is silent as to the workers' right to strike, it seems unlikely that this right would come under the aforementioned "freedom to demonstrate." The constitution pictures the workers as collective masters of the society. Being masters, they could not go on strike against themselves; backing wage demands with a strike, for instance, would surely not be "in accordance with the interests of socialism and of the people." On the contrary, it would be a way of misusing democratic freedom to "violate the interests of the state and the people."

Trade unions do take part in management: workers are allowed to elect their own representatives to help manage corporations and cooperatives. However, almost on the eve of the election, all workers must submit to study sessions under the leadership of the VCP cadres in their union about who should be elected. As a result, those who are elected to management are invariably party members.

In 1976 the VCP claimed more than three million workers and public employees among its members, and the figure was expected to rise to five million by the end of 1980. Nguyen Van Linh, the Politburo member who headed the General Confederation of Trade

Unions, said that 1.5 million of these were technical workers.[38] Unfortunately he did not give any figures for union membership in South Vietnam, although he did say that "in the most recently liberated areas, the trade unions have quickly mobilized and educated the workers and public employees of the old regime and enrolled a large number of them in the unions."[39]

Membership in trade unions is voluntary, but it is also a privilege handed out by the VCP. Union members spot "good workers" (that is, hardworking employees), then induce them to join a two-week evening training program. After that they may join the union and so become one of the four categories of persons in the corporation to whom the state grants material privileges (the other three are party members, state employees, and members of the Youth League). All union leaders must be high-ranking party members. I do not know if many of them are southerners, but it seems unlikely that they would be.

The Youth League

The right arm of the VCP is the Ho Chi Minh Communist Youth League (also translated as "Youth Union" or "Youth Organization"). The league helps to implement party policies, but its principal duty is to screen, recruit, and train members for the party.[40] There is a saying among Vietnamese Communists: "To be admitted to the Party, you must have gone through the [Youth] League."

Formerly the Ho Chi Minh Labor Youth League, the league changed its name in 1976, after the Vietnam Workers Party had become the Vietnamese Communist Party. Its responsibility for party development remains the same. The league is the communist school of youth; it nurtures the revolutionary generation of the future. Building a strong and widespread Youth League is therefore a matter of pressing importance to the VCP in its drive to organize the South. The league's recruiters have been particularly active in high schools and colleges, but they also operate at the ward and village level. They are looking for young people who fall into either of two categories: those who come from revolutionary families, that is, families with a record of activity in behalf of the VCP; and "elite youth" (that is, from the poorer classes) who, because neither they nor their families were involved with the American "imperialists" or the "puppet government," may be considered politically clean. Both categories are recruited locally by members of the local Youth League chapter.

The qualities that chiefly catch a recruiter's eye are being a hard worker or an outstanding student. The young person who has those qualities, plus the right political background, is selected and sent to a training program. After graduation, he or she becomes a *doi tuong doan*, or "target for the Youth League"—in other words, someone who is a candidate for official recruitment into the league. After a year of challenge and trial, the candidate may become a league member upon recommendation by two members and approval by the local league. In almost all colleges and high schools in South Vietnam the classes are subdivided into teams of fifteen to twenty students. Usually, five students in each team are Youth League members. In practice many young people from rich families or families who worked for the Americans or the former South Vietnamese government are recruited as *doi tuong doan* so that the authorities can keep an eye on them.

VCP cadres help Youth League chapters to organize "assault youth units" on the economic, cultural, and social fronts. These units may be nothing more formidable than soccer teams or technical study groups, but they are still part of the VCP's effort to mobilize the masses in support of its policies.

Will the System Work in South Vietnam?

It is clear from official sources as well as the accounts of refugees that southerners have been very reluctant to join mass organizations. After several years of living under communism they have had their fill of meetings. Working hard all day is not enough; in the evening, they already have to go to study sessions, self-criticism sessions, ideological instruction classes, and other meetings they cannot avoid. People who belong to two or three organizations—for example, their neighborhood solidarity cells (membership in which is compulsory), neighborhood committees for the protection of residents, and the organizations belonging to their trades or occupations—have to attend the meetings held by all of them. Some find they have to attend as many as three meetings in one evening. A mass organization, for the ordinary citizen, is just one organization too many.

Another reason why southerners are not joining mass organizations is that in such meetings, members are required to express their opinions. If they do not do so in an appropriate manner, they may be suspected of opposition to the regime and sent to a re-education camp. The meetings, in any case, achieve nothing constructive; their only real purpose is propaganda. Moreover, southerners have learned one thing from northerners after so many years of being cut off from them: passive resistance to the communist regime, if practiced with finesse, need not lead to arrest or imprisonment.

Finally, southern peasants who oppose cooperativization (as the great majority of Vietnamese peasants always have) can afford to be quite outspoken in their opposition if they helped the Communists during the war. The party cadres dare not arrest them because to arrest the party's former supporters would be too visible a form of betrayal. Other peasants rally round the ones who speak out, and the party has great difficulty in getting any of them to join mass organizations.

The socialist transformation of the South, then, is still a long way off. With the help of northern cadres, who occupy all positions of importance, the VCP installed its organs of local control very rapidly. But it has failed to mobilize the peasants and has been forced to call off its program of collectivization. In the cities it has failed to persuade ordinary workers or employees that enthusiastic participation in VCP front organizations is as much in their own interest as in the VCP's. Above all, despite the most vigorous efforts, it has failed conspicuously to control the black market, which (as in the case of the seafood processing plants) has made a mockery of its economic programs.

On the other hand, no fair-minded observer can deny the VCP a certain measure of success. It has succeeded, for instance, in imposing food rationing on the South Vietnamese people, and in using the chronic shortage of food to suppress all organized opposition and strengthen party control. The state security network, too, has been eminently successful in controlling people's movements, in keeping track of them, and in hounding them into concentration camps and NEZs if they get out of line. In their ultimate objective, however, the Communists have not succeeded: they have not broken the people's spirit.

6

Repression—and Resistance

The Vietnamese Communists are experts in mass murder: they have had nearly 40 years' practice at it. Their principal victims have been members of the various nationalist parties—the parties that, immediately after World War II, fought for Vietnamese freedom and independence while the Communists allied themselves with the French.[1]

The communist tactic was successful. Between mid-1945 and late 1946, the guerrilla forces of the Viet Minh, an anti-French front that had soon fallen under communist domination, systematically exterminated the nationalist leadership in North Vietnam and crushed all nationalist opposition. Thousands of Nationalists were interned; others fled to the Highlands, where they regrouped and continued their resistance.

Understandably, the VCP has rewritten the history of this period so that only the Viet Minh and its collaborators appear patriotic. This is not the place to set the record straight. A few incidents, however, should be recalled to show that communist methods were ruthless from the beginning. I will then show that these methods have not changed.

The 1945–46 Massacres

The two most important rivals of the Communists were the Vietnam Quoc Dan Dang (Vietnam Nationalist Party), or VNQDD, which had been founded in 1927 in close imitation of the Chinese Kuomintang; and the Dai Viet Quoc Dan Dang (Greater Vietnam Nationalist Party), commonly known as the Dai Viet Party, which began (in 1939) as a splinter group of the VNQDD. Both parties were dedicated to the cause of Vietnamese independence; both of them wanted to establish a Vietnamese republic.

Early in 1946 the Viet Minh decided to eliminate the Nationalists, who were still formally allied with it. A series of Viet Minh attacks were followed by massacres of nationalist prisoners and their families. The VNQDD withdrew northwards, but continued to maintain a secret headquarters in Hanoi, in a house facing Lake Halais, on On Nhu Hau Street. The Communists, from whom nothing was hidden, smuggled a large number of corpses into the headquarters and then accused the VNQDD of conducting a bloodbath. In reality, these were the corpses of Nationalists murdered by the Communists during their purge. Several years later, when the French regained control of Hanoi, many more corpses were found in sandbags at the bottom of the lake. The victims, according to the most plausible account, had been dumped there in 1946, when the Viet Minh ruled the city.

Having been expelled from Hanoi, the nationalist forces attempted to set up bases nearby but suffered a series of crushing defeats at the hands of the Viet Minh. At last they were encircled at Phu Tho. Nearly all the nationalist units were captured and detained in the Luc Yen Chau concentration camp. Here several thousand Nationalists, with their relatives and friends, were buried alive.

The Bridge at Lao Cai. The Dai Viets, who were never wholly defeated, succeeded in rallying the remaining nationalist forces at Lao Cai, a city on the railroad near the Chinese border. However, the Viet Minh cut their supply lines. They were forced to flee across the border or starve. Those who could not flee were rounded up by the Viet Minh and put in prison camps.

News of the ensuing mass murders leaked out via the few prisoners who survived. Every night, according to one of these prisoners, a group of 25 to 30 Nationalists, their hands tied, were taken to the Ho Kieu Bridge, on the Hong Ha River in Lao Cai, and lined up in single file. A Viet Minh cadre stood on the bridge holding a sledgehammer, while another called each prisoner by name. As the prisoner stepped forward, he was hit in the head with the hammer and pushed by a third cadre into the river. The same scene was repeated night after night; every village in Viet Minh territory had its own version. The man who told this story survived because he was the last on that night's list of victims, and the executioner, being tired, hit him on the shoulder instead of the head. He was pushed into the river anyway, and so lived and made his way to Hanoi.

The Land-Reform Program of 1953–1956

The North Vietnamese Politburo, as I explained in Chapter 2, based its land-reform program on the principle that the wealthiest 5 percent of the population owned 95 percent of the land and had therefore to be eliminated.[2] This figure of 5 percent was applied indiscriminately to every village and hamlet; if, for instance, a village had 1,000 inhabitants, then the 50 who were alleged to be the wealthiest had to be killed or sent to concentration camps. Under this program, even high-ranking communist party members were killed (the party considered it unwise to imprison them, since they might one day return to seek revenge). The killing was carried out by special land-reform teams stationed in each village; they acted on orders from provincial party headquarters, after it had reviewed the report of the village land-reform team. The latter compiled its lists of prospective victims from party cadres who worked with landless peasants and schooled them in the party line. These peasants, having become tools of the party, would denounce the upper-class landlords before the people's court.

The Hue Bloodbath of 1968

During the Tet offensive of 1968 the city of Hue was overrun by Viet Cong forces, who held it for three weeks. The Communists wasted no time. Underground communist agents provided names and addresses of persons considered hostile to the communist cause. The agents guided V.C. units that arrested people in their own homes. Most of those arrested were civil servants, military men, medical persons (including four from West Germany), religious leaders, or political activists, especially members of nationalist parties and their families. After the Viet Cong forces withdrew, several thousand people were found to be missing. Almost a year later, through children who were caring for water buffalo in a remote area, large pits full of corpses were discovered. Some pits held only a few hundred bodies, while others held over a thousand. Eventually, more than four thousand corpses were discovered.

Repression

Given the events I have described, it is reasonable to conclude that physical liquidation of opponents has long been a standard and indeed indispensable tool of VCP policy. Such a tool is not likely to be discarded after a military victory, nor was it.

Public Trials, Clandestine Reprisals

When the North Vietnamese conquered the South, they began a widespread liquidation campaign; they did so behind a cover of moderation, having profited from their earlier experience. They had learned by then to handle such matters quietly, secretly if need be, and with dispatch. The early days, immediately after the military victory, offered the greatest opportunities in these respects, and it was then that they struck.

VCP propaganda, by emphasizing the deliberate lack of reprisals in Saigon and ignoring what went on elsewhere, has given the West a completely distorted impression of this period. It is now generally accepted, even by those with no ideological stake in the matter, that there was no bloodbath after the communist takeover of South Vietnam. I do not know how much blood has to be shed in order to count as a bloodbath. If, however, the implication is that there were no widespread or systematic reprisals made by the Viet Cong after their victory, then I believe that the evidence indicates otherwise. That evidence, gleaned from articles by or interviews with refugees, is of course incomplete, but it does seem authentic, and there is enough of it to suggest that the killings they have described were not isolated incidents.

Consider, for instance, the account of Nguyen Cong Hoan, who escaped from Vietnam to Japan in 1977 and now lives in the United States, not far from me. As a witness to history, Hoan is in the almost unique position of having been a legislator both under the Thieu regime, when he was elected to the Vietnamese House of Representatives by his native province of Phu Yen, and under the SRV, which allowed him to be elected to the National Assembly on the strength of his record as a left-wing Buddhist and antiwar activist. A teacher by profession, with a B.S. from Saigon University, he is a shrewd observer who had unusual opportunities, because of his special position, to travel and make inquiries. He writes:

Over five hundred people in the villages of Hoa Thang, Hoa Tri, Hoa Quang, and Hoa Kien (all in the Tuy Hoa District) were murdered during the first days of [the communist] occupation. These were the villages with the greatest number of communist cadres who had been regrouped to North Vietnam. Everywhere in my province—in districts such as Song Cau, Tuy An, Dong Xuan, and Hieu Xuong District—the same situation occurred: the more communist cadres, the more killings. Members of the Dai Viet Party, former government employees, military officers, police, and intelligence agents were the first to be picked up. They were ordered by the VCP to go to re-education classes. The Communists then selected about five hundred people from the classes and sent them to the elementary school at Hoa Thang, where they were confined. On the following night, all of them were taken to a jungle area near the village and murdered en masse. The Communists kept the villagers from coming near the place until, half a month later, a boy taking care of cattle discovered the crime. Relatives of the victims were then permitted, after they had been sworn to secrecy, to go and search for their bodies and give them decent burial.

Truong Tu Thien, a member of the Dai Viet Party, had been a colleague of mine in the National Assembly under the Thieu regime. He was arrested, barbarously tortured, and then taken off (he is still detained in North Vietnam). A number of other personalities were similarly treated: Tran Pho, an old teacher, was stabbed to death at Le Uyen after the liberation (he was the uncle of Tran Quang Hiep, my secretary under the communist regime). He had made statements opposing the new regime because his 15-year-old son was killed by the Viet Cong in 1969. Thich Dieu Bon, a Buddhist monk and deputy representative of the Vietnamese Unified Buddhist Church in Tuy Hoa, was accused of being an agent of the U.S. Central Intelligence Agency, and was taken away during the first days of [the communist] occupation because the American consul in Phu Yen had commended him for helping in the search for MIAs.

The predicted bloodbath did not occur in Saigon. It really occurred in my native province, however; in fact, it is still going on there. Later, I made inquiries in several places, especially in Central Vietnam in Binh Dinh, Quang Ngai, Quang Nam, Thua Thien, and Quang Tri provinces. I found that the situation there was very much the same.

How sad it is that the VCP has prevented anyone at the United Nations from seeking the truth about these events. Instead, they praise their political system to the skies, although my fellow coun-

> trymen have suffered much under their tyrannical, inhuman oppression. They are engaged in a cover-up.[3]

The reprisals made by the Viet Cong can be grouped into two main categories: so-called people's trials followed by official (and in some cases public) executions; and secret liquidations.

People's Trials. Many officials and military officers of the former regime were publicly denounced before people's courts installed by the VCP. The ones that the Communists wanted to liquidate were always charged with the same crimes: being lackeys of the American imperialists and owing a blood debt to the people. It was a foregone conclusion that they would be condemned and executed. Such trials took place all over South Vietnam.

For example, in Bac Lieu Province the following victims were executed after two days of trials in late May 1975 (the trials were held at the Bac Lieu soccer field).[4]

1. Le Van Si, chief of the Gia Ray District. After the court pronounced the death sentence, guerrillas tied him to a pole and shot him. To make sure, they crushed his skull with a rock. His corpse was buried face downwards with the hands still tied.
2. Village Chief Nguyen Van Diem, An Thach Village, Gia Ray District. After being sentenced to death, he was sent back to his village for execution. However, on the way back home, he was stabbed in the side. On the village outskirts a Viet Cong guerrilla blew his head off with a burst of automatic rifle fire.
3. Sergeant Nguyen Van Lac, chief of Phong Thanh Tay Village, Phuoc Long District. Sergeant Lac had been wounded before April 30, 1975; he appeared in court on crutches. The death sentence was carried out at his village. His bullet-riddled corpse was dragged around the village by a Viet Cong guerrilla who had fastened a rope to one foot.
4. A lieutenant colonel who was the chief of Kien Thuan District, after receiving the death sentence, was tied to a pillar and shot. After the fusillade one man stepped forward, grasped the victim's hair to raise his head, and gave him a last shot in the face. His wife and children had been brought there to watch; they were denied permission to take the corpse for burial.

Some five or six hundred people were brought to the soccer field to watch the trials. The executions, here and in other provinces, were carried out in the villages or districts in which the victims were performing their duties at the time South Vietnam fell.

Secret Liquidations. Firsthand accounts of the secret liquidations are understandably hard to come by. Probably the full truth will never be known. Nevertheless, there is strong evidence that massacres took place. In particular, I should cite the sworn account of Nguyen Dong Da, a peasant from Phu Khanh Province, in the Central Highlands, concerning five incidents that took place there almost simultaneously in early April 1975, soon after the city of Phu Yen, which is about 300 km northeast of Saigon, had fallen to the Communists. In July 1978, being detained in a camp at Phu Khanh, Da escaped from Vietnam by boat. He was admitted to the United States and made his way to Los Angeles, where he still lives.

His original account was given to a group of Vietnamese students who interviewed him in Los Angeles for a refugees' magazine.[5] Later I talked to him myself, by phone, obtaining additional details of the incidents and of how he came to know of them. In the following summary I have presented the incidents in the same order as they appear in Da's signed statement, which is available in English.[6]

The Lu Ba Incident

At 5:30 P.M. on April 8, 1975, at the Dinh Thanh Camp, Hoa Dinh Village, Le Liem, commander of the Tuy Hoa District II Security Forces, ordered all prisoners (an estimated fifteen hundred persons) to turn out and stand in line. He then had the camp commandant, Lt. Nguyen Chat, read a long list of prisoners who, supposedly, were being sent to the city for re-education. The prisoners so named were made to step forward and stand in a separate corner of the yard where they were surrounded by armed guards. They were tied together in groups of nine. At 8:00 P.M. all of them were ordered to walk to Lu Ba, a hill near Mount Dinh Ong, not far from the village. Each group of nine was headed by a guerrilla armed with a Russian AK automatic rifle. Two-and-a-half hours later, the prisoners were slaughtered by fire from these rifles and from submachine guns.

The incident was disclosed five days later by one of the guerrillas who had taken part in it. He told a comrade whose father, Le Van Cuong, had been a policeman under the RVN and was one of those killed there. The son began to search for the corpse of his father, and soon parents, wives, and children of other prisoners rushed to the place in search of their loved ones. Finally, they uncovered a total of 225 corpses. The corpse on top of the pile was recognized as Dang Thanh Thuoc, former member of the Hoa Thong Village Council, and the one lying at the bottom as Nguyen Hoang, a South Vietnamese government employee in the rural development program. The majority of the victims were identified from their sandals—their names were written on the underside—and their clothes. Nguyen Dong Da was one of those who took part in the search for corpses and helped bury them. He was told the rest of the story by the son of Le Van Cuong, the murdered policeman.

The Ho Ngua Incident

Ho Ngua is a mountain pass near the Hoa Dinh railway station; it is actually part of Hoa Quang Village. The bodies of 27 persons were discovered there in late April by relatives who had been looking for them. Nguyen Dong Da was among the relatives. The corpse of Maj. Dao Tat Thuyen of the Logistics Department, Phu Cat Retransmission Center, Binh Dinh Province, was found on top of the pile, and that of Lt. Huynh Van Diem, Phu Yen Military Sector, at the bottom. It was presumed that the massacre had taken place on the night of April 4, since at 6:00 P.M. on that day the victims had been taken from their homes for "re-education."

Discovery at Mount Tho Vuc

The mountain in question is about 3.5 km north of Lu Ba, near Phu Yen. On the evening of April 8, 1975, communist security forces took 85 persons from the camps at Tuong Quang and Ngoc Phong and led them up the mountain. Three months later, according to Da, the remains of 85 corpses were found on the mountain. Only skeletons remained; no one could be positively identified.

Reprisals at Cay Xop

About 3 km from Lu Ba is the hamlet of Lien Tri. At Cay Xop, an area in that hamlet, local people in search of captured relatives discovered a pit with six corpses in it. Among them was Dang Kim Hung, an officer from the Phu Yen Interrogation Center. His wife, who witnessed the sight, recounted later that the victims had been tied together and their heads smashed in. Another victim was Captain Nhuong, deputy chief of the Field Police at Phu Yen.

The Cau Dai Bridge Massacre

On the evening of April 8, 1975, Huynh Xanh, a South Vietnamese militiaman, was hiding under the Cau Dai Bridge, which carries Route 1 of the national road system across the Da Rang River south of Tuy Hoa. He saw communist soldiers approaching with 30 prisoners of war. The prisoners had been tied together in groups with the leader in each group linked to a Honda motorcycle ridden by a soldier. Each group was dragged to the bridge and then shoved off it into the river. Huynh Xanh was later arrested and taken to a prison camp in Phu Yen. There he met Nguyen Dong Da and told him what he had seen.

The extreme cruelty and barbarity of these killings were part of the Communists' plan to terrorize the population. Beheading, stabbing, denial of proper burial—such practices, reminiscent of those of ancient emperors, were no more lethal than others, but they did serve to outrage and humiliate the victims' families. When the Communists, as they sometimes did, beheaded the corpses of those they had just massacred, they knew that any relative who came for the bodies would view such a death as particularly shameful, and that the memory of it would remain with those families for generations.

Freedom for Sale

The massive refugee exodus from Indochina is not merely a result of the harshness of life there, but is part of Vietnamese diplomatic strategy in Southeast Asia. The refugees impose military, social, and economic strains on the countries that receive them. Their presence has also divided the members of the Association of Southeast Asian Nations (ASEAN) and, perhaps more seriously, is being seen as cover for infiltrating agents and agitators into the outside world. Moreover, the taxes that the communist authorities impose on refugees before they leave are swelling an impoverished national treasury. It is the Ministry of the Interior and Ministry of Finance in Hanoi that actually oversee the traffic in refugees. Rough estimates put Hanoi's receipts from this traffic at U.S. $115 million for 1978 alone—about 2.5 percent of the total estimated gross national product.[7] The ministries in effect issue departure orders to southern provincial capitals. There, local officials negotiate contracts with boat organizers for the journey overseas. A tax of about four taels of gold is levied on each registered passenger (a tael is 37.5 g, or 1.21 oz.).

Not all these departures are strictly legal, but most involve bribing officials. Some classes of citizens, notably the ethnic Chinese, have been formally expelled as undesirable, while others—capitalists, bourgeois intellectuals, and others considered social misfits—have merely been encouraged to leave. The risks are terrible; probably half of those who left in small boats have been drowned. Nevertheless, for thousands of Vietnamese, the prospect of death at sea is less terrible than the prospect of life under communism.

The VCP has argued that most of these refugees are not political but economic. It is true that not all of them have equally urgent reasons for leaving, but these reasons, even when ostensibly economic, can be shown to be rooted in politics. The VCP, on the other hand, has both economic and political reasons for wanting them to leave; indeed, of the four discernible types of refugee, there is only one type that they might wish to retain. The four ways of becoming a refugee are as follows:

1. *Escape* (di chui). People who choose this method risk almost certain arrest if caught. They organize the escape by themselves, in secret; if some of the preparations are visible, they disguise them to look like something else. For instance, they may build a fishing boat and then get a fishing license. With the license, if they sell their fish to the state, they are allowed to buy gas. They save gas and escape.
2. *Escape with Permission of Local Authorities* (mua bai, *literally*, "*purchase of a loading place*"). People offer money (usually gold) to the local security authorities in charge of a coastal area (a river mouth or other suitable point of departure). The escape must be made at night. There is some risk if higher-echelon officials have been forewarned or if Naval Patrol Forces detect them before they have reached international waters. In that event, they are arrested and put in prison; all their property is confiscated. The usual bribe is 6 taels of gold per refugee. Whether or not the higher echelons take the bribes too is unknown to this day. It is assumed, however, that they do, because otherwise the local security authorities could not bypass other local agencies and their higher echelons. The arrests made by the Naval Patrol could be just for show.
3. *The Semiofficial Way* (di ban chinh thuc). The provincial party committee is in charge of this matter. Each refugee has to pay 12 taels of gold to the one who organizes the exodus. This person buys a vessel of some kind, with the necessary fuel and food; he also pays 6 to 8 taels of the gold to the provincial party committee. Each such vessel contains at the most a few

hundred people. Before they can leave, the refugees have to offer their main possessions—their houses, cars, and so on—to the local party committee; they actually have to hand over the keys, with the title deeds and other papers. Their vessel, while it is sailing out to international waters, is escorted by a naval forces ship and then shown which way to go.

4. *Official Registration* (di dang ky chinh thuc). This program is supervised by the central government.[8] It is concerned exclusively with ethnic Chinese. Those who want to leave must register at one of several offices in Saigon. They have to turn in their family books so that the names in them can be cross-checked; they also have to pay 12 taels of gold. The program was responsible for the steel-hulled refugee ships, each carrying three to four thousand people, that arrived in Malaysia, Singapore, Indonesia, and Hong Kong. These ships made an official departure from Saigon Pier and, like the semiofficial refugee ships, were escorted to international waters by communist naval forces. A few non-Chinese escaped through this program after they had bought identification papers with Chinese names and learned to speak a few words of Chinese.

The Policy Behind the Program. Over half a million people were released under Hanoi's human trafficking scheme. The exodus caused serious problems to countries in the region; many boats were sunk and a great number of refugees drowned. This awakened the Western countries, and there was pressure on Hanoi to attend the July 1979 Geneva Conference on Refugees organized by the United Nations. Hanoi, already concerned at the number of clandestine escapes, committed itself to an Orderly Departure Program (ODP) that would aim principally at reuniting families.

Nevertheless, refugees under this program have to fulfill the same conditions as those under ways 3 and 4 above, that is, they have to pay gold and surrender all their real and personal property. Hanoi's expulsion policy, then, remains the same as before. I would list the aims of that policy as follows:

1. *Collection of Gold.* The regime is in desperate need of hard currency. Its debts to the Soviet Union are huge. We may reasonably assume that the gold collected from refugees as the price of freedom is being used to pay those debts. At any rate, Western journalists have reported seeing Vietnamese gold,

which comes in thin, pocket-sized sheets embossed with the words *Kim Thanh*, in several Eastern European countries.

2. *Seizure of Personal Property.* The VCP needs to seize as much property as possible from the South Vietnamese middle classes, both in order to break the power of those classes and in order to reward its own senior officials with material privileges.
3. *Removal of a Potential Ethnic Chinese Fifth Column.* After the break with China, all Chinese-Vietnamese in North Vietnam, even those whose parents and grandparents had been born in Vietnam and who no longer spoke Chinese, were rounded up by armed militiamen and transported to a center in Haiphong. From there they were loaded onto small boats and dispatched to China under naval escort. The ethnic Chinese in the South were not only considered security risks; they were also considered to be members of the comprador bourgeoisie.
4. *Dividing the ASEAN Countries.* Hanoi hoped that the refugees would become a bone of contention among the ASEAN countries—Thailand, Singapore, Malaysia, Indonesia, and the Philippines—which would not be able to agree on a common refugee policy and would try to unload the refugees on each other. This hope was not fulfilled, since although the refugees were a problem for ASEAN, the ASEAN countries united against Hanoi more firmly than ever when it invaded Cambodia.
5. *Making a Virtue of Necessity.* So many people were already escaping clandestinely (ways 1 and 2, above) that the regime abandoned hope of preventing the exodus—the Vietnamese coastline is, after all, some 1,200 km long—and decided instead to profit from it. The regime even tried to use the exodus as proof of its moderation, although many of the refugees, if they had stayed, would certainly have been imprisoned or liquidated.
6. *Moral Blackmail.* The VCP leaders have stated repeatedly that the refugees have been leaving Vietnam for economic reasons. Because of the war, their argument runs, the Vietnamese economy has been devastated, and this is the fault of the United States. The only way to stop the flow of refugees, then, is for the United States to comply with article 21 of the 1973 Paris Agreement and provide $3.25 billion for economic reconstruction. I have dealt with this specious argument in previous chapters.

7. *Infiltration of Agents.* Communist agents masquerading as refugees have been infiltrated into many Western countries, where they keep an eye on refugee activities and engage in various types of espionage.
8. *Repatriation of Refugees' Earnings.* Incredible though it may seem, the VCP has now established a special Office for Vietnamese Overseas, in Ho Chi Minh City on Nguyen Du Street, whose duty it is to solicit gifts from Vietnamese refugees. Every month, Vietnam receives some 220 tons of goods—food, clothing, medicine, beauty products, kitchen equipment, and many other things that are scarce or unobtainable there—that refugees send to their families. These gifts, which also include sums of money in hard currencies, total millions of dollars and help to shore up the sagging Vietnamese economy.

The Exodus Continues. The flood of refugees has diminished since 1979, but it has not been contained. In May 1981 a total of 12,718 Vietnamese boat people were recorded as arriving in Malaysia, Thailand, and other countries of refuge—the most since July 1979, when the official U.N. total was 56,941.[9] By the following April the number had dropped to 4,602, an indication not so much of diminishing incentives to leave as of less favorable opportunities to do so.[10] The major routes followed are shown in Figure 14.

The reasons for this mass migration have not changed much, but its social composition has. The first wave, in 1975, consisted of educated people. The majority were military men and their families because the military had the necessary ships and planes. Many who were American dependents or associates were airlifted out by American helicopters. Some fishermen came with this wave, since they too had boats.

The next wave, after the Communists established control over South Vietnam, consisted mainly of fishermen or peasants living in coastal areas and along major rivers such as the Mekong. They, too, had boats, and could get away quickly. Most of them had little or no formal education.

The next wave consisted overwhelmingly of ethnic Chinese. Early in 1978, when relations between China and Vietnam were strained to the breaking point, the VCP, as I have already described, instituted an official registration program for ethnic Chinese in Saigon who wished to emigrate; similar facilities were provided in the southern provinces under the semiofficial program.[11] In the North,

Figure 14: Main Routes of the Boat People in the Southeast Asia Region

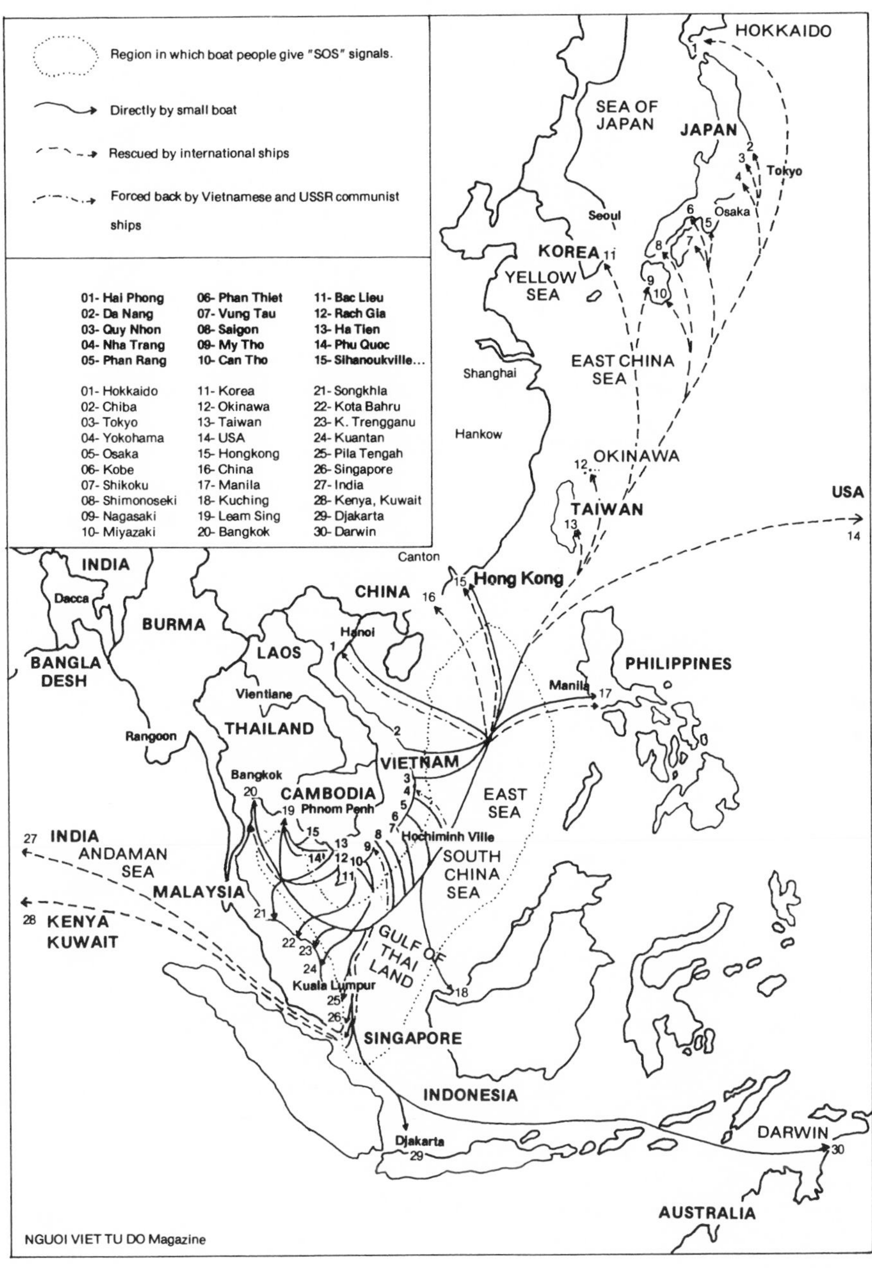

over 300,000 ethnic Chinese were simply expelled; China admitted some 260,000 of them. About a million ethnic Chinese lived in the South before the official registration program. It is possible that as many as half of them left under the program, but without seeing the registration figures there is no way of knowing. Here in the San Francisco Bay Area it was very noticeable during the 1980–81 period that the majority of refugees arriving from South Vietnam were ethnic Chinese. It did not appear that they had been quite so badly treated by the communist regime as the earlier refugees; rather, having realized that they could have no economic future under the regime, they had used their money to get out.

The totally racist nature of the expulsions of ethnic Chinese from North Vietnam can be judged from the following statement by one of them, a former resident of Hanoi. After being towed out to sea with his family in a small boat, he was interned in Hong Kong and, in mid-1979, allowed to enter Canada.

> My family has lived in Vietnam for three generations. I had two sons who joined the resistance movement in 1945. My oldest son was killed in the Cao Bac Lang military campaign in 1950. As a result, my family was awarded the title of Family of Soldiers Killed for the Country. My second son was promoted to lieutenant colonel in the North Vietnamese Army. However, in 1965 he was expelled from the army, and also from the party, for having connections with the Hoang Minh Chinh Revisionist Group, which followed the Soviet line as opposed to the Red Chinese line. He was demoted and sent to Dien Bien Phu to perform the duties of a carpenter.
>
> My two daughters are married to Vietnamese; one is a party district committee member, the other a high-ranking professional in the communist regime. In March 1979 my four little sons and myself were put on a military truck by an armed military unit. We were taken from our home to Mong Cay [a coastal town in the northeast corner of North Vietnam] where my family and many other persons were concentrated. All of us were forced into sailing boats, which were then towed by ships to the open sea. One thing I'd like you reporters to tell people is that, after we had been put on the boats, the Communists added a number of [common] criminals, six or seven to a boat, who had been taken straight from North Vietnamese prisons. These criminals robbed us of all our belongings even on the boats and created problems in the Hong Kong camps such as disturbances or robberies.[12]

Since the winter of 1978–1979, when Vietnam took over Cambodia, there has been another type of refugee: land people. The only country to which these refugees can escape is Thailand. Some have walked through the jungle to Cambodia, and then through Cambodia to the Thai border. Others have paid for a permit to travel by bicycle to the Vietnam-Cambodia border and then, with a guide, reached the Thai border by bicycle or ox cart. Still others have bribed members of the NVA to truck them, disguised in army uniforms, to somewhere in West Cambodia. Many of them have got no farther; either the soldiers shot them as they dismounted or they were hunted down by Pol Pot's guerrillas. The best available figures on the total number of refugees from Indochina, both land people and boat people, are shown in Table 3; it will be noted that they run only through April 1982, and that they do not include ethnic Chinese deported to China.

The very latest wave of refugees consists in part of persons released under the ODP. The program is supposed to reunite families, but I know of at least one case in which a refugee in the Bay Area was sent the wrong wife and children. I do not believe this was accidental; the Communists have often done such things in Vietnam.

Since the refugees keep on coming, my American friends often ask me what reasons besides economic hardship there might be for leaving Vietnam now that the war is over. I can think of quite a few. Imagine a society in which you have to keep attending political meetings, usually when you are tired or have better things to do. Any chance remark that you let fall at one of these meetings could result in your being denounced as a reactionary and sent to a concentration camp or—what amounts to the same thing—an NEZ. Or suppose that you happen to meet two friends at a café and strike up a conversation with them. If a security agent or government informer happens to see you, you will all three be invited to visit the ward security office. There you will be separated from each other and required to make declarations as to what you talked about. If there is any discrepancy between the declarations, you can be sent to a concentration camp for the rest of your life. At the least, your name will be placed on a list of suspicious persons. Once your name is on the list, you could be rearrested and interned at any time. Even your children may be interned.

Is it any wonder that the illegal departures from such a society continue to outnumber the legal departures by more than twenty to one?

TABLE 3. ARRIVAL OF INDOCHINESE REFUGEES AND DISPLACED PERSONS IN COUNTRIES OF TEMPORARY ASYLUM, 1977–1982

Countries of Temporary Asylum	Until end of					1982				
	1977	*1978*	*1979*	*1980*	*1981*	*Jan.*	*Feb.*	*Mar.*	*Apr.*	*Total*
Australia	861	747	497	—	30	—	—	—	—	—
Brunei	38	35	—	29	—	—	—	—	—	—
China	—	—	70	220	54	—	—	—	—	—
Hong Kong	1,007		72,020	11,170	8,475	389	310*	793	779	2,271
Indonesia	679		48,651	6,821	9,328	225	382	749	607	1,963
Japan	851	722		1,278	1,026	—	13	48	153	214
Korea	161	98	150	20	168	—	—	—	—	—
Macau	25	945	3,350	2,270	448	—	—	2	—	2
Malaysia	5,817	63,120	53,996	18,263	23,113	2,150	1,065	1,701*	1,803	6,719
Philippines	1,153	2,582	7,821	4,932	8,353	350	219	142	—	711
Singapore	308	1,828	5,451	9,280	9,381	91	11	93	126	321
Thailand	4,536	6,325	11,928	21,549	18,378	972	788	836	1,046	3,642
Other countries	221	464	372	1	—	—	—	—	—	—
Subtotal (boat people)	15,657	88,736	205,489	75,833	78,754	4,177	2,788	4,364	4,514	15,843
Thailand (land people)	31,214	61,662	65,393	43,569	24,414	825	783	879	519	3,006
Grand Total (boat + land)	46,871	150,398	270,882	119,402	103,168	5,002	3,571	5,243	5,033	18,849

SOURCE: U.N. High Commissioner for Refugees, Geneva.

*Amended figure

Resistance

The War Continues

It is clear from various sources—refugees, Western journalists, even the heavily censored Vietnamese press—that the war is still going on in South Vietnam. In 1977 *Time* magazine reported that the U Minh Forest, the area bordering the Parrot's Beak of Cambodia, and most of the Central Highlands harbored resistance forces that were giving the communist regime considerable trouble.[13] Since then the regime claims to have brought the resistance under control, but not to have eliminated it.

Later reports, chiefly from refugees, indicate that the most effective resistance forces are those of FULRO, the Montagnard organization that I mentioned in Chapter 3. The militant Hoa Hao sect, despite heavy losses, also continues to offer resistance, as does, to a lesser extent, the sect known as the Cao Dai (the fate of both sects since 1975 will be discussed more fully in Chapter 8). Other resistance comes from regrouped elements of the Army of the Republic of Vietnam (ARVN), from Catholics, from ethnic Khmer living in Vietnam, and from disaffected anticommunist youth.

Evidence that armed resistance continues is fragmentary but convincing. A recent refugee, formerly a lieutenant colonel in the ARVN, told me that early in 1979 he traveled to Vung Tau in search of ways to escape. On his way there, near the marker that shows the highway has reached a point 80 km from Saigon, he saw communist infantry units with tank and helicopter support engaged in mopping-up operations. Since early 1980, if the Communists' own news reports are any indication, such operations have become larger and more frequent.

In May 1980, Van Tien Dung, the SRV's minister of defense, visited Seventh Military Region Headquarters to address a conference of cadres and party organizations. He called on the Seventh Military Region to be "comprehensively strong and firm and able to fulfill all the military and political tasks."[14] Already in March Pham Hung, the minister of internal affairs, had attended a conference on public security in Ho Chi Minh City in order to discuss "measures to intensively ensure political security, public order and safety." Attending the conference were leading cadres of the public security service in the South and of the Interior Ministry's southern organs and departments. The minister urged them to struggle against "negativism" among units of the public security forces in order to complete the pacification of South Vietnam.[15] During the same period, an editorial in *Quan Doi Nhan Dan* (People's Army), the army's magazine, admitted that "our people and armed forces have been compelled to cope with many new ordeals resulting from the frenzied counter-attacks of the reactionaries among the Beijing ruling circles in collusion with the U.S. imperialists."[16] In May 1980 another conference on the security of South Vietnam, held in Ho Chi Minh City with Pham Hung presiding, resolved to combat "armed reactionary activities" and smuggling along the frontier with Cambodia. Western analysts noted that "for the second time in less than a month [communist authorities were] officially admitting the fact that armed reactionaries were operating on Vietnamese soil."[17]

Pham Hung continued to tour the South in 1981. In January he visited the provinces of Phu Khanh (formerly Phu Yen and Khanh Hoa provinces), Gia Ray, and Cong Tum in order to review the public security forces. The "new situation," he told them, required "the people's public security forces to make an all-out effort to improve their quality and strengthen their ranks both ideologically and organizationally."[18] By March, the Vietnamese service of the British Broadcasting Corporation (BBC) was carrying reports of increased FULRO activity in the Central Highlands, between the Twelfth and Fifteenth Parallels.[19] These reports were confirmed in April by an interview that Agence France Presse (AFP) obtained with interim head of state Nguyen Huu Tho.[20] To these a special correspondent in Vietnam for the Paris newspaper *Le Monde* added reports of guerrilla activities, also in the Central Highlands, by former members of the ARVN. In the same correspondent's view, such resistance was low-level and uncoordinated; nevertheless, he added, it was giving the authorities trouble.[21] Refugees have told me the same thing: the resistance is under no unified command. Not yet.

Because of deteriorating security on the border with Laos, where the FULRO units are operating, and on the border with Cambodia, where the former ARVN elements are concentrated, the regime has established a special Border Control Police, as a department of the Ministry of the Interior. In January 1981, after the new department had been in existence for a year, Col. Le Thanh congratulated it on having foiled "many schemes and acts of sabotage of the Beijing expansionists, of the lackeys of the imperialists and other criminals."[22] Evidently the department has been coordinating its patrol and investigation efforts with the Ministry of Defense.[23] Such coordination is evidence of more than routine security problems.

Security in Ho Chi Minh City. In 1981, six years after the liberation, there was still a curfew in Ho Chi Minh City from midnight to 5:00 A.M. All ordinary citizens were subject to it. The Ministry of the Interior, according to *Le Monde*'s correspondent, had announced that it was seriously worried by a "new wave of lawless activity . . . and by the existence, in increasing numbers, of resistance cells, that is, of reactionaries both civilian and military."[24] The official report of a conference held that January by the City Military Command noted that "despite numerous difficulties in the past two years," the command, with the help of the public security forces, had succeeded in eliminating "thousands of counterrevolutionary cases."[25] Pham Hung, during a speech in Ho Chi Minh City the following month, referred to the "cruel hoodlums" who were committing "robberies and murders" there, as well as to the threat from "intelligence agents, spies and reactionaries."[26] No doubt the worsening economic conditions noted by such observers as Tiziano Terzani have contributed to the rising crime rate.[27] Unemployment, shortages, and the corruption that is the communist regime's hallmark, together are producing a situation that threatens to become unmanageable.

From time to time, we catch glimpses of what the "reactionaries" have been up to. On July 13, 1979, the Vietnam News Agency (VNA) reported that a court in Ho Chi Minh City had tried a ring of twenty reactionaries who had secretly set up a Front for National Salvation in late 1975. The ring had "carried out psychological warfare to sow confusion among Vietnamese, plotted murders of government officials and hoarded weapons to prepare for the formation of their armed forces with the intent to topple the revolutionary administration." The leader was Vo Van Nhi, a former captain in the ARVN. He was condemned to death.[28] In a report on the internal security of Ho Chi Minh City a communist cadre of the Security Agency, speaking at the Institute for Study in the Social Sciences, stated that the total number of communist cadres assassinated in the city during the twelve-month period from May 1975 through April 1976 was three hundred. In the countryside, during the same period, cadres collecting taxes were killed by villagers. The cadres' heads were left on the rice-field levees.[29] In Ho Chi Minh City, communist cadres dare not walk the streets alone. In rural areas, military forces withdraw to their stockades at night. Government officials dare not move freely in the southern countryside.

Passive Resistance

Most of the resistance to communism in Vietnam is of course passive or unarmed. But it is nonetheless damaging to the regime, and its existence, which is widespread, gives the lie to communist propaganda about the joyous reunification of the country. It also shows up the nature of the Vietnamese communist system. So far from being embraced enthusiastically by the masses, for whose benefit it was allegedly designed, the system clearly makes little sense to anyone not a member of the tiny elite that is imposing it. Indeed, except for those whom the regime is actively persecuting, peasants and workers would appear to be the most disaffected classes. This is as true of the North as of the South.

Details are lacking, but the pattern is clear enough. During the war, the North was mobilized to fight the so-called foreign aggressor. In official propaganda the foreign aggressor is now China, not the United States, but even the VCP has been unable to make effective use of this threat. The war, as far as most North Vietnamese are concerned, is over, and morale has plummeted. Despite repeated calls for greater production, peasants north and south take a "negative attitude." Industrial workers do not heed the calls either. In 1977, the number of hours actually worked by the average industrial worker amounted to only 1,900 of the required 2,400. Le Duan, in 1978, appealed to the working class and the trade unions to carry out "a fierce struggle every day and every hour against the thought and habits of small-scale production, lax discipline, arbitrariness, fragmentation, lack of planning, superficiality, slowness, dragging things out, indifference and doing things as a matter of form."[30] Refugees from no matter what part of the country confirm that Le Duan was not exaggerating; except for the piecework contractors, who work at home and deliver what they make to state enterprises, people are just not exerting themselves. Whether in state agencies or production cooperatives, the general picture is one of underemployment. One practice that has become widespread is for workers to take turns filling in for each other. The worker whose turn it is that day reports for work then sneaks off home while someone else takes care of his duties. Some agencies keep rosters for this purpose.

Paradoxically, this regime that aims to control so much of its citizens' private lives has made it easy for them to practice passive resistance in the workplace. It has done so because it has organized work in such a way as to simultaneously destroy incentives and encourage irresponsibility. For instance, two workers may be on the same production team of a furniture cooperative. One of them can make a fine table in a day; the other takes two days to make a shoddy one. Both are paid according to the same wage scale, so the superior craftsman is actually discouraged from doing superior work. Since the team, not the individual, is the basic unit, responsibility becomes harder to fix. A typical incident might go as follows. Team *A* has been assigned to do a certain type of work—planting rice, let us say—in a specific area for a certain number of points. On their way to the designated work area, the team members walk along the rice-field dikes. In one dike they see a hole through which water from an upper rice field is flowing down to a lower rice field. If this is allowed to continue, the rice plants in the upper field will die. But the team members decide to forget they've seen anything. The hole is management's responsibility, not theirs, and they do not see what they have to gain by helping management out. Their behavior is a form of passive resistance.

Sometimes the resistance is more than passive. Instances are recorded of factory workers, especially technicians trained under the former regime, sabotaging their machines before turning them over to the communist workers they are forced to train as their replacements. Of course, the sabotage is done unobtrusively, by breaking some small but important part. This happens even in hospitals.

A more obvious index of the regime's unpopularity in the South is the eagerness with which people accept and circulate stories unfavorable to it. The city named after Ho Chi Minh is continually swept by rumors of communist defeats by troops of the Front for National Salvation, of assassinations of high-ranking communist cadres, and of communist ineptitude or corruption in everything from agriculture to foreign affairs. Despite the most rigorous censorship, despite floods of propaganda in which communism and friendship with the Soviet Union are incessantly equated with patriotism, the VCP has not yet succeeded in imbuing the great mass of southerners with the correct socialist spirit.

As a result, the regime finds itself in the embarrassing position of publishing books and newspapers that nobody wants to read and showing movies that nobody wants to see. Schoolchildren are compelled to buy Vietnamese translations of such hoary Stalinist classics as *How the Steel Was Tempered*, but nobody reads them. The more humane Soviet literature of the post-Stalinist era is rarely imported and never widely distributed. Employees of state enterprises are given time off to attend propaganda movies that would otherwise be ignored. Only by subterfuge can the general public be induced to attend them. Thus in March 1981 the public in Ho Chi Minh City was invited to an open-air showing of what, to judge from the posters advertising it, was the classic American movie *Gone with the Wind*. There was a rush for tickets. On the appointed evening the audience was packed in so tight that no one could move. At last the show began. The movie was a Russian one. Spectators who objected were told they had been promised, not *Gone with the Wind*, but a Russian movie as good as *Gone with the Wind*. When they looked at the poster they saw that, indeed, the name of the Russian movie was on it in very small letters, next to GONE WITH THE WIND in very large ones.

Unpopular, too, are the ever-present propaganda slogans, verses, and songs. The people of South Vietnam have found ways of retaliating to such stuff. For instance, the initials XHCN stand for *xa hoi chu nghia*, which means "socialism." What they really stand for, though, according to a widely circulated joke, is *xao het cho noi*, which means "so deceitful you can't tell the difference." Then there are the songs that all children have to learn in school. One of them begins

> Last night I dreamed of meeting Uncle Ho.
> His beard was long, his hair was grey.
> I kissed him tenderly on both cheeks . . .

An alternative version runs

> Last night I dreamed of meeting a lost wallet.
> In the wallet I found 4,400 dong.
> I was so happy I ran and showed it to Uncle Ho.
> He smiled at me. "Let's split it," he said.

Another VCP children's song is called "The Great Victory."

> It's just as if Uncle Ho were present
> On the joyful day of the Great Victory.
> His words are now a glorious victory,
> After thirty years of struggle for independence and
> freedom . . .

The version told me by refugees is a little different.

> It's just as if Uncle Ho were being kept
> In the Cho Quan Mental Hospital.
> His words, after thirty years of struggle,
> Have made the whole country crazy . . .

Photographs

1. *Prisoners at Ha Tay Re-education Camp* (Courtesy: *Der Spiegel*)

2.–5. *Scenes from Hanoi* (Courtesy: *Der Spiegel*)

6. *Refugee "boat city"*

7. *Unseaworthy refugee boat towed out to sea by Malaysian Navy*

8. *The daily wait for water, ferried from another island, at Pulau Bidong, a warehouse-island for 43,000 refugees*

9. *Waiting for ship with drinking water*

10. *Refugee children, Mersing, Malaysia*

11. *Overcrowding in Pulau Tengah Camp, Malaysia*

7
Culture with a Socialist Content

The Revolutionary Program

The VCP's education policy is designed to bring everyone in Vietnam a rich moral and cultural life in line with the general objective of socialism. Education, in this ideological-cultural revolution, will be the means of satisfying the ever higher material and cultural demands of society. Educational institutions have accordingly been given the twin tasks of "building a society with [an] elevated culture having a socialist content and a national character," and of "moulding a new socialist man who nurtures correct thinking, develops noble and beautiful sentiments and acquires adequate knowledge and abilities as both worker and master of the community, society, nature and himself."[1]

Education, since the communist victory, also has a more immediate task. Le Duan, in a major report to the 1976 Party Congress, put it this way.

> The important task of ideological and cultural work is to combat bourgeois ideology, to criticize petty bourgeois ideology, and other nonproletarian ideologies; to sweep away the influence of the neo-colonialist ideology and culture in the South; to spread thorough-going propaganda and education about Marxist-Leninist ideology and the lines and policies of the Party in order to give absolute pre-

> dominance to Marxism-Leninism in the political and spiritual life of the entire people; to carry out education reforms in both zones, step by step to build a new culture with a socialist content and a national and popular character, to build and foster a type of socialist man in Vietnam.[2]

In this report, the congress formally adopted "wide educational reforms throughout the country." The reforms were based on the principles of "linking schools with society" and "combining education with productive labor." As for general education, Le Duan called it "the cultural foundation of a country" and said that "all children and young people" should pass "all the degrees of general education."[3]

These basic guidelines are now in the process of being implemented. For instance, in January 1979 the Politburo resolved that "for the younger generation, education must be carried on continuously from childhood to maturity." The aim of such education was to "train a new labor force having revolutionary morality, scientific and technological knowledge, technical capacity and good health to respond to the increasing needs of the socialist construction."[4] Adult education, too, was to be revolutionary and political as well as scientific and technological. The same kind of language is found in chapter 3 of the 1980 Constitution, which affirms that "the state has the sole responsibility for education" (article 41).

The arts, as one would expect, are also under government control; in fact, they are to be "developed on the basis of the perspective of Marxism-Leninism, and in keeping with the Communist Party of Vietnam's line with regard to literature and art" (article 44). Lip service is paid to the people's "aesthetic needs," and there is official encouragement for literary and artistic activities, whether professional or amateur. The main function of such activities, however, is clearly intended to be "as a means of educating the people in the line and policies of the party and the state" (ibid.). Once again, the new constitution echoes Le Duan's 1976 report, which speaks of combating "all bourgeois and opportunist tendencies in literature and [the] arts."

Suppression of Decadent Materials

In the South, soon after the communist victory, the party officials and military commanders on the spot declared open season on the previous regime's culture. Gangs of young enthusiasts were secretly ordered or incited to destroy as much of this culture as they could. Early in May 1975, Communists burned every book in the libraries of the Saigon University Faculty of Law and Faculty of Letters; the books, they said, came from a "decadent culture." Circulation of all other books, as well as art works such as music tapes, records, films, and even paintings, was prohibited. Communist youths went from door to door to search out and confiscate books and materials considered antirevolutionary. When found, they were replaced by socialist books extolling the virtues of democracy in the USSR. All materials branded as decadent were burned there and then. An editorial in the July 16 issue of *Saigon Giai Phong* defined antirevolutionary materials as "reactionary, decadent, literary and artistic works, especially those which we still overlook or cannot yet enumerate, like boxing novels and various types of books from other cultural fields which abound with reactionary thoughts or propagandize the viewpoints of the decadent bourgeois culture."[5] It called for elimination of the "poisons" that had impregnated people's minds for so long. More militantly, *Quan Doi Nhan Dan* called for a complete eradication of "anticommunist culture." The magazine left no doubt as to the official origin of the book burnings.

> Under the leadership of the local Party Committee and Governmental Administration, our people and soldiers have begun to eliminate a very large volume of bad poisonous works left behind by the old regime. They are reactionary, decadent cultural works of all types, including nude movies, gangster films, decadent and adventuristic literature and somnolent or provocative records and tapes. The works are dangerous "sugar-coated" pills.[6]

By means of such works, the "U.S. imperialists and their lackeys" had not only spread capitalist and nationalist propaganda but had infected the people with pessimism and fatalism, all the better to enslave them.

The original book burnings and house-to-house collections had been the work of local officials who, since they lacked a clearly articulated policy, had applied a literal and in some cases overly zealous interpretation of the party's general line (even some scientific works were burned). By early 1976, the communist authorities were struggling to formulate a policy that could be administered in an orderly fashion. The task proved to be an extremely difficult one. Materials that were either overtly anticommunist or affronted communist no-tions of decency could be branded as reactionary without any trouble and their sale forbidden. But what about the vast mass of material situated somewhere between these two extremes? According to a writer in *Saigon Giai Phong*, the materials published under the old regime could be classified into several types.

> A. [A] type which is directly politically reactionary and anti-communist, distorts the Revolution and praises the United States, the puppet army and puppet government.
> B. [A] type which is provocative and poisonous, [and] encourages a decadent licentious way of life [, praising] crime and racial discrimination.
> C. [A] type which is deceptive[;] provokes negative, unrealistic and general war thinking; confuses right and wrong[;] and has the effect of benefiting imperialism.[7]

Type *C*, it should be noted, is extremely varied. According to this writer, it is distinguished by its plaintive and melancholy character, and by its popularity among students. It includes so-called golden music (a term used to denote music, especially love songs, with a languid or pathetic beat), romantic poems, gloomily romantic novels, ghost stories, and books written from the "feudalist, [petit] bourgeois viewpoint." Materials of types *A* and *B* had already been forbidden by the Ministry of Information and Culture; the author suggested that materials of type *C* should be included in that policy. The remaining two types, however, were to be encouraged. Type *D* comprised works that were neither "lewd" nor anticommunist, but encouraged struggle against or opposition to the United States. Type *E* included works that condemned the feudal colonists and the crimes of the old regime.[8]

However, the policy of banning works of types *A* and *B* and restricting works of type *C* has met with very little success. Golden music has become a black-market commodity, even among Communists. Escapist material such as science fiction and fantasy continues to be passed from hand to hand. The flow of such materials from the South to the North has been so heavy that the VCP has called for its elimination.[9] "Decadent music," complained a northern journal in 1976, "has been slipped to the North. Most of those records and tapes have reactionary contents and the singing is lethargic, pathetic. They are poisonous . . ."[10] By 1978 the VCP was forming "cultural army units" in each party chapter to launch an all-out attack on these remnants of "neocolonialist culture."[11] This program could not have been successful either, for in May 1981 the Executive Committee of the Ho Chi Minh City Party Committee issued a directive to carry out a "decisive struggle" and eliminate all vestiges of the enemy culture. In implementing the directive, a three-day campaign launched in eleven precincts resulted in seizure of "more than 2,500 phonograph records and cassettes, dozens of movie reels, and over 4 tons of reactionary books secretly circulated by the enemy and bad elements." In addition, "owners of hundreds of coffee shops, and undercover music halls—the major threats to our society in the field of culture, literature and arts"—were "appropriately punished."[12]

The problem is one that preoccupies the VCP at the highest level. Also in May 1981, the party convened a meeting of all party officials in charge of culture, literature, and the arts in all the provinces of South Vietnam. The meeting was chaired by Vo Van Kiet, alternate Politburo member and secretary of the Ho Chi Minh City Party Committee. All the delegates concluded that "numerous negative phenomena" were appearing in the region's culture.[13] As examples of such phonemena a reporter for *Tien Phong* magazine cited the latest songs by Pham Duy, Hung Cuong, and other composers who had fled to the United States after the communist takeover. The songs were available in Ho Chi Minh City's numerous coffee houses. There, during the late evening, tables and chairs were stacked against the walls, rock music was played, and people danced. Tran Quang Khai Street, in the city's first precinct, had 21 such coffee houses/dance halls. A raid on them in April had turned up "hundreds of tapes of decadent music."[14]

The taste for decadent culture is not confined to the South. Indeed, there are signs that, at the cultural level, it is the South that is influencing the North rather than vice versa. Alarmed at this threat to revolutionary morals, the VCP in May 1981 launched the same kind of cultural search-and-destroy campaign in Hanoi as it was launching in Ho Chi Minh City. A veritable ring of cultural deviationists was uncovered. On May 26, *Nhan Dan* reported, the Hanoi People's Court tried and convicted a number of people on charges of possessing and spreading decadent cultural works. Six were named as employees of the Hanoi Film Production and Movie Projection Agency, of the Hanoi Handkerchief and Towel Factory, of the Hanoi Federation of Trade Unions Club, as a teacher, and as a decorative designer at the Bat Trang porcelain factory. These six showed dozens of decadent films not only for their own enjoyment but for that of "hundreds of other people at various locations," including a small apartment belonging to the Hanoi Federation of Trade Unions Club.[15]

Abolition of Civil Rights

Freedom of Speech

The state has a monopoly over the mass media. This is now as true in the South as it has been in the North since 1954. Private citizens may not discuss political issues in the newspapers. They may raise them in local government or party meetings. However, the majority of those who do raise such issues have been accused of harboring a "reactionary" spirit. They run the risk of being sent to reeducation camps. Even a congressman or a government minister may not speak freely. Nguyen Cong Hoan has described the situation in detail.

> Even as a congressman, I was not allowed to express my own opinion on the floor. Moreover, I couldn't refuse to read a prepared statement there if I was called on to do so. Such statements were either prepared by the individual congressman, in conformity with the line presented by his team leader, or prepared for him by someone else. After each session, the teams of congressmen had to report the results to their constituents exactly as prescribed by the Standing Committee.
>
> A congressman may not freely meet with foreign reporters, unless he is permitted by the team to do so. I was warned that all foreign reporters, including reporters from communist countries, are intelligence agents. As for ordinary citizens, conversations between two or three unrelated people are [in practice] forbidden. If such a conversation does occur, local security agents take them to a security office for the purpose of making a declaration of what has been discussed. Each party is made to sit in a separate corner and write down everything the group talked about. If there are inconsistencies between the parties, they are brought in for additional interrogation.
>
> Family meetings such as weddings, anniversaries, and funerals are not permitted unless authorized by the local government and with the presence of a security agent.
>
> In the schools, teachers teach only what has been written in communist textbooks. The textbooks are [protected by] state law. If there is an error in printing a formula, a postulate even, teachers may

not correct it. Correcting a textbook is an act in contempt of the communist state and therefore a violation of state law.[16]

Freedom of Movement

The Vietnamese Communists have deprived the Vietnamese people of their right to travel, now effectively denied by a policy of "household management." According to this policy, each member of the household must file an adequate statement of his or her identity and background. On this basis, the Communists designate the place where the household resides as its permanent location. No one, without special permission, is allowed to move to another location except for moving to an NEZ.

If a person does need to go somewhere, he or she must obtain a permit from the local security office by pleading sufficient reason for the journey. The longer the journey, the higher the level of security office that must be applied to—of course through the communist administrative hierarchy. In South Vietnam the permit bears the signatures and seals of the local people's revolutionary committee, in North Vietnam of the people's committee.[17] Any visitor who comes to a private house must be checked in. The block security agent, aided by a network of informants, follows up the matter. Anyone in the household who left the residence without permission would be detected immediately and his or her family members could be called to the local security office for interrogation.

Life and Liberty

Food rationing is another means employed by the VCP to keep the general population under control. Without being adequately fed, people are not able to revolt. Rationing is based on the household management system. Citizens of all ages must have their names registered in a "family book." They are then registered members of that household. Each registered member is allowed to purchase a prescribed amount of food at the official price. Accordingly, if a person voluntarily moves to another place, that person will automatically lose the right to an official food quota. Noncompliance with an order from the secretary of the local party chapter or any activities contrary to the secretary's decision may result in a person being sent to a reeducation camp, in which case that person's food quota is also cut off. The crops raised in the camps are shipped elsewhere. Prisoners are fed mostly on inferior and inadequate rations brought in from outside (the camps contain no food-processing mills). To lose one's food quota, then, is to be sentenced to a slow death from starvation.[18] Because of the general food shortage and because of this rationing policy, a house guest usually has to carry a personal supply of rice.

Thought Reform

Re-educating the People

Every adult citizen, as I explained in Chapter 5, must join at least one party-sponsored organization appropriate to his or her age, sex, occupation, religion, or other distinguishing characteristics. Accordingly, there are plenty of organizations where Marxist-Leninist ideology is taught to members and where party policies are discussed. All heads of housholds must go to such training sessions in the organizations appropriate to their status. Generally, criticism and self-criticism are also on the agenda at these sessions.

Former military, administrative, and political officials have received special treatment. Dr. Le Kim Ngan, ex-president of Phuong Nam University, a conservative Buddhist institution in Saigon before the takeover, escaped from Vietnam in 1977 and arrived in Canada the same year. He has given the following account of VCP policy toward this group.

> This policy has two objectives:
>
> 1. *Elimination of individual thought and forcing each individual to think as the party wants—that is, along Marxist-Leninist lines.* In order to implement [these policies] the VCP has taken a number of measures. First, people are given so much work and so many meetings to attend that they have no time to think. Everyone in Vietnam has to get up at 5:00 A.M. to do physical exercise and clean the streets. After that they go to work, returning only in the evening. They must cook and eat in a hurry because they are required to go to meetings or training classes in their wards or hamlets. These go on until 11:00 or 12:00 P.M., when they may at last come home and go to bed.
> 2. *Terrorizing the populace.* Local armed security forces or state political security teams can arrest anyone at any time if he or she is suspected of counterrevolutionary conduct. A statement at a meeting or at work that is not consistent with party policy; behavior or language that unwittingly betrays disrespect for a communist leader; a phrase that the local party secretary may interpret as an objection to his oppressive be-

havior; any of these may be considered counterrevolutionary activities. Accused of being counterrevolutionary, the victim will be taken away at midnight. This policy of permanent terrorism is aimed at every citizen and as a consequence, people must pretend to follow rigidly the thought patterns of Marxism-Leninism. The following are used [to implement this policy]: (1) forcing all citizens to continuously "reform their thoughts" by daily studying the party lines and policies at their work places and at local government offices; (2) sending to re-education camps—that is, imprisoning—people who are not "fully aware" of the party line and policies; (3) instituting a state monopoly of education—a one-way education the party calls "the educational policy of the proletarian dictatorship"; (4) instituting a state monopoly of newspaper publishing.[19]

Thought reform, then, is something from which there is no escape: one must either undergo it as part of one's daily life or be sent to a concentration camp and undergo it there. The concentration-camp version of thought reform will be described in Chapter 9. The general public in South Vietnam, together with low-level government employees and former ARVN personnel from privates to NCOs, were for the most part allowed to take a modified version of it lasting from three to ten days. I refer here to the period immediately following the communist victory, when thought reform was used both to inform people what the new regime expected of them and to screen out security risks. Thought reform at this stage included much instruction in the communist view of the Anti-American War and the allegedly patriotic and nationalistic role of Ho Chi Minh and the VCP. University professors and other intellectuals had to take an advanced course that covered the entire range of Vietnamese history from the Marxist-Leninist point of view.

Le Kim Ngan's account of these courses makes clear that they were not just ordinary lectures but actual training sessions.

A trainee class was organized into teams of ten to twenty. After the whole class had listened to a lecture given by an instructor, the trainees returned to their teams, each of which was led by a team leader (usually a party member) and a deputy leader (usually a trainee elected by the other team members). Each member was expected to express his or her opinion on the subject of the lecture. Those who failed to make a statement would be considered guilty of displaying a "negative attitude," or of "passive opposition" to the revolution. Those who made improper statements would be considered reactionaries or agitators inciting others to oppose the revolution.[20]

After a final discussion, according to Dr. Ngan, the team leader made notes on each member's political attitude and reported his findings to higher party authorities. Before the course ended there was a team discussion during which each member had to read his own statement of self-criticism—a statement of all his strong and weak points with respect to morality, honesty, duties to be performed, labor assigned, and so on. After he had read it, all the other members had to participate in discussing it in order to determine its correctness. This, of course, was a grand opportunity for some members to denounce others in order to curry favor with the party. The entire course also provided much valuable information for the VCP security apparatus, since the team leaders could make fairly accurate estimates of each trainee's political attitude.[21]

The Captive Press

The press in South Vietnam is now a mere appendage of the VCP. The daily newspapers—*Saigon Giai Phong, Tin Sang*, and others—carry only information intended as propaganda for the regime: local production of rice and other foodstuffs, activities of state and party officials, meetings of people to laud the regime, attacks on foreign enemies, praise of allies, and ideological editorials aimed at the general populace. Information and pictures reflecting discredit on the regime are banned. There is no such thing as commercial advertising.

Everything published under the communist regime, whether book, magazine, or newspaper, exhibits the same characteristics of monotony, predictability, dependence on ideological catchwords, and continued paeans to Uncle Ho and the VCP. Authors who cannot master this official style soon find themselves in trouble. Events such as assassinations of communist cadres are hardly ever reported. Acts of resistance against the regime are reported as common crimes while common crimes are neglected unless some propaganda purpose is served by reporting them. Such newspapers serve the regime, not the people. Refugees from Hanoi as well as from Saigon often say that the daily newspapers are "too dry." Readers can usually tell an article's contents just from knowing its subject.

Foreign news is strictly censored before being printed. For example, the election of an international figure to some key position in a certain organization or in a government will be dismissed in a few lines. Strikes in Poland are ignored or, if reported, will be misrepresented and downplayed. Strikes or demonstrations in the United States, on the other hand, will be given full coverage if they can be made to fit the communist line. Censorship of this kind naturally creates a demand for hard news, and Vietnamese in North and South Vietnam often listen to BBC and Voice of America (VOA) broadcasts just to find out what is going on in the world. They also tape songs of love and romance, transcribe the lyrics, and pass them from hand to hand. Novels, too, are circulated clandestinely. Especially popular are novels of the 1930s and 1940s that, because they dealt forthrightly with social problems, were banned both during the war against the French and—in the DRV—after the French had been driven out. Northerners born under communism like to read these books for a picture of the old days that the VCP does not give them.

Education and the New Socialist Man

Education in South Vietnam until 1975 was patterned after the classic French model. In other words, it was elitist rather than egalitarian (though anyone with sufficient ability could join the elite), and valued pure intellectual achievement more highly than the acquisition of vocational skills.

Communist education policy, especially since 1979, has aimed at introducing certain reforms, such as increasing the number of vocational schools, that were probaby overdue, while subjecting education at every level to a degree of political interference that promises to make those reforms self-defeating. The ostensible purpose of education in the SRV is to institute a scientific and technological revolution—considered the most important of the three revolutions—that will enable socialism to create "a civilized and happy life, with the new culture and the new socialist man."[22] In practice, it replaces the old system of intellectual elitism, which did at least produce intellectuals, with the new and no less elitist system of party control. The new system does indeed pay lip service to educational values. Its guiding principle, however, is blind loyalty to the party line.

Education Under the RVN

Since even the main features of the old system may be unfamiliar to some readers, I will briefly describe them before going on to discuss the VCP's innovations. Compulsory education extended from grades one through five, that is, through elementary school. Graduation from the fifth grade was not easy: it required excellent spelling, the ability to write essays involving both description and moral reasoning, plus a command of mathematics equivalent to the ninth-grade level in an American school. There was no automatic promotion from one grade to the next; students who failed to make the grade had to repeat it. Junior high school, which concentrated on general education, extended from grades six through nine. Admission to public high school was by competitive examination; many of those who failed to gain admission went to private schools instead. In high school (grades ten through twelve) students began to major in one of four subjects: mathematics, science, literature, and classics. All students, however, continued to receive a balanced general education. Just before the communist takeover there were some 2.5 million students in public elementary schools and some 900,000 in public high schools. The private schools, both elementary and secondary, held some 1.2 million.

The indispensable requirement for admission to all higher education, even at the community college level, was the baccalaureate, awarded after a two-part examination of which the first part was generally taken in the eleventh grade and the second part in the twelfth. Holders of the baccalaureate were entitled to register at any university faculty, though some faculties, to avoid overcrowding, might also require a placement test. Of the eight faculties at Saigon University before the communist takeover the two that absorbed the most students were my own Faculty of Law, with 58,000, and the Faculty of Letters, with over 30,000. The total number of university students throughout the country was about 150,000. Besides the university faculties there were various schools or institutes, such as the Institute of National Administration, that functioned outside the university system although, like the universities, they granted a B.A. degree after a four-year course of studies. These schools were funded by the Ministry of Education and run by whatever ministry had the greatest interest in employing its graduates. Thus the Institute of National Administration, a training ground for future government administrators, was directly answerable to the prime minister's office. The university faculties were funded in the same way, but—within the limitation of their budgets—were entirely autonomous; the minister of education had no right to tell the members of any faculty how they should spend their money. Individual professors, too, had full power and authority to prepare instructional materials, choose textbooks, and so on, provided they followed the curriculum, which was established by an independent Council of Professors.

Efforts were being made in the early 1970s (for instance, at Quang Da) to establish two-year community colleges of the American type, but these, like the few existing technical colleges, still required entrants to have the baccalaureate. Weakness in availability of technical instruction, then, was one feature of higher education in South Vietnam under the RVN, though it certainly was not weak in pure science or in professional medicine. Another feature was the size and vitality of the private sector. Saigon alone had four private universities, two of them Buddhist and one Catholic, while the Hoa Hao and Cao Dai sects had established their own universities at An Giang and Tay Ninh, respectively.

Nationalization of Schools and Colleges

In October 1975 the communist administration convened a meeting of private-school principals to plan the conversion of all private schools to public.[23] To facilitate the conversion, the Communists pressed school owners to offer their schools to the state; it was, they argued, the owners' patriotic duty to do so. Nguyen Ho, deputy chairman of the Ho Chi Minh City National Liberation Front Committee, had stated at a meeting of private school teachers held in Saigon the previous day:

> We must annihilate the subservient and reactionary education of the American imperialist and lackey administration in order to achieve a national education that serves the interests of the people, particularly the strata of poverty-stricken working people, and [that] is capable of training a body of young people having the abilities to continue the revolutionary undertaking and to build a prosperous and strong country. In order to do this, education must be unified in terms of its substance and organization and placed under state management. Consequently the revolutionary administration adopts the policy of turning private into public schools in order to guarantee and create favorable conditions for everybody to go to school.[24]

A total of 1,087 private schools were nationalized during 1975. They were reopened in October of that year as public schools under a single state education policy.

The next stage, after elimination of the private sector, was to purge both the teachers and their textbooks. All South Vietnamese textbooks, even scientific and mathematical ones, were banned. Over a million textbooks were imported from North Vietnam. Teachers, of course, had to undergo re-education. The regime, it appears, at first intended to send them all to re-education camps. Faced, however, with the prospect of bringing education to a standstill, it released some teachers early from the camps and substituted a short local training course for others. Nevertheless, a large proportion (I have been unable to obtain a reliable estimate) were sent to the camps, where some remain to this day.

The situation of the younger male teachers was made perilous by the fact that most of them were technically still members of the armed forces. Under the RVN's policy of general mobilization, all men aged 18 to 45 were drafted. Some essential services, including education, were left so understaffed by this policy that the Ministry of National Defense agreed to make up the deficiency by returning the men in question to their civilian duties after only a short period of military training or service. Being, in effect, soldiers in civilian clothes, these trained reservists were accused by the Communists of being agents of the American CIA, and were therefore sent to long-term re-education camps. (All NVA officers in civilian agencies had in fact to be agents of the DRV's Bureau of Central Research, which was the equivalent of the CIA, so the North Vietnamese assumed the ARVN followed a similar policy.) Women teachers, however, and male teachers over 45 were sent to local re-education classes for about three months and then permitted to teach again. Once a year, during the summer vacation, they must take a month-long refresher course.

Blueprint for Utopia

Under a resolution issued by the VCP Politburo on January 11, 1979, Vietnam is to undergo major educational reforms. Only through education, according to the text of the resolution, can socialism create the "new Vietnamese," the working people who will be "masters of society, nature and their selves." Education will help to create "a beautiful civilized and happy society even though the economic conditions have not yet been highly improved."[25] Twenty successful years of socialist education in the North, the resolution continues, have shown the way.

At the same time, the resolution admits that socialist education has remained poor in overall quality even while its quantity, as measured in terms of literacy rates, numbers of schools, and so on, was being expanded. Serious weaknesses are admitted, including the system's failure to attract more preschool children to state day nurseries and kindergartens, and to provide sufficient vocational education, particularly for technical and scientific workers. The current generation of working people, the resolution implies, is not up to the revolutionary demands being made of it, and the skilled manpower needed for socialist construction is not being produced by the schools.

The balance of the resolution is in effect, a blueprint for meeting and permanently solving the manpower crisis. Reforms are to be implemented in all areas, from preschool to university.

1. Day-care nurseries and kindergartens are to be set up everywhere, even in the countryside, as an "all-important" segment of the educational system. Here children aged two through six will be taught "love for the socialist fatherland" and will be prepared for general education and for life in the new Vietnam.[26]
2. Compulsory general education is to be extended through grade nine—that is, through age fifteen. Primary general schools for grades one through nine will stress not only traditional subjects (interpreted in a revolutionary manner, of course), but "methodical labor education to promote labor readiness" and "the habit of working in an organized manner." Social activities at this level will be under the direction of the Ho Chi Minh children's unit and the Ho Chi Minh vanguard teenagers' unit.[27]
3. Students who graduate from primary general schools may go either to secondary general schools (grades ten through twelve), which may lead to college-level and other advanced training, or to vocational and trade schools, which lead directly to jobs. Most vocational education is to be organized and managed at the local level.[28]
4. In colleges and advanced schools the emphasis is to be on scientific research and the training of specialized, high-level technical cadres. Curricula are to include "the newest scientific and technical achievements of the world."[29]
5. Adult education is to proceed on two levels: supplementary education classes for older workers, to bring them up to an acceptable general level; and on-the-job training for cadres, civil servants, or other workers who may need to upgrade their job skills.[30]

Ideology and Control

A blueprint, of course, is only a blueprint, and this one is considerably less impressive in practice than on paper. In the text of the resolution, although continual reference is made to the need for strengthening political and ideological education, this need is made to seem on the same footing as the need to raise educational standards and foster individual achievement. In practice, however, politics and ideology are all-important.

For instance, although all children, including children of the so-called former oppressor classes, are permitted to attend elementary and high school, college recruitment is strictly along class lines. This fact does not appear in official documents such as the Politburo resolution just quoted. Official policy is that students who graduate from the twelfth grade are eligible to take an examination for admission to any college they want. First, however, applicants have to go to the ward committee (security section) of the area where they reside in order to get a Certificate of Confirmation of Identity. The chief of the security section issues the certificate after investigating the applicants' backgrounds (that is, whether their fathers were ARVN officers, civil servants, comprador bourgeoisie, or other discredited elements). The applicants hand-carry the certificates and other documents such as their birth certificates and high school diplomas, and file them at the local bureau of student recruitment. The bureau is a special state organ subordinate to the Ho Chi Minh City People's Committee; it reviews the application forms and makes decisions as to who is allowed to take the admission test. Those who are allowed to take the test receive notification of its date, time, and place; the rest do not. Thus only politically clean students can be sure their applications will be allowed.

Official policy statements also fail to note the extent to which key positions in the educational hierarchy are filled or at least closely supervised by party cadres. In South Vietnam, moreover, holders of such positions are nearly always northerners. This is true even of most high school principals—all of them, in Ho Chi Minh City—though some of the smaller high schools are headed by southerners who formerly belonged to the NLF. The local VCP chapter, the secretary of which is a party cadre, checks up on all school activities. Party control is particularly tight at the college level. Every college is under the direction of a board, the members of which generally come from North Vietnam. The college principal always has two or three deputies or vice-principals. One of these, the vice-principal in charge of political affairs, supervises and directs the party cadres who report on the loyalty and attitudes of teachers in every department and who organize the local chapters of the Students Party and the Youth Union. The power that accrues to this vice-principal's position reduces the principal himself to a figurehead, especially since another vice-principal is placed in charge of finances. One of the vice-principals is always secretary of the local party chapter and the others are at least party members. At every level of the institution, the only leadership is party leadership.

Much of this leadership is based on measures taken in secret. Thus each college, in addition to offices in charge of political education, financial services, and management, has an office of organization that secretly investigates the backgrounds of the college's teachers, staff, and students. There is also a protection section, headed by a party member who quietly directs a network of informants made up of other party members or sympathizers, including members of the Youth League. Any teacher or student who openly condemns or criticizes the regime, or who makes statements contrary to state policy or the party line will be secretly reported to protection. Censorship, too, is effectively maintained by the college's printing office, to which all political materials, lectures, worksheets, slogans, banners, and research materials must be sent for reproduction. The office reviews all of them, even if they are meant only for limited circulation. Unauthorized mimeographing or photocopying, if one had access to the equipment, would be a serious offense.

Libraries, too, are heavily censored. The old university libraries having been burned, the new ones consist of books sent from North Vietnam. Most of these books were published before 1975, and many of them are in Russian. There is also a superabundance of political materials such as party resolutions. One refugee told me that the library of the Ho Chi Minh City Comprehensive University contains over 100,000 copies of the collected resolutions of the VCP Fourth Congress.

Building the Socialist Personality

The party resolution on educational reform places great emphasis on the practical side of learning. Theory divorced from practice, the resolution states, must henceforth be banned. Scientific thinking must be linked to revolutionary sentiments; knowledge must become faith and faith a guide to action. The task of building the socialist personality requires no less.

Education in South Vietnam has certainly become more practical than it was under the old regime. In secondary schools each class has to spend two hours a week performing some kind of labor—making chalk, knitting, making plastic shoes and hats, and so on. Classes are given other duties such as cleaning the school or raising chickens and pigs in the school yard. Whole schools are sometimes conscripted for emergency work on dams and other public works. During the summer vacation, the local ward committee will direct students to do such work as street cleaning during the day and take political education classes or engage in cultural activities during the evenings.

At the same time, the dividing line between education and political propaganda has been abolished. For instance, first-grade children learning how to add may be faced with such problems as

> In 1970 agricultural cooperative *A* produced 300 tons of rice and in 1971 350 tons. How many tons did it produce in both years together?

or

> Our troops went to the battlefield and killed 5 American imperialists and 3 puppet troops. How many troops did our troops kill?

Primary reading texts are full of stories about soldiers who killed American imperialists and their puppets in battle or workers who outproduced their fellow workers in some task of socialist construction. In art class children are encouraged to draw grenades and other weapons, and to invent scenes in which American imperialists are being slaughtered. Even science textbooks, translated from the Russian, are full of communist jargon. A teacher I interviewed in 1981 (he had escaped from Vietnam in 1979) exclaimed to me:

> The purpose of such education is to create and nurture hatred in the minds of children. For twelve years their heads are crammed with "American imperialism," with killings, with "socialist construction," "production targets," "labor emulation," "collective ownership," and all the rest of it. The insidious thing is that such stuff is made an integral part of every subject taught, and that children in the classroom must repeat it all the time, so that they get used to it.[31]

Secondary education builds on these foundations. Study of Vietnamese history begins with the resistance against the French and soon proceeds to the founding of the VCP and its subsequent activities. The doctrine of the three revolutions is expounded as historical fact. Political studies, of course, are exclusively Marxist-Leninist and tell how to become a good Communist. Study of Vietnamese literature centers on the writings of party leaders, especially Ho Chi Minh, and on works that are anti-Catholic or in other ways highly critical of the former regime.

Even school routine is designed to enhance party control. Each class of about 50 students is divided into six or seven teams that resemble party cells. Because of these teams, there is no class roll call; the team leader, who is always a member of the Youth League, knows who is present. The class leader is generally some North Vietnamese student whose parents have come south to work in a government agency. Representatives of the school's VCP chapter often visit the classroom in order to hear what the teacher is saying and even take part in classes. Once a week, with a teacher in the chair, the class conducts a formal self-criticism session. The class leader and team leaders report on the class's activities, its academic progress, and the state of its discipline. Students who have been lazy or talking out of turn are publicly criticized and the more serious offenders sent to the school's administrative office. Really serious offenses, however, are dealt with by other means. Thus anyone caught circulating leaflets critical of the regime will be quietly taken away.

8 Measures Against Religion

Religion has always played an important part in Vietnamese life. Ninety percent of the total population—almost fifty million people—are Buddhists. In almost every village, north and south, there is a pagoda where the faithful come to worship Buddha. Most Buddhists are peasants.

Almost 7 percent of the total population or between three and four million are Roman Catholics.[1] To most Vietnamese Catholics, parish and community are synonymous; the parish priest or vicar is the community leader. The Catholic population in South Vietnam is nearly double the one in North Vietnam because half of all northern Catholics (about 700,000 people) were evacuated to South Vietnam in 1954 when Vietnam was partitioned pursuant to the Geneva Agreement. Most Catholics, like most Buddhists, are peasants. Despite its minority status, the Catholic church was very influential in Vietnam under the French and under successive regimes until 1975.

Two other religious groups should be mentioned here because of their great political importance. The Hoa Hao sect is composed of almost 2 million members. They live in villages, primarily in the western provinces of South Vietnam—An Giang, Dong Thap, Cuu Long, and Hau Giang. Many villages in these provinces are inhabited only by the Hoa Hao faithful. The Hoa Hao sect is a modified Buddhist church and therefore calls its creed Hoa Hao Buddhism. Its followers are peasants. The Cao Dai sect comprises about 500,000 members concentrated in Tay Ninh, Long An, and Ben Tre provinces. The sect is an eclectic, multireligious cult whose followers worship Buddha, Jesus Christ, Confucius, Mohammed, and other religious figures. The followers are peasants and live in villages that are actually religious communities.

Religion and the Revolution

In theory, the VCP has a three-point policy regarding religion:

1. Respect both the right to freedom of religion and the right to atheism.
2. Educate and motivate both the masses and religious groups to implement political tasks set forth by the party.
3. Help free the churches from "imperialist shackles," and return them to the people.[2]

Such a policy is far removed from the "three no's" policy—no family, no religion, and no country—taught to communist cadres during the war against the French. The policy was never officially publicized, and the Viet Minh, to all appearances, was not antireligious. Nevertheless, communist guerrillas had standing orders to do nothing to help the cause of religion. It was no coincidence that they so often used Catholic and Buddhist places of worship as antiaircraft posts: the French planes, having been fired on, would return and reduce the church or temple to rubble.

After the partitioning of Vietnam the communist government in the North proclaimed its official policy to be that (in the words of a resolution passed by the Third Party Congress in September 1960) "Marxism-Leninism must absolutely dominate the moral life of the country, become the ideology of all the people, be the basis on which to build a new morality."[3] This policy was already in force by summer 1955, when the party carried out its land-reform program, and it met with opposition by Catholics. The fiercest fighting was in the Vinh area, where some ten thousand Catholics who claimed that they had been prevented from moving to South Vietnam resisted all official efforts to placate them and proceeded to sack government and party offices. In less than a year the antireligious policy had backfired. By October 1956 the VWP was confessing its errors and firing those responsible—not soon enough, for a widespread revolt erupted the following month. Despite their eventual defeat the Catholics had proved they were still a force to be reckoned with. The VWP was forced to adopt a milder line on religion. The Catholic cathedral in Hanoi became a showcase of religious freedom to which foreign visitors were regularly taken. In practice, however, all religious activities were closely regulated, and this was the policy the Communists brought to the South.

Regulation and Restriction

Citizens of the SRV, according to article 68 of the 1980 Constitution, "enjoy freedom of worship, and may practice or not practice a religion." To practice a religion is, however, the riskier course, since the freedom to do so is subject to a proviso: "No one may misuse religions to violate state laws or policies." That the communist regime expected religion to be used for such purposes is evident from the care it took, beginning in 1977, to subject every type of religious activity to detailed government regulation.

The new policy, as is customary in the SRV, was first outlined by a government apologist in an authoritative journal, in this case the *Communist Review*.[4] Quoting the political report of the VCP Central Committee to the Fourth Party Congress, the author explained the party's resolute opposition to "all imperialist plots to capitalize on religion" and its determination to stamp out "all distorting propaganda allegations of the imperialists and reactionaries hiding behind religion." At the same time, the regime was not attacking religion as such. "Reactionaries under the cloak of religion have at times frantically sabotaged the Revolution, and our state has been compelled to apply laws to deal with them. However, this does not mean in any way a policy of terrorism against religion."

A few months later, on November 11, 1977, the Council of Ministers issued Resolution No. 297, signed by Premier Pham Van Dong.[5] The resolution contained a comprehensive set of regulations effectively subordinating religion to the state. Besides ordinary religious services, the following religious activities now required permission from the people's committees of villages, districts, provinces, or cities:

1. Services attended by many people coming from other areas;
2. Religious teaching classes;
3. Such religious meetings as the summer sessions and congresses of the Buddhist Church, of the Great Council of the Protestant Church, of the meditation retreats of Christian priests, etc. [article 1a, para. 3].

The resolution also prescribed clergymen's duties toward the state: "Clergymen while propagating religion, besides preaching religious teachings, have the duty to mobilize followers to perform well citizen's obligations and to carry out well the policies and laws of the state [article 1b]." Local governmental agencies might take over church premises if they felt it necessary: "Grassroot People's Committees (local Administrative Agencies), whenever necessary, may use places of worship temporarily as schools, meeting places, etc. [article 2]." The status of priests was to be regulated as follows: "Those selected for training must be good citizens, have a spirit of patriotism and love for socialism. A certificate of good citizenship must be issued by the People's Committee of the place of birth. Teachers must have a permit from the Provincial People's Committee. Classes must be authorized by the Provincial Committee.

As for appointment to the priesthood, state control in this area was one of the first principles affirmed by the Communists after the fall of Saigon. On August 15, 1975, at a meeting of Catholic clergy that the new regime had organized, Mai Chi Tho, Le Duc Tho's brother, who was vice-chairman of the city's Military Management Committee, affirmed this principle in unmistakable terms.

> To place a bishop in the position of heading a diocese is not a matter related only to religion. To say that it is a matter of religion, [that] means to separate Catholicism from the Nation. Each Vietnamese Christian family is a unit of the Vietnamese Society. Therefore, the appointment of a person to head a diocese must be approved by the revolutionary administration.[6]

The occasion for his speech was the arrest of Bishop Nguyen Van Thuan, a nephew of former President Ngo Dinh Diem, who had been appointed deputy to Archbishop Nguyen Van Binh of the Saigon diocese a few days before the communist victory. Bishop Thuan's present whereabouts are unknown; he has been reported under house arrest in Nha Trang, but there are also rumors that he is in Hanoi. In order to avoid the necessity for such arrests, the new regulations provided that all investitures and appointments of priests must be approved by the corresponding local people's committee, except that for appointments involving several provinces a decision by the premier's office may be required.[7] In general, religion has been placed under local control. Thus transfers of clergymen from one parish to another have to be approved by the people's committee of the receiving parish. Nobody can assist a clergyman in the performance of his religious duties without first being approved for that purpose by the local grassroots-level people's committee (article 3). Church-owned lands may be requisitioned and run by local cooperatives, but—so that no one may accuse the VCP of outright confiscation—25 to 30 percent of the income so realized must be paid to the church in question (article 5, para. d).

Despite the regime's claim that it regulates religion only for security's sake, on balance its policies are antireligious. Nguyen Cong Hoan testified at a hearing of the U.S. Congress in July 1977 that in North Vietnam organized religious activity had virtually ceased.

> For example, in Quynh Luu District, Nghe An Province . . . only old men and women went to mass on Sunday. The main pagodas in Hanoi have been reduced to tourist attractions. I didn't see a single young monk, only old ones; probably before long they'll be dead and there'll be no replacements . . . Nguyen Xuan Huu, a member of the VCP Central Committee and leader of the Phu Khanh Province Congressmen Team (of which I was a member), declared at a meeting of the Fatherland Front on June 16, 1976, that "being a priest is a betrayal of the country and priests are only dishonest proletarians."[8]

Hoan went on to describe the regime's extensive antireligious propaganda. A film, *Holy Day*, depicted a Catholic priest who raped a girl in a confessional; it had been completed after the communist takeover of South Vietnam. In January 1977 the congressmen gathered in Hanoi for that month's assembly meetings were invited to a dramatic performance by the Central Classical Drama Group at the Ba Dinh Hall. Once again, the story dealt with a priestly rapist; this one, in fact, was also an accomplished seducer (the victims were all parishioners). Since the action took place under the previous regime, the priest was also a CIA agent. In this capacity he went around dynamiting the public facilities in his village. More vicious nonsense of this type was to be found in novels written to order by party hacks. One such novel, *Water Buffalo Flies*, had been translated from the Russian.

Measures Against Catholics

Communist policy was more concerned with restricting the Roman Catholic Church than other religious groups because the latter had never been so well organized or so powerful. In communist eyes, the Catholic hierarchy had become "a force opposed to all movements for national liberation and social progress" and "a state within a state."[9] The entire Vietnamese Catholic way of life, practiced as it was in self-contained enclaves, impressed the Communists as alien to Vietnamese culture.

The communist attitude, as I have indicated, had deep historical roots. In 1945, after the August Revolution, Ho Chi Minh and his collaborators in the Viet Minh government were finally revealed as Communists. They were faced with strong opposition from Catholics. There were Catholic uprisings in Thanh Hoa, Nghe An, Nam Dinh, and Ninh Binh provinces. Ho Chi Minh was compelled to invite Msgr. Le Huu Tu, bishop of the Phat Diem diocese in North Vietnam, to join the government as supreme adviser. Secretly, however, the Communists increased their terrorist attacks against Catholic leaders. In order to protect the Phat Diem area, Monsignor Tu directed Fr. Hoang Quynh and Fr. Nguyen Gia De to organize a Catholic Youth Self-Defense Group. The former was appointed its general commander and the latter his deputy. The standoff between Catholics and Communists persisted until 1949, when the French army dropped paratroops in the Phat Diem and Bui Chu areas and the communist forces had to withdraw. Father Hoang Quynh sent his troops to take over previous communist strongholds. In this way the area became the so-called Autonomous Region, which also included the Bui Chu diocese under the jurisdiction of Msgr. Pham Ngoc Chi. There were other areas, too, in which Catholics did not cooperate with Communists. In 1954, after the Geneva Agreement, Monsignors Huu Tu and Pham Ngoc Chi, with Father Hoang Quynh, moved south. Almost half of the Catholic population of North Vietnam followed them. They were settled in various parts of An Giang, Gia Dinh, Bien Hoa, Lam Dong, Long Khanh, and other provinces, as well as, of course, in Saigon. They were organized into parishes under the same leaders as before.

Southern Catholicism Since 1975

Because of the events I have described, there are more Catholics in the South than in the North. In April 1975 the southern church had about 1.9 million members, including 3,000 regular and lay priests, 1,200 friars, and 6,000 nuns in 870 parishes grouped into 75 dioceses. Most of them are still in Vietnam, though by the time the Communists took Saigon about 400 priests and friars had fled abroad with around 56,000 of the faithful.[10]

The new regime wasted no time in taking various measures against the southern Catholic community. Its first aim was to get rid of all foreign clergy. His Excellency the Most Reverend Henri Le Maître, apostolic delegate to Vietnam, was expelled immediately after the communist takeover. The Reverend Le Maître had tried to get the Vatican to ordain the aforementioned Bishop Thuan, a strongly anticommunist priest from the Nha Trang diocese, as deputy to Archbishop Binh in order to strengthen the anticommunist forces in the Saigon diocese. In order to make his expulsion seem like the people's will, communist authorities resorted to the standard tactic of a staged demonstration. On this occasion, however, the tactic backfired and resulted in tragedy. The demonstrators, officially a group of ordinary Catholic students, were actually Communists or communist sympathizers under the leadership of left-wing Catholic priests.[11] It was these same priests who, under the Thieu regime, had published an antigovernment magazine called *Doi Dien* (Confrontation) and were now sponsoring the Renovation and Concord Movement, which was a communist front for Catholics. On the afternoon of June 3, 1975, these suborned protesters gathered in front of the Apostolic Office in Saigon and began to shout that Le Maître must go. Finally, in symbolic fulfillment of their demands, they broke in and carried him on their shoulders to the gate of the office compound.[12] All this took place without any interference from the security forces—unmistakable evidence, in a city under martial law, that the demonstration was communist-inspired.

Meanwhile, around 10:00 P.M., a group of Catholics in Bui Phat parish assembled at the parish church on Truong Minh Giang Street. They had heard the bell ringing, though it was not time for worship. A worried vicar received them and bade them go immediately to the Apostolic Office and save the Reverend Le Maître. A small crowd of Catholics soon gathered with the intention of holding a counterdemonstration (the parish is composed largely of northern Catholics who came south in 1954). With the vicar at their head, they soon set off in the direction of the Apostolic Office. Contrary to some reports, they carried no slogans but only two flags, those of the Catholics and of the NLF. They had got as far as the Truong Minh Giang Bridge when they were stopped by security forces. It was about 11:00 P.M., with only an hour to curfew. Shots were fired, and one of the counterdemonstrators lay dead. Many others were arrested.

Anxious to avoid any further incidents, the authorities quickly removed the dead body. All but about ten of those arrested were released after curfew was over. The vicar who had called for the counterdemonstration was arrested and held for a year. Nevertheless, on June 5 the Reverend Le Maître was expelled, and his replacement, Fr. Sesto Quercetti, S.J., met the same fate a year later.[13] All other foreign Catholic priests were gradually forced to leave Vietnam. On October 9, 1978, eighteen were expelled in one day.

Besides eliminating foreign clergy, the communist regime has succeeded by one means or another in neutralizing the native Catholic leadership. Father Hoang Quynh, that doughty leader of the former Autonomous Region, was arrested; little is known of his fate except that he died in jail, possibly in 1976. The fate of Fr. Tran Huu Thanh, who escaped arrest under the Thieu regime despite his opposition to it, is somewhat better documented. Father Thanh's background is worth recalling: it shows the type of Vietnamese patriot that the communist regime fears. By 1972 the corruption of the Thieu regime was so notorious that a group of nationalist congressmen and other dignitaries united under Father Thanh's chairmanship to form what they called the Anticorruption Campaign. Although its purpose was to overthrow Thieu, it was strongly anticommunist; in fact, its main objection to Thieu was that—as actually happened in April 1975—the corrupt and self-seeking nature of his regime would be the downfall of South Vietnam. The Anticorruption Campaign boldly organized a number of demonstrations at which it revealed facts on the regime's corruption and urged Thieu to resign in order to raise the morale of his troops.

On the evening of February 15, 1976, Father Thanh had dined with a friend and was on his way home. He never got there. Communist security agents arrested him and took him to Saigon police headquarters, where he was confined in a cell 2 m square. Since he had to sleep on the cement floor, the gout from which he had long suffered flared up and tormented him for nearly two months. He was later moved to Chi Hoa Prison, Saigon's main detention center, where he remained for a year.[14] After that his relatives lost all contact with him, and he was believed dead.

In June 1979 communist authorities revealed that he was being held for re-education in Hanoi. In July a French journalist was permitted to interview him in the presence of the prison director and an alleged interpreter (who was not needed, since Father Thanh spoke excellent French).[15] As courageous as ever, he refused to admit to any "crimes" against his fellow countrymen, though he did admit to "errors"—for instance, in having thought that communism was only a utopian creed that could not be realized. He claimed not to have been brainwashed, but recounted how, since coming to Hanoi, he had been kept in a private cell, where he was made to read the party newspaper and listen to Radio Hanoi every day. No definite decision seemed to have been taken on his case, although the prison director said he would be released in a year's time if the Ho Chi Minh City People's Committee approved. Latest reports from refugees state that he is still in a prison camp in North Vietnam.

From "Vietnamese Catholics" to "Catholic Vietnamese." The new relationship between church and state in Vietnam requires the Catholic church to endorse the party line even on ecclesiastical matters. Officially, there can be no serious conflict between the church's goals and the VCP's. Such, at least, is the impression given by statements such as the following one by Archbishop Binh, who, besides caring for the Ho Chi Minh City diocese, is dean of the Council of Bishops of South Vietnam.

> We are Vietnamese living on Vietnamese soil. Over recent years, we have begun calling ourselves "Catholic Vietnamese" instead of "Vietnamese Catholics" to underscore the fact that while we are Catholics we are first of all Vietnamese. Conscious of the position and role of the Vietnamese people, who are now masters of their nation, the Catholics—clergy and laity—are making an effective contribution to the reconstruction of their country. One may say that on the state farms and construction sites, in the public offices and factories, in the newly settled decentralized regions and new economic zones, in fact everywhere, Catholics are present and they are [so] in a positive manner.[16]

Even though church activities such as the ordination of priests have been strictly regulated by the state, he declares that "the relations between the Catholic Church and the Vietnamese Socialist State have improved day by day." He agrees with the Communists that "their goal is nothing but happiness of all and of each," and that for this reason the Catholic church in South Vietnam is pleased to hand over church social, educational, and medical establishments to the state. He goes still further when he openly adopts the VCP lines criticizing "foreign powers" for having "created a profound gap" among the Vietnamese people, sowing division among different groups in order to invade Vietnam.[17]

Refugees interviewed by the author report that, when they objected to the archbishop that he was making propaganda for the VCP, he replied, "You people should not believe what I said publicly." Others questioned him when he came to conduct a mass in Bui Phat parish as to why there were two North Vietnamese soldiers on his car wherever he went. He replied that they were there to clear traffic.

It is true that Archbishop Binh was placed in a very difficult position after the Reverend Le Maître had been expelled. At that time the archbishop met with local authorities and with Premier Pham Van Dong, who issued a call for national unity. It seems clear, however, that he already wanted a compromise with the VCP. If the archbishop had openly opposed communism, as Cardinal Trinh Nhu Khue, dean of the Council of Bishops of North Vietnam, did after 1954, the VCP could not have suppressed Catholicism in South Vietnam as easily as it has done. Even Ho Chi Minh, according to Janos Radvanyi, was not successful in reconciling with the North Vietnamese Catholic church because it remained "obdurately uncooperative."[18] He asked for advice on church-state relations from a Hungarian delegation that visited Hanoi in 1959. The delegation's answer was that he should keep both the party and the state strong, so that the Catholic hierarchy would come to accept and respect this fact and not dare to engage openly in oppositionist political activity. Having already tried this method in the past, he said, he thought that "the best way for him to deal with Catholicism in the North was to do nothing better than keep the Catholics under tight surveillance and control."[19]

A more resolute voice than Archbishop Binh's was heard at Hue on April 15, 1977, when the Reverend Nguyen Kim Dien, archbishop of the Hue diocese, spoke at a meeting of the Fatherland Front of Binh Tri Thien Province and the city of Hue. The context of his remarks was the recent arrest, in Ho Chi Minh City, of six leading monks of the Unified Buddhist Church (the arrest is further discussed below, in the section on measures against Buddhists). The speech was not, of course, officially reported in this form; Archbishop Dien himself circulated it a few days later, in a version representing his best recollection of remarks that were originally extemporaneous.

> I want to talk about two things only: (1) freedom of religion, and (2) equality of civil rights . . .
>
> 1. *On Religious Freedom.* After the day of Liberation, when I heard the government proclaim the policy of religious freedom, I was very happy and encouraged. This was reflected in my remarks

made at that time. But two years have elapsed since and I no longer feel happy, because freedom of religion has not really existed.

Worship services have been restricted, and Catholic priests prevented from circulating to serve the Catholic population, for example, in the New Economic Zones. There are churches that have been seized and others prevented from holding worship services. I appreciated the wisdom of the government when it proclaimed the policy of freedom of worship; this was stated clearly in the five decrees and communiqués on religion. But these are only the written proclamations. As far as oral orders [are concerned], they often contradict the spirit of the published proclamations. May I ask the government: Should I obey the text or should I obey the oral orders? I want to believe that the texts reflect correctly the government's policy; but the oral orders are given by government agents. Perhaps I should not identify the government with government agents who practice wrongly the policy of the government . . .

2. *Equality in Civil Rights.* During the last two years, let me be honest, Catholic citizens did not feel all right. Wherever they found themselves, whenever they did something, they always felt they were suspected and oppressed.

At school, students always heard anti-Catholic teachings, and the teachers tried to smear Catholicism. Of course, there were shortcomings during the history of Christianity, but, compared to the many good things done by Christianity during 2,000 years and which are not mentioned, these shortcomings are only a small part. Furthermore, each time has its own principles, but criticizing former times by using the criteria of our times is not a scientific way.

Concerning Catholic workers, employees, teachers, social workers: even if they are recognized as good workers, they cannot continue their job[s], just because they are *Catholic*. If you are a Catholic, and if you are refused a job, or if you have difficulties in continuing your job, and if you want to know the reason, you will be told privately that if you abandon Catholicism or if you quit going to church, things will go better for you.

During the Assembly of the Fatherland Front of Viet Nam recently held in Ho Chi Minh City, a member of the Central Committee of the Fatherland Front made remarks that suggested to us that Catholics are regarded only as second-class citizens.

The government contends that everybody is equal, that every ethnic group is equal. We are a people of fifty million. There are forty-five million Kinh people [ethnic Vietnamese] and from five to six

> million people of about 60 ethnic groups. There are at least three million Catholics, yet in practice *they do not have the right to equality in civil rights*.[20]

There is confirmation of Archbishop Dien's account. For instance, a 26-year-old Catholic refugee, formerly an ARVN soldier, was reported in 1977 as saying that he and his fellow Catholics had not been able to go to mass for two years, although there were services on Sunday. The authorities, he added, did not officially force them to give up their religion, but the work and re-education schedules had been organized to coincide with the hours of the mass.[21]

The Siege of Vinh Son Church. There have been reports of armed resistance by Catholics, but it is hard to tell how much of this is spontaneous and how much due to communist provocation (or outright fabrication). For instance, on February 13, 1976, communist security forces laid siege to the famous Vinh Son (St. Vincent de Paul) Church in Saigon and, after thirteen hours during which shots were exchanged and three people killed, captured its defenders. The latter included the vicar, Fr. Nguyen Quang Minh, former Lt. Col. Nguyen Ngoc Thiet of the ARVN Airborne Corps, and an attorney, Nguyen Khac Chinh. All were northerners by birth, as indeed were the majority of Father Minh's parishioners (they had followed him south in 1954). As a result of the siege, which was given a great deal of publicity, communist authorities claimed to have uncovered "an impressive cache of arms, transmitters, teleprinters, radio equipment, a modern printing press and equipment for counterfeiting currency."[22] The counterfeiting equipment was said to be capable of producing 300,000 dong, or about U.S. $160,000, in ten hours, and the printing press had allegedly been used to print leaflets with news of a Movement for National Salvation whose forces were led by former Gen. Ngo Quang Truong. Moreover, according to the official report, the conspirators were being aided by the American CIA.

I have no way of telling how much of all this is true. I did, however, obtain a somewhat different account from a refugee whose uncle and aunt lived in the vicarage with Father Minh. On the morning of February 13, the refugee said, three soldiers of the security forces came to the vicarage saying that they had just returned from a mission and wanted to stay a while. Father Minh saw that they got lunch, but they did not leave. At 6:00 P.M. more soldiers came and arrested everyone in the house, including the refugee's uncle and aunt. There was a gun battle at the church, according to the refugee, but it was provoked by the security forces, who then persuaded an old retired vicar who lived with Father Minh to call for his surrender through a megaphone. The refugee also believed that it was the communist troops who had planted the weapons cache, printing press, and other aids to conspiracy inside the Vinh Son Church. He admitted that his own uncle had secretly been acting as a contact between Father Minh and a group of former ARVN officers who had joined the National Salvation forces. However, since the uncle was released from detention only a few months later, it seems likely that the purpose of the raid was to remove Father Minh permanently from the scene rather than to get to the bottom of any real conspiracy. Such an interpretation is supported by the occurrence, not long after, of another anti-Catholic raid, this one on the fortified Catholic village community of Tam Hiep, 40 km north of Saigon. Potential centers of Catholic resistance were being neutralized before they could become troublesome.

Harassment of Jesuits. A similar pattern can be seen in the regime's treatment of the Jesuit order. At the time of the communist takeover there were 34 Jesuit priests left in South Vietnam. To the best of my knowledge, no Vietnamese member of the order even attempted to flee the country. On the contrary, the order made every effort, from 1975 to 1976, to strengthen its position by establishing four additional centers in which new priests could be trained. The Communists, however, not only sent armed troops to prevent young people and others from attending these centers, but also began to confiscate facilities at the existing Jesuit centers. First they confiscated the farm at the Thu Duc Center, 15 km north of Saigon, then the facilities of the Alexandre de Rhodes Center, in Saigon itself. The latter included a television studio (the order had produced its own programs), living quarters for university students, a library, and a chapel. The Communists appropriated the television studio and converted the rest into facilities for their own research.[23]

The Jesuit order continues to exist in Vietnam, but is being harassed and restricted, according to the latest reports, by measures that range from censorship to arrests of its leading members. By August 1981 at least eight of the latter were known to be in jail, the most recently arrested being Fr. Dinh Cong Chinh and Fr. Khuat Duy Linh; Father Chinh's offense was that in his capacity as censor, he had allowed the order to publish a religious journal of which the Communists disapproved. Nevertheless, a handful of postulants and novices were still preparing for admission to the order.[24]

Northern Catholicism: A Dying Church?

What the Catholic church in the South may be reduced to before long can be seen from the fate it has already suffered in the North. The Catholic population there is 5 percent of the total population, that is, from 1 to 1.2 million people. For these there are only 400 priests, who are old and infirm, ten bishops, two archbishops, and one cardinal in one archdiocese. North Vietnam's nine dioceses comprise 522 parishes with 3,578 churches.[25] The communist regime limits the number of vicars by allowing each diocese to train only two theology students at a time. The monsignor of the Thanh Hoa diocese has been forced to turn away more than two hundred young people who want to be priests and nuns. All religious activities are subject to censorship and restriction by the Secret Police; the giving of sermons is as strictly controlled as the training and recruitment of priests. No priest may cross the boundary of his parish without a permit issued by the VCP. All parishioners who are active in church affairs get called to their local police stations for questioning.[26]

The methods that have been used to repress Catholicism in North Vietnam are the same as the ones now being applied to the South. For instance, in 1955, the VCP founded a front organization called the Liaison Committee of Patriotic and Peace-Loving Vietnamese Catholics. It was led by procommunist priests. The committee helped reinterpret the Gospels for priests in accordance with the party line: the worship of God must involve love of country; freedom of belief required the independence and freedom of the homeland. The committee appealed to the church and its followers to support the regime. At the same time it attacked "reactionary priests" and upheld the VCP. The policy has continued. In 1975 Father Phan Quang Phuoc wrote in the government-sponsored religious journal *Chinh Nghia* (Just Cause): "[As for] retraining of new priests: the foremost requirement of [candidates for the priesthood] is that they be patriotic and accept Socialism."[27] He also criticized priests for noncooperation with the regime. Most of them, he added, were "not yet very old," yet they acted as if they were. "They are shy and are fearful. When people visit them or when they are invited to participate in meetings, they wrap scarves around their necks and claim to be ill, to have rheumatism or a headache."[28] The southern equivalent of *Chinh Nghia* is *Cong Giao va Dan Toc* (Catholicism and the Nation), written and edited by such procommunist priests as Chan Tin, Nguyen Dinh Thi, and Nguyen Ngoc Lan—the same group that was prominent in the demonstration against the Reverend Le Maître. Both journals, like their corresponding front organizations, are used by the VCP to attack the church from within.

In this, as in their other measures against religion, the Communists are aiming at results over the long term. They appear to be getting them. The consequences are that in North Vietnam, after over twenty years of communist domination, very few priests, if any, have been ordained, while the incumbent priests get older and older. Adequate religious education for Catholic children is rarely available in their homes. Fr. Nguyen An Ninh, now a refugee in Los Angeles, has recounted his experience with some of the young northern soldiers who took and occupied Saigon. They came to him, he said, and asked for a confession. "Our parents taught us that we are Catholics," they told him, "and that we must never give up our religion. However, because of obstacles created by the regime, they did not teach us what Catholicism is, nor did we go to church when we were in North Vietnam."[29]

Measures Against Buddhists

As I said at the beginning of this chapter, some 90 percent of the total Vietnamese population are Buddhists. The recent history of Buddhism in Vietnam is a history of struggle. The Buddhist church was discriminated against by the French and actually persecuted under the Diem administration. After such repressive measures of President Diem's as the arrests of monks and nuns in 1963, there was a Buddhist uprising that led to Diem's collapse. After this the Buddhist church became very influential. However, it also began to split into two sects. One sect was led by monks evacuated from the North in 1954, the other by monks from Central Vietnam in cooperation with monks from the South. The latter, since it used the An Quang Pagoda in Saigon as its headquarters for directing its activities throughout South Vietnam, was dubbed the An Quang Church. It was very militant; in fact, from 1964 onwards it was usually opposed to the government of South Vietnam, whatever that happened to be.

A turning point in the An Quang Church's political fortunes came in 1973, when it had a slate of ten candidates elected to the Senate. It also had its own members in the House of Representatives. With this amount of political clout, it was able to mount a serious appeal for American withdrawal and an end to the war. Finally, it adopted a middle-of-the-road position, between the Nationalists and the Communists, by announcing a program of national conciliation and concord. The de facto leader of the An Quang Church was the Thich Tri Quang (*thich* means "reverend"), who had played a key role in the Buddhist struggle against Diem.

Because of its middle-of-the-road position during the war, and because of its campaign to end the war and secure an American withdrawal—a goal that, in general, coincided with the VCP's—the An Quang Church was considered left-wing. Whether it was or not, it was certainly infiltrated by communist agents, and many communist students worked to further its political program.

The VCP has used the same measures against Buddhism as against Catholicism. Soon after the communist takeover the La Boi Buddhist Church printing house was confiscated.[30] An officially sponsored Buddhist journal named *Hoa Sen* (The Lotus) began to be published; its only purpose was to explain and justify government policy. The An Quang Church's hard-core leftists were separated from it and used to help found a communist front organization with the innocuous title of the Patriotic Buddhist Liaison Committee, which proceeded to attack the An Quang Church.

When the leaders of the An Quang Church—or rather, to use its official title, the Unified Buddhist Church of Vietnam—attempted to keep up the same kinds of political activities that had made Buddhism such a force under the previous regime, they were quickly disabused. I think it is true to say that no event during the Vietnam War made a greater impression on world opinion than the self-immolation of Buddhist nuns and monks protesting for peace. From October 23 to 25, 1975, the twelve members of the Duoc Su Monastery at Tan Binh, a village in Can Tho Province, had planned to hold their annual service in memory of the two nuns, Dieu Han and Dieu Nguyen, who had died in this way, the first in 1972 and the second in 1974. Instead, the service was banned by the Tan Binh Revolutionary Committee, from which the abbot of the monastery received the following orders:

1. Display of the Buddhist flag in front of the monastery is formally prohibited.
2. Inclusion of religious praying for President Ho Chi Minh and the dead liberation fighters [in] the rituals is formally prohibited.
3. Monks and nuns are not allowed to go into religious retreat and observe silence. They must eat and talk normally so as to learn the way of the Revolution.
4. The Abbot is responsible for expounding the glorious, his-

torical, and great victory of the Revolution among the monks and nuns of the monastery.
5. Monks and nuns are required to participate in the political activities of revolutionary organizations.
6. Acceptance and admission of followers who leave or stay in their homes for the practice of their faith is formally prohibited.[31]

Rather than comply with these orders, the twelve members of the monastery, both monks and nuns, assembled at midnight on November 2 and followed the martyrs for peace into the flames. Their remains were confiscated by the communist authorities, who also placed the monastery under quarantine. Two Buddhist women who came there to make inquiries were arrested and taken away. Thich Tri Thu, president of the Unified Buddhist Church's Executive Council, related these happenings in an open letter to the PRG because, he complained, the government had continually refused to grant him an audience to discuss religious matters.[32]

Relations between the Unified Buddhist Church and the regime continued to deteriorate throughout 1976. Buddhist church properties were being confiscated all over South Vietnam, while Buddhist monks and nuns were being turned out of their monasteries and forced to lead secular lives. Soon the Unified Buddhist Church was as much in opposition to the government as it had been under Diem. In January 1977 the committee for the organization of the church's Seventh Congress refused to allow the representatives of Tay Ninh, Minh Hai, and Hau Giang provinces to be seated on the grounds that they were members of the Patriotic Buddhist Liaison Committee and of the NLF. Thich Vien Giac, the representative from Minh Hai Province, who was in fact a member of the Liaison Committee, counterattacked in a press conference on January 22. The decision to bar him and his colleagues from the congress, he said, came from "bad elements" in the council of the "Buddhist Institute" (that is, of the Unified Buddhist Church, which the VCP does not recognize). The congress, he continued, should clear-sightedly eliminate such elements from the council and elect truly religious and virtuous personages to the council's leadership committee.[33]

His words were ominous. Such leading figures in the Unified Buddhist Church as Thich Tri Quang were already under police surveillance. At the beginning of April the An Quang Buddhists decided to stage a mass demonstration of the type with which they had helped to bring down Diem and discredit Thieu.[34] They prepared banners with slogans demanding freedom of religion, return of church properties, and release of monks and nuns from secular employment. The banners were draped round the An Quang Pagoda fence while loudspeakers called from inside the pagoda for public support. The security forces moved swiftly. On April 6 every street and alley leading to the pagoda was blocked by plainclothesmen warning people, under pain of arrest, to go home and stay there. When night fell security forces broke down the pagoda gates and searched the building.

Among the Buddhist leaders arrested were Thich Huyen Quang, the church's vice-chairman in charge of Buddhist reconstruction activities, Thich Thuyen An, head of religious instruction, and Thich Quang Do, the church's secretary-general. They were taken to an undisclosed place of detention. Little is known of their fate. Thich Thien Minh, deputy to Thich Tri Thu, was arrested soon after. He died in jail in 1978. As for Thich Tri Quang, who had gained worldwide fame for leading the Buddhist opposition to Diem, his fate was perhaps harder still. Placed at first under house arrest, he was later detained for sixteen months in Chi Hoa Prison under conditions reserved for those who have committed what the Communists regard as major crimes. The prisoner is kept in a partly underground dungeon that is little more than a poorly ventilated hole just large enough for one person—or rather, not quite large enough, since the prisoner cannot even sit without assuming a fetal position. In comparison with such holes, the much-publicized Con Son tiger cages (which the Communists have used) appear large and well-appointed. Thich Tri Quang was let out for only fifteen minutes a day, during which he had to wash and relieve himself. After sixteen months of this treatment, he was reduced almost to a skeleton and his legs atrophied. He was then permitted to return to the An Quang Pagoda, where he is now confined to a wheelchair.[35]

With the leaders out of the way, the Communists redoubled their persecution. Thich Man Giac, former vice-president of Van Hanh University, reported after his escape from Vietnam in 1977 that the new regime was pursuing "a policy of shattering the religious communities of our country." Hundreds of monks had been arrested, hundreds of pagodas confiscated and converted to government buildings. Celebration of Buddha's birthday as a national holiday had been prohibited and statues of Buddha smashed.[36]

Another eyewitness estimated that 80 percent of all Buddhist priests and nuns had been stripped of their religious status. By 1978 the regime was boasting that nearly 1,300 monks and nuns from 486 pagodas had been forced to take part as production workers in agriculture, growing and processing native medicines, rice growing, and handicrafts such as weaving rattan and bamboo and knitting sweaters for export.[37] (The source of this information was the privately owned newspaper *Tin Sang*, but since the communist victory its publisher Ngo Cong Duc, who under the Thieu regime was a congressman and secret communist sympathizer, has let it be used as a vehicle for VCP propaganda.) In March 1978, as a final show of strength, militant Buddhists marched three thousand strong through the streets of Ho Chi Minh City.[38] After the inevitable breakup of this demonstration by communist security forces, the more determined elements went underground, some by joining resistance movements in the countryside.[39]

Buddhist opposition has evidently not been smashed, since the repression of Buddhism continues. The regime has found some new labels to pin on that opposition. The Buddhist faithful, like any other sincerely religious people, are now accused of cooperating with "U.S. imperialists and Beijing reactionaries" and of conspiring to "create disturbances [and] conduct psychological warfare by spreading false rumors to distort governmental policies."[40] However, the regime still does not dare to be officially antireligious; it needs the cooperation of religious groups and it needs the legitimacy that their endorsement can bring. For these reasons, and in order to extend its control of Vietnamese Buddhism, it has established an institution called the Committee for the Unification of Buddhist Organizations in Vietnam, which is to serve as an alternative Buddhist church with procommunist leanings. The committee made its first public appearance at the Quan Su Pagoda in Hanoi on April 9, 1980. It is headed by Thich Tri Thu, who is acceptable to the VCP because of his leftist political record during the war and to the church because of his senior position in it. Thich Minh Chau, former president of Van Hanh University, who in April 1981 was elected to the National Assembly, is the committee's first secretary. The committee has of course joined the Fatherland Front and has been officially received both by Acting President Nguyen Huu Tho and by Mai Chi Tho, chairman of the Ho Chi Minh City People's Committee.[41] It has not, however, put an end to the arrest and arbitrary imprisonment of Buddhist clergy. In February 1981, according to *Le Monde*, an appeal was made by the Paris-based Vietnamese Human Rights League and the Committee for Defense of Political Prisoners in Vietnam for the immediate release of such clergy. The two committees provided the names of 77 priests and 36 monks who are imprisoned.[42] This list did not even include the numerous Buddhist intellectuals who have suffered the same fate.

Measures Against Sects

The close association between religion and politics in South Vietnam has been further complicated by the presence of two militant sects, the Hoa Hao and the Cao Dai.

The Hoa Hao

The Hoa Hao sect, an offshoot of Buddhism, was founded in 1939 by Huynh Phu So, regarded by his followers as a prophet, in An Giang Province, South Vietnam. Huynh Phu So was also an astute political leader. In 1945 he founded the Union of Buddhist Associations and the Movement for Vietnam Independence. After the Japanese defeat, he and other Vietnamese leaders set up a National Unified Front that was promptly merged with the Viet Minh. However, after the treaty of March 6, 1946, that Ho Chi Minh signed with the French, So joined the others to create the Front for National Union. In September 1946 he founded the Dan Xa Dang Social Democratic Party. On September 8, 1945, the Hoa Hao faithful held a demonstration in the South Vietnamese city of Can Tho to dramatize its campaign for democracy. The demonstration was bloodily repressed. Several attempts were made to assassinate So during this period, but they were not successful. In April 1947, the Communists invited him to a meeting at Dong Thap Muoi. He went there—and disappeared. At the same time, communist armed forces arrested and secretly assassinated hundreds of leading Hoa Hao Buddhists. It was in order to prevent such events from reoccurring that the Hoa Hao reactivated its military forces and maintained them in a high state of readiness. With two million followers, all of them living together in the same Mekong Delta communities, the sect was able to preserve its internal security as successfully as its perimeter.

In July 1975, communist authorities announced that caches of arms and ammunition had been found in a Hoa Hao community, and that two of the sect's churches in that area were therefore to be closed down.[43] Their action seems to have been the prelude to a more sustained pacification effort. By fall 1976 there were official reports that a Cuu Long group had been set up to work with the Hoa Hao religious sect in the Mekong River (Cuu Long) area. The group—in effect, a military unit—had to maintain security in the area inhabited by the sect's followers; to assist local authorities in implementing government and party policies; and to apply the revolutionary principle of the "three togethers," that is, to help the local people by eating, living, and working with them on such tasks as irrigating rice fields and digging ditches. The group's methods were paying off: it had discovered and captured nearly 100 "enemy elements" who had refused to report to the authorities.[44]

Because the sect's members were so numerous and so highly organized, special precautions were necessary for dealing with them as a group. Nevertheless, the VCP's policy toward the Hoa Hao sect was in essence the same as its policy toward the Buddhist and Catholic churches: to confiscate its property and destroy its leadership. In addition to the sect's armed forces, which had been a thorn in the flesh of every South Vietnamese government since 1954, the VCP dissolved the sect's organizations for youth, women, and veterans, as well as its numerous charities. The sect's facilities—schools, clubs, offices—were converted to adminstrative offices for the new regime. Its publications and writings were prohibited from circulating, and efforts were made to persuade its faithful to abandon their beliefs. Even its cemeteries were destroyed.

Of the arrested leaders, Ngo Van Ky, an adviser to the sect's Central Executive Committee, and Lam Thanh Nguyen, a former commander of its armed forces, are known to have died in concentration camps. Phan Ba Cam, former chairman of the Dan Xa Dang Social Democratic Party and later secretary-general of the Hoa Hao Central Executive Committee, died in prison in 1979. Trinh Quoc Khanh, secretary-general of the Social Democratic Party, is believed to have met the same fate. Huynh Van Lau and Nguyen Thanh Long, former ARVN officers who were also members of the Hoa Hao, were summarily executed by the Communists, the former in Chau Doc and the latter in Cai Rang.[45] Meanwhile, as proof that they permit freedom of religion, the Communists have installed one Muoi Tri as their own official head of the Hoa Hao church.[46]

The Cao Dai

The Cao Dai sect was founded in South Vietnam in the early 1920s. Its main church is (or rather was) in Tay Ninh. One of its founders was Pham Cong Tac. A southerner, he was trained in French schools. After leaving school, he became a civil servant in the French colonial government. He could be called "an early Nationalist" in the South because he was involved there in fighting for Vietnamese independence against the French. Like Hoa Hao Buddhism, Cao Daism is a peasant-based religion. It came into existence in South Vietnam before the VCP had organized its own infrastructure. The sect was therefore able to join in preventing the VCP from expanding as rapidly and successfully as it did in North and Central Vietnam. With over a million adherents, the Cao Dai sect had great influence in Tay Ninh, Long An, Ben Tre, and Minh Hai provinces. The faithful lived in their own communities, and in each Cao Dai village or hamlet there was a Cao Dai church.

By 1945 the Cao Dai sect had its own military forces consisting of two brigades (equivalent to two regiments). The VCP tried to negotiate for the integration of these forces with their so-called national armed forces, but the Cao Dai leaders realized the Communists' intentions and refused. However, the Cao Dai did cooperate with the Viet Minh in fighting the French, who retaliated by freeing Pham Cong Tac, whom they had been detaining in Madagascar, and bringing him back to South Vietnam to lead the sect. Pham Cong Tac ordered the Cao Dai forces to cooperate with the French against the Communists. The French helped the Cao Dai activate twelve mobile platoons. With Trinh Minh The as their commander they were successful in eliminating communist forces from the Tay Ninh area. In 1951 the Cao Dai forces withdrew to their resistance base in a jungle area of Tay Ninh and established the National Resistance Front.

In 1954, Trinh Minh The and his forces cooperated with Ngo Dinh Diem, who made him a brigadier general. In 1955, however, he was killed in a battle against a pro-French group in Saigon. As to the cause of his death, some people at that time concluded that Ngo Dinh Nhu, Diem's brother, had his supporters eliminate The as a potential threat. However, Cao Dai members close to The were convinced he was killed by French agents. They had two main grounds for believing this. First, Diem's position was very weak in his struggle for power against the pro-French group; therefore, he still needed The's support and did in fact make him commander of the anti-French forces. Second, the circumstances surrounding The's death point to a pro-French plot. During the operation, while he was walking on a bridge across a small river in the Saigon suburbs toward the pro-French positions, he was hit in the head from behind by a rifle bullet. He was being followed at the time by some armored vehicles on which pro-French officers were later identified.

Diem proceeded to suppress the Cao Dai as a military power. During the Second Vietnam War (1958–1975), the Cao Dai forces seemed paralyzed. In 1956, Pham Cong Tac had to escape to Cambodia. From there he declared that the Cao Dai was observing a neutral position in the war, and that the faithful were engaged only in practicing their religion. In 1968 the South Vietnamese government changed its policy and began recruiting Cao Dai youth to regional and local armed units. After taking over South Vietnam, the VCP arrested and detained all Cao Dai leaders. Tran Quang Vinh and Ho Duc Trung were only two of such leaders who died in prison. The main Cao Dai church in Tay Ninh was confiscated and converted to an office of the Tay Ninh Provincial Party Committee. All the village churches were closed.[47] The harshness of these measures was to be expected, since the Cao Dai, like the Hoa Hao, had been active in fighting communism for over three decades.

The Future of Religion in Vietnam

The VCP's attack on the Roman Catholic church in South Vietnam is part of its attack on the bourgeoisie, which it claims to have eliminated as a class. The church's anticommunism, its identification with every previous South Vietnamese government, and its considerable wealth together make it a natural target for the new regime's hostility. The communist leaders also regard Catholicism as a subversive foreign influence. Ho Chi Minh remarked in 1959 that he considered it quite as dangerous as American imperialism and neocolonialism.[48]

Catholicism, however, is not being persecuted merely because it is anticommunist, middle-class, or foreign. Any religion that organizes people into groups is a threat to the dominance of the VCP and a potential source of opposition to it.

Religion is also a stumbling block to Marxist doctrine, which derides it as the "opium of the people." The truth is that any religious world view is, on all fundamental points, incompatible with the Marxist one. Some well-meaning but misguided religious people have deluded themselves that this is not so, but the Marxists know that it is. Over the long term, then, the VCP seeks to eliminate religion.

In my opinion, it will not succeed. No government can eliminate something that is inherent in human beings, who cannot live without religious beliefs. Most Vietnamese are peasants, and peasants are probably more conscious of this truth than other people. Moreover, it is in times of distress that people turn most often to their religion for comfort. The Communists, by plunging most of the population into permanent distress, can only strengthen their religious beliefs. Communist measures against religion—prohibition of religious practices, confiscation of church property, restriction of recruitment to religious office—have not succeeded in the North; even Ho Chi Minh confessed himself at a loss in this area of policy. They will not be successful in the South.

9

Vietnam's "Bamboo Gulag"

During the war against the French, the Vietnamese Communists used the most brutal and repressive methods to silence all political opposition in the areas under their control. Among these methods was the concentration camp, which there and then became part of their repertoire. The most notorious of their camps was Ly Ba So, in Thanh Hoa Province. Hundreds died there.

The camps were no less indispensable after the French had been driven out. Indeed, the camp system was now extended from the former Viet Minh areas to cover the whole of North Vietnam. Even at the district level, camps existed for those opponents of the regime who could not be dealt with by house arrest.

Whether detained at home or in one of the camps, all political prisoners in communist North Vietnam had to undergo *cai tao tu tuong*, or thought reform. In official documents it was always referred to as *cai tao* ("thought reform," or "re-education") or simply as *hoc tap* ("education" or "study"), but it was a more extensive process than these innocuous terms suggest. Prisoners were systematically indoctrinated by being made to read party newspapers and magazines, listen to government radio broadcasts, and attend classes held by party instructors. After each class session they had to write reports on the subject matter presented. At regular intervals, they also had to write statements of self-criticism.

The process, modeled on the techniques long used by Chinese

Communists, is undoubtedly a form of brainwashing, since continuous exposure to such materials under such conditions does have a conditioning effect. The subject must acknowledge that his past, with the entire way of thinking connected with it, has been a mistake, and that there is no hope for him unless he begins to think differently, not just in factual terms but with a different sense of right and wrong. "Thought reform is a process enabling the mind to part with what is bad and to assimilate what is good."[1] This definition, published in *Saigon Giai Phong* only six weeks after the communist victory, might just as well have read: "The Party will decide what is good and what is bad. You no longer have any say in the matter."

The Camps and Their Prisoners

Most discussions of thought reform center on the question of its psychological effectiveness. From the experience of South Vietnam under communism we can see that it may be effective in quite another way: as a pretext for keeping anyone in a concentration camp indefinitely, without any charges being brought, and with no hope of a proper trial. By concealing this latter use of thought reform from its victims until they were safely incarcerated, the Communists succeeded in hoodwinking an entire nation into believing it was being offered clemency and a fair chance to join the new society as citizens. The truth, however, was that it was being cruelly punished and that its former leaders were about to lose their citizenship, if not their lives. Since the measures taken have been widely misreported in the Western press, I will describe them here at some length.

From Registration to Deportation

On May 3, 1975, a communiqué from the communist Military Management Section that had taken charge of ARVN General Headquarters directed all former South Vietnamese military men and all civilians employed at the headquarters to register with the new regime at designated offices from May 4 to 6. At the same time they were to turn in all ARVN documents, equipment, and weapons in their possession.[2] This communiqué, overlooked in most subsequent accounts, was a portent of things to come.

Also on May 3, the Saigon Gia Dinh City Military Management Committee made its well-known Order No. 1 regarding the registration of current ARVN personnel. To implement the order, the committee issued a communiqué, dated May 7, that specified in detail the times and places at which various categories of persons were to report, register, and turn in their weapons. Thus generals were to report from May 8 to 9, colonels from May 8 to 11, and other commissioned officers from May 8 to 14. NCOs and private soldiers, plus all military personnel detached to civilian agencies, were ordered to report and register in the same way as others on active duty. Registration for the entire ARVN was to be completed by the end of the month.[3] On the same day, the committee issued a separate communiqué stating similar requirements for all police, from top-ranking officers to ordinary civilian employees; all members of government administrative agencies down to the rank of deputy director; all senators and congressmen; and all justices of the Supreme Court.[4] On May 23 a communiqué issued by the Saigon Education Section (part of the City Education Department) required all teachers to report for registration.[5] At the same time, former ARVN men were given until the end of May to register.[6]

Nothing had yet been said about thought reform. However, it soon became clear that registration and thought reform were inextricably linked. On June 10 the Saigon Military Management Committee appealed to both civilian and military subjects of the former regime to "reform themselves and to cleanse their wrongs in order to quickly become honest citizens, loving the fatherland and peace, and to return to the nation." The appeal encouraged them to "make quick progress," an outcome that would favorably affect consideration of whether their rights as citizens should be restored.[7] On the same day, the committee issued a communiqué on how this opportunity for self-reform would be administered. It began, for reasons that later became only too clear, with those of lower rank. All NCOs, privates, civilian employees of ARVN, and lower-echelon civil servants were to undergo three days of instruction (*hoc tap*) at designated places in the localities where they had already registered.[8]

The conduct of this vast program of instant, on-the-spot thought reform was reported in detail in the Western mass media by journalists largely favorable to the communist cause. Their reports gave an impression of great leniency being shown by the new regime toward its former enemies. This impression was precisely the one that the regime wanted to convey. *Saigon Giai Phong*, in its "Daily Topic" column of June 13, commented on the *hoc tap* classes under the headline "A Policy Imbued with Vietnamese Humanitarianism." The "puppet personnel," claimed the article, had simply been "ordered to report for registration and turn in their weapons . . . there have even been efforts to educate and reform them."[9] When most of the NCOs and privates, except those who had served in the intelligence, marine, airborne, or ranger corps, were actually released after undergoing the three-day classes, the impression of leniency was reinforced. True, failure to report to class was considered a serious offense. But the communist authorities permitted those who had registered in one area and worked in another to report to a class in the latter. Reeducation, since it did not usually involve being detained, did not seem so bad, and the use that communist security agents were to make of information gained from the classes was not yet clear. These were the classes described by Dr. Le Kim Ngan (see Chapter 7).

On June 13 the Military Management Committee, for the first time, began to disclose its plans for ARVN officers. All junior officers, from the ranks of captain to second lieutenant, who had already registered would have to "attend reform classes in order to become genuine citizens." Since no details were given, it was generally assumed that there had been no change in policy.

The details came on June 20, in a flurry of communiqués signed by Gen. Tran Van Tra himself. The one referring to junior officers read as follows:

> All officers, policemen and intelligence agents who have reported for registration shall perform thought reform at the following places:
>
> A. Captains to Second Lts. detached to civilian agencies will gather from June 23 [to] 24, 1975, at a number of designated centers.
> B. Captains (not detached to civilian agencies) will gather from June 23 [to] 24, 1975, at a number of different centers.
> C. Lts. will gather at designated centers from June 25 [to] 26, 1975.
> D. Second Lts., police officers from Chief Warrant Officers to Captains [and] intelligence junior cadres report from 27 [to] 28, 1975, at designated centers.
>
> Those people gathering for education shall bring along enough paper, pens, clothes, mosquito nets, food or money for use in 10 days beginning from the day of gathering.[10]

As I explained in Chapter 7, military men detached to civilian government agencies were considered to be CIA agents. They were therefore ordered to report to separate centers.

Similar communiqués were issued for senior officers and for senior government officials, civil servants, and legislators, including the president, vice-president, and prime minister. There was one small but significant difference in the instructions given to this group: they were to bring enough food and personal articles for 30 days, not 10.[11] Teachers, too, were ordered to report for re-education under the same conditions.[12] Although it was now clear that all persons in these categories would be moved to camps, there was no widespread panic or resistance. The government's own request that they should bring, at most, a 30-day supply of food seemed to guarantee that they, like the NCOs and ordinary soldiers, would be released after a brief course of instruction. Nearly all of them, including the elderly and infirm, presented themselves at the centers on the days appointed.

In this way, according to Tiziano Terzani, who was in Saigon at the time and has since revisited it, "some 250,000 people disappeared into the remote jungle concentration camps that are distributed over the whole country."[13]

Duration of Confinement

Sometime in early July—at least ten days after the officers had left Saigon for re-education—a truck convoy carrying junior ARVN officers to the Trang Lon concentration camp in Tay Ninh was involved in an accident. As far as I have been able to discover, one of the Molotova trucks overturned.[14] Its North Vietnamese driver and some of the detained officers were injured.

Rumors of the accident filtered back to Saigon, where they soon took the form that some officers—perhaps a substantial number—had been killed in an ambush set by anticommunist guerrillas. Since the junior officers were expected home any day, about 50 of their wives and other family members went to the offices of the Military Management Committee at Doc Lap Palace and demanded to know the truth.[15] They were chased away by armed guards. Later the committee issued a communiqué that there had been no deaths and that those who spread such rumors would be severely punished. After 30 days, the truth could no longer be concealed: no one was being released.

> In a political education session for intellectuals in Saigon, someone asked how long the education and thought-reform sessions would last, since a month had now elasped and the trainees had not returned home. Mai Chi Tho, then secretary of the City Party Committee, replied: "The government's communiqué said they were asked to bring food for only a month. The communiqué did not say that the education period is one month."[16]

Faced with rising public indignation, the regime at last disclosed what it alleged was its policy on the duration of camp-based thought reform. That policy, as summarized in *Saigon Giai Phong* on August 24, called for the release of detainees in the following four categories:

1. Good people who were caught in enemy sweeping operations and then were forced to join the enemy army [but while they were in it] did not commit crimes against the people.
2. Relatives of revolutionary cadres (father, mother, wife or husband, blood siblings).
3. People [with] family member[s] (father and mother, wife and husband, siblings) [who] "have merit" toward the Revolution and whose family has had a good political attitude toward the Revolution in the locality, and who themselves, while in the puppet army administration, did not commit crimes and are acknowledged [as blameless] by the local people.
4. People engaged in specialized scientific-technical, educational, economic and other work who while working for the puppets did not commit crimes and did not participate in reactionary political parties and organizations.[17]

The detainees' relatives, the summary concluded, would be responsible for their good behavior after release, as well as for the education, care, and reform of their children.

Although this policy sounded magnanimous, announcement of it did not presage any substantial release of detainees from the camps. Indeed, practically the only ones released, as far as I have been able to discover, were the teachers I referred to in Chapter 7, a number of needed professionals such a doctors and engineers, and the seriously ill. However, the announcement made a good general impression because most South Vietnamese did not feel that they or their relatives had committed "crimes against the people" or could be blamed for having been drafted into the armed forces. After all, the detainees had not been formally charged with any crimes. Hope for their release grew accordingly.

What the detainees' relatives did not yet realize was that the regime had no intention of bringing formal charges. Its main basis for deporting people to the camps was the set of administrative categories it had drawn up at the time of general registration. Anyone who fell into one of the wrong categories—in effect, anyone the Communists feared or suspected, however groundlessly—was ipso facto classified as deportable. The deportation policy, which by a stroke of the pen converted prisoners of war into political prisoners, lacked even a facade of legality. The administrative justification for it was delivered retroactively. There was no way, as the regime itself tacitly acknowledged in its use of deception, by which such a policy could be reconciled with a policy of national reconciliation. The longer the deportees stayed in the camps, the harder it was to let them out, since if they were not at first hostile to the regime they certainly became so as a result of imprisonment. In any case, the official story that they would be re-educated and then returned to society was a deliberate propaganda myth. Informally, as Le Kim Ngan has related, communist cadres freely admitted that they had written off as irreconcilable not only the entire former governing class of South Vietnam but also their children.[18]

The official line, however, was that all the detainees would be either re-educated to the point of reconciliation or brought to justice for their crimes. The period set for completing this process was—as the public learned from a PRG policy statement issued a full year later, on May 25, 1976—three years from the initial date of detention.[19] The policy was a more elaborate version of the one issued in August 1975, and it had the same air of leniency. Officers, NCOs, and ordinary members of certain branches of the armed services, including paramilitary and security forces, intelligence and psychological warfare units, and police, with civil servants at various levels of the administrative apparatus of the former regime, would have to attend re-education courses for three years (article 9). However, the following were exempted from this requirement:

1. Persons allowed to attend short-term, on-the-spot reformation courses who had not perpetrated any open or secret actions against the republic (article 2)
2. Public servants of the former administration allowed to attend short-term, on-the-spot reformation courses (article 3)
3. Members of reactionary political parties who, having been forced to join or having mistakenly joined these organizations, were allowed to take short-term reformation courses (article 4)
4. Technical people such as engineers and doctors who had been drafted into the former regime's military services (article 5)
5. Those who were old, weak, or suffering from serious diseases; pregnant women; those who had children under three years of age; those who retired prior to 1975 (article 7)

6. People at central education camps who made noteworthy progress (article 6)[20]

The statement added that others, such as *hoi chanh* (article 10) and those who had committed crimes against the revolution (articles 11 and 12), would be tried by the revolutionary administration.[21] No mention was made of how long they would have to stay in the "central education camps," that is, in the jungle concentration camps to which it had already deported them. It was uncertain, then, to whom—if anyone—the three-year limit would be applied. In fact, it was not so much a limit as an indeterminate sentence, since it was applied simultaneously to those "who must continue their re-education course" and to those "who must be brought to trial." The latter category included: (1) "persons who have committed many crimes against the people and dangerous evildoers who have incurred many blood debts to their compatriots"; (2) "persons who were in the ranks of the resistance and betrayed the country"; and (3) "persons who have not submitted to the revolutionary administration, who refuse to report to the Administration for re-education courses."[22] Even if (1) and (3) are excluded from the PRG's list, the number of persons aimed at was very large, since more than 250,000 Vietnamese had taken part in the *hoi chanh* program since its inception in the early 1960s. The purpose of the program, which was administered by the Chieu Hoi (Open Arms) Ministry of the South Vietnamese government, was to win over V.C. cadres, both military and political. Those who took advantage of the program were called *hoi chanh* ("political returnees"). They first received indoctrination, then were placed in a rehabilitation program. The program, financed by the U.S. government, had a uniform policy of eventually integrating the returnees into South Vietnamese society. In contrast, under the VCP's re-education program it was impossible, in the absence of formal criminal charges, for the prisoners (let alone their relatives) to tell if they "must be brought to trial." By the end of 1976 the many complaints and inquiries about the camps had placed the regime on the defensive. Thus Vo Van Sung, the Vietnamese ambassador to Paris, attempted in February 1977 to justify his country's policy in the following terms.

> More than one million people who worked for the enemy but who have shown repentance and demonstrated their wish to serve the nation, have been enfranchised. However, there are people who have committed unpardonable crimes and who have tried, since the liber-

> ation, to obstruct the reconstruction of the country. To release them now would be detrimental to the interests of the nation. Those people will be judged according to the Constitution of Vietnam which is the sovereignty of Vietnam.[23]

According to an article in *Nhan Dan* dated a few days before this statement, 95 percent of the "puppet administration's personnel" had been set free and enjoyed citizenship.[24] Such a percentage would refer to about a million people.

Leaving aside for one moment the question of numbers, I can state with some certainty that persons released from the camps are not treated as full citizens. According to Nguyen Cong Hoan, who was in a position to know, the very few released by 1977 "could be arrested, even killed at any time without any good reason."[25] On national holidays, according to Hoan, they were rounded up by local authorities and put under guard. Neither they nor their wives and children could get jobs, and their children had a hard time even getting education. In the end, all of them had to go to the NEZs.[26] He also discloses that many detainees' families were induced to depart for the NEZs by promises that their loved ones would be released sooner. Once they got there they found that the promises were illusory and that they were completely at the mercy of the local authorities, who treated them like slaves. Meanwhile the homes and property they had left behind were seized and allocated to party cadres.

The Vietnamese communist authorities classify those who have once been sent to re-education camps as *thanh phan tap trung* ("concentration elements"). Such "elements" are blacklisted and at any time can be arrested and sent back to the camps. Communist North Vietnam has always had a similar policy. A refugee who was a classmate of mine in the eleventh grade told me that after leaving Saigon for Hanoi in July 1954 he was jailed three times, the third time in 1965 when the United States began systematic bombing of the North. A great many others, he said, were arrested at the same time as himself. A large proportion of them were still in re-education camps when he fled Vietnam in 1980.

How Many Prisoners?

There is something decidedly strange about the SRV's official figures on its political prisoners. Vo Van Sung, in the statement already quoted, was following the official line when he said that there were only 50,000 of them, and that they had all committed "major crimes" either during or after the war. By December 1979 the regime had apparently misplaced 10,000 prisoners, since it told the representatives of Amnesty International then in Hanoi that only 40,000 soldiers and civilians had been detained for long-term re-education since the communist victory.[27]

No well-informed person believes either of these figures. I have already mentioned Terzani's estimate of 250,000—the estimate of someone who was at first favorably disposed toward the regime. In May 1981, when Terzani returned to Saigon, he found no one willing to give a straight answer to the question, How many have been released? People's guesses, he added, ranged from 20,000 to 200,000.[28] He did not mention the government's official reply to Amnesty International, which was not publicly disclosed until June: some 14,000 of the original 40,000 had been released by December 1979, according to this. By September 1980, according to an official memo, the regime had released another 6,000.[29] These figures, whether interpreted literally or as indicating true proportions of the whole, are equally fantastic. What, for instance, has become of the more than 250,000 Vietnamese who, by 1975, had passed through the Chieu Hoi program? The Communists hated these men as traitors and would certainly have interned any they were able to identify. Despite many inquiries I have heard of very few refugees who are also *hoi chanh*, nor have I been able to learn what happened to the ones still in Vietnam.

Simply by considering the classes of persons interned, one can see that figures of a much larger order than 40,000–50,000 would have to have been involved. A former ARVN field officer who uses the pseudonym "Phu Yen" has made a systematic study of the re-education camps on the basis of his own five-year internment in several of them and on what he has been able to learn from interviews and written reports.[30] According to Phu Yen's estimate, some 343,000 persons had been interned by the end of 1975. Except for a number taken prisoner in the Central Highlands and on Highway 7 and the central coastal area by the advancing communist armies, these persons could be classified, in round numbers, as follows:

1. 8,000 elected officials (village and provincial councillors, congressmen and senators)
2. 5,000 civil servants with the rank of deputy director or above; officials of the South Vietnamese Central Intelligence Organization (CIO)
3. 20,000 members of the nationalist political parties such as the

Can Lao Nhan Vi, Dan Chu, Vietnam Quoc Dan Dang, and Dai Viet

4. 60,000 members of the Rural Development Corps, of Operation Phoenix (CIA-sponsored counterintelligence), and of the Chieu Hoi program
5. 60,000 ARVN officers with the rank of second lieutenant and above
6. 10,000 police officers with the rank of second lieutenant and above
7. 100,000 NCOs from political warfare, intelligence, the Special Forces, the airborne, and the marines
8. 50,000 NCOs from police field forces and from the Special Police
9. 30,000 others, including anticommunist religious leaders, writers, actors, artists, students, and so forth

These figures, Phu Yen continues, are consistent with the communist claim, which was published in *Saigon Giai Phong*, that 400,000 persons—that is, ARVN officers, senior government officials, and other notables—had registered for re-education.[31] Most of those who registered with local authorities, it appears, did in fact report for re-education at the prescribed times and places. In Saigon alone, 345 colonels, 1,800 lieutenant colonels, and about 5,000 majors registered with local authorities; 336 colonels, 1,752 lieutenant colonels, and 4,700 majors actually reported to local officers for re-education. Phu Yen estimates that more than 229,000 of those who reported are still interned.

Another major source of information on the camps is the American embassy in Bangkok, which extensively debriefs many (though by no means all) of the refugees who have escaped from them into Thailand. The embassy's statistics on the camps are strictly cumulative, that is, it reports only what the refugees tell it and makes no attempt at statistical projection or estimation as Phu Yen has done. In December 1981 the embassy reported that 50 re-education camps had so far been identified by former inmates as operational during the 1980–81 period, and that their combined population, according to these sources, was "in excess of 126,000."[32] This, too, is consistent with Phu Yen's estimate, since one would not expect every camp in Vietnam to be represented among the refugees debriefed at the embassy. Moreover, for the entire period from 1975 through 1981, refugees at the embassy have reported on over a hundred operational camps.[33] It so happens that the fourteen camps described in detail by refugees in embassy despatches of December 1981 and January 1982 have an average population of slightly over 3,000.[34] Since 3,000 × 100 = 300,000, it would seem that Phu Yen, unlike the SRV's official spokesmen, is at least dealing in figures of the right magnitude.

According to Phu Yen, by far the greater proportion of the camps' inmates—some 200,000, he believes—are detained in the South.[35] This would accord with the personal observations of Nguyen Cong Hoan, who happens to be a native of Phu Khanh Province. There, he recalled in 1977, there were only 300,000 inhabitants but seven large re-education camps with a total of 50,000 prisoners.[36] One of these camps, located at Dong Tre, Xuan Phuoc Village, in Dong Xuan District, held more than 1,400 refugees who, after being evacuated from South Vietnam in May 1975, chose to return under American auspices in November on the Vietnamese-owned ship *Thuong Tin*. Communist authorities arrested them on arrival and accused them of being CIA agents. They have been interned ever since. The prisoners in Phu Khanh Province, according to Hoan's 1977 article, came from all levels of society. Although many of them were former ARVN officers, there were others who had opposed the old regime or stayed aloof from it.

> Nguyen Trong Quy, vice-chairman for the Phu Khanh branch of the National Reconciliation and Concord Movement, has so far been kept in solitary confinement for two years.
>
> Tran The Khang, chairman of the provincial Red Cross (Hoi Hong Thap Tu), had no connection at all with the former regime. He was nonetheless arrested and sent away for long-term re-education. All his property has been confiscated.
>
> Thich Khe Hoi, representative of the Phu Khanh Province Unified Buddhist Church and a close friend of Thich Tri Quang, has suffered the same fate.[37]

The prisoners in these camps, according to Hoan, lacked all legal protection or recourse. The principal basis for their imprisonment was that they had been denounced by local communist cadres.

Camp size, as one would expect, is reported to vary a good deal, both among camps and, as prisoners die or are transferred, at the same camp over time. Some hold as many as 5,000–6,000 prisoners, but a more typical size, to judge from figures given by former inmates, is 2,000–4,000. According to the American embassy in Bangkok, the Suoi Mau Camp in Dong Nai Province holds about 6,000 prisoners (as of January 1981) and the Gia Trung Camp in Gia

Lai-Cong Tum about 5,000 (May 1981). On the other hand, Gia Ray, in Dong Nai Province, holds 4,000 (April 1981); Xuyen Moc, also in Dong Nai, 4,000 (May 1981); Ham Tan, in Thuan Hai, 4,000 (September 1981); Phuoc Long, in Song Be, 3,600 (February 1980); Vinh Quang, in Vinh Phu (North Vietnam), 2,700 (May 1981); Nghe Tinh, in Nghe Tinh, 2,300 (May 1981); Cay Cay, in Tay Ninh, 3,500 (July 1980); and Nam Ha, in Ha Nam Ninh (North Vietnam), 3,650 (January 1981). The smallest camp described by recent refugees is Con Cat, in Hau Giang Province, with about 900 prisoners (October 1980).[38] Nguyen Cong Hoan tells of four camps located in the mountains near Ngan Dien, a hamlet in the Son Ha District of Phu Khanh Province, with 500 prisoners each.[39] It is clear, however, that these were all subcamps of the same general camp, and subcamps of 500–1,000 prisoners have often been reported by other sources.

There would appear to be no uniform system for naming the SRV's concentration camps. Refugees report that they are generally known by the name of the nearest village or hamlet. The communist regime usually designates each camp by a code number. Sometimes, it changes the name or the code. For example, Ly Ba So was the name of a camp in Thanh Hoa in the 1940s and 1950s. The camp is located in the Thieu Yen District, Thanh Hoa Province. It was renamed Camp No. 5, possibly because, in a subcamp, it contains several hundred Biet Kich (Special Forces, similar to the Green Berets) who were trained by the Americans and sent to North Vietnam. Many of them were arrested and have been interned since the late 1950s or early 1960s.[40]

Each *tong trai*, or general camp, is generally divided into a number of subcamps under the direction of a single camp headquarters. For security reasons, so that prisoners' relatives can send them mail without being told where they are, each camp is officially known by its own code number and each subcamp by a serial number that is appended to the code number. Thus the huge camp in the Western area of Phu Khanh, which from 1975 to 1977 held 50,000 prisoners, is coded TH-188 and has four camps designated Tuy Hoa, A-20, A-30, and T-5 (Camp A-20 is reserved for the luckless passengers of the *Thuong Tin*). Figure 15 shows the provinces and their prisons, north and south.

Attempts have been made by some observers to classify the camps according to the types of prisoners they contain and the relative severity of the sentences meted out to them. As to the types of prisoners, I believe that a very rough classification may be possible. The highest-ranking prisoners, plus those of all ranks who were said to have "committed serious crimes against the people" and to "owe a blood debt to the people," were sent to camps or prisons in the North. Besides senior ARVN officers, then, the northern camps tend to contain members of the airborne, marines, and rangers; members of nationalist political parties; and police and intelligence officers.

I say "tend to" because such northern camps as Vinh Phu, with about 6,000 prisoners, and Subcamp A of Nam Ha, with about 1,100 prisoners, are known to have mixed populations. The latter's population, for instance, includes officers and NCOs captured during the Lam Son 719 operation of July 1971, in which ARVN units sent to deny the NVA its extensive sanctuaries and infiltration routes in southern Laos found themselves up against seven or eight NVA divisions. Refugees report that different categories of prisoners are often assigned to different subcamps; thus all the prisoners classed as "political" may be in Subcamp A, for instance, and all the prisoners classed as "criminal" (that is, as perpetrators of common crimes, not "crimes against the people") in Subcamp B. But general camps for one category only would seem to be rare in the North. Proximity to Hanoi undoubtedly reflects the seriousness with which a prisoner's "crimes against the people" is regarded. The most important prisoners are held in Hoa Lo Prison in Hanoi itself; Gen. Bui Van Nhu of the police and Col. Tran Van Thang, former director of ARVN military security, are among them.[41] Many of South Vietnam's former political leaders, including Premier Nguyen Van Loc, Minister Cao Van Tuong, Senator Nguyen Thon Do, and Ambassador Nguyen Xuan Phong, who was head of the South Vietnamese delegation at the Paris Peace Conference, are in Subcamp A at Nam Ha, 45 km south of Hanoi.[42] The showcase camp of Ha Tay, with its 460 or so high-ranking prisoners, is only 20 km north of Hanoi.

The southern camps, since they hold the largest categories of prisoners, tend to be more specialized. Thus the inmates of Da Nang, Pleiku, Suoi Nuoc Trong, Trang Lon, Katum, Suoi Mau, and Phuoc Long are nearly all ARVN officers.[43] Ben Keo, Cay Gua, and Tac Van, among others, are for persons arrested while attempting to flee the country.[44] Even in the South, though, there may be a great variety of prisoners at a single camp. For instance, Cay Cay Camp in the province of Tay Ninh was reported in July 1980 to contain not only ARVN officers and NCOs but also "women's army corps personnel, former RVN district, provincial and central government officials, Cao Dai religious leaders, common criminals, and resistance fighters."[45] Buddhist monks and Catholic priests are often found among

Figure 15: Prisons and Re-education Camps in Vietnam, 1975–1981

(by province)

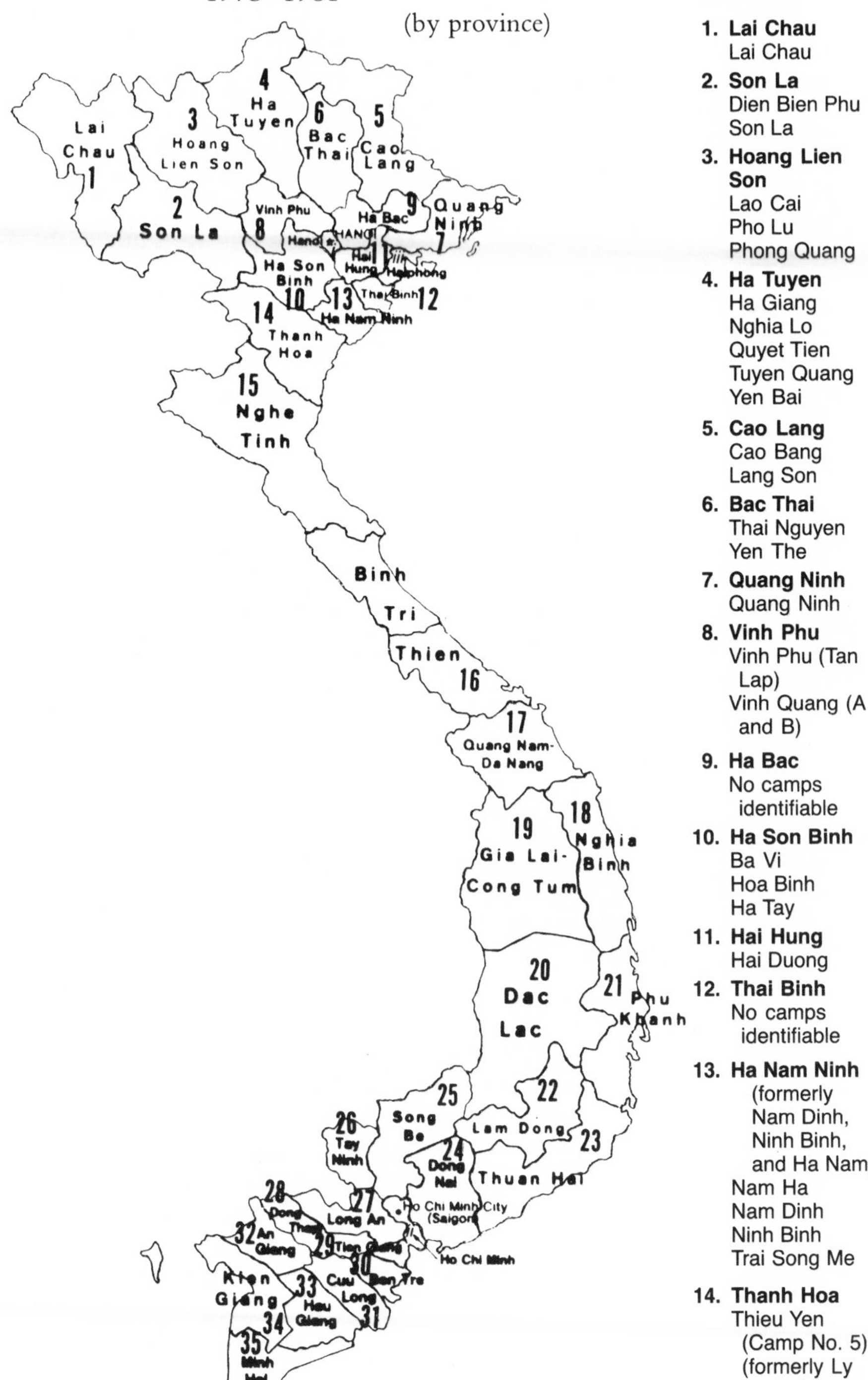

Thanh Lam
Vinh

15. Nghe Tinh
(formerly Nghe An and Ha Tinh)
Con Cuong
Ha Tinh
Nghia Dan
Nghe Tinh

16. Binh Tri Thien
(formerly Quang Binh, Quang Tri, and Thua Thien)
Dong Hoi
Mui Ron
Hue
Khe Sanh
Lao Bao
Quang Tri

17. Quang Nam–Da Nang
An Diem
Da Nang
Quang Nam

18. Nghia Binh
(formerly Binh Dinh and Quang Ngai)
An Lao
Ba To
K–18
Mo Duc
Quang Ngai
Qui Nhon
Tam Quan
Tra Bong

19. Gia Lai–Cong Tum
Gia Trung
Cong Tum
Le Trung
Pleiku

20. Dac Lac
Ban Me Thuot
Duc Lap

21. Phu Khanh
(formerly Phu Yen and Khanh Hoa)
Cam Ranh
Khanh Duong
Nghia Phu
Nha Trang
Tuy Hoa
Lac Chi (A–30)
Dong Tre (A–20)
Ngan Dien (T–5) (includes T–51, T–52, T–53, and T–54)

22. Lam Dong
Bao Loc
Da Lat
Dai Binh
Don Duong
Madagui
Minh Dong
Trai May

23. Thuan Hai
Binh Tuy
Chan Chua
Da Mai
Ham Tan (Z–30D)
Phan Rang
Phan Thiet

24. Dong Nai
(formerly Bien Hoa, Long Khanh, and Vung Tau)
Ba Ria
Bien Hoa
Gia Ray (Z–30)
Ho Nai
Long Giao
Long Thanh
Phuoc Le
Suoi Mau (Tan Hiep)
Trang Bom
Xuan Loc
Xuyen Moc
Trang Tao

25. Song Be
Bu Gia Map (includes Bu Dang, Bu Dop, and others)
Loc Ninh
Phuoc Binh
Phuoc Long
Binh Duong
Phu Cuong

26. Tay Ninh
Bau Co
Dong Ban
Katum
Bo Tuc
Trang Lon
Cay Cay (A and B)
Suoi Nuoc Trong
Ben Keo

27. Long An
Long Nguyen
Phu Loc
Tan An

28. Dong Thap
(includes former Kien Phong)
Moc Hoa and others

29. Tien Giang
Cai Be
My Tho
Vuon Dao

30. Ben Tre
(formerly Kien Hoa)
Ben Tre
Bau Sen
Ben Gia
Con Ong
Phu Vinh

31. Cuu Long
(formerly Can Tho)
Bau An
Can Tho
Cau Binh Dong
Go Nhum
Long Tuyen
Nha Dai (Vinh Long)
Khanh Hung
Vinh Chau
Vinh Long

32. An Giang
(includes former Chau Doc)
Cai Lang
Chau Doc
Chi Lang
Long Xuyen

33. Hau Giang
Bac Lieu (Vinh Loi)
Chau Thanh
Chuong Thien (D–18)
Quyet Thang
Thang Loi
Soc Trang
Con Cat

34. Kien Giang
Ha Tien
Kinh Mot
Phu Quoc Island
Rach Gia
U-Minh
Cau Van
Ta Nien
Kinh Nam

35. Minh Hai
(formerly An Xuyen)
Cay Gua
Con Son Island
Kinh Ngang
Quan Long
Rach Ruong Nho
Tac Van

Hanoi City
Hoa Lo

Haiphong City
Hoa Lo Haiphong

Ho Chi Minh City
An Duong
Chi Hoa
Gia Dinh (Phan Dang Luu and Cau Bang Ky)
Hoc Mon
Mac Dinh Chi Police Station
Thu Duc
Saigon Police Headquarters
National Police Headquarters
Fatima Catholic Church

SOURCES: Reports, U.S. Embassy, Bangkok; interviews with refugees; Aurora Foundation; various articles, books, and documents written by former prisoners who fled the country.

the political prisoners, as are journalists and members of nationalist political parties.

It is much harder to reach any definite conclusion about whether the camps can be classified according to the length of their inmates' sentences. According to Douglas Pike, there are three types of camps involved in re-educating the former government's employees, who have been detained for "crimes against the people." These camps, he claims, have been officially classified into five levels, as follows:

1. Re-education camps, composed of two levels: level one, for those allowed to come in for study during the daytime, for a total of 30 days; and level two, for those who need to be re-educated on a full-time basis
2. Collective reformatory camps, for thought reform
3. Production socialist reform camps (indoctrination plus forced labor) with two levels: level four (three years' detention), and level five (five years' detention)[46]

In practice, however, ex-prisoners who have gone through different camps from the South to the North, then back to the South, state that there are only three types of camps:

1. *Three-day Thought Reform Classes.* These were classes organized at the end of May 1975 for ARVN NCOs, enlisted men, and low-ranking civil servants. After three days they were released and awarded certificates of graduation in noisy ceremonies. This, as I have explained, was merely a tactic to trap ARVN officers and high-ranking civil servants with visions of the new regime's clemency.
2. *Camps for Forced Labor and Indefinite Detention.* These are the camps that make up Vietnam's Bamboo Gulag. After being lured into them, ARVN officers and high-ranking civil servants of the former government have been incarcerated indefinitely, doing forced labor. Some have been released from time to time for propaganda purposes. However, as my research shows, the number of those released is much smaller than the number still detained in over 100 camps throughout the country.
3. *Thought-Reform Classes for University Professors and Teachers.* These have been described by Dr. Le Kim Ngan in the passages quoted in Chapter 7.

I do not mention here the camps, administered by provincial, district, and village party committees, in which only small numbers of prisoners are detained. In brief, it is my opinion that official classification of the camps into five levels does not reflect the reality, but aims at misleading world opinion.

If the authorities are applying the three-year limit, they certainly are not doing so uniformly or consistently, since one hears more often of prisoners being released as individuals than in batches. The only verifiable mass releases have been those of teachers and other needed professionals. Although a prisoner in the "serious crimes" category (someone who served in a psychological warfare unit, for example) is still likely to be shipped north even after admission to a southern camp, the present chances of being released would seem to be much the same north and south—that is, highly unpredictable. Prisoners are being released, but not usually for reasons that the regime cares to publicize. Thus former inmates of Vuon Dao, a camp in Tien Giang Province (South Vietnam) with a population of about 1,800, report that from 1977 to 1979 some 150 prisoners were released, ostensibly because they had completed their re-education, but actually, for the most part, because their relatives had bribed camp officials (the bribes allegedly included sexual favors granted by prisoners' wives to the camp commander).[47] Mention of such bribery is extremely common; the going price of release is 5 taels of gold. Almost as common, it appears, are releases of prisoners who are related to high-ranking government or party officials. Some prisoners are released because they are disabled or seriously ill, or because their families have moved to NEZs. Neither policy, however, is applied consistently, while bribery and nepotism are universal.

10

Re-education or Revenge?

"This camp," a Western journalist has written in the guest book at Ha Tay, "is beyond all doubt a demonstration for humanity."[1] According to Tiziano Terzani, who was allowed to visit the camp in 1981, the regime's purpose in throwing it open to foreign visitors is only too obvious.

> The detention cells are clean; flowers bloom in the garden; the food is excellent; the guards smile. Everything looks like part of a model prison readied for foreign visitors. Occasionally the visitor is offered too much of a good thing, so that perfection changes into perversion, the smiles into grimaces.
>
> In a classroom a prisoners' orchestra plays a waltz. Twenty-four former generals, colonels, and judges of the Supreme Court under the Thieu regime rise up and applaud while the camp commander examines them all in turn and explains, on the basis of such questioning, that one or the other man has made great progress and that—alas!—there are still inmates who have not yet written a full and frank report on their misdeeds.[2]

No waltzes are heard in the mountainous and jungle areas where nearly all the other camps are located. Prisoners live for the most part in huts of bamboo or mud with earthen floors and roofs of palm leaves; a lucky minority enjoys concrete floors and roofs of corrugated iron. The climate is often unhealthy, but blankets and mosquito nets are not allowed. The principal foreign visitors to these camps are from other communist countries, and even they are kept apart from the prisoners. Representatives of international organizations such as Amnesty International and the Red Cross are seldom allowed to set foot in them, and then only after the prisoners have been sent off to work in the fields.[3] Even if international officials were allowed to talk with prisoners, they would not learn very much. Nguyen Cong Hoan explains why.

> I accompanied a number of relatives in visiting prisoners in camps within my provinces. Once, taking advantage of my position as a congressman and also of my acquaintance with Lt. Col. Xuan, T-52 camp commander, I asked permission to come and visit his camp. However, I was allowed to come and observe only some showcase areas in the camp and to make contact with a few prisoners who, I know for sure, are not so stupid as to tell me the whole truth about their prison—that is, if they don't want to die. The party leaders themselves have told me that they are very proud of their talent for deceiving world opinion. "We've been worse than Pol Pot," they joke, "but the outside world knows nothing."[4]

The relatives' visits were considered a privilege, not a right, and might end in insults or physical abuse by camp authorities.

> It was the authorities who decided if and when families might visit prisoners. The date, time, and place of the visit—everything was prescribed by the authorities.
>
> A visitor was allowed to bring cookies, candies, sugar, and fruit up to a maximum total of 2 kg. Fish, meat, or medicine was not allowed. Those who violated this rule might be eliminated from the visitor list and never allowed to return. Moreover, the prisoners in question could be severely punished for throwing doubt on the Party's official claim that all prisoners had plenty to eat.
>
> During the New Year holiday I came and visited a cousin at T-52 at Ngan Dien Camp [in Phu Khanh Province]. I personally witnessed a scene in which an old mother who had brought a bottle of fish sauce to her son, a detainee, was viciously insulted before everyone and then denied permission to see him. The old lady went down on her knees, but her plea was denied. When the prisoners were allowed to line up to receive their gifts (her son, of course, was not among them), the V.C. cadres loudly asked them: "Do you need fish

> sauce here?" All the prisoners shouted back: "No, we have quite enough fish sauce here!" The truth was that, so far from having fish sauce, they didn't even have salt.[5]

At Camp A-30 of Phu Khanh, according to Hoan, visiting relatives had to stay overnight because the camp site was so deep in the jungle. They were lodged in a guest hut, built by the prisoners, that had been divided into cubicles and supplied with double beds. During the night, prisoners who had been informants for the camp authorities were given official permission to force themselves on the women sleeping in the hut. This privilege, the camp cadres made known, was a reward for progress in re-education.[6]

Prisoners such as former police officers and intelligence agents, who are automatically assumed to "owe blood debts to the people," lack even the right to receive mail, let alone visitors. To their relatives, they are as good as dead.

The Process of Re-education

Dr. Le Kim Ngan, whose analysis of VCP thought-reform policy I quoted in Chapter 7, provides a well-authenticated outline of the classroom curriculum in a typical re-education camp. The curriculum is taught in two stages.

> *Stage I.* Ten weeks, with eight subjects:
>
> 1. History of Vietnam
> 2. American imperialism (or neocolonialism), an enemy of the people
> 3. Crimes committed against our people by American imperialism
> 4. Reasons why the Vietnamese people were victorious
> 5. History of the Vietnamese people's struggle (from Chinese domination to French domination)
> 6. Treaties that brought about victories for the Vietnamese people (from the Geneva Agreement of 1954 to the Paris Agreement of 1973)
> 7. Socialism
> 8. New men in the New Society
>
> Another week is added to study "crimes committed by oneself." On the one hand, each trainee, before the whole class, must analyze

his own crimes against the people. On the other hand, each trainee must participate in team discussions in the course of which self-criticism and self-denunciation are made to the team by each participant. Each team member must comment on the participant's statements and remind him of points he may have forgotten or details he may have distorted. This is an opportunity for participants to denounce one another in order to avenge a friend and as a result curry favor with the VCP, because the party policy is to encourage such practices. In that case, he will be considered progressive and will have hopes of being released from the camp.

Finally, each trainee still has to make a written twenty-page report on the outcome of his own case. In this he describes all his past crimes, begs the Revolution for a pardon, and promises to study hard to become a good citizen of the socialist regime.

Stage II. This includes several weeks with the four following subjects:

1. Reports of the communist leaders such as those of Le Duan, Truong Chinh, Pham Van Dong
2. Direction of the South Vietnamese economy
3. The Vanguard Youth
4. Construction of New Economic Zones

Approach: for each subject, three days are allocated for listening to lectures, and another three for team discussions. They are followed by one day for answering questions and by one or two days to make a written six-page report on what each participant got out of the subject.[7]

Le Kim Ngan's account is easily confirmed from other sources. For instance, I was told the following by a refugee physician who arrived in the United States in 1980.

> During my 32 months at different camps in South Vietnam, I had to write at least 30 self-criticism reports. A really daunting thing was that communist cadres in the re-education camps usually compared the details of one report with those of another. If one of your reports is inconsistent with another, you're in serious trouble. As a result, prisoners all the year round live under pressure, because no one can remember the details of what he declared two or three years earlier.

He added that you have to be careful of what your friend writes, too, since they compare your report with his. Such a self-criticism report, it appears, is regarded by the authorities as an admission by the prisoner of the commission of crimes. To him, it serves as a sentence by which he could be imprisoned for life in re-education camps. No one, including his family, can protest the sentence, because the written admission is taken as proof of the accusation.

Life in the Camps

Seven years after the communist victory in Vietnam it is sufficiently clear, from the reports of ex-prisoners, that the main purpose of the new regime's prison camps is not re-education but revenge. This revenge is being exercised indiscriminately, against whole classes of people, with scarcely a pretense of legality and with total disregard for human rights.

Such considerations weigh little with the regime, which appears to have taken the attitude that anyone who had anything to do with the Americans or with the former Republic of Vietnam deserves the worst that can be done to him. The notion that torture, summary execution, deprivation of medical care, or slow death from malnutrition are likely to improve anyone's attitude toward the government that inflicts them upon him is one that even a communist theoretician would not attempt to make plausible. What the regime has done, then, is to call its concentration camps by another name, and then to deny that most of them exist. In the previous chapter I exposed the regime's "big lie" that the camp population is much smaller than it really is. Here, by reviewing the policies actually pursued in the name of re-education, I shall contend that a concentration camp by any other name is still a concentration camp.

Control by Hunger

The VCP, as Nguyen Cong Hoan has well said, uses the stomach to control the spirit.[8] All prisoners have to perform physical labor. The type of labor tends to vary by locality. In one, it may be digging canals or building dams; in another, clearing jungle for crop cultivation; in another, repairing railroads or removing mines from minefields. In all camps, however, the prisoners are systematically and deliberately underfed. Their diet consists mainly of rice mixed with sorghum, manioc, or maize. Rations are tiny. The amount most frequently reported is less than 500 g of such food a day. In many camps, prisoners receive only two small bowls of these staples a day, or just enough to survive on. Mixed with the staples are camp-grown vegetables such as sweet potatoes and, occasionally, a very small piece of salted dried fish. The daily allowance may also include a small bowl of thin vegetable soup. Only on a few national holidays are prisoners given meat, in the form of camp-raised duck or pork. Former prisoners stated that two or three ducks are given to a company of over 100 persons, or one pig to a whole battalion of 500 to 600. Since it is impossible to divide so little meat fairly among so many, the prisoners invariably make soup of it.

The purpose of this policy is twofold. First, it aims to keep prisoners in a permanent state of hunger and physical exhaustion. This, when combined with hard labor, makes them incapable of revolt. Second, it subjects the prisoners to as much public humiliation as possible by making them compete with each other for food or even resort to stealing it. VCP cadres appear to derive a sadistic pleasure from seeing these former oppressors and representatives of the bourgeoisie scrabbling over a pot of gruel. The prisoners who secretly dig manioc or other edible roots are so many silent witnesses to the efficacy of control by hunger. Mealtimes in the camps are a solemn sight, though ex-prisoners remember them with hilarity. Since the guards never divide the food into individual rations, everyone has to shift for himself. Prisoners are given only 30 minutes for lunch and rest. Therefore, they have just a few minutes to down their food. As a result, no one talks or even coughs; the only sound to be heard is that of chopsticks hitting the bowl, which never leaves the mouth.[9]

Former prisoners from the Bu Dang Camp, near the Cambodian border, told me that, each week, each prisoner was allowed to have 100 g or about half a cup of rice. However, 50 percent of the 100 g was reserved for patients laid up in the camp's sick bay. To replace their rice, the other prisoners were given manioc and maize. They were also given wheat flour, said to be imported from the Soviet Union (prisoners suspected that it originated in the United States). They mixed the flour with water to make a round cake with an estimated weight of 100 g, and then cooked it in plain water. Each prisoner had one in a meal with a little soy sauce or salt. For two other meals in the day, he or she was given manioc, sweet potatoes, or sorghum. Twice a year, at the Vietnamese New Year and on September 2 (National Day), prisoners were allowed a piece of pork the size of two fingers. Every week or two each was also given a dried fish of the same size. As to soup, a 25 g package of noodles cooked with vegetables grown by the prisoners made do for a whole platoon of 30 persons.

Under these conditions, as one would expect, the prisoners' health speedily deteriorates. Former prisoners who are now refugees report that many of their fellow inmates died of malnutrition. Well-attested cases include those of ARVN Majors Luan, Van, and Phong at Vinh Quang Camp, Vinh Phu Province, in North Vietnam.[10] In all other camps from which reports are available, including Gia Trung, Gia Ray, Ben Gia, and Xuyen Moc, the situation would appear to be similar. Without relatives' food parcels, which get through only because camp authorities are bribed, many prisoners would not have survived.

Deprivation of Medical Care

There are no communist camp doctors; only nurses are provided. In some camps such as Vuon Dao in Tien Giang Province and Bu Dang in Song Be Province, prisoners who are themselves doctors are allowed to serve under the supervision of communist nurses. There is little they can do, however, since no drugs or other medical supplies are available; traditional remedies, based on jungle herbs and leaves, must do instead, unless patients can get drugs from their relatives.

No camps, not even the largest, have hospitals. At the Suoi Mau Camp in Dong Nai Province, which has 6,000 prisoners, there is a dispensary located in Subcamp K-5; ex-prisoners note that it has little to dispense.[11] Most general camps have only one such dispensary; the only readily available treatment is at so-called first-aid stations. Accordingly, prisoners often die of diseases, especially malaria, that go untreated. At Gia Ray Z-30, twenty deaths are reported to have occurred due to lack of medication.[12] Deaths also occur from botched operations by communist nurses. Prisoners who are very seriously ill are sometimes transferred to provincial hospitals. Torture victims, however, are often just finished off. Such was the case with Huynh Van Luc, a former captain in the Rangers, who was interned at T-54 of Ngan Dien Camp, in Phu Khanh Province. Since one of his hands was injured, he could no longer fulfill his work quota. He was therefore confined with his feet chained to a wooden bar. "The resulting sores on his feet became infected. He was fed a handful of rice at each meal and was allowed to bathe once a week. If he showed no progress in re-education, his food ration could be reduced."[13] Luc was shot dead in July 1976. He never received a decent burial, nor were his relatives informed of his death.

Terrorization, Torture, and Summary Execution

Terrorization. As if months of thought reform were not sufficiently intimidating, prisoners are subjected to other stress-inducing devices. Every camp has a loudspeaker system that is used without warning to summon prisoners who did not show enthusiasm for their work or who, according to informants, made unfavorable remarks about the revolution. They are ordered to report to the camp headquarters at midnight. Such prisoners never come back. Usually, a few hours after they have been summoned, the other prisoners hear rifle fire in the nearby jungle. Perhaps these are mock executions, and the "executed" prisoners are secretly moved to other camps; perhaps they are not. I have inquired of ex-prisoners and they cannot tell me. I do know, however, that these midnight arrests have an effect on the prison population that is absolutely terrifying. Even in his dreams, a prisoner is haunted by the thought that he may be summoned and taken away like his friends.[14]

The classification of prisoners into different categories also contributes to their nervous apprehension. Those who are said to have committed only minor crimes against the people and who are making progress in re-education, or do not have any reactionary attitudes, may stay in the camp. In contrast, those who are said to have committed capital crimes are suddenly called up and sent somewhere else for what is called "more thorough education." The process of classification is repeated over and over, so that everyone is made to feel that, bad though his present camp is, he might be transferred to a worse one. It is of course possible that in some cases whole groups of such reclassified prisoners are sent from southern to northern camps. However, it is equally possible, from what I have heard, that prisoners are just transferred from one southern camp to another for psychological effect, and to forestall prison revolts.

The re-education classes that follow the day's work are also a source of tension, since they place the prisoner in an agonizing dilemma. If he does not stoop to follow the party lines and policies, his future is foreseeable: a slow death in the camps. If, on the other hand, he zealously denounces his friends—and the camp authorities do all they can to set the prisoners against another by making them compete at work, in class, and so on—then he can at least hope to be released sooner. Moreover, he will certainly receive extra food rations, especially of meat or fish. No wonder some prisoners—a minority, I believe—take the second option. Others, in the hope that they can at least stay out of trouble, have been driven to feign stupidity. This option has been celebrated in the following poem, well known among refugees, who recognize in this anonymous prisoner's words the camp society from which they have escaped.

> I meet with people who are stupid, so stupid that
> their lives are quiet
> As the lives of priests, and I am one among the
> stupid.
> I have become half priest, half prisoner.[15]

Torture and Execution. According to all reports, prisoners in the camps are punished by being shackled, in many cases in a small, dark punishment cell or in a connex container (a steel box of about 8 m^3 formerly used by the U.S. military to store ammunition) exposed to the sun with only a little hole for air. Such punishment, which may last from three to six months, is handed out for such infractions as violating camp rules, refusing to work, and voicing opposition to communism. At Con Cat Camp, in Hau Giang Province, Roman Catholic Father Nguyen Van Tinh was shackled for four months and ten days for having attempted to teach English to other prisoners.[16] At Gia Trung Camp, in Gia Lai–Cong Tum Province, a writer and teacher named Nguyen Sy Te was shackled in a punishment cell for having planned to "organize a government in jail."[17] At Cay Cay Camp, in Tay Ninh Province, prisoners were placed in stocks or pinioned night and day with both hands tied to a bamboo pole for having joked about the regime or shown reluctance to work.[18] Hoang Qui, an ARVN first lieutenant and former seminarian, was suspected of saying mass for Christian prisoners at the same camp. He was placed in stocks from July 1977 to October 1978.[19]

In addition to being shackled and (as previously mentioned) put on short rations, prisoners are frequently beaten, sometimes with fatal results. At Gia Ray Z-30, guards are reported to have struck prisoners with rifle butts and used sticks wrapped in cloth to hit them on the chest.[20] Sadistic punishments are also reported. A refugee who was held at Phuoc Long Camp in Song Be Province says that guards there burned prisoners' hair and mustaches using Molotova motor gas as a combustion agent.[21] A female prisoner named Mrs. Lieu who had been an ARVN member was not only beaten by guards at Ham Tan Z-30D, in Thuan Hai Province, but suffered serious injuries when they violated her with a stick. Her offense had been to display an RVN flag.[22]

Executions are reported in cases where prisoners have attempted to escape or displayed an obdurate attitude in other ways. Nguyen Manh Con, a writer, was shot at Xuyen Moc Camp in Dong Nai Province because he had begun a hunger strike in an attempt to gain his release.[23] Nguyen Duc Xich, Gia Dinh province chief under the Diem regime (he was a retired lieutenant colonel when Diem fell in 1963 and later on became the RVN's inspector general) was shot to death at Vuon Dao Camp, Tien Giang Province, after having been incarcerated in a dark cell for four months, then held in a connex container for two months.[24]

Some Well-Known Victims

So many former South Vietnamese notables, including antiwar activists whose sympathies the Communists exploited while the war was going on, have met their end in communist prisons and concentration camps that we can only conclude the VCP always planned to dispense with them once it gained power. The following members of this tragic and ever-expanding company represent only a small fraction of the known total.

1. Hoang Xuan Tuu, a senator from 1967 to 1973 and a member of the Dai Viet Party, was detained in various camps. Tuu was once vice-president of the RVN Senate. He died at Nam Ha Camp, Ha Nam Ninh Province (North Vietnam), in September 1980. The official story was that he contracted a fatal illness.[25]
2. One-term senator Tran The Minh (1967–1973), a political independent, was also interned at Nam Ha. He died in October 1977. One of his relatives offered the communist authorities 5 taels of gold for a permit to go to Ha Nam Ninh in search of his body. At the camp, through a prisoner friend, he learned that Minh had been poisoned. By using his wits he was able to find out from the camp commander where Minh was buried. It was in a large cemetery with the graves of thousands of "puppet officers and civil servants." He then sought for a permit to exhume the corpse and bring Minh's bones back to Saigon. The condition of the bones appeared to support the allegation of poisoning.[26]
3. Tran Van Tuyen, noted attorney and a former president of

the Saigon Bar Association, was a congressman before 1975 and leader of an opposition group that demanded President Thieu's resignation. Tuyen was detained in various re-education camps, but died in the showcase camp of Ha Tay. Terzani reports that, when he asked the camp commander about the cause of Tuyen's death, the latter replied it was a cerebral hemorrhage. However, one of Tuyen's friends in Saigon told the same reporter that Tuyen could no longer stand being interned and committed suicide sometime in October 1976 by cutting the veins in his wrists.[27]

4. Fr. Hoang Quynh, former commander-in-chief of the Catholic anticommunist forces in the Autonomous Region of the Bui Chu and Phat Diem dioceses in North Vietnam before 1954, was arrested in his home at Binh An Thuong, a suburb of Saigon, then tortured to death, probably at Chi Hoa Prison in Saigon, in early 1977.[28]
5. Mai Van An, justice of the RVN Supreme Court, has been held in various camps since 1975. He, too, is now detained at Nam Ha, where his health is said to be deteriorating rapidly. He is over 60 years old.[29]

The fate of Thich Thien Minh (1921–1978), vice-president of the Unified Buddhist Church (An Quang Buddhist Church) and concurrently its commissioner-general for youth, merits a few extra words. He died in Ham Tan Z-30D on October 17, 1978. Although few details are known, it is clear that his death resulted from long torture and mistreatment by communist authorities. He had been arrested on April 13, 1978, for objecting to the regime's treatment of political prisoners, its measures to suppress religion, and the hardships imposed on the general population. The arrest put an end to a period during which the Venerable Minh, having been expelled from his room at the Buddhist Youth Center, wandered from pagoda to pagoda in search of a place to live, but was continually denied a residence permit by the police.

At first he was confined in a re-education camp in Gia Dinh, Ho Chi Minh City, where he was stripped of the monk's robe he had worn for 41 years and forced to live naked in a dark cell. In September 1978, he was tranferred to Ham Tan, a notorious camp in Thuan Hai Province that contains a large number of religious leaders of all faiths, and where prisoners are regularly beaten and otherwise mistreated. News of his death reached the An Quang Church on October 18, 1978. On October 23, Radio Hanoi announced that he had died of a cerebral hemorrhage. Church dignitaries were allowed into the camp to identify the body but were not allowed to touch or inspect it (only the head was uncovered). In protesting these measures, Thich Tam Quan has written: "And why, every time an important figure dies in prison, is his death explained as having been caused by cerebral hemorrhage?"[30]

During the war, Thich Thien Minh was a senior monk of the An Quang Church. He was one of the Buddhist leaders who called for immediate cessation of U.S. bombing in the North, a cease-fire in the South, and a policy of national reconciliation and concord. Since this line was consistent with the official line of the NLF, the Venerable Minh was accused of being a communist agent. As a result, in 1966, an attempt was made to assassinate him, and he was left unable to walk without a stick. In persecuting him, the communist authorities were persecuting a cripple.[31]

How the Camps Are Organized

The atrocities I have just detailed cannot be dismissed as the work of a few isolated camp commanders. The camps are in fact organized in typical communist fashion, with each commander strictly answerable to his bureaucratic superiors.

Some camps are under the direct control of the Department of Prison Management of the Ministry of the Interior, in Hanoi. These camps are organized, in quasi-military fashion, into divisions, regiments, and so on, all the way down to platoons (Figure 16).

Other camps are run by provincial or city people's committees, which means in practice that they are controlled by local security departments. Here the logistics are less complicated but the division of functions is essentially the same.

Concentration Camps Without Fences

Every province has a bureau of New Economic Zones, but some provinces have more of such zones than others; the number seems to depend less on the nature of the terrain than on the capabilities of the provincial party apparatus.

The purpose of the NEZs is twofold.

1. *Political.* Through them the VCP aims to concentrate potential opposition elements and put them under control of NEZ party organs. In so doing, the party also disperses them from

Figure 16: Organization of a Thought-Reform Camp

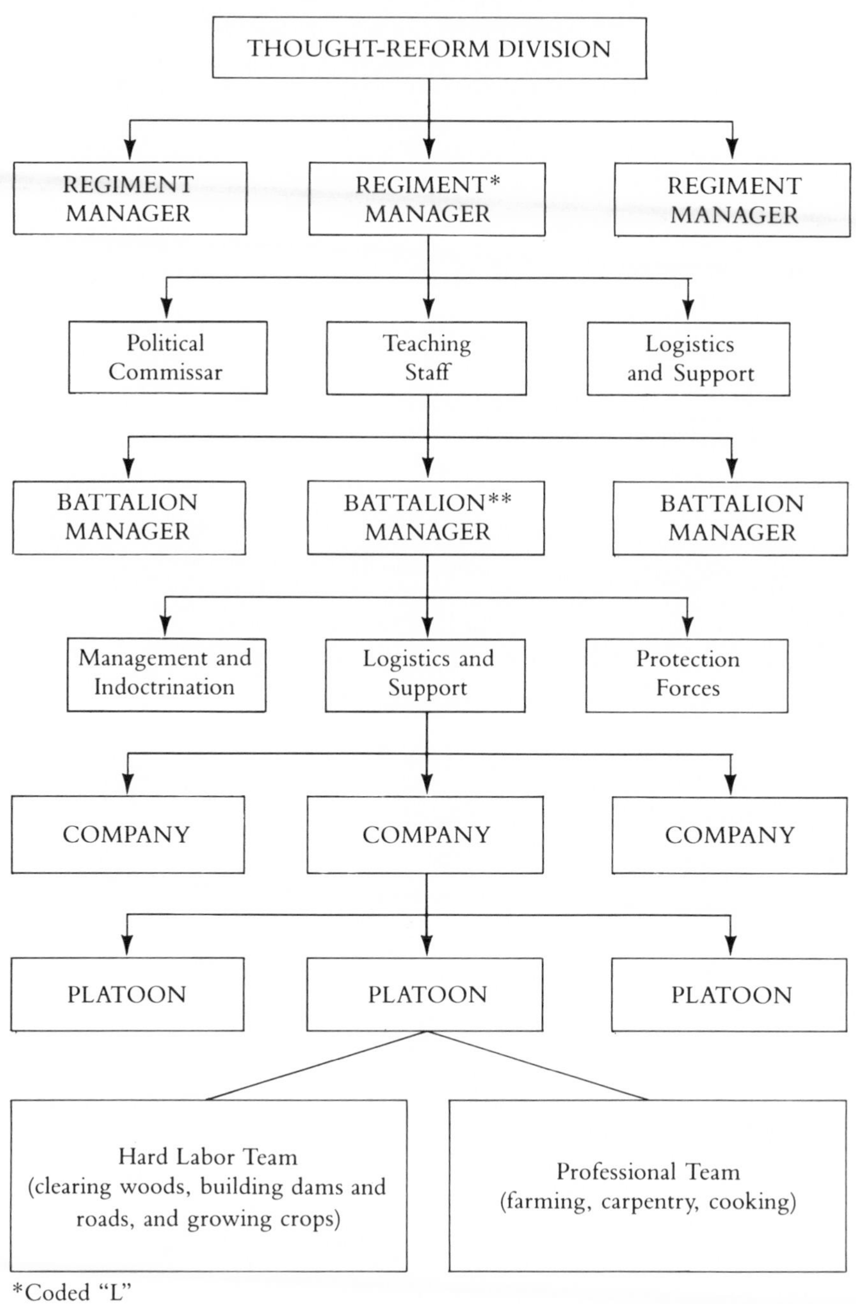

*Coded "L"
**Coded "T"

the cities, where they could easily unite and start an uprising, and places them in a collectivized situation so that they become familiar with the socialist state.

2. *Economic*. The NEZ program is an opportunity to redeploy the work force and population for the purpose of increasing production through land development and collectivized agriculture. All this, of course, is part of the Five-Year Plan.

The Vietnamese population, as I pointed out in Chapter 2, is growing at the rate of 3 percent a year. The communist regime is afraid that current patterns of population distribution, if allowed to persist, will become politically and economically unmanageable. It has therefore developed long-term plans for correcting the situation. In the words of Che Viet Tan, vice-chairman of the State Planning Commission, these plans will require "the relocation of about 10 million people in the overpopulated delta in the North and the Central Vietnam plains." Part of this number, according to Tan, will go to the Central Highlands and the northern mountain areas, while most will go to the Mekong Delta.[32]

Knowing that the NEZs are concentration camps in all but name, the general population has actively resisted being sent to them. Whole groups of people, according to Pham Anh Hai, have therefore been designated for relocation. The first victims were families of former government officials, army officers, and businessmen. At the same time that they were informed of the government's decision to move them to the NEZs they were instructed not to sell or transfer the homes where they were residing; not to sell vehicles or household necessities, including their dishes and chopsticks; and not to destroy any real property or factories they owned. All such property was requisitioned and distributed to party cadres, the great majority of whom, as I have said, were northerners.[33] In order to force citizens into the NEZs, the VCP has also used such techniques as threatening to send them to re-education camps, withdrawing their ration cards so that they can no longer purchase daily necessities such as rice and cloth at official prices, and not allowing their children to attend school.[34]

Self-Sufficiency and Survival

The NEZs are organized into two sectors, a public one and a private one.

Private Land for One's Own Production. Each household is given a lot of 500 m^2 as "basic production land." A small lot of 24 m^2 (6 m × 4 m) is used to build a house for a family (even a large one), including kitchen. The result is an instant rural slum, such as the one described by Pham Anh Hai.

> In the Vam Co Dong New Economic Zone live 3,000 people who came from a section west of Saigon. They are housed in 400 thatched huts built on low foundations. The huts are spread out along a canal in the middle of a forest that abounds in poisonous snakes, mosquitoes, and clouds of insects. Because the water in this area is brackish, the only crop that can be grown there is pineapples.[35]

After eight hours working on the collectivized farm, settlers can work on their private lands to raise additional crops for their families. The government will support them for only the first six months; after that, they must be self-sufficient. Even the thatched huts were built by the settlers who first arrived in the area.

Collective Farms. This, in the Vam Co Dong NEZ, is a large low area covered by bushes. The settlers had to dig a drainage canal within 30 days of their arrival. When Hai visited the area, the 1,200-m-long canal had been completed.

> The point was that the Communists had intentionally used human labor to do the job, instead of using a bulldozer to dig the canal and the bushes. A member of the farm told us that within the first week of clearing the bushes, seven people died because they were bitten by snakes. Others died later of malaria.
>
> As to the farm's income, the government decreed as follows:
>
> > Thirty percent was used to pay government taxes.
> > Twenty-five percent was sold to the government at the official price.
> > Fifteen percent was reserved to pay the salaries of the cadres managing the economic zone.
> > The remaining 30 percent was divided among the workers based on the work points earned by each.[36]

Return from the NEZs. A few NEZs have succeeded. In Dong Nai Province, for instance, the land in the NEZs is fertile, and the settlers have been able to live off it. Accordingly, they are willing to stay put. Most NEZs, however, are not merely falling short of expectations; they are disastrous failures. Terzani, reporting from Vietnam in 1981, estimated that only some half-million acres had really been brought under cultivation; the greater part remained unproductive.

> Le Minh Xuan, for example, was a famous New Economic Zone—one of the first—about 30 km northwest of Saigon. Visitors were regularly taken there in order to inspect this model of Vietnam's future.
>
> Today visitors are no longer allowed at Le Minh Xuan because in the interval it has once more become a wilderness. The huts are deserted, the fields lie exposed to the scorching heat of the sun, the unpaved street that runs through it is empty.
>
> The 4,000 hectares of land that, with appalling labor, were filled and made ready for planting, are now lying fallow. No one had suspected that in this district, 30 cm below the surface, there was a layer of particularly acid soil. This soil, when mixed with water, poisoned the entire planting area.[37]

The party cadres in charge of the project had neglected to take even one soil sample before ordering the land plowed and diked. The hundreds of families involved had no alternative but to make their way back to Saigon, where, since their homes had already been confiscated and there was no work for them, they joined the thousands already sleeping in the streets.

Le Minh Xuan is not an isolated case. In Minh Hai Province, for example, the settlers, who were ordinary city people, were just dumped in a NEZ where the land was inundated with salt water. The only way to live off such land, as the mounds of empty shells testified, was to dig clams, and there were not nearly enough of these to go round.[38] In Song Be Province the area chosen for a NEZ was so primitive that many settlers fell sick and died.[39] There are similar reports of the NEZs in Gia Lai–Cong Tum and Dac Lac Provinces and in the Mekong Delta. In general, these tragic fiascoes are due not only to the authorities' technical incompetence but to their failure to create an economic infrastructure or provide even the most elementary tools for creating one. Settlers have been sent into areas to which there were no roads and where no irrigation system was ever set up. They have often been kept short of hand tools, especially the ones they needed to cut down trees and clear land for cultivation. Sometimes they have lacked even seed.

Concentration Camps and Forced Labor in the SRV

It is clear from a growing body of reports—reports that numb the mind with their revelations of Nazi-style atrocities—that the so-called re-education camps and New Economic Zones are nothing but concentration camps and forced labor projects. Moreover, so far from being a temporary response to postwar conditions, they are built-in features of the Vietnamese communist system.

The re-education program is vital to the regime's system of internal security. It is a means of incarcerating all those citizens, no matter how numerous, who either oppose the regime or, according to communist ideology, can have no place in it except that of prisoner and slave laborer. Communist re-education camps have existed in North Vietnam for almost 30 years; there were some even before the Communists took power in 1954. They are still everywhere. The more totalitarian a regime, the more extensive a camp system it needs in order to stamp out opposition. That is why so many concentration camps are being built in Vietnam today and why they will continue to be built as long as Vietnam is communist.

The VCP claims that its camps exist for the purpose of helping its wartime opponents adjust to the new socialist reality, and that those who cannot adjust are too dangerous to let out. In reality, it has incarcerated many of its former political allies, who realize now that the "socialist reality" is not something that they can or should adjust to. And the number of such maladjusted people, from peasants to intellectuals, is growing daily. It is therefore hardly surprising that, in addition to central re-education camps, the regime has set up smaller camps at the provincial and district levels. It has also placed innumerable persons under house arrest in villages and remote hamlets.

The NEZs, which I have compared to concentration camps, are punitive in the sense that, like other penal colonies, they are settled by forced labor. But they also exemplify the spirit of collectivism. Each NEZ is in effect an agricultural cooperative, with the difference that its members are usually not seasoned peasants but urban dwellers who have been selected for anything but their experience of agriculture. In this way, even those suspected of antisocialist tendencies can be used to build socialism.

"An Extremely Humanitarian System"

In December 1979 the government of the SRV received a mission from Amnesty International, the well-known human rights organization that has dedicated itself to the cause of all persons imprisoned solely for political reasons. The mission stayed in Vietnam for only ten days. It was allowed to visit only three camps and Chi Hoa Prison in Ho Chi Minh City. At all these locations the mission evidently had very limited contact with the prisoners.[40]

In June 1981 Amnesty International made public what it described as "a detailed written dialogue" between itself and the authorities in Hanoi. It did so with a sense of frustration, since the dialogue had borne little fruit. The mission's report, already communicated to Hanoi, had centered on the following recommendations.[41]

1. The Vietnamese government should publish a list of its re-education camps and all other places of detention, with "detailed figures on individuals and categories of those still imprisoned."
2. Action should be taken against prison officers found to be abusing their powers, and such action should be publicized.
3. Those aged, sick, or infirm prisoners who, according to the government's own declared policy, were eligible for release, should be released forthwith.
4. International standards of human rights, based on recognized international agreements, should be observed in the camps and prisons, so that the prisoners could be protected somehow.

As for those prisoners classified by the regime as "people who committed serious crimes against the people" and who "owed a blood debt to the people," so that they had to undergo "long-term re-education," the Amnesty International mission stated its belief that a number of these had really been "imprisoned for the expression of their conscientiously held beliefs." These people, the mission stated, "had no connections with the former administration of South Vietnam, nor were they arrested in 1975."[42] Finally, the mission recommended that the Vietnamese government "abolish the present system of compulsory detention without trial for the purpose of re-education." Instead, an independent commission should be set up to examine the grounds for detention in each case.[43]

Hanoi's answer to these suggestions has been that everything it does is justified by national security. In May 1975, it told Amnesty International in September 1980, it had been faced with the task of disarming a hostile armed force of 1.3 million. "Re-education," under these circumstances, represented a policy of national reconciliation rather than vengeance. Then, "during the past two years," it had been faced with "new and unexpected security considerations" (presumably the Chinese invasion) that had made it impossible to release all the detainees from the re-education camps within the three-year period allegedly first envisaged. It claimed, as I said earlier, already to have released about half of those originally detained for long-term re-education, and refused to admit that the latter had ever numbered more than about 40,000.

To defend its policy of never bringing these people to trial, it argued that "re-education without judiciary condemnation is an extremely humanitarian system which is very advantageous to [the detainees], compared with the usual system of trial before [a] court." One reason they had not been tried, it appeared, was that "in Vietnamese psychology the absence of judiciary condemnation spares the person concerned a tarnished judiciary record which may adversely influence his whole life and that of his children."[44]

I leave the reader to judge whether, in the light of the information presented in this chapter, the government of the SRV has been motivated, in its thought-reform program, by humanitarianism or tender regard for Vietnamese psychology. I do feel, however, that if any reply is made to the government's claim, it should come from one of the prisoners. A poet named Nguyen Chi Thien has been interned in North Vietnamese prison camps for over sixteen years. Nearly four hundred of his poems were smuggled out of Vietnam through diplomatic channels and published in the United States in August 1980. Here is one of them.

From Ape to Man

From ape to man, millions of years gone by.
From man to ape, how many years?
Mankind, please come to visit
The concentration camps in the heart of the thickest
    jungles!
Naked prisoners, taking baths together in herds,
Living in ill-smelling darkness with lice and
    mosquitoes,
Fighting each other for a piece of manioc or sweet
    potato,
Chained, shot, dragged, slit up at will by their
    captors,

Beaten up and thrown away for the rats to gnaw at
their breath!
This kind of ape is not fast but very slow in action,
indeed
Quite different from that of remote prehistory.
They are hungry, they are thin as toothpicks,
And yet they produce resources for the nation all
year long.
Mankind, please come and visit![45]

11

Hanoi's Foreign Policy: I. Expansion and Isolation

Getting off the Tightrope

Foreign Relations and the VCP

Vietnam today is isolated from the Free World because it has committed itself to the Soviet Union. Wittingly or unwittingly, it has to serve the Soviet interest in Southeast Asia, helping the Russians to expand their influence in the region. Its territory is used as a base for Soviet forces to maintain their presence as far as the Indian Ocean—a major threat to the region's security. Vietnam also plays the role of henchman in continuing to accept massive Soviet military aid, which it has used to invade Cambodia and occupy Laos.

The Vietnamese communist leaders have always tried to play off one foreign enemy against another. Right now they are very interested in reconciling with America so that they can use it as a counterweight against the Chinese (of course, they also want to receive assistance from the American people to rebuild their shattered economy). America should beware of any such overtures from Hanoi. There are several reasons for caution. First, Vietnamese in general, not just the Communists, are imbued with extreme chauvinism. For almost a thousand years, foreigners have been trying to conquer and assimilate them. They have preserved their national identity only by their willingness to die for it. Second, the Vietnamese communist leaders were involved in clandestine activities from the first, when they opposed their French colonial rulers in the 1930s. In order to escape from dangerous situations, they used to lie. They did this so often that lying became a way of life for them, although ordinary Vietnamese do not like to practice deceit. Third, the communist leaders, since they are thoroughgoing Marxist-Leninists of the old school, have adopted treason and betrayal as key tools in the struggle against capitalism, and even in the daily struggle for existence. As a result, morality and self-respect have little place in the Vietnamese communist regime today. Finally, the pattern of action that includes all these features has been tested and improved for almost a half-century and has been proven successful, especially in all the VCP's greatest historical exploits. It has therefore become common practice.

From Soviet Assistance to Soviet Embrace

In October 1975 Le Duan went to visit the Soviet Union. The result was a joint communiqué announcing that the Russians would send highly qualified experts to Vietnam to train economic, scientific, technical, and cultural personnel. The Soviet Union would also provide assistance in the study of the technical and economic aspects of a number of major national economic projects and would lend Vietnam money on a most-favored-nation basis for carrying out socialist industrialization, pushing ahead with agricultural production, and increasing public welfare—all this, to be incorporated in the Second Five-Year Plan (1976–1980).[1] The communiqué also promised, without further specification, cooperation between Hanoi and Moscow within the "frameworks of multilateral cooperation of socialist countries." Normally this would have indicated membership in the Eastern bloc's Council for Mutual Economic Assistance (COMECON), but Vietnam did not join it yet.

Before accepting the role of Soviet satellite, the VCP had resisted the Soviet Union's influence on its policies. Deputy Foreign Minister Phan Hien, for instance, declared during his tour of Southeast Asia in mid-1976 that Vietnam did not subscribe to the Soviet Union's view of ASEAN as an imperialist creation—a successor to SEATO—or to its proposal for an Asian Collective Security Treaty.[2] Premier Pham Van Dong ostentatiously snubbed his host, the Soviet ambassador to Hanoi, at a 1976 reception marking the anniversary of the October Revolution.[3] Despite pressure from Soviet Politburo member Mikhail Suslov, who in December 1976 attended the VCP's Fourth Party Congress, to join COMECON, Hanoi did not respond. Instead, immediately after its victory in South Vietnam, Hanoi made

Moscow unhappy by joining the World Bank, the International Monetary Fund (IMF), and the Asian Development Bank.

Despite the lack of direct evidence, it is fairly clear why Hanoi was reluctant to join COMECON. (1) The members of COMECON were socialist countries that were not nearly prosperous enough to give postwar Vietnam the kind of aid its government wanted. (2) If Vietnam joined COMECON, it would be committed to the Soviet line and so isolated from the Western countries. (3) The aid required to build socialism in Vietnam would be on such a massive scale that only the United States could provide it; any part played by other Western countries would be welcome but incidental. Probably for these reasons, the Communists made a great show of moderation in the period immediately following their military victory. There was, as they continually pointed out, no general bloodbath (although, as I have shown, there were not a few clandestine atrocities). Although they began by demanding that the United States accept responsibility for war damages before relations could be normalized, they soon dropped this condition and hinted strongly that they would accept normalization on almost any terms. They even tried to use the mortal remains of American MIAs as pretexts for a diplomatic exchange.

The decisive factor, in my opinion, was Hanoi's failure to obtain large sums from Western sources as soon as it had expected. By 1978, Hanoi had still not complied with World Bank and IMF regulations for receiving major development loans. It had already received some small grants from Western countries, but it was also under pressure to accept more aid from the Eastern bloc. Suslov, in December 1976, had remarked pointedly that there were "many new and still greater possibilities to further deepen the relations of economic cooperation among the socialist countries."[4] The Second Five-Year Plan, by my estimate, required not less than $10 billion for its realization. The plan was two years old in 1978. Hanoi joined COMECON that year out of desperation, and because of its deepening rift with China, which had slowed down most aid in 1976 and canceled it altogether in 1978. Moreover, in November of that year, Hanoi and Moscow signed a 25-year Treaty of Friendship and Mutual Cooperation. Under Moscow's aegis, Hanoi moved to occupy Cambodia. In February 1979 China sent several divisions to invade Vietnam. The Soviet Union, however, did nothing to help Vietnam under the 25-year treaty, but paid only lip service to it. The VCP's response has been to make the most of the concessions, particularly in opening Vietnamese military bases to Russian use, which the Soviets had been demanding. Nevertheless, the Soviets have continued to draw the line at intervention. In early March 1982, President Leonid I. Brezhnev's proposal in Tashkent to improve Soviet relations with China caused Hanoi much anxiety. It is reported that, as preliminary conditions for opening the talks, China proposed the end of Soviet support for Vietnam. Continued Soviet overtures to the Chinese have the VCP's leaders on tenterhooks, although the latter still seem likely to follow the Soviet line, whatever it may be.

An Asian Cuba?

Having finally committed itself to Moscow, Hanoi supported the Soviet foreign-policy line at the conference of Third World countries that was held in Havana, Cuba, in 1979. Hanoi also openly defended the occupation of Afghanistan by Soviet armed forces in early 1980. As the recipient of some $3 million a day in Soviet military aid, the SRV has been used as a force to menace China's flank. It also seems to many observers to be playing the role of an Asian Cuba by supporting revolutionary movements in the region. However that may be, the SRV has undoubtedly sent its armed forces into Cambodia with Soviet matériel and equipment.

Vietnamese naval bases and airfields have been used by the Soviet Union. In December 1978, during the period of the Cambodian invasion, Soviet ships carried Vietnamese troops and matériel from Haiphong to Saigon. The Russians operated an airlift with giant AN-22 transport planes to rush in urgently needed ammunition and spare parts. Since 1979, about a dozen AN-12s have been in Vietnam to ferry troops and military supplies all over Indochina. Two Soviet LSTs (landing craft for tanks) have been plying between Ho Chi Minh City, Danang, and Haiphong carrying troops and matériel.[5] A diesel-powered Foxtrot class Soviet submarine entered Cam Ranh Bay in May 1979. Soviet warships seen there have included a guided-missile frigate and a minesweeper.[6] The aircraft carrier *Minsk* was spotted at anchor in Cam Ranh Bay in November 1980 by a Japanese television crew. This carrier, capable of handling helicopters and vertical takeoff warplanes, joined the Soviet Pacific Fleet in 1979.[7] Shortly afterwards, U.S. intelligence sources revealed that the Soviets were setting up an electronic listening post at the Cam Ranh Base in order to monitor ships of the U.S. Seventh Fleet.[8]

Soviet TU-95D Bears, which are long-range reconnaissance aircraft, have gone to South Vietnam. In mid-April 1979 the Bears reportedly flew missions over Cambodia, the Gulf of Tonkin, and Southeast Asia. Regarding the Soviet Backfire long-range supersonic bomber, Gen. Lew Allen, chief of staff of the U.S. Air Force, said during a visit to Australia in November 1980: "Our area of concern with the Backfire was that it was being introduced into the Pacific and represented a new capability in the Soviet East. It had not yet been introduced to Soviet bases in Vietnam but I believed its naval version could be deployed there in future."[9] Western sources have estimated that some five thousand Soviet technicians are in South Vietnam to maintain and refuel the aircraft as well as to train Vietnamese in the use of such advanced equipment. If the Soviet Union is allowed to use the huge South Vietnamese naval bases, especially the one at Cam Ranh, that were built by the Americans at such expense, then it will be able to service its ships and rest their crews without sending them back to Vladivostok. The new bases will extend its range as far as the Indian Ocean.

Hanoi is understandably anxious to stress what it calls the normality of the large Soviet military presence in Vietnam. The regular visits of Soviet warships, submarines, and planes, Pham Van Dong has said, are "normal practice."[10] According to a statement later issued by the Vietnamese Ministry of Foreign Affairs, "the access of the Soviet military ships to Vietnamese harbors is a normal arrangement for countries having friendly relations." The truth is that Vietnam, heavily dependent upon Russia for its economic survival, much of its food, its military supplies, and more besides, is in a weak position to resist any Russian request, and this dependence increases daily. Hoang Van Hoan, whose defection to China was described in Chapter 3, has analyzed the situation as follows.

> In fact, under the control of Le Duan and company, Vietnam today is no longer an independent and sovereign country but one subservient to a foreign power economically, politically, militarily, and diplomatically. If this state of affairs should be allowed to continue, it would not be long before Vietnam turns into a source of raw materials, a processing plant, and a military base serving the interests of a foreign power.[11]

According to P. J. Honey, a leading expert on Southeast Asia, Hoan is "better qualified than almost any other person to know what the truth is."[12] The judgment that Vietnam has become a Soviet satellite, with a quasi-colonial status, is not one that Hanoi can easily dismiss now that Hoan and his friends are making it.

Relations with the West

Hanoi Blackmails the United States

Immediately following the fall of South Vietnam, the new government officially stated that it wanted to establish diplomatic relations with the United States. At the same time it imposed a number of preconditions for the establishment of such relations and also insisted on a fixed order of subjects for discussion in joint talks.

In December 1975 Hanoi gave some publicity to an earlier letter from President Nixon to Premier Pham Van Dong in which Vietnam was promised $3.25 billion from the United States in reconstruction aid "without any political conditions." This letter had been sent on February 1, 1973, at the time of the Paris Agreement. The United States, however, now took a different view of that agreement, since the Communists had broken it so often (a scaling down of DRV military activity in the South had in fact been one of the preconditions for U.S. aid). The Carter administration was under domestic pressure to do something about the American servicemen still missing in action (MIA) in Vietnam. The Paris Agreement authorized machinery for dealing with this issue.

Hanoi, in the hope that the reconstruction clause of the agreement could be reactivated, attempted to use the MIA issue, on which it was prepared to be conciliatory, as leverage. In February 1977 Vo Van Sung, Hanoi's ambassador in Paris, stated:

> As we have many times declared that we are prepared for an exchange of views on questions concerning both parties, we are ready fully to discharge our obligations concerning the provisions of article 8*b* of the Paris Agreement.
>
> The American side must also assume its obligation concerning its contribution to the healing of the wounds of war and to postwar reconstruction of Vietnam, and implement what was agreed upon in Paris in 1973 by the joint economic commission. This is not only a question of law, but also a question of honor, responsibility, and conscience.[13]

To back up this demand, Hanoi reissued the Nixon letter, which was as follows.

> The President wishes to inform the Democratic Republic of Vietnam of the principles which will govern United States participation in the

postwar reconstruction of North Vietnam. As indicated in article 21 of the Agreement on Ending the War and Restoring Peace in Vietnam signed in Paris on Jan. 27, 1973, the United States undertakes this participation in accordance with its traditional policies. These principles are as follows:

1. The Government of the United States of America will contribute to postwar reconstruction in North Vietnam without any political conditions.
2. Preliminary United States studies indicate that the appropriate programs for the United States contribution to postwar reconstruction will fall in the range of 3.25 billion dollars of grant aid over five years. Other forms of aid will be agreed upon between the two parties.[14]

Hanoi's appeal to morality backfired. Despite the long ordeal of the MIAs' families, the House Select Committee on Missing Personnel in Southeast Asia, after fifteen months of investigation, stated in its report in early 1977 that it strongly opposed "any conditions even faintly resembling blackmail" that Hanoi might impose before it would give an accounting of the MIAs.[15] Hanoi then became more conciliatory. It set no conditions for agreeing to meet with a delegation headed by United Auto Workers president Leonard Woodcock that, at President Carter's request, went to Vietnam in March 1977 specifically in order to discuss the MIAs. Previously, it had refused even to discuss the issue before the United States began paying war reparations.[16] In 1978 Hanoi sent technicians to visit the U.S. central identification laboratory in Hawaii to study the latest methods of identifying human remains.

Meanwhile the Carter administration made a number of concessions to Hanoi. In May 1977, after the return of the Woodcock mission, the Paris talks were renewed. Their main focus was Hanoi's often-repeated desire for bilateral U.S. aid and for an end to the U.S. trade embargo. Washington did make known to Hanoi that it was no longer opposed to Vietnam's entry to the United Nations and that, as part of the normalization process, it was prepared to lift the embargo, though it did not do so. However, it permitted private American organizations to send aid worth several million dollars to Vietnam; it also sent $34 million in aid to Vietnam indirectly, through grants to international aid organizations. At the same time it gradually ceased to demand a full accounting of the MIAs.[17]

These concessions fell far short of what the Communists wanted.

Under pressing need of economic assistance to rebuild the national economy, the Hanoi administration changed its tactics again. Speaking to Tatsuzo Mizukami, president of the Japan Foreign Trade Council, who headed a private economic goodwill mission to Vietnam in May 1978, Premier Pham Van Dong said he would welcome the United States as his country's prospective friend if only it would extend a helping hand in Vietnam's economic reconstruction.[18] More aggressively, Hanoi in a discreet message to Washington, sent through a third country, made known its willingness to shelve the issue of American aid in healing the wounds of war and to proceed with the normalization of diplomatic and commercial relations.[19] These messages were repeated in 1978 and in the following year through intermediaries in Japan and throughout Southeast Asia.

Hanoi had badly miscalculated the American mood. As early as May 1977 the U.S. House of Representatives, by voting 266 to 131 against negotiating with Vietnam on the aid question, had given unmistakable notice to the Carter administration that normalization was not to be bought with concessions.[20] To Hanoi the progress of normalization was far too slow; to Congress even the few concessions that had been made were excessive. It was inevitable that, with the exodus of refugees and Hanoi's invasion of Cambodia in 1978, its normalization process should be endangered. When Hanoi, on November 3 of that year, signed the Treaty of Friendship with the Soviet Union, it killed all prospects of renewing the talks, at least for the time being. The Cambodian invasion followed less than two months later.

How could the supposedly astute communist leaders of Vietnam have been responsible for such a debacle? Their need for American aid and investment was more urgent than ever, but their own behavior guaranteed that neither would be forthcoming. The answer lies in the communist mentality and world view. Hanoi believed that the United States, as a capitalist country, was bound to return to Vietnam for economic reasons, in order to promote exports and to exploit new oil reserves available in Vietnamese territory. Hanoi thus felt confident enough to impose rigid conditions for the restoration of diplomatic relations. Having failed in its initial approach, Hanoi was forced to drop all preconditions and simply call for the restoration of diplomatic relations. This it did in spring 1978, using various Asian and Third World countries as intermediaries. Hanoi considered that normalization would of itself lead to American economic assistance, or at least to the lifting of the U.S. trade embargo. It counted on being able to manipulate American public opinion just as it had manipulated it during the war. In fall 1978 Foreign Minister Nguyen Co Thach came to New York with a delegation to work out the details of a normalization agreement. The agreement was never signed. In December of the same year the United States took the momentous step of extending formal recognition to the People's Republic of China. Hanoi then changed its tactics. The Cambodian invasion and the appalling spectacle of the boat people strengthened the misgivings of those Americans who felt that too much had been conceded to Hanoi already. By August 1979 Thach was complaining that the United States had reneged on its agreement.[21] His words were hollow. Hanoi's own policies had made the prospects for normalization too remote to discuss.

In desperation, Hanoi has continued to use the mass exodus of refugees as a means of putting pressure on the United States and other countries. According to official Vietnamese spokesmen, the refugees left their homes because of the economic difficulties occasioned by U.S. intervention—for instance, because of chemical warfare or bombing. According to Hanoi, only U.S. economic aid to Vietnam can now stop the mass exodus of refugees.[22] This argument, too, has backfired. It is obvious that the latest waves of refugees have occurred only since the Communists have wrecked the Vietnamese economy and antagonized the people they were supposed to have liberated.

Normalization: Arguments Pro and Con. Those who sympathize with Hanoi have blamed its diplomatic isolation, and consequent move into the Soviet camp, on the United States. They argue that the United States, for a variety of selfish reasons, does not want to establish normal relations with Vietnam. Among these alleged reasons are:

1. The United States still wants to discredit the nationalistic nature of the Vietnamese revolution. According to this school of thought, if Vietnam is dependent upon the Soviet Union its revolution will lose credit, since it will only have traded one master (the United States) for another (the Soviet Union). Therefore the United States must want Vietnam to be a Soviet satellite.
2. The United States would have no leverage or control over an independent nationalistic Vietnam. Therefore, it is alleged, the United States hopes that, after making Vietnam weak and dependent on the Soviet Union, it can prevail on Moscow to pressure its ally into acceptable behavior.

On the contrary, runs the argument, the best way for the United States to deal with Vietnam would be to establish full diplomatic relations and treat it as an independent sovereign nation.[23] Taking this step would be a decisive factor in stabilizing the region because it could help prevent more fighting or even a full-scale war between Vietnam and China. It would also signal to the Chinese that the United States has an interest in avoiding bloodshed in Southeast Asia. Perhaps it might also open up new channels of communication between China and Vietnam.[24] The proponents of this point of view also tend to echo Ambassador Vo Van Sung's statement, quoted above, that direct U.S. aid to Vietnam is "not only a question of law, but also a question of honor, responsibility, and conscience."

To take the last argument first, I would object that, as far as law is concerned, it was Hanoi that broke the Paris Agreement by using force to annex South Vietnam. If the United States were to ignore this gross violation, it would have to ignore all future violations. In any case, negotiating and signing treaties are, for the Communists, merely the continuation of war by other means—a mere extension of military strategy. Nothing is more characteristic of their behavior than the way in which they feel free to break treaties while insisting that non-Communists should keep to them.

As for honor, responsibility, and conscience, I do not know how the Hanoi government can appeal in their name to the United States after its use of the MIA issue to blackmail the Carter administration. No doubt Hanoi will return to the issue, since all it can offer the United States in exchange for normalization is the corpses of American servicemen. The anxiety and grief of the MIAs' families will be exploited by Hanoi to keep open the channels through which it hopes to discuss economic aid.

But the most contemptible of Hanoi's blackmailing tricks is its use of the refugee issue. The refugees, Hanoi says, are leaving Vietnam for economic reasons; therefore, if it wants no more refugees, the United States should provide Vietnam with economic aid.[25] I leave it to the reader to judge whether the collapse of the Vietnamese economy, which has been systematically mismanaged for purely political and ideological reasons, should be considered a political or an economic disaster. What kind of a government is it, though, that can so cruelly exploit the suffering of people who would rather risk their lives at sea than spend one more day on the soil that it governs? Hanoi's appeals to morality are like its appeals to legality: a merely tactical use of rules that it expects others to observe while itself preparing to break them at will.

Relations with Western Europe

Hanoi at the time of its military victory was by no means as isolated from the West as it is now. It has in fact received substantial economic aid from several Western European countries, particularly its former colonial master, France.[26]

France. Since late 1973 France has given Vietnam about $363 million, including funds unused by the former South Vietnamese government and reallocated to unified Vietnam in mid-1976. The majority of the aid is in long-term loans or loans guaranteed by the Compagnie Française du Commerce Extérieur. France has signed several contracts with Vietnam, for instance to expand the cement plant at Ha Tien ($60 million) and to deliver $40 million worth of heavy agricultural and dredging equipment. The most important such contract was signed at Hanoi in November 1977 between Vietnam and the French steel group Creusot-Loire; it called for reconstruction of the Thai Nguyen $200-million smelter complex, which has a prospective yearly output of 250,000–500,000 tons. Another protocol was signed in order to increase economic assistance to Vietnam, should such assistance be needed in the future.

In April 1977 Premier Pham Van Dong visited Paris and personally signed an agreement with Elf Aquitaine, a state-run oil company, for offshore oil exploration. The following year French and Vietnamese representatives signed contracts for the construction in Vietnam of a plywood plant and a paper mill. Following a 1977 agreement, construction was begun on a cotton-spinning mill in Ho Chi Minh City by the Société Alsacienne de Construction Mécanique; it was scheduled to cost F200 million. France has also financed construction of a new building for the French Section of the Institute of Foreign Languages in Hanoi.

Two mixed Franco-Vietnamese companies have been formed: Rhone Poulenc, a pharmaceutical company; and Helivifra, a helicopter service set up in late November 1978 in order to ferry workers from Vung Tau to the oil rigs off the coast. Air France runs a weekly Boeing 747 to Ho Chi Minh City, and the French have done work on Hanoi's new airport. French foreign minister Louis de Guiringaud visited Hanoi in September 1978.

Despite the evident interest of both parties in starting suitable projects, French and Vietnamese cooperation in the economic field has not been good. The main reason has been Vietnam's inability to use the available funds, grants, or long-term loans. Thus work under the Creusot-Loire contract was postponed at Hanoi's request, probably due to the incompetence of the Vietnamese state management and its misapplication of the project funds.[27]

France halted its aid in protest at the Vietnamese invasion of Cambodia, but resumed it in December 1981 after the French electorate returned a socialist government to power. The new aid package totaled F200 million (about U.S. $35 million), of which 20 percent went to compensate French firms in Vietnam whose assets the VCP had confiscated, and the remainder to finance various industrial projects.[28] In the face of strong objections from ASEAN, France did stop short of endorsing the Vietnamese presence in Cambodia. However, it acceded to Vietnam's request, in April 1982, for emergency food shipments, and it promised to ask the European Economic Community to resume its program of food aid, suspended since December 1978.[29] France's lead in these respects may well prove influential.

Other Western European Countries. At least eight other countries in Western Europe have followed France's example.

Sweden. From 1969 to 1970 and again from 1976 to 1977, $450 million in grants was made available. Most of the grants were used to construct a huge paper mill and two hospitals. Swedish bank loans totaling $34 million were also made.
Holland. In 1977 $20 million in grants was pledged to finance various projects, particularly irrigation.
Italy. Through 1977 $40 million had been provided in oil exploration equipment, tractors, and tires.
Denmark. In 1975 a total of $28 million was allocated—$6 million in grants and $22 million in loans—toward the construction near Haiphong of a plant to produce 7 million tons of cement a year.
Belgium. Aid from Belgium to Vietnam amounted to $6 million.
Finland. After providing $10 million in loans and grants, Finland undertook from 1976 to 1980 to fund a program, costing $4 million a year, to develop harbor equipment and dockyards.
Norway. Between 1973 and 1975 grants worth $16 million were provided for fertilizers and medical drugs. For the period 1976 to 1979, $23 million in grants was earmarked to finance fisheries and oceanic research.
Austria. Grants for agricultural development amounted to $4 million.

Early in 1977 the Vietnamese government promulgated a foreign investment code with the purpose, in the words of economic planner Dang Viet Chau, of attracting investment from the "Western and Third World countries."[30] As of 1982, no country has accepted the invitation. Moreover, after Vietnam invaded Cambodia, all Western European countries except Sweden suspended their aid to Vietnam.

Hanoi's Cambodian Adventure

After signing the 25-year Treaty of Friendship and Mutual Cooperation with the Soviet Union in November 1978, Vietnam moved to take over Cambodia and established the puppet Heng Samrin government. The invasion marked an expansion of the VCP's power under the aegis of the Soviet Union and with its military assistance.

The development should have surprised no one who knew the VCP's history. In Chapter 3 I mentioned that it was founded in the 1930s under the name of the Indochinese Communist Party, or ICP. Here I should add that although it was, as the name implies, intended to cover Vietnam, Cambodia, and Laos, in practice it consisted only of Vietnamese. By 1945 the ICP was very weak. Ho Chi Minh knew that the nationalist parties were strong; moreover, the Allies sent the anticommunist Chinese forces to accept the Japanese surrender in Vietnam. Faced by these difficulties, Ho declared the ICP dissolved on November 11, 1945. His purpose was to divert his opponents' attention. "In reality, he noted later, "it [the ICP] went underground . . . And though underground, the party continued to lead the administration and the people."[31] At the same time, Ho created the so-called Marxist Studies Association headed by ICP Secretary-General Truong Chinh. The association was merely a front for underground party activities. Not until 1951 did the party hold its Second National Congress, which took place at Tuyen Quang in North Vietnam from February 11 to 19. Ho Chi Minh read a lengthy political report in which he said, "This is the Vietnam Workers Party [Dang Lao Dong Vietnam]." He further stated that "as regards theory, it adheres to Marxism-Leninism."[32] The VWP, then, was organized to replace the ICP. It did not hide its communist nature; Ho Chi Minh was its chairman and Truong Chinh its secretary-general. It was meant to serve as a Vietnamese nucleus in the Communists' struggle for Indochina. The other two Indochinese parties were independent of it only for the time being. In order to explain these tactics to lower-echelon party members who questioned the policy, the VWP issued a lengthy circular emphasizing that "after the victory is won, the three parties will be integrated into the Indochinese Federation."[33]

The desperate and brutal conduct of Pol Pot should be judged against this historical background. In order to break free of the Indochinese Federation, and so escape being dominated by the Vietnamese Communists, he murdered every pro-Vietnamese agent in his Cambodian Communist Party. According to Deputy Prime Minister Ieng Sary, Vietnam made unsuccessful attempts to overthrow the Pol Pot regime in 1975, 1976, and 1977.[34] Pol Pot knew that he was scheduled to be eliminated sooner or later and replaced by a pro-Vietnamese agent. He was motivated, P. J. Honey has written, "not only by feelings of extreme nationalism but also by the knowledge that the Vietnamese Communists [would] never accept [the Cambodian leaders] under any circumstances and [would] work unremittingly for their replacement by men more amenable to Vietnam's official policy of creating an Indochinese Federation under Vietnamese hegemony."[35] It was his anti-Vietnamese nationalism that earned Pol Pot support from China. He failed, having decimated his country's population.

On December 25, 1978, the VCP sent thirteen army divisions supported by artillery, tanks, and planes, to attack Phnom Penh. On January 7, 1979, the Pol Pot regime collapsed. Pol Pot had to withdraw to a jungle in western Cambodia. Heng Samrin rules Cambodia today. He stays in power with the support of some sixteen Vietnamese divisions, or about 200,000 soldiers. He represents much more than a pro-Vietnamese faction in the People's Revolutionary Party of Cambodia (as the ruling party is officially known). The policy that he is implementing is the policy of Indochinese federation that the ICP conceived in the 1930s. The Lao People's Revolutionary Party likewise stays in power with the support of 60,000 Vietnamese troops and is in the same position as the Heng Samrin party. All the internal and foreign policies of the two countries are determined by the VCP. As a result, the three countries of Indochina have been termed "Greater Vietnam."

The VCP has not, however, completely eliminated Pol Pot's armed forces. On the contrary, the Vietnamese armed forces in Cambodia are under attack from Pol Pot's guerrillas. The VCP has had to send more troops in order to maintain its hold on Cambodia and prop up Heng Samrin. In addition, in order to legitimize the Heng Samrin government, the VCP had it publish a new constitution and organize elections in 1980. Finally, it appears that Vietnam has begun a large-scale exchange of populations. Refugees coming from South

Vietnam report that hundreds of Cambodians, including women and children, have been taken to various places in South Vietnam, and that Vietnamese have been sent to settle in Cambodia. Evidently the VCP's intention is to assimilate the Cambodians, on the one hand, and to colonize Cambodia, on the other.

The Sino-Vietnamese Conflict

An Ancient Conflict Is Renewed

The invasion of Cambodia and expulsion of ethnic Chinese from Vietnam by the VCP, in the context of Vietnam's close relationship with the Soviet Union, are proximate causes of the current Sino-Vietnamese conflict. In fact, Vietnam's destruction of the Pol Pot regime is widely regarded as a public humiliation of China that is bound to diminish China's position as a major power, both in Asia and in the rest of the world. It was to retaliate against the invasion of Cambodia and to protect its own prestige that China, in February 1979, took action against Vietnam by crossing their common border. After destroying important installations at Lang Son, the Chinese troops began their withdrawal.

The way was now open for peace talks, but the prospects for lasting peace did not appear promising. To counter the Chinese move, in the midst of rising resentment against China for its support of Cambodia, the VCP in March 1978 had ordered the nationalization of private trade. It proceeded to confiscate the stocks of the ethnic Chinese merchants in Cholon and elsewhere and precipitated a flight of ethnic Chinese from the country. As the exodus swelled to 200,000, Beijing had angrily attacked Hanoi for "persecuting and expelling ethnic Chinese." However, there were even more profound causes for the war between the two communist countries. Historically, Vietnam had been dominated by China at various times over a period of almost a thousand years, up to the tenth century. But China had never succeeded in assimilating the Vietnamese. A vast territory in China's Yunnan and Kwangsi provinces had belonged to Vietnam. China pushed the Vietnamese southward centuries ago and annexed this territory, a deed for which the Vietnamese never forgave them.

In modern times, as we have seen, China and Vietnam have been at odds for ideological reasons. Vietnam has now adopted the Soviet party line, not China's. During the twenty years prior to 1978, China gave Vietnam an estimated $14 billion in aid. In 1964 Deng Xiaoping, then secretary of the Chinese Communist Party (CCP), secretly flew to Hanoi. In an attempt to wean the Vietnamese away from Moscow, he offered them $1 billion in aid per year. He failed.[36] Starting in 1973, the year of the Paris Agreement, China began to reduce its aid to Hanoi. After Hanoi won the war, China made a new offer of $2 billion per year in aid if Vietnam would join the Chinese camp. Since the VCP was still unable to compose its differences with the CCP, the Chinese withdrew all their technical aid in August 1978.

Why is Hanoi no longer able to walk the tightrope between the Soviet Union and China in order to take advantage of both? During the war against the United States, Hanoi had successfully taken a middle-of-the-road position. Both the Soviet Union and China had supported their "little brother" in the war effort. If either of these two great powers had failed to support the Vietnamese Communists, it would have lost credit with other communist parties and so-called liberation movements. It would also have been unable to expand its power in other parts of the world. While the war lasted, both great powers thought they had something to gain. The Soviet Union as well as China still had confidence in the respective factions they had secretly supported inside the VCP; each power thought its own faction would gain control of the party. Finally, the Soviet Union as well as China had its own reasons for gaining control over the VCP. The Soviet Union believed in its strength, its advanced position in technology and science, and its abundance of natural resources. During the war against the United States, Soviet aid was estimated at 80 percent of Hanoi's war expenses. China, in contrast, relied on cultural and geographic conditions. The Vietnamese, Chinese leaders reasoned, were Asian, not white, and had a culture similar to theirs. China's vast territory was contiguous to Vietnam's, thereby making Soviet assistance to Vietnam extremely difficult. In addition, China had given substantial support to Vietnam during the two wars. Wei Guoqing, a Chinese general, commanded Vietnamese troops, provided weapons and ammunition, and supplied Chinese reinforcements to help defeat the French at Dien Bien Phu. After the war had ended, both communist giants required Vietnam to adopt their own line; they would no longer tolerate a middle road.

Why Hanoi Chose Moscow

Hanoi, as I said, finally elected to side with the Soviet camp. The reasons for its choice were as follows. First, the Soviet Union did not threaten Vietnam's territorial integrity. There was a high probability that, in siding with China, Vietnam would be dominated and assimilated by it. With a billion hungry people, China need only peacefully move 1 percent of this total tc Vietnam in order to achieve that objective.

The Chinese might not have been as close to starvation as formerly, but Vietnam had never forgotten the hungry Nationalist Chinese troops, commanded by Gen. Lu Han, who came to North Vietnam in 1945 to disarm the defeated Japanese. Although I was very young in 1945, I well remember seeing these Chinese troops as they marched along a provincial road close to my village. Their clothing was poor; many of them did not even have shoes, and looked like beggars. Could these be soldiers? we all wondered. More likely, they were Chinese who had come to Vietnam for food. They moved to Hanoi. Next to the railroad station there was a row of one-story houses where they were billeted. They used straw or wood for cooking there, and the walls got darkened. People saw this from the train and shook their heads.

The Soviet Union, on the other hand, could not conquer Vietnam owing to geographic, logistic, and political factors—or so Hanoi reasoned. The Soviet Union had the advantages already described. Hanoi expected protection from it against a Chinese or any other invasion. Vietnam needed foreign economic aid in order to build socialism, and the Russians were already the major source of such aid. China could not provide aid on this scale.

The Soviets, of course, do not give their aid for nothing. When Vietnam occupied Cambodia, the Vietnamese leaders were serving not only their own territorial ambitions but also Moscow's desire to expand its influence in Southeast Asia. Soviet military aid will remain indispensable to Vietnam as long as Vietnam remains bogged down in Cambodia. Vietnam also contributes to the Soviet containment of China.

Finally, there is a serious territorial issue outstanding between China and Vietnam. In 1974 China forcibly regained control over the Paracel Islands, a considerable group southeast of Hainan Island, from South Vietnam; the latter still controlled the Spratly Islands, a smaller group to the southwest. The position of both groups is strategically important. They are located on one of the world's most important sea-lanes, through which trade from Malacca pours into the basin of the South China Sea and is either routed southwest, dividing at the Spratlys, or northeast, skirting the Paracels. After taking over South Vietnam, the communist regime tried to negotiate with China for return of the Paracels, but without success. The discovery of oil in the South China Sea has made these islands doubly important. The presence of offshore oil has become increasingly tempting to both

Vietnam and China, whose economies need oil to generate reserve capital for economic expansion. Whoever owns the territory, owns the oil reserves. The dispute became especially bitter when China signed contracts with American oil companies for exploration of the disputed waters around Hainan Island. Vietnam is much concerned over these contracts because its only deep-water port, Haiphong, could easily be blockaded by Chinese naval forces deployed from Hainan to the Paracels.

The 1979 Peace Talks. In March 1979 China declared it had taught Vietnam a sufficient lesson and that peace talks could now begin. Its troops were withdrawn from Vietnam after inflicting, according to some reports, about 50,000 casualties (killed and wounded) and taking about 2,000 prisoners. Chinese casualties were estimated at 20,000; the Vietnamese appear to have taken under 1,000 prisoners.[37]

Although Vietnam had declared it would not come to the peace table as long as China occupied some ten disputed points on the border, peace talks finally got under way on April 18, 1979. Phan Hien, the chief Vietnamese negotiator, proposed three points:

1. In order to secure peace in the border region and facilitate the exchange of prisoners there, a demilitarized zone should be created.
2. Normal relations between the two countries, including rail, air, and postal communications, should be restored.
3. The border and territorial dispute should be settled on the basis of the Franco-Chinese agreements of 1887 and 1895.

Chinese troops, Phan Hien added, still occupied "ten points on Vietnamese territory," and the Vietnamese people would "resolutely refuse to accept this."[38] The Vietnamese proposals, then, implied that China was the aggressor. The Chinese delegation, headed by Vice-Minister for Foreign Affairs Han Nianlong, countered with eight proposals, of which the fourth called for recognition of Chinese sovereignty over the Paracel and Spratly Islands and the sixth for the Chinese who remained in Vietnam to be well treated. The Vietnamese delegation's three points were downplayed or bypassed. Instead, the Chinese delegation placed great emphasis on a proposal that neither side should seek hegemony in Indochina, Southeast Asia, or elsewhere (point 7); and that neither side should join any military blocs aimed at the other, or (in an obvious reference to the invasion of Cambodia) provide military bases to other countries or use the territory and bases of other countries to threaten or subvert the other.[39]

Since the Chinese proposals were nothing less than an invitation to Vietnam to withdraw from Cambodia and renounce its treaty of friendship with Russia, it is not surprising that, after only two rounds of talks, the peace negotiations were broken off. Han Nianlong, interviewed in April 1980, put the Chinese viewpoint in a nutshell when he said: "The Vietnamese are not prepared to solve anything. Going further, it is because the Vietnamese want to engage in regional hegemonism and China is opposed to that."[40]

12

Hanoi's Foreign Policy: II. Relations with Noncommunist Neighbors

Hanoi's noncommunist neighbors may conveniently be divided into, on the one hand, the Association of Southeast Asian Nations (ASEAN), a group of nations interested chiefly in economic development, and, on the other, an economic superpower—Japan. In this chapter I will review Hanoi's generally ineffective moves to inaugurate an era of neutralism and anti-Western isolationism in Southeast Asia and will conclude with a few thoughts on where this type of policy is likely to take Vietnam in the future.

Vietnam and the Members of ASEAN

It will be recalled that the members of ASEAN, founded in 1971, are Thailand, Singapore, Malaysia, Indonesia, and the Philippines. Unlike the now-defunct Southeast Asia Treaty Organization (SEATO), which was founded in reaction to the communist takeovers in Mainland China and North Vietnam, ASEAN is not a military organization. Although it was very active after the fall of South Vietnam, its declared goal is and always has been the economic development of countries in the region. It would be quite willing to admit Vietnam as a member, if only the Vietnamese Communists would share its goals.

Le Duan, in his political report to the Fourth Party Congress in December 1976, said that the VCP "fully supports the just struggle of the peoples of Southeast Asia for national independence, democracy, peace, and genuine neutrality, without foreign military bases and troops on their lands, [and] stands prepared to establish and develop relations of friendship and cooperation with the other countries in the Southeast Asian Region."[1] This statement was merely a smokescreen for the VCP's customary tactic of divide and rule. By dealing with each member of ASEAN separately rather than as a bloc, it hoped gradually to remove all five from the U.S. sphere of influence. ASEAN, to Hanoi, is simply an organization set up by U.S. imperialists for military no less than economic domination of the region. In the name of "national independence" and the "people's struggle," Hanoi would encourage the members of ASEAN to sever all ties with the United States. The fact that these are no longer colonial countries but independent nations does not seem to deter Hanoi from its endless denunciations of what it calls imperialism.

The denunciations had some initial success. In May 1975, shortly after the communist victory in Vietnam, the government of Thailand, under pressure from Hanoi, asked the United States to withdraw its military forces from Thai bases. The following year Thailand did in fact close the Utapao Air Base, from which U.S. bombers had flown missions against Vietnam during the war. Indonesia was also attacked by Hanoi as "the regional policeman" of the United States, which had "openly committed an armed invasion of East Timor."[2] The target of such criticism was any promotion of ASEAN cooperation in security matters. Hanoi continually castigated individual ASEAN members for their role in maintaining a U.S. military presence in the region (though neither Malaysia nor Singapore had U.S. bases) and claimed that the United States had tried "to use ASEAN to rally all pro-American reactionary forces to oppose the revolutionary movement in Southeast Asia."[3] It is obvious, then, why Vietnam did not join ASEAN, though invited by the latter to do so. ASEAN, to the hard-liners in Hanoi, was an American puppet, a military alliance, and a factor causing instability in the region. Instead, Hanoi advanced proposals for setting up a regional organization dedicated to the common good, to replace ASEAN. This organization was to be "based on new foundations," would adopt "new forms," and would be "attuned to the new situation." Its watchword should be "peace, independence, and neutrality"—a slogan that implicitly condemned a rival Malaysian proposal for a "zone of peace, freedom, and neutrality" (ZOPFAN).[4]

When this approach proved fruitless, Hanoi switched policies and proposed to establish cordial and mutually beneficial relations with each country of ASEAN. The proposal, however, was made on a strictly bilateral basis, with the "purpose of mutual protection of independence and sovereignty, of help in economic and technical fields and of opposition to 'coercion' and exploitation by imperialism and neocolonialism."[5]

No More Subversion?

In a joint communiqúe, issued by the Lao People's Revolutionary Party and the VCP in early 1976, the two parties expressed "complete support for the revolutionary movement of Southeast Asia." The movement, they continued, "is stronger and has a better position from which to work since the victories of Indochina. Laos and Vietnam will participate in making southeast Asian countries independent, peaceful, and truly neutral."[6] Among the countries whose "independence" and "neutrality" are of strategic concern to Hanoi is Thailand. For this reason, the Thai Communist Party was one of the three communist parties from noncommunist Asia invited to the VCP's Fourth Party Congress. Radio Hanoi noted the success of the "patriotic armed forces" that had forced the Thai government to declare an emergency in ten provinces. The station concluded that "not content with past success, the Thai people remain vigilant and continue to struggle resolutely for their objectives."[7]

Asked by ASEAN to stop offering such support to insurgent organizations in Southeast Asian countries, Vice-Minister Phan Hien made no response. Later, however, in autumn 1978, Premier Pham Van Dong during his visit to ASEAN members offered assurances that Vietnam would cease all aid and support for subversion in the region.[8] In theory, then, the ASEAN countries no longer have anything to fear from Vietnam in this respect. In practice, however, one may wonder if Pham Van Dong's gesture was really so magnanimous. The VCP could accomplish very little in most of these countries even if it wanted to. In the Philippines, for instance, the Moro (Moslem) secessionists owe no allegiance to Vietnam; neither do the principal parties and factions opposing President Marcos. If the Philippine Communists have a mentor, it is more likely China than Vietnam. The communist parties of Indonesia and Malaysia are notoriously close to the CCP, and therefore immune to the VCP's influence. Singapore does not appear to have a communist party and in any case lacks the social conditions that make communism thrive. The one country in the ASEAN bloc that offers easily exploited opportunities for subversion by the VCP is Thailand. It is to Vietnam's relations with Thailand, then, that we should look for a test of its sincerity in promising not to subvert its noncommunist neighbors.

Vietnamese Aggression Against Thailand. The VCP has long championed the Vietnamese minority, some 50,000 strong, that has been established in Thailand for decades. Many members of this group tend to favor Hanoi—a capital opportunity for subversion. One Vietnamese refugee from Thailand tells me that he has seen Vietnamese communist agents being infiltrated into Thailand as refugees. They land on the Thai coast and disappear on the following day.[9] According to another informant, a Vietnamese lady married to a senior Western diplomat, trucks come and remove them to an unknown destination. She also told me, when I talked to her in 1980, that the Vietnamese embassy in Bangkok had been enlarged to provide accommodation for transients, some 40 at a time.

Internal subversion is not the only threat. Hanoi continually stages military incidents on the Thai border. The frequency of these incidents makes clandestine activities superfluous. The bad relations that exist between the two countries are clearly not Thailand's fault. Thailand established diplomatic relations with Vietnam on August 6, 1976, only two weeks after the deadline set for the withdrawal of U.S. military forces from Thailand. The Thai military leaders who came to power in the subsequent coup were content at first to pursue a policy of détente toward the communist states of Indochina. In September 1978 Pham Van Dong visited Thailand and promised that Vietnam would refrain from attacking or subverting it.[10] All this diplomatic activity was fruitless. After Hanoi's invasion of Cambodia, Thailand was subject to repeated attacks by Vietnamese troops stationed along its eastern border. The Thai leaders were forced to readopt the same hard line against Vietnam that they had abandoned in 1976.

The list of border incidents is a long one. They have not been mere skirmishes. On June 11, 1980, two days before U.S. Secretary of State Edmund S. Muskie arrived in Kuala Lumpur for a meeting of ASEAN foreign ministers, a Vietnamese squad attacked two Thai border listening posts.[11] On January 22, 1981, in the second such incident that month, Vietnamese armed forces attacked Thailand with units from different divisions and regiments.[12] On March 17, 1981, Vietnamese forces ambushed a Thai inspection party and killed two naval officers.[13] It is little wonder that Thailand has once again begun buying large quantities of arms from the United States: the Thais need to have the same kind of strategic alliance with a superpower that the Vietnamese already have with the Soviets. Little wonder, too, that ASEAN has begun to think more in terms of its collective security.

The political purpose behind Vietnam's attacks on Thailand is an issue that deserves the closest scrutiny from the United States. The short-term purpose, of course, is often sufficiently obvious. On June 17, 1980, Thailand announced it would begin repatriation of Cambodian refugees, the great majority of them from the refugee camp at Sakaeo, which was controlled by Pol Pot's guerrillas, the Khmer Rouge.[14] Thailand was burdened with over 150,000 such refugees, and the repatriation was being undertaken with the cooperation of the High Commissioner for Refugees at the United Nations. To Vietnam, however, it was as if its own tactic of encouraging massive refugee outflows was about to be turned against it. It denounced the repatriation as intervention by Thailand in the Cambodian conflict. On June 22 Thailand was invaded by Vietnamese troops.

The attitude of Vietnam toward Thailand is anything but defensive. On July 19, 1980, Hanoi officially proposed to establish a demilitarized zone along the Thailand-Cambodia border. After it was established, the two governments would work out the withdrawal of part of the Vietnamese armed forces from Cambodia. To this the Thai government replied that the proposal was unacceptable because it assumed that Thailand was at war with Kampuchea (Cambodia). In addition, the proposal was deeply offensive to Thailand because it would have given the Vietnamese a legitimate excuse to bring their troops up to the Thai border. Despite this provocation, Thailand's answer was a diplomatic one. With four other members of ASEAN, the Thai delegation to the United Nations sponsored a resolution demanding the withdrawal of Vietnamese troops from Cambodia. The resolution included the following points.

1. Total withdrawal of Vietnamese troops within a specific time and with U.N. verification
2. U.N. measures during the withdrawal "to prevent Cambodian armed elements from seizing power"
3. U.N. guarantees against interference by external powers
4. Free elections in Cambodia under U.N. supervision
5. A conference to reach an agreement to prohibit the introduction of foreign forces into Cambodia
6. Respect for the country's sovereignty, independence, and territorial integrity

7. Assurance that Cambodia would not be a threat to any of its neighbors

This resolution, introduced at the U.N. General Assembly meeting of November 1979, won the support of 91 of the 141 members.[15] In 1980, 97 members adopted it; and in November 1981, the resolution passed for the third time with 100 members in favor.[16]

Addressing the General Assembly in 1980, Vietnamese foreign minister Nguyen Co Thach condemned the ASEAN proposal as interference in "Cambodia's internal affairs."[17] The intransigence of his reply bodes ill for future relations between Vietnam and Thailand. Continual border attacks on Thailand serve the Vietnamese Communists' long-range political interests. I say this for two reasons. First, there can be no doubt that these attacks help to raise the morale of the insurgents the VCP is sponsoring in Thailand. Probably, also, the attacks help the insurgents to build their organization and gain experience in subversion. Second, the routine presence of Vietnamese troops on the Thai border has a lulling effect on Western public opinion. Since Hanoi's military activity, with its incursions into Thai territory, has become a permanent feature of the area, Hanoi could prepare a large-scale invasion of Thailand without attracting any special attention at all.

Relations with Other ASEAN Countries

Hanoi has not succeeded, even on a bilateral basis, in establishing favorable relations with the remaining countries that make up ASEAN. These relations can be briefly summarized.

Singapore. Of the five ASEAN countries the most outspoken in its opposition to communist Vietnam has been Singapore. Foreign Minister Sinnathanby Rajaratnam, when asked in a 1978 interview how he felt about the Soviet Union and China in general and about Vietnam in particular, replied: "None of them have abandoned their long-term objectives of one day bringing [the] ASEAN countries under their shadow. ASEAN should not mistake the shadow for the substance. The shadow is very friendly but the substance is a big question mark as far as we are concerned."[18] Singapore is not prepared to tolerate Communists in its midst; of them Rajaratnam said curtly, "We know the game."[19] Despite this uncompromising diplomatic posture, Singapore has established commercial relations with Vietnam. The value of its imports from Vietnam increased from U.S. $22 million in 1977 to U.S. $49 million in 1980; exports for the same years have shown a like pattern, increasing from U.S. $29 million to U.S. $39 million.[20] For the time being, at any rate, Singapore has ceased to see Vietnam as a threat. Premier Lee Kuan Yew, interviewed in early 1982 by *U.S. News & World Report*, stated: "For the present, with China squatting on Vietnam's northern border and the Khmer Rouge and the Khmer People's National Liberation Front harassing Vietnamese forces in Cambodia, the danger of Vietnamese expansionism is contained."[21]

The Philippines. Four months after the Communists took over South Vietnam, a Filipino diplomat traveled to Hanoi to arrange for the repatriation of Filipino nationals who were still in Saigon and for the normalization of relations. Later in 1976, Vice-Minister Phan Hien visited the Philippines and signed an agreement in Manila establishing full diplomatic relations between the two countries. In November of the same year, President Marcos quietly dispatched a three-man television team to Vietnam that filmed in the North as well as the South and obtained interviews with Premier Pham Van Dong. It may be doubted, however, whether Hanoi's relations with Manila are either close or cordial, since Hanoi's idea of showing friendship for the latter has been to denounce it for maintaining U.S. bases on its territory. Hanoi started taking this tone after its initial denunciations of the United States for "using" the Philippines made little impression on the Marcos regime.[22]

Malaysia. The Thai-Malaysian border operation against communist insurgents on January 18, 1977, elicited strong protests from Hanoi, which described the massive bombing and artillery attacks on the Communists' jungle hideouts as "America's ASEAN schemes." The Malaysian Foreign Office issued a statement telling the Vietnamese Communists to keep out of the matter; these were "internal problems" that the Malaysians would solve by themselves.[23] Malaysia, however, is prepared to have friendly relations with Vietnam, and has received Vietnamese delegations including one headed by Premier Pham Van Dong. Like other ASEAN countries, it took the initiative in seeking and establishing diplomatic relations with the SRV. This initial reservoir of goodwill would appear to have been dissipated by Hanoi's support for the insurgents, and by Malaysia's difficulties with Vietnamese boat people.

Indonesia. Hanoi, as we have seen, calls Indonesia "the regional policeman for the United States," and has accused it of invading East

Timor and of rallying all the pro-American reactionary forces against revolutionary movements in Southeast Asia. Hanoi has also criticized Indonesia for promoting ASEAN cooperation in security matters after the ASEAN summit meeting in early 1976 on the Indonesian island of Bali. At the summit, the ASEAN leaders let it be known that other countries of Indochina would be welcomed as signatories to their regional Treaty of Amity and Cooperation. To Hanoi, on the other hand, Indonesia's role at that meeting was merely one of promoting U.S. interests. ASEAN, in which Indonesia plays a pivotal role, was united in its opposition to Vietnam's invasion of Cambodia. Nevertheless, Indonesia has taken the initiative in offering Vietnam a way to end its regional isolation. Jusuf Wanandi, head of the Public Affairs Department of Indonesia's semiofficial Center for Strategic and International Studies, proposed in May 1981 that Vietnam accept a compromise settlement in Cambodia.[24] By this he seems to have meant that if Vietnam withdrew from Cambodia, ASEAN would recognize the Heng Samrin government. The proposal fell on deaf ears.[25]

Vietnam Confronts ASEAN

I have already mentioned Malaysia's initiative to set up a "zone of peace, freedom, and neutrality" (ZOPFAN) for Southeast Asia. This initiative, which has found favor with ASEAN, calls for a Southeast Asia free from great-power influence and neutral between the two conflicting ideological blocs.

Hanoi's reply was to call for a Southeast Asian "zone of peace, 'genuine independence,' and neutrality."[26] In July 1978, Singapore's foreign minister Rajaratnam asked Vice-Minister Phan Hien, during the latter's visit to Singapore, about the true meaning of this "genuine independence." Phan Hien replied that it was a mistake in translation; Vietnam's plan, according to Hien, was for a "zone of peace, independence, and 'genuine neutrality.'"[27]

The incident was more than semantic. To the Communists, the Southeast Asian countries must be completely independent of the United States. None of the ASEAN countries is independent by Hanoi's standards. The ASEAN countries retort that Hanoi has let Soviet naval forces use Cam Ranh Bay as a base from which they could move to the Indian Ocean and so threaten the stability of the entire region. The Soviet presence in Vietnam itself is another concern of ASEAN.

These differences of viewpoint have not been settled, and therefore Vietnam has not joined ASEAN. Instead, Vietnam has repeatedly emphasized bilateral relations with individual ASEAN countries. However, Pham Van Dong's tour of ASEAN capitals in September 1978 yielded not one signatory for his treaties of friendship, cooperation, and nonaggression. The reasons for his failure were twofold: any country that signed such a bilateral treaty would have been seen as leaning towards Hanoi; and the treaty would not only have alarmed China but would have been a step toward a Soviet-dominated system of collective security for Southeast Asia.

After its lack of success in wooing the ASEAN countries bilaterally—the divide-and-rule strategy—Hanoi in 1979 put ASEAN on notice that the time had come to choose between China and Vietnam. By continuing to side with China, Hanoi warned, ASEAN members would only be harming their own interests.[28] At the same time, the foreign ministers of Vietnam, Laos, and Cambodia met in Phnom Penh on January 5, 1979, to sign a communiqué. The main point of the communiqué was that as long as China, the United States, and other reactionary forces continued in their hostility to the three countries, the Vietnamese military presence in Laos and Cambodia would remain essential.[29]

Vietnam and Japan

During the war in Vietnam the Japanese government took a middle-of-the-road position, avoiding criticism of the American involvement yet refusing to associate Japan too closely with it. However, formal diplomatic relations between Tokyo and Hanoi were not established until 1973, when it appeared that peace was at hand.

After the communist victory this new relationship was tested by three issues. First, would Hanoi honor the debts incurred by the former South Vietnamese government? The issue was of concern to Tokyo because it had extended some ¥30,000 million in loans to that government, and over half of the amount had yet to be repaid. At first Hanoi repudiated the debt. Tokyo's reply was that unless the debt were honored, the Japanese government would be unable to give Vietnam any aid, whether loans or grants, in the future.

Hanoi finally backed down and, for the sake of Japanese aid, acknowledged the debt. Tokyo thereupon offered Hanoi a grant of ¥8,500 million (U.S. $28.6 million), with which it purchased machinery essential for reconstruction. This was in 1975. In September 1976 Vietnam negotiated and signed an agreement with Japan for credits amounting to ¥5,000 million (U.S. $17.5 million), to be used for Japanese materials and equipment to construct a cement plant in Haiphong.

Japan showed similar goodwill toward Vietnam in disposing of the other two issues. A claim against Japan by the Vietnamese Communists for World War II reparations was settled in October 1975 by a Japanese grant of aid totaling ¥13,000 million, mainly in the form of Japanese commodities. After this Hanoi ceased to make a serious issue of the Japanese claim to be compensated for assets appropriated in South Vietnam after the communist victory. The principle that Vietnamese concessions would be rewarded by Japanese aid had been established as the basis of relations between the two countries, at least in the eyes of the Communists.

The Japanese government took this conciliatory attitude because it saw many possible advantages in developing a full range of economic relationships with the new Vietnam and because it believed that the communist leaders of Vietnam would place no difficulties in its path. The government's optimism was shared by Japanese business leaders, who were quick to take the initiative. A Tokyo-based group of consulting engineers, Nippon Koei, sent technicians to Vietnam to discuss the restoration of a hydroelectric power station it had designed and that had been damaged in the war (the power station had been part of Japanese World War II reparations to South Vietnam). Matsushita Electric, part owner of a joint venture called Vietnam National, resumed sending parts and components to its radio and television assembly plant in Saigon.[30] The Japanese government, ever conscious that Japan must import nearly all its oil, was keenly interested in signing an agreement with Vietnam for offshore oil exploration, and in December 1975 sent Foreign Ministry officials to Hanoi for preliminary talks on the subject. Apparently the response was favorable. Seichi Matsuma, chairman of Alaskan Petroleum Development, declared early in 1976 that Hanoi wanted Japanese and French participation. A delegation from the Japanese oil exploration industry soon visited Hanoi, and there seemed to be prospects for a regular oil rush.[31] Another large Japanese delegation, representing six steel mills and trading companies, visited Hanoi in June 1977 to negotiate a contract for delivery of 200,000 tons of steel. This contract, worth U.S. $50 million, was the largest one between Vietnam and Japan since 1975. Many other Japanese corporations, including Japan Air Lines, Sanyo Electric, and Hitachi Shipbuilding & Engineering, attempted to make trade deals with Vietnam during this period. Trade delegations from Japan, besides officials from numerous government departments, included representatives from the Bank of Tokyo and other major Japanese banking corporations.

Few of these contacts progressed beyond a certain point.[32] The rigidity of the Vietnamese Communists' thinking—to them Japan was just another capitalist country, a tool of American imperialism—inhibited them from giving Japan any substantial role in the task of building socialism in Vietnam. The Communists seemed incapable of realizing that the Japanese, although they certainly wanted to make money, were also prepared to export their technical experience for the sake of mutually agreed interests. They were anxious to treat the Vietnamese as Asians first and Communists second.

In December 1979, after the Vietnamese invasion of Cambodia, Japan broke off its aid agreements and adopted a hard line in its dealings with Hanoi.[33] Once again the Vietnamese leaders had succeeded in alienating a nation whose friendship they sorely needed.

Outlook for the Future

The key to understanding Vietnamese foreign relations today is Vietnam's chosen status as a Soviet satellite. By using its military forces to invade Cambodia and attack Thailand, Vietnam is playing the role of an Asian Cuba. In addition, it is allowing Vietnamese territory to be used as a base for Soviet military expansion in the Pacific region.

This policy has resulted in Vietnam's isolation. Many countries—Japan and France are the outstanding examples—were at first in sympathy with the SRV, but have now turned their backs on it. One must admit, however, that the communist leaders have been consistent. The world situation being what it is at present, the VCP has no alternative, in the light of its own beliefs, but to implement the Soviet Union's policy in Southeast Asia. The crucial decisions, then, will henceforth depend on Moscow rather than Hanoi. How long, for example, will Moscow be able to continue its military aid program to Vietnam now that Soviet forces appear to have bogged down in Afghanistan? Certainly, the Soviet Union has no incentive to develop the Vietnamese economy, for, if it does, Vietnam will attempt to escape from Soviet control once it is strong enough.

Even Ho Chi Minh, if he were alive, would not be able to see a way out of Vietnam's dilemma, though he was a capable leader who knew exactly how far to go and how to earn and keep his followers' respect. Today the situation is more difficult. No one in the VCP is capable of occupying the same position as Ho Chi Minh. Internal conflict, then, is as inevitable as it is serious. Those who hold real power in Vietnam for the time being are Le Duan, Le Duc Tho, and their families. Lacking any natural or even earned superiority over other party members, they depend on the Soviet Union for support and survival. Since this is so, the United States will not be able to exert any influence on them and will have no way of controlling their actions in the future.

Meanwhile, the VCP's leaders have achieved their objective: conquest of Cambodia. To the Free World, they have declared that the situation there is "irreversible." Premier Pham Van Dong, in reply to questions about Cambodia, said: "More nations will see the justice in our action, but it will take time."[34] As he sees it, this fait accompli will be recognized by capitalist countries sooner or later. The VCP, he believes, has taken the historically correct path, and history will confirm the party's legitimacy as ruler of Vietnam. To the Vietnamese people, however, the Vietnamese Communists are blunderers who have brought innumerable sufferings upon them and have destabilized Indochina. As P. J. Honey has said, the Communists, "through ambition, ineptitude and one suspects, plain stupidity . . . have brought their own country to the brink of famine and economic ruin, have provided a foothold for the Soviet Union in Southeast Asia, and have brought the possibility of large-scale conflict once more into the region."[35]

Epilogue

The Paris Agreement of 1973 that helped end U.S. involvement in Vietnam actually led to the takeover of South Vietnam by the Communists in April 1975.

In order to conclude the agreement, the Vietnamese Communists had followed general communist rules. For them, negotiation at a peace conference is merely a continuation of war under another form. Similarly, concluding an agreement is a strategy by which they weaken or immobilize the enemy; then they apply force to conquer by surprise. To accept talks proposed by the Communists or negotiation on terms initiated by them is merely to be trapped by their strategy for the future.

South Vietnam, in 1975, fell victim to such a trap.

American Mistakes, Communist Gains

The U.S. government, as we review its past dealings with the Vietnamese Communists, can be seen to have made mistakes, among these that peace talks were not held at an appropriate time. In 1967, the Vietnamese Communists built up their forces in the South in order to launch a general offensive the following year—the Tet offensive. They were defeated. They mounted another offensive in May, but it was not successful either. At that very moment, the United

States entered into negotiations with them to end the war. Until the Tet offensive, the Communists had not been thought of as being capable of mounting a large-scale attack in South Vietnam.

There were other obvious indications that the United States was not in a strong position to accept the Communists' proposal for peace talks. First, the antiwar movement in the United States had just reached its peak. As a result, the Vietnamese Communists had become convinced that it was their agents in the United States who had been successful in leading the movement and in forcing the U.S. government to enter into negotiations to end the war. VCP officials used to declare that they would defeat the Americans in Washington, D.C., just as they had the French in Paris in 1954. Being in a strong position, they demanded peace talks and peace terms that favored themselves.

Second, during the negotiations, the American team did not seem to improve its position and consequently conceded too much. In fact, there was little difference between the ten-point proposal made by the NLF on May 8, 1968, and the final agreement signed in Paris in 1973. Among the terms of the agreement were that a coalition government should be set up; that the United States should be required to respect "the fundamental rights of the Vietnamese people"; that American troops should be withdrawn from South Vietnam and American military bases there dismantled; and that the responsibility for wartime losses and devastation should be imposed on the United States. These concessions had a very great impact on the situation.

Third, the Paris Agreement conferred upon the Vietnamese Communists the status of a legal, fully authoritative government ruling a certain portion of the population in certain areas of South Vietnam, though they were merely a subversive organization. This recognition was really what they had longed for, and implementing the agreement led to unfavorable consequences for the South Vietnamese people.

1. *Communist morale was raised to a high level.* The fact that the U.S. government entered into negotiations with a communist delegation in 1968 made the Communists, in general, feel that the Americans had no other choice than to accept their proposals.
2. *The South Vietnamese people and their troops were demoralized.* The Communists emerged as a lawful government with their military forces officially stationed in the different areas they

had occupied. Their delegation came and lived at Tan Son Nhat Air Base to implement the agreement, often attacking the South Vietnamese government openly. This had a great impact on South Vietnamese morale, both civilian and military.

3. *South Vietnam was immobilized for the Communists to attack at will.* On the American side, all military forces were gradually withdrawn from South Vietnam and all military bases were dismantled as agreed upon. Furthermore, supplies were cut to comply with the agreement. On the communist side, commanders were free to send to the South larger units and heavy war materials to gain superiority on the battlefield. In many cases, reportedly, South Vietnamese outposts were overrun by the Communists because defenders had no ammunition and no grenades. Trucks and planes were left parked in garages and hangars for lack of spare parts and fuel. The South Vietnamese army, in its fight against the enemy, was like the proverbial "son born to a poor family." Truly, the Paris Agreement was an opportunity for the Vietnamese Communists to tie the hands of the South Vietnamese and, at the same time, increase their own military forces to a level at which, in April 1975, they were able to seize power.

After taking over South Vietnam, the Vietnamese Communists, with an arrogance born of their success in defeating the United States, one of the world's leading anticommunist powers, showed themselves, by setting up preconditions for normalizing relations, to be in no hurry to establish diplomatic relations with their enemy. The preconditions were: removal of the American embargo on trade and investment and a substantial American contribution of aid for the postwar reconstruction of Vietnam as projected in article 21 of the Paris Agreement. The amount they claimed was U.S. $3.25 million, as promised by President Nixon. The American reply was negative.

Later on, in 1978, the Vietnamese Communists dropped the preconditions and just asked for plain diplomatic relations. There were two reasons for this change in strategy. First, they believed that diplomatic relations with the United States would lead to economic aid. Only the United States, they now realized, was capable of supplying sufficient capital for them to build socialism. They had shopped around for development capital but found little available. The Soviet Union was contributing less than one-fourth of the capital needed for the Second Five-Year Plan, on a loan basis. Although the interest rate was low, Vietnam was having trouble paying back its debts. Other countries' contributions were very minimal.

The second reason was that, by 1980, Vietnam had reached a dead-end position. On one side, it was being threatened on its northern flank by China; on the other, it was bogged down in Cambodia with almost 200,000 troops, not including the 60,000 troops or so being deployed in Laos. Its economy was shattered due to the incompetence and corruption of party cadres, general mismanagement, lack of specialists, and, above all, the fact that the ideology that guided its economic planning was out of date. Maintaining a huge army of a million troops, reportedly the world's third largest, it depended heavily on the Soviet Union, receiving some U.S. $3 to $6 million a day for military expenditures. This of course made Vietnam yield more favorable terms to the Soviet Union. In order to relieve itself from such pressures (from China no less than the Soviet Union), it needed to bring the United States into the scene and use it as an instrument to break the deadlock.

In the hope of achieving this objective, the Vietnamese Communists have used various methods of keeping channels to the United States open. The refugee exodus has been one way. They claim it is for economic reasons that the refugees are risking their lives to escape, and that the present economic situation in Vietnam is the consequence of American bombing during the war. The only way of stopping the exodus, they say, is for the United States to contribute economic aid. With that condition met, neither the United States nor other countries, particularly the countries of Southeast Asia, will have any more trouble with Vietnamese refugees. The MIA issue has been another such method. The Vietnamese Communists know that the issue is of great concern to any U.S. administration. Therefore, from time to time, they release some American remains in order to wake up the American people, who in turn press the government to do something to solve the problem. Another is the Agent Orange controversy; this and other chemical agents used during the war are said to have caused birth defects—some 100,000 cases are claimed—and also to have slowed down production. Aid is demanded on both counts. Withdrawal of Vietnamese troops from Cambodia is yet another issue that the Vietnamese Communists hope to exploit. They will not withdraw those troops until their cadres have been placed in all the local Cambodian communist party chapters. By then, even if no Vietnamese military units are seen in Cambodia, the situation would not be reversible. Such a withdrawal would, however, open the road to diplomatic relations with the United States.

As this book went to press, two other issues were being exploited. In June 1982 Nguyen Co Thach told Mike Wallace on CBS's "Sixty Minutes" that he would like the United States to take all the people still detained in re-education camps. What Thach did not say was that if the U.S. government wants to admit them, there will have to be negotiations, in the course of which diplomatic relations or at least removal of the trade embargo could be asked for. Hanoi officials were also attacking the U.S. government for an alleged lack of responsibility for the admission of children fathered by Americans during the war. Hanoi was noisily publicizing the matter and, at the same time, expecting to establish negotiations of some kind with the U.S. government.

U.S. Interests in Vietnam

It is obvious, from the diligence with which the Vietnamese Communists have been seeking normalization of U.S.–Vietnam relations, that they consider it to be in their own best interests. Is it also in the interests of the United States? Before answering that question, we need to determine what interests the United States really has in Vietnam.

Political-Strategic Interests

Vietnam needs to be viewed in the light of the U.S. interest in Asia as a whole and in Southeast Asia in particular. The stability and peace of the Pacific region affect both the world situation and U.S. security; a seedbed of one world war, it may yet produce another. Recognizing this fact, the United States maintains a regional presence by keeping the Seventh Fleet there with its bases in the Philippines and Japan. The purpose of this presence is to create what Richard Holbrook, assistant secretary of state for Asian affairs, called in 1979, "a stable, peaceful system of nation states" in Southeast Asia.

Contrary to the U.S. interest, the SRV's policies are creating a destabilizing situation in the Pacific region. The SRV has deeply committed itself to the Soviet Union. It joined COMECON upon the latter's request, then signed a 25-year Treaty of Friendship with it in 1978. As a Soviet surrogate, the SRV used its military forces to invade Cambodia in 1978 and to subdue Laos after the local communist party came to power there. At least seven Vietnamese corps were stationed on the northern border to face the Chinese threat. The SRV's military units in Cambodia were repeatedly attacking Thailand. During a visit to Singapore in July 1982, Nguyen Co Thach threatened to wage subversive warfare against any member of ASEAN who maintained "unfriendly policies" toward Vietnam-occupied Cambodia. More important was the fact that SRV territory, especially the former U.S. bases, was being used by the Soviet Union for military purposes. This directly challenged the U.S. presence in the region, including the bases essential to maintaining that presence.

Furthermore, because of the SRV's substantial contribution to the buildup of Soviet naval forces in the Indian Ocean, the Soviet Union was being encouraged to cast an envious eye on the vital Middle Eastern oil reserves. The same forces were backing up the Soviet offensive in Afghanistan—an offensive aimed at the Persian Gulf. The situation also posed an immediate threat to the sea-lanes by which oil reached Japan, an indispensable U.S. ally in the Far East. In short, the contribution of the SRV to the Soviet Union in the Pacific was great enough to cause radical reconsideration of U.S. naval strategy to counter the new situation.

Economic-Commercial Interests

There has been no trade between the SRV and the United States since 1975. The outlook for improvement is not promising, due to the inefficiency and consequent corruption of party officials and the vagaries of party policy. Japanese businessmen have not had good experiences in dealing with the SRV. Vietnam may well have oil resources. In the early 1970s there were some small discoveries; if there is more oil, the quantity has yet to be established, and any income from it is still a decade away. The continual presence of Soviet naval forces would of course have implications for U.S. trade with Asia, the value of which was estimated at U.S. $240 billion in 1980.

Humanitarian Interests

The United States cannot turn its back on the sufferings incurred by the peoples of Indochina under the yoke of the VCP. Thousands have lost their lives in the open sea as they sought freedom. Many are still escaping by any means available. Meanwhile, in Vietnam, some 250,000 persons have been detained in re-education camps to perform hard labor. Hundreds of thousands more are confined in NEZs. Over half a million have been sent to Siberia and East European countries as slave laborers to build oil pipelines and work on construction sites. Other oppressive measures, not discussed here, have had an equally wide impact.

Should U.S.–Vietnam Relations Be Normalized?

Given the nature of its interests in Vietnam, it is doubtful that the United States could maintain them more effectively through normalization. The reasons are many.

First, such a decision would imply approval of the SRV's policies. The SRV, in all likelihood, would be encouraged to continue on the same path. Such an outcome would be very dangerous to the stability and peace of Southeast Asia and would also threaten the lives of many in Indochina, because an American office in Hanoi could not exert any influence on the SRV to change its policies. On the contrary, the decision to normalize could show that the United States is in a very weak position, merely by replying to and complying with the SRV's demands. In this case, the United States could not gain anything. President Carter committed this error. In the hope of solving the MIA issue, he sent a commission, headed by Leonard Woodcock, to Hanoi a month after his inauguration. Because the SRV promised to provide the United States with all available information on MIAs and return their remains as soon as recovered, President Carter acquiesced in Vietnam's admission to the United Nations in September of that year. However, the failure of the United States to use its veto at the United Nations was not interpreted by the SRV as a conciliatory and cooperative gesture but rather as a sign of submission to the new regime. The Hanoi media said as much. It is no wonder that, in the talks held in Paris following the Woodcock mission's visit to Vietnam, the SRV demanded removal of the U.S. embargo on trade and investment and fulfillment of what it saw as the U.S. obligation to contribute aid for the postwar reconstruction of Vietnam. We all know how much information and how many remains President Carter subsequently got from the SRV. We all also know that it is still using and still plans to use the MIA issue as a bargaining counter.

Second, we should never expect such diplomatic contact or even economic aid to the SRV to turn its leaders into Vietnamese Titos, though the suggestion is often made. In the 1940s, Ho Chi Minh and his followers received no aid from Stalin to fight the Japanese or the French; on the contrary, in order to attract aid from the United States, they pretended to be nationalists. Many Westerners still naively believe that Ho would never have become a Communist but for the U.S. denial of aid. Despite their many bitter experiences with the

Soviet Union, the VCP leaders have never abandoned the Soviet ideology and never relinquished a position of dependence on the Soviet Union. Clearly, the VCP leaders are so dogmatic that they will never want to accept a change of position; whatever Marx or Lenin said is gospel to them. If, by some fluke, they were to deviate from the Soviet line, they would not know where to go.

Besides, when a communist party, especially one like the VCP, has a collective style of leadership, it is likely to have great difficulty in reaching a Yugoslavian type of compromise. With Ho Chi Minh gone, no one in the VCP Politburo has been able to emerge as a Vietnamese Tito. If anyone were to attempt such a role, there is no doubt that the pro-Soviet faction would purge him immediately.

Even if the U.S. government were to establish an official relationship with the SRV, what could the U.S. office in Hanoi do to exert influence on the VCP leaders? Would they, for example, dismantle the Soviet naval base in Cam Ranh, or—in compliance with the three U.N. resolutions on the subject—withdraw Vietnamese troops from Cambodia? And if they refused to do such things, what action should the United States take against the SRV? Of course, military action would not be appropriate. The most obvious recourse would be a break in diplomatic relations and an embargo on trade. The United States would be back where it started!

To sum up: those who create political instability in a region and increase the chances of regional conflict should not be rewarded.

Conditions for Normalization

If the United States should normalize its relations with the SRV, negotiations must be slow and cautious. Even so, the United States must obtain preconditions for such negotiations, or its interests will suffer. A hard stance needs to be taken; without one, the SRV will never compromise. A precedent might be President Nixon's decision, in December 1972, to resume heavy bombing of North Vietnam. It was this decision that forced Hanoi to return to the conference table in Paris and sign the agreement ending the war.

The preconditions essential for preserving the U.S. interests in Vietnam should at least include:

Political-Strategic Concessions. Dismantling of Soviet naval bases at Cam Ranh; withdrawal of Vietnamese troops from Cambodia and Laos; compromise and peaceful coexistence with nations in the region; withdrawal of Vietnamese experts in subversive warfare from El Salvador and elsewhere.

Economic and Commercial Concessions. An open-door policy for international trade and investment in Vietnam, with adequate guarantees that private investments will not be nationalized.

Humanitarian Concessions. Full accounting of MIAs and release of all living MIAs still detained; release of over 250,000 prisoners of conscience who have been confined since 1975 without trial, including over 200 Biet Kich; dissolution of all NEZs, which are merely concentration camps under another name; genuine recognition of the fundamental rights of the Vietnamese people in conformity with the 1948 Universal Declaration of Human Rights and the 1975 Helsinki Agreement. Those 500,000 Vietnamese sent to Siberia and Eastern European countries to work as slave laborers must be brought back and liberated. Humanitarian aid, including food, clothing, and medicine, could be given to the poor.

All the conditions, once agreed upon, should be accompanied by detailed inspection, follow-up, and sanctions. Without such measures, recognition of the Hanoi regime would be a reward and an encouragement to tear up the agreement as it has torn up two other agreements—the Geneva Agreement of 1954 and the Paris Agreement of 1973.

Several examples of the Vietnamese Communists' former behavior could be adduced in formulating appropriate guidelines to ensure their good conduct. In particular, the United States should be on guard against their practice of releasing spies and common-law criminals in place of prisoners of conscience. Another such practice is their diversion of international aid for political purposes. In order for medicine and food to reach those who need them, relief agencies should have the right to give them directly. The agencies must have a full list of recipients with their addresses. Agency staff must check the next day to see if VCP cadres have forced aid recipients to make donations to the party. Such checks must be carefully made. During the war against the Americans, VCP cadres visited South Vietnamese villagers at night and forced them to dispose of all medicines received from U.S. army medical teams during the day. The alleged reason was that the American imperialists were giving the villagers poison, which should be turned over to the party for destruction. In many cases the VCP cadres called the villagers together and then, by using an overdose of some medicine, poisoned a dog before their eyes. The medicines turned over were later secretly distributed among the cadres. No one should have been surprised, then, when French visitors to Hanoi in 1979 reported they had seen food there in containers indicating it had been given directly by international relief agencies to Cambodian refugees on the Thailand-Cambodia border.

The preconditions set forth here are consistent not merely with American interests in Indochina but also with America's commitment, as a major power leading the Free World, to a responsible ideal of world peace.

Notes

The following abbreviations are used in the Notes:

AE	American edition
AFP	Agence France Presse
CNA	*China News Analysis*
DS	domestic service
FBIS	Foreign Broadcast Information Service
FEER	*Far East Economic Review*
JE	Japanese edition
JPRS	Joint Publications Research Service
NHK	Nippon Hoso Kyokai (Japan Broadcasting Corporation)
NVTD	*Nguoi Viet Tu Do*
OS	overseas service
TCCS	*Tap Chi Cong San*
VNA	Vietnam News Agency
YB	*Yellow Book*, familiar name for the FBIS *Daily Report on Asia Excluding China*

The principal periodicals cited, with their places of publication, were as follows (**J** = journal; **M** = magazine; **N** = newspaper):

A. Vietnamese

Chinh Nghia (Just Cause)	**M**	Hanoi
Cong Tac Ke Hoach (Work and Planning)	**M**	Hanoi
Dai Doan Ket (Great Unity)	**M**	Hanoi

Giao Thong Van Tai (Communications and Transport)	**M**	Hanoi
Hanoi Moi (New Hanoi)	**N**	Hanoi
Hoa Sen (The Lotus)	**M**	Saigon
Lao Dong (Labor)	**M**	Hanoi
Lien Lac (Liaison)	**M**	Mountain View, Calif.
Lien Lac (Liaison)	**M**	Manila
Nghien Cuu Kinh Te (Economic Studies)	**J**	Hanoi
Nguoi Viet Tu Do (Free Vietnamese)	**M**	Japan and USA
Nhan Dan (The People)	**N**	Hanoi
Quan Doi Nhan Dan (The People's Army)	**N**	Hanoi
Su That (The Truth)	**M**	Stuttgart
Tap Chi Cong San (Communist Review)	**M**	Hanoi
Tap Chi Quan Doi Nhan Dan (The People's Army Review)	**M**	Hanoi
Tin Sang (Morning News)	**N**	Saigon
Vietnam Courier (in English)	**M**	Hanoi
Vietnam Hai Ngoai (Vietnam Overseas)	**M**	San Diego, Calif.
Vietnam	**M**	San Jose, Calif.
Vietnam Pictorial (in English)	**M**	—

B. Other Periodicals

Asahi Evening News	**N**	Tokyo
Asahi Shimbum	**N**	Tokyo
China News Analysis	**M**	Hong Kong
Chuo-Koron	**M**	Tokyo
Courier Mail	**N**	Brisbane
Est & Ouest	**M**	Paris
L'Express	**M**	Paris
Far Eastern Economic Review	**M**	Hong Kong
Il Giornale	**N**	Rome
Le Matin	**N**	Paris
New Straits Times	**N**	Kuala Lumpur
Southeast Asia Record (now *Asia Record*)	**N**	Palo Alto, Calif.
Der Spiegel	**M**	Hamburg
L'Unità	**N**	Rome

Like any student of Southeast Asian affairs, I can only regret that *Indochina Chronology*, a quarterly publication of the Institute of East Asian Studies, University of California, Berkeley, did not begin publication until spring 1982. It promises to become an indispensable guide to the mostly fragmentary and inadequate coverage of communist Vietnam in the world press.

A few words of comment on the method of citation employed here: Original Vietnamese titles are given only when I am citing the original Vietnamese documents. Most Vietnamese sources are cited from the translations provided by the FBIS and JPRS; the original titles (and sometimes page numbers) were therefore not available to me, although the original date of publication or broadcast usually was. If FBIS citations carry no year, the reader can assume the year of publication by the FBIS was the same as the year of broadcast. Readers puzzled by shortened citation forms, which are used for works cited more than once, are advised to consult the Bibliography, where all such works are listed in full.

Chapter 1

1. Van Tien Dung, *Dai Thang Mua Xuan* [Great spring victory] (San Diego, Calif.: *Hon Viet Magazine*, 1976), pp. 16–17.
2. Ibid., p. 15.
3. George H. Nash, "The Dissolution of the Paris Peace Accords," in Anthony T. Bouscaren, ed., *All Quiet on the Eastern Front: The Death of South Vietnam* (Old Greenwich, Conn.: Devin-Adair Co., 1979), p. 30.
4. The same point was later made by Truong Chinh, now the SRV's chief of state. In 1970, during an interview with East German playwright Peter Weiss, Truong Chinh remarked that "the line followed by the party and the people of Vietnam in armed and political struggle is the line of revolutionary power" (Peter Weiss, *Notes on the Cultural Life of the Democratic Republic of Vietnam* [New York: Delta Books, 1970], p. 170). He further stated: "At present in the South, there is but one effort: the military victory of the armed forces of the people" (ibid., p. 167). Vietnam's problems, he stressed, would be resolved primarily on the battlefield and only secondarily at the conference table (ibid., p. 168).
5. Nguyen Van Canh, *Chien Tranh Chinh Tri Cua Cong San* [The communist political warfare] (Saigon University Law Faculty, 1974), pp. 223–24.
6. Olivier Todd, "Comment Hanoi nous a trahis: Une interview de Truong Nhu Tang, ancien ministre du G.r.p." [How Hanoi has betrayed us: An interview with Truong Nhu Tang, former minister of the Provisional

Revolutionary Government], *L'Express*, June 14, 1980, p. 93. See also Tran Dien and Vu Van Khoa, "Con ngua thanh Troie," interview with Truong Nhu Tang, *Vietnam Hai Ngoai*, no. 74 (June 16, 1980): 42.

7. Radio Saigon, DS, FBIS, *YB*, May 5, 1975, pp. L3–L4.
8. VNA, in English, May 25, 1975, FBIS, *YB*, May 27, p. L9.
9. Pham Van Dong, Speech at opening session of National Assembly, June 3, 1975, Radio Hanoi, FBIS, *YB*, June 3, p. K7.
10. Provisional Revolutionary Government of the Republic of South Vietnam (PRGRSV), Circular, dated June 1, 1975, on the celebration of the sixth anniversary of the PRGRSV, cited in Allan W. Cameron, *Indochina: Prospects After the End* (Washington, D.C.: American Enterprise Institute for Public Policy Research, 1976), p. 7.
11. Pham Hung, Speech to South Vietnamese Congress of National Reunification, Dec. 22, 1975, Radio Saigon, DS, FBIS, *YB*, Dec. 24, p. L5.
12. Author's interview with Dr. Tran Xuan Ninh, M.D., former professor at the Saigon Medical School, who escaped in a fishing boat and arrived in the United States in March 1979; and with Vu Van An, a high-ranking expert of the RVN's Agricultural Development Bank who, after being re-employed by the communist National Bank in a similar capacity, escaped and arrived in the United States in 1979.
13. Author's interview with Pham Nghia, former ARVN captain, who escaped and arrived in the United States in 1979.
14. Todd, "Comment Hanoi nous a trahis," p. 93.
15. Nariko Sugano, "Dan Saigon, Dan Hanoi" [Saigonese and Hanoians], *NVTD*, AE, Dec. 15, 1979, pp. 29–30. Originally published in *Chuo-Koron Monthly Magazine*, June 1979.
16. Le Kim Ngan, "Su sup do tat yeu cua Cong San Vietnam trong thap nien 80" [The necessary collapse of the Vietnamese communist regime in the 1980s], *NVTD*, AE, July 1979, p. 28.
17. A list of the participants was read on Radio Hanoi in Vietnamese, Nov. 15, 1975, FBIS, *YB*, Nov. 17, p. L1. For the heads of delegations and their deputies, see "Final Communiqué of the Political Consultative Conference," VNA, in English, Nov. 21, 1975, FBIS, *YB*, Nov. 24, p. L2.
18. Hoang Van Hoan, "Unite as One in Spirit, Emulate in Productive Labor, Struggle for Good Result in the General Election" (Speech on reunification at a public meeting in Hanoi, Nov. 28, 1975), *Nhan Dan*, Nov. 29, p. 2, JPRS, no. 66694, *Vietnam*, no. 1764 (Jan. 29, 1976): 9.

19. Ibid.
20. Nayan Chanda, "Speeding Towards Reunification," *FEER*, Dec. 5, 1975, p. 23.
21. Quoted in Nayan Chanda, "Elections . . . 20 Years After," *FEER*, Apr. 30, 1976, p. 13.
22. P. J. Honey, "Duoc Lam Vua," *Asian Affairs*, 3, pt. 3 (Oct. 1978): 264.
23. Todd, "Comment Hanoi nous a trahis," p. 93.
24. Cameron, *Indochina: Prospects After the End*, p. 13.
25. Chanda, "Speeding Towards Reunification," p. 23.
26. Todd, "Comment Hanoi nous a trahis," p. 93.
27. Pham Van Dong, Speech at Ho Chi Minh birthday celebration, Hanoi, May 19, 1975, VNA, in English, FBIS, *YB*, May 20, p. K3.
28. Nayan Chanda, "Promoting the Spirit of Friendship," *FEER*, Aug. 8, 1975, p. 22.
29. JOAK TV, Tokyo, "Interview with Wilfred Burchett by NHK Correspondent Nagata," News Center Nine O'Clock [Program], Sept. 19, 1975, JPRS, no. 65867, *Vietnam*, no. 1711 (Oct. 7, 1975): 40–41.
30. V. Q. V. [author's initials], "National Unification of *Legislation*," *Vietnam Courier*, June 1977, p. 13.
31. Author's interview, May 6, 1980, with Tran Quan, a former law student who had arrived in the United States as a refugee the previous month.

Chapter 2

1. Douglas Pike, *History of Vietnamese Communism, 1925–1976* (Stanford: Hoover Institution Press, 1978), p. 100.
2. Le Duan, "Outline of the Draft Political Report of the Central Committee of the Vietnam Workers Party to the Fourth Party Congress," *Vietnam Courier*, Dec. 1976, p. 14 (hereafter cited as Le Duan, "Outline").
3. Nguyen Tien Hung, *Economic Development of Socialist Vietnam, 1955–1980* (New York: Praeger, 1977), p. 22. Hung's well-documented book is my source for the rest of this paragraph.
4. As quoted in Nayan Chanda, "Towards Socialism—on the Double," *FEER*, July 9, 1976, p. 10.
5. Nguyen Van Linh, Interview in *Dai Doan Ket*, Nov. 5, 1977, JPRS, no. 70463, *Vietnam*, no. 2003 (Jan. 11, 1978): 21.
6. Ibid., p. 23.

7. Ibid., p. 24.
8. *Saigon Giai Phong*, "The Welfare Committee of Phu Nhuan District Looks for Jobs for Youths and Helps People Who Have Little Capital Establish Handicraft Cooperatives," Sept. 10, 1975, JPRS, no. 66587, *Vietnam*, no. 1755 (Jan. 14, 1976): 70.
9. P. J. Honey, "Vietnam's New Policies and Perspective," *CNA*, Dec. 15, 1978, p. 2.
10. Philippe Devillers, "Vietnam in Battle," *Current History*, Dec. 1979, p. 217.
11. *Nhan Dan*, "Specific Efforts to Resolve the Grain Problem," Editorial, Feb. 2, 1977, Radio Hanoi, DS, Feb. 1, FBIS, *YB*, Feb. 4, p. 22.
12. Jacques de Barrin, "Le Socialisme à pas lents," *Le Monde*, Mar. 18, 1981, p. 5.
13. Jean Thoroval, "*Nhan Dan* Official Declares 'VWP to Be Reorganized,'" AFP Hong Kong, in English, August 29, 1976, FBIS, *YB*, Aug. 30, p. 11.
14. Information on the schools for land-reform cadres from Bui Xuan Vinh, interviewed by the author in Saigon in late 1967. Vinh was a North Vietnamese agricultural engineer. In 1953 he was recruited into a training program for cadres of the land-reform team assigned to work in the Hong Ha River Delta from 1954 to 1956. The program was held at a secret training school in a jungle area on the border with China, in the Cao Bac Lang area. Vinh was drafted into the NVA and sent to the South in 1966. In 1967 he defected to the RVN. For the 1953 directive, see Hoang Van Chi, *Tu Thuc Dan den Cong San* [From colonialism to communism], translated from English into Vietnamese by Mac Dinh (San Jose, Calif.: Nguoi Viet Tu Do, 1980), p. 214.
15. Tran Chat, "Content and Method of Setting up Planning Tasks for State Farms," *Cong Tac Ke Hoach*, Aug. 1975, pp. 11–20, JPRS, no. 66319, *Vietnam*, no. 1742 (Dec. 9, 1975): 17.
16. Thanh Giang, "An Investigation of the Division of Classes in a Number of Hamlets Within the Mekong River Delta," *TCCS*, no. 5 (May), 1979: 53–58, JPRS, no. 73850, *Vietnam*, no. 2130 (July 16, 1979): 58–59.
17. To Huu, "Completely Eradicate Exploitation and Unite the Laboring Peasants to Vigorously and Steadily Advance the Agricultural Cooperativization Movement" (Speech at Nov. 21–23 Conference on Agricultural Transformation in the South), Radio Hanoi, DS, broadcast in segments on Jan. 3, 4, 5, 8, and 9, 1979, JPRS, no. 72678, *Vietnam*, no. 2094 (Jan. 1979): 19.

18. SRV Council of Ministers, Decision on Nov. 15, 1978, re socialist transformation of private mechanized and agricultural forces in Southern Provinces, in execution of Directive 57/TW of VCP Politburo, *Nhan Dan*, Dec. 18, 1978, JPRS no. 72858, *Vietnam*, no. 2100 (Feb. 26, 1979): 21.
19. VNA, in English, Jan. 29, 1977, FBIS, *YB*, Feb. 8 (in "News Briefs"), p. K17.
20. To Huu, "Completely Eradicate . . . ," p. 13.
21. Ibid., p. 17.
22. Ibid., p. 18.
23. *Saigon Giai Phong*, "On State Policy for Restoring and Expanding Industry and Commerce and on Eliminating Comprador Bourgeoisie," Question-and-Answer Column, Sept. 14, 1975, JPRS, no. 66200, *Vietnam*, no. 1734 (Nov. 24, 1975): 28.
24. P. J. Honey, "A Vietnamese Domesday Book," *CNA*, June 9, 1978, p. 2.
25. Ibid., p. 3.
26. VNA, "Socialization of Private Transport," in English, Apr. 22, 1979, JPRS, no. 73392, *Vietnam*, no. 2116 (May 7, 1979): 27.
27. P. J. Honey, "A Unified Currency," *CNA*, June 9, 1978, p. 4.
28. SRV Council of Ministers, Decree No. 27 CP, June 8, 1979, on civil servants and cadres, Radio Hanoi, DS, June 10, JPRS no. 73736, *Vietnam*, no. 2125 (June 21, 1979); 17.
29. P. J. Honey, "Eliminating Private Commerce from the South," *CNA*, June 9, 1978, pp. 1–2.
30. Kim Son [reader], "Mot sang kien can ngan can" [An initiative needs to be stopped], *Nhan Dan*, Sept. 22, 1976, *NVTD*, JE, Dec. 1976, p. 36.
31. *Tin Sang*, "Contribute to Opposing Theft of Socialist Property," Oct. 29, 1977, JPRS, no. 70410, *Vietnam*, no. 2001 (Jan. 4, 1978), p. 2.
32. Le Giao Vien, "Sach chui" [Smuggled books], *Nhan Dan*, date omitted, *NVTD*, JE, Aug. 1978, p. 37.
33. Nhu Van Lo, "Cho troi Thai Nguyen" [Flea market in Thai Nguyen], *Nhan Dan*, date omitted, *NVTD*, JE, Jan. 1978, p. 36.
34. Bang Vu, "Restricting the Theft of Coal and the Transporting of Contraband Goods," *Giao Thong Van Tai*, Oct. 31, 1977, p. 3, JPRS, no. 70410, *Vietnam*, no. 2001 (Jan. 4, 1978): 8.
35. Jean Thoroval, "Hanoi Observers Note Return of Tipping, Bribing," AFP Hong Kong, Oct. 16, 1975, JPRS, no. 66029, *Vietnam*, no. 1722 (Oct. 29, 1975): 17.

36. Katsuichi Honda, "Nan tham nhung tai Vietnam moi" [Instances of corruption in the new Vietnam], *Asahi Shimbun*, May 1, 1978, *NVTD*, AE, June 1978, pp. 20–21.
37. Tran Dien and Vu Van Khoa, Interview in Feb. 1980 with Hoang Huu Quynh, *Vietnam Hai Ngoai*, Mar. 16, 1980, p. 51.
38. François Nivolon, "Correcting Past Mistakes," *FEER*, May 16, 1980, p. 61.
39. Ibid.

Chapter 3

1. Le Duan, keynote speech to National Assembly, June 26, 1976, as quoted in Nayan Chanda, "Towards Socialism—on the Double," *FEER*, July 9, 1976, p. 10.
2. "'Full Translation' of New SRV Constitution," VNA, in English, Dec. 19, 1980, chap. 1, art. 4, FBIS, *YB*, Dec. 22, p. K3 (hereafter cited as *SRV Constitution*).
3. VCP, "General Resolution of the Fourth National Congress of the Communist Party of Vietnam," *Vietnam Courier*, Jan. 1977, p. 5.
4. Ibid., p. 6. See also Le Duan, "Outline," p. 7.
5. Le Duc Tho, "Report Summarizing Party Building Work and the Amended Party Charter" (read at Fourth Party Congress, Hanoi, Dec. 1976), *Nhan Dan*, Dec. 20–23, pp. 2–6 (hereafter cited as Le Duc Tho, "Report"), FBIS, *YB*, Feb. 3, 1977, vol. 4, no. 23, supp. 6, p. 64.
6. Ibid. The report (pp. 68, 69) also establishes party caucuses in the state's "leadership agencies."
7. See, for instance, Truong Chinh, "Hold Fast to the Proletarian Dictatorship," *TCCS*, no. 1 (Jan.) 1977, Radio Hanoi, DS, Feb. 6, 1977, FBIS, *YB*, Feb. 10, p. K14.
8. *TCCS*, "Learn from President Ho's Ethics, Improve Revolutionary Qualities," Editorial, no. 5 (May) 1981, Radio Hanoi, DS, May 17, 1981, FBIS, *YB*, May 21, p. K5.
9. *Nhan Dan*, "Strictly Punish Those Who Practice Corruption, Bribery and Oppression of the Masses," Editorial, May 20, 1981, Radio Hanoi, DS, May 19, FBIS, *YB*, May 20, p. K7; SRV, "Law on Punishment for Bribery Offenses," promulgated by Nguyen Huu Tho on May 23, 1981, Radio Hanoi, DS, May 24, 1981, FBIS, *YB*, May 28, p. K4.
10. Tan Phong, "Investigative Report," from a "recent" issue of *Tien Phong* [no further details], Radio Hanoi, DS, May 24, 1981, FBIS, *YB*, May 28,

p. K9. See also *Nhan Dan*, "Campaigns Underway Against Decadent Culture," May 27, 1981, Radio Hanoi, DS, FBIS, *YB*, May 28, p. K8.

11. Nayan Chanda, "A Massive Shock for Vietnam," *FEER*, August 16, 1979, p. 8.
12. Allen W. Cameron, *Indochina: Prospects After the End*, p. 5.
13. Tran Dien and Vu Van Khoa, Interview in February 1980 with Hoang Huu Quynh, p. 52.

Chapter 4

1. Nguyen Huu Tho, Report to joint conference held by the NFL and VANDPF [Vietnamese Alliance of National Democratic Peace Forces], Radio Saigon, DS, May 13, 1976, FBIS, *YB*, May 17, p. L1.
2. PRG, article 22 of order signed by NFLSV Chairman Nguyen Huu Tho and President Huynh Tan Phat dated February 20, 1976, Radio Saigon, DS, Feb. 27, 28, 1976, JPRS, no. 66938, *Vietnam*, no. 1780 (Mar. 10, 1976): 8–9.
3. Electoral Council's official announcement of April 26, 1981, election results, Radio Hanoi, DS, May 17, 1981, FBIS, *YB*, May 18, p. K7.
4. Le Duan, *On the Socialist Revolution in Vietnam* (Hanoi: Foreign Language Publishing House, 1965), p. 205.
5. *Nhan Dan*, "A General Revolution," Editorial, June 30, 1976, Radio Hanoi, DS, June 29, FBIS, *YB*, July 1, p. K8.
6. Ibid.
7. Ibid., p. K9.
8. Vo Nguyen Giap, "On the Scientific and Technological Revolution in Vietnam" (Speech at Fourth Party Congress, Hanoi, Dec. 1976), *Vietnam Courier*, May 1977, pp. 8–10.
9. Tran Dien and Vu Van Khoa, Interview in Feb. 1980 with Hoang Huu Quynh, pp. 52–53.
10. Ibid.
11. *Nhan Dan*, "A General Revolution," pp. K9, K10.

Chapter 5

1. SRV Council of Ministers, "The Tasks, Powers, and Responsibilities of the District Election State Administration in the Sphere of Economic Management (Supplement)" (Excerpt from SRV Council of Ministers

Directive No. 33, Jan. 4, 1978), *Cong Tac Ke Hoach*, April 1978, pp. 7–16, JPRS, no. 71904, *Vietnam*, no. 2063 (Sept. 21, 1978): 26.

2. *Nhan Dan*, "Election of Members of People's Councils at the District, Village and Equivalent Levels," Feb. 3, 1979, p. 4, JPRS, no. 73106, *Vietnam*, no. 2109 (Mar. 29, 1979): 6; State Planning Commission, Institute of Planning and Management Research, "Draft of Study on Building the Districts into Agro-industrial Economic Units," *Cong Tac Ke Hoach*, Oct. 5, 1977, pp. 7–33, JPRS, no. 70445, *Vietnam*, no. 2002 (Jan. 9, 1978): 2–51.
3. "Election of Members of People's Councils . . . ," *Nhan Dan*, Feb. 3, 1979, pp. 6–7.
4. Nguyen Dinh Nam, "The District and the Inevitable Need to Build a District Agricultural and Industrial Economic Structure," *Nghien Cuu Kinh Te*, no. 2 (Apr. 1979): 13–19, JPRS, no. 74134, *Vietnam*, no. 2137 (Sept. 5, 1979): 3–10.
5. Author's interview with Pham Tien Khoan, financial expert employed by RVN and re-employed by communist regime, Palo Alto, Calif., Mar. 10, 1980.
6. Hanoi Municipal People's Committee, "Temporary Regulations Regarding the Missions and Authority of the Precinct People's Committees" (Promulgated in accordance with Decision No. 5417/QD-CQ-UB, Dec. 21, 1979, of the Hanoi Municipal People's Committee), *Hanoi Moi*, Dec. 28, 29, 1978, JPRS, no. 72984, *Vietnam*, no. 2105 (Mar. 13, 1979): 14.
7. Le Duc Tho, "Report," FBIS, *YB*, Jan. 31, 1977, vol. 4, no. 20, supp. 5, p. 7.
8. Ibid.
9. Ibid., pp. 8, 101.
10. Ibid., pp. 9, 11.
11. Ibid., pp. 11, 12.
12. Ibid., pp. 32–34.
13. Katsuichi Honda, "Che Do Thu Lai tai Viet Nam Ngay Nay" [Bureaucracy in present Vietnam], *Asahi Evening News*, n.d. (October 1977?), *NVTD*, JE, Nov. 11, 1977, p. 32.
14. Le Duc Tho, "Report," FBIS, *YB*, Feb. 3, 1977, vol. 4, no. 23, supp. 6, p. 57.
15. Nayan Chanda, "A New Type of Commissioner," *FEER*, Feb. 1, 1980, p. 14.
16. Ibid.

17. Ibid.
18. Le Duc Tho, quoted by Nguoi Xay Dung in "Discipline Must Be Strict and Rigid," *TCCS*, no. 12 (Dec. 1978): 65–68, JPRS, no. 73043, *Vietnam*, no. 2107 (Mar. 20, 1979): 70–71.
19. Nguoi Xay Dung, "Party Line: The Sense of Organization and Discipline," *Hoc Tap*, no. 1 (Jan. 1976): 71–74, JPRS, no. 66835, *Vietnam*, no. 1773 (Feb. 23, 1976): 49.
20. Nguoi Xay Dung, "Party Line Unity," *TCCS*, no. 9 (Sept. 9), 1977: 61–64; FBIS, *YB*, Sept. 30, 1977, p. K9.
21. Ibid.
22. Vu Trong Kien, "Several Experiences in Strengthening the Basic Organizations of the Party in the Countryside," *TCCS*, no. 8 (Aug.), 1978: 86–87; JPRS, no. 72158, *Vietnam*, no. 2074 (Nov. 1, 1978): 96.
23. Nguoi Xay Dung, "Discipline Must Be Strict and Rigid," *TCCS*, no. 12 (Dec.), 1978: 65–68, JPRS, no. 73043, *Vietnam*, no. 2107 (Mar. 20, 1979): 70–71.
24. Le Duan, "Political Report Before the National Assembly," *Vietnam Courier*, July 1976, p. 6.
25. Nguoi Xay Dung, "Waste," *TCCS*, no. 10 (Oct.), 1978, JPRS, no. 72546, *Vietnam*, no. 2088 (Jan. 2, 1979): 109.
26. *Nhan Dan*, "Nearly 3,000 Gondola Cars Need to be Used," Readers' Opinion Column, May 10, 1979, p. 3, JPRS, no. 73805, *Vietnam*, no. 2128 (July 5, 1970): 70.
27. Nguoi Xay Dung, "About Public Property, Private Property," *TCCS*, no. 6 (June), 1978, JPRS, no. 71733, *Vietnam*, no. 2057 (Aug. 29, 1978): 119.
28. *Lao Dong*, "Unusual Phenomena Which Must Be Overcome," Aug. 2, 1975, pp. 1–4, JPRS, no. 65915, *Vietnam*, no. 1717 (Oct. 17, 1975): 1–2.
29. Thuy Mai, "Tai sao tri thuc Viet Nam roi xa que huong?" [Why did intellectuals flee Vietnam?], *NVTD*, AE, Mar. 15, 1980, pp. 36–37.
30. Carlo Belihar, "Conspiracy of Silence on South Vietnam," *Il Giornale*, Jan. 10, 1976, p. 5, JPRS, no. 66733, *Vietnam*, no. 1766 (Feb. 4, 1976): 11. However, this judgment may have been premature. In July 1981 Nguyen Huu Tho became chairman of the Standing Committee of the National Assembly and concurrently a vice-chairman of the Council of State, while Huynh Tan Phat, in July 1982, also became a vice-chairman of the Council of State.
31. P. J. Honey, "Duoc Lam Vua," p. 261.

32. Katsuichi Honda, "Viet Nam moi va Chu Nghia Quan Lieu" [The new Vietnam and officialdom], *Asahi Shimbun*, n.d., *NVTD*, JE, Dec. 1977, pp. 24–28.
33. To Huu, "Let Us Endeavor to Bring the Best Possible Results to the Party Organization Congresses on Various Levels" (Speech at VCP Organization Cadres Conference, held Nov. 15, 1978, by the Organization Department of the Party Central Committee), *TCCS*, no. 1 (Jan.), 1979: 23–30, JPRS, no. 73308, *Vietnam*, no. 2114 (Apr. 25, 1979): 35.
34. Nguyen Van Tien, "VFF's Role in Election of People's Councils," *Dai Doan Ket*, May 1, 1977, Radio Ho Chi Minh City, DS, May 2, FBIS, *YB*, May 10, p. K3.
35. Hoang Quoc Viet, political report read at National United Front Congress, Radio Hanoi, DS, FBIS, *YB*, Jan. 31, 1977, p. K4.
36. The Hung, "The United Front—the Vietnamese Revolution's Source of Strength," *Vietnam Courier*, March 1977, p. 3.
37. VNA, "Details of VGFTU Political Report Given," in English, June 22, 1977, FBIS, *YB*, June 22, pp. K4–K5.
38. *Vietnam Pictorial*, Interview with Nguyen Van Linh on role of working class, July 1978, p. 11, JPRS, no. 72397, *Vietnam*, no. 2083 (Dec. 8, 1978): 5.
39. Ibid.
40. Robert Turner, *Vietnamese Communism: Its Origins and Development* (Stanford: Hoover Institution Press, 1975), p. 121.

Chapter 6

1. Pike, *History of Vietnamese Communism*, p. 82.
2. Hoang Van Chi, "Tu Thuc Dan den Cong San."
3. Nguyen Cong Hoan, "Van De Lao Tu tai Viet Nam" [Problems of imprisonment in Vietnam], *NVTD*, JE, June 1977, pp. 30–31.
4. Author's interview, May 1980, with Nguyen Tam, Vietnamese refugee who came to the United States in 1979, in Palo Alto, Calif.
5. Nguyen Dong Da, "A Horrible Massacre in Phu Yen," *NVTD*, AE, July 1979, pp. 14–51.
6. Nguyen Dong Da, "The Terrible Massacre of 373 Nationalist Vietnameses [*sic*] at Phu Yen Province, Vietnam," unpublished typescript (Los Angeles, July 4, 1979).
7. Guy Sacerdoti, "How Hanoi Cashes In," *FEER*, June 15, 1979, p. 24.

8. Paul Wilson, "How Vietnam Profits from Human Traffic," *FEER*, Jan. 12, 1979, p. 10.
9. *Asia Record*, July 1981, p. 60.
10. *Refugee Reports* 3, no. 13 (June 1982): 8. For detailed information on the refugees and their plight, see *Boat People: Today's Untouchables* (Tokyo: Asian Relations Center, Sophia University, 1978), a compilation in Vietnamese, French, and English; and Barry Wain, *The Refused: The Agony of the Indochinese Refugees* (New York: Simon and Schuster, 1981), a study by the diplomatic correspondent of the *Asian Wall Street Journal*.
11. Wilson, "How Vietnam Profits . . . ," pp. 10–11.
12. *Dan Quyen Magazine*, "Phong Van Can Bo Ha Noi Ty Nan Cong San" [Interview with a Hanoi cadre who fled the communist regime], Sept. 20, 1979, *NVTD*, AE, Nov. 15, 1979, p. 38.
13. *Time*, "Insurgents: A New Old Battle," July 4, 1977, p. 14.
14. Radio Hanoi, DS, May 16, 1980, FBIS, *YB*, May 20, p. K9.
15. Ibid., Mar. 17, 1980, FBIS, *YB*, Mar. 19, p. K11.
16. *Quan Doi Nhan Dan*, "Our Inevitably Victorious Strength," Editorial, Apr. 30, 1980, Radio Hanoi, DS, FBIS, *YB*, May 7, p. K11.
17. AFP Hong Kong, "Security Conference on Smuggling," in English, May 20, 1980, FBIS, *YB*, May 20, p. K10.
18. Radio Hanoi, DS, Jan. 24, 1981, FBIS, *YB*, Jan. 27, p. K14.
19. BBC, OS, in Vietnamese, Mar. 18, 1981.
20. AFP Hong Kong, in English, May 20, 1980, FBIS, *YB*, May 20, p. K10.
21. Jacques de Barrin, "Vietnam: Le socialisme à pas lents," *Le Monde*, Mar. 17, 1981, p. 5.
22. Radio Hanoi, DS, "Border Control Department[,] Subordinate to Ministry of Interior, Established by the Council of Ministers on January 25, 1980," news conference, Jan. 17, 1981, FBIS, *YB*, Jan. 22, p. K11.
23. Ministries of Defense and Interior, Joint Directive No. 01/CTLB, cited by Pham Hung, Greetings to Public Security Forces, Radio Hanoi, DS, Jan. 13, 1981, FBIS, Jan. 15, p. K1.
24. Barrin, "Vietnam: Le socialisme à pas lents," p. 5.
25. Radio Hanoi, DS, "Ho Chi Minh City Military Command Holds Conference on January 29, 1981," Jan. 20, 1981, FBIS, *YB*, Jan. 22, p. K11.
26. Radio Hanoi, DS, Feb. 3, 1981, FBIS, *YB*, Feb. 4, p. K5.
27. Tiziano Terzani, "Wir sterben und haben keinen Sarg" [We are dying and have no coffin], *Der Spiegel*, Aug. 24, 1981, pp. 110–18.
28. *Southeast Asia Record*, "Leaders of Underground Opposition Sentenced to Die, Others Imprisoned," via Reuters, July 13, 1979, p. 10.

29. Le Kim Ngan, "Su Sup Do Tat Yeu cua Cong San Viet Nam trong Thap Nien 80" [The necessary collapse of the Vietnamese communist regime in the 1980s], *NVTD*, AE, Aug. 15, 1979, p. 30.
30. Honey, "Duoc Lam Vua," p. 261.

Chapter 7

1. *Nhan Dan*, "A General Revolution," pp. K8–K10.
2. Le Duan, "Political Report of the VWP to the Fourth Party Congress, December 1976," *Vietnam Courier*, December 1976, p. 15.
3. Ibid.
4. Politburo Resolution No. 14-NQ/TW, January 11, 1979, on educational reform, full text, *Nhan Dan*, Aug. 25, 1979, JPRS, no. 74380, *Vietnam*, no. 2145 (Oct. 16, 1979): 29.
5. *Saigon Giai Phong*, "Continue Wiping Out Neo-Colonialist Literary and Artistic Vestiges," Editorial, July 16, 1976, Radio Ho Chi Minh City, DS, FBIS, *YB*, July 19, p. K15.
6. Nguyen Nguyen, "Completely Eliminate Neo-Colonialist Culture and Art in the Newly Liberated Areas," *Quan Doi Nhan Dan*, July 1975, pp. 29–36, JPRS, no. 66054, *Vietnam*, no. 1725 (Oct. 31, 1975): 141.
7. Lu Phuong, "Concerning the Sale and Circulation of Cultural Items Printed and Produced in Saigon Prior to April 30, 1975," *Saigon Giai Phong*, Jan. 21, 22, 1976, p. 3, JPRS, no. 66918, *Viet Nam*, no. 1778 (Mar. 8, 1976): 39.
8. Ibid., pp. 40–41.
9. *Hanoi Moi*, "Be on Guard Against Bad Cultural Works," Feb. 13, 1976, p. 2, JPRS, no. 67051, *Vietnam*, no. 1788 (Mar. 30, 1976): 1–2.
10. Phong Vien, "Two Often Contagious Diseases," *Hanoi Moi*, Feb. 15, 1976, p. 4, JPRS, no. 67051, *Vietnam*, no. 1788 (Mar. 30, 1976): 3.
11. N. N. [author's initials], "From Now Until the End of 1978, Strongly Attack and Wipe Out the Traces of Neo-Colonialist Culture," *Tin Sang*, Mar. 7, 1978, pp. 1–8, JPRS, no. 71309, *Vietnam*, no. 2038 (June 16, 1978): 66.
12. Radio Hanoi, DS, "Campaign to Eliminate Enemy Culture in Progress," May 16, 1981, FBIS, *YB*, May 20, p. K8.
13. Radio Hanoi, DS, May 17, 1981, FBIS, *YB*, May 20, pp. K8–K9.
14. Radio Hanoi, DS, "Ho Chi Minh City Raids," May 24, 1981, FBIS, *YB*, May 28, p. K9.

15. *Nhan Dan*, "City Campaign Under Way Against Decadent Culture: Sentences in Hanoi," Radio Hanoi, DS, May 27, 1981, FBIS, *YB*, May 28, p. K8.
16. Nguyen Cong Hoan, "Van De Nhan Quyen tai Vietnam" [Human rights problems in Vietnam] (Statement at U.S. House Subcommittee on International Organizations, on human rights, July 26, 1977), *NVTD*, AE, Aug. 1977, p. 18.
17. Tran Uu Tu [reader], "We Request the Administration to Simplify Travel Formalities," *Saigon Giai Phong*, Readers' Opinions Column, Nov. 29, 1975, p. 2, JPRS, no. 66671, *Vietnam*, no. 1762 (Jan. 26, 1976): 20.
18. Le Kim Ngan, "Toi Ac Huy Diet Quyen Lam Nguoi cua Cong San Viet Nam" [Crimes of destruction of human rights by the VCP), *NVTD*, AE, Jan. 15, 1980, p. 24.
19. Ibid., p. 25.
20. Le Kim Ngan, "Cai Tao Tu Tuong" [Thought reform], *NVTD*, JE, June 1977, p. 27.
21. Ibid., p. 24.
22. Politburo Resolution No. 14-NQ/TW, p. 28.
23. L.T.–P.T., "Owners of Private Schools Enthusiastically Respond to Policy of Turning Private into Public Schools," *Saigon Giai Phong*, Oct. 10, 1975, pp. 1–4, JPRS, no. 66543, *Vietnam*, no. 1754 (Jan. 9, 1976): 60.
24. Ibid.
25. Politburo Resolution No. 14-NQ/TW, p. 28.
26. Ibid., pp. 32–33.
27. Ibid., pp. 39–40.
28. Ibid., pp. 40–42.
29. Ibid., p. 43.
30. Ibid., pp. 44–45.
31. Author's interview with Trung Ho, refugee teacher, Redwood City, Calif., July 14, 1981.

Chapter 8

1. Projected from official church figures of 2.49 million, or 6.5 percent of the total population, in 1970. See Rev. Bui Duc Sinh, "Lich Su Giao Hoi Viet Nam," *Lien Lac*, June 29, 1981, pp. 49–50.

2. Tran Huu Tien, "The Socialist Revolution and Freedom of Religion," *TCCS*, no. 6 (June 1977): 60–63, 68, FBIS, *YB*, June 24, p. K5.
3. Quoted in Pike, *History of Vietnamese Communism*, p. 108.
4. Tran Huu Tien, "The Socialist Revolution and Freedom of Religion," p. K5.
5. SRV Council of Ministers, Resolution No. 297, Nov. 11, 1977, "On Some Policies Concerning Religion," *Chinh Nghia*, Dec. 20, 1977, p. 6, JPRS, no. 70656, *Vietnam*, no. 2012 (Feb. 17, 1978): 6.
6. *Saigon Giai Phong*, Aug. 17, 1975, p. 4; JPRS, no. 66029, *Vietnam*, no. 1722 (Oct. 29, 1975): 59.
7. SRV Council of Ministers, Resolution No. 297, p. 8.
8. Nguyen Cong Hoan, "Human Rights Problems in Vietnam," p. 19.
9. Anh Phong, "Catholicism in Vietnam and Reintegration into the National Community," *Vietnam Courier*, Nov. 1977, p. 24.
10. Ibid., p. 28.
11. Contrast the misleading account in Tiziano Terzani, *Giai Phong* (New York: St. Martin's Press, 1976), p. 260. Refugees from Vietnam who witnessed the event have told the author that it was the left-wing priests (Fathers Phan Khac Tu, Nguyen Ngoc Lan, and Chan Tin) who led the demonstration for expelling Le Maître.
12. These details are from a communist source, Anh Phong, "Catholicism in Vietnam . . . ," p. 29.
13. Author's interview with Nguyen Tieu, Catholic refugee who came to the United States in early 1981. Tieu witnessed the event. The interview was held in Hayward, Calif., in Oct. 1981.
14. Patrice Barrat, "Un prêtre Vietnamien en cours de reeducation parle," *Le Matin*, July 25, 1979, as reprinted in *Lien Lac*, Aug. 1979, pp. 9–11.
15. *Le Matin*'s prefatory note states that the interview "was conducted directly in French" (ibid., p. 9).
16. VNA, "Ho Chi Minh City Bishop on Catholics' Position, Role," in English, June 10, 1978 (Interview with Archbishop Nguyen Van Binh by Emilio Bargi Amada, correspondent of *L'Unità*), JPRS, no. 71376, *Vietnam*, no. 2041 (June 28, 1978): 53.
17. Ibid., p. 55.
18. Janos Radvanyi, *Delusion and Reality* (South Bend, Ind.: Gateway Editions, 1978), p. 22.
19. Ibid.
20. Archbishop Philippo Nguyen Kim Dien, "Where is Freedom? Where Are Civil Rights?" *NVTD*, JE, Oct. 1977, p. 41.

21. André Tong, "Life in Communist Vietnam," *Est & Ouest*, Dec. 1, 1977, pp. 8–9, JPRS, no. 70463, *Vietnam*, no. 2003, Jan. 11, 1978, p. 19.
22. Nayan Chanda, "Vietnam's Parish of Resistance," *FEER*, Feb. 27, 1976, p. 12.
23. *Su That*, "Giao Hoi Mien Bac" [Catholicism in North Vietnam], no. 2, NVTD, JE, Dec. 1976, p. 33; and author's interview with Nhan Luu, now living in San Jose, Calif., who had been involved before 1975 with the TV Education Program of the Jesuit Order at its Alexandre de Rhodes Center, Yen Do Street, Saigon (Luu fled Vietnam in 1979).
24. Personal letter from a refugee postulant, *Lien Lac*, Sept. 1981, pp. 1–2.
25. Anh Phong, "Catholicism in Vietnam . . . ," p. 26.
26. *Su That*, "Catholicism in North Vietnam," p. 33. See also Rev. Bui Duc Sinh, "Lich Su Giao Hoi Vietnam" [The history of the Catholic Church in Vietnam], *Lien Lac*, Jan. 27, 1981, pp. 46–47.
27. Pham Quang Phuoc, "Participate in the Discussions of Young and Old: The First Step. Young Catholic Priests Urged to Keep Up with Times," *Chinh Nghia*, Nov. 6, 1975, p. 3, JPRS, no. 66613, *Vietnam*, no. 1758 (Jan. 19, 1976): 7.
28. Ibid.
29. Author's interview with Fr. Nguyen An Ninh, Aug. 1980, in Orange County, Calif.
30. Letter dated Mar. 3, 1976, from a monk in Saigon.
31. Thich Tri Thu, open letter to chairmen of PRG, Presidium of NFL Central Committee, and Ho Chi Minh City Military Management Committee, Nov. 28, 1975 (distributed Nov. 29 by Executive Council, UBCVN, Ho Chi Minh City, to all executive committees of local UBCVN chapters and to all monasteries, temples, and Buddhist institutes), English translation, p. 1. Available, with photocopy of original, from Vietnamese Buddhist Peace Delegation, 69 boulevard Desgranges, 92330 Sceaux, France.
32. Ibid., p. 2.
33. Radio Ho Chi Minh City, DS, Jan. 23, 1977, FBIS, *YB*, Jan. 27, p. K2.
34. Author's interview, October 1981, with Nguyen Tieu, a refugee from Vietnam, in Hayward, Calif. In April 1977 Tieu resided next to the An Quang Pagoda.
35. *New Straits Times*, "Religious Groups Plan Resistance Movement," July 14, 1979, p. 4 (based on interview with Thich Thien Quang in Tanjung Pinang, Indonesia, July 13, 1979), JPRS, no. 74034, *Vietnam*, no. 2134 (Aug. 17, 1979): 10.

36. *Courier Mail*, via AFP and Reuters, Nov. 11, 1977, p. 6, JPRS, no. 70410, *Vietnam*, no. 2001, Jan. 4, 1978, p. 65.
37. K. T. [author's initials], "Production Labor Movement Developed Among Buddhist Clergy," *Tin Sang*, Apr. 12, 1978, p. 1, JPRS, no. 71391, *Vietnam*, no. 2042 (June 30, 1978): 42.
38. *New Straits Times*, "Religious Groups Plan Resistance Movement," p. 10.
39. Ibid.
40. *Quan Doi Nhan Dan*, "Maintain Political Security," Editorial, Feb. 27, 1980, pp. 1, 4, FBIS, *YB*, May 20, p. K5.
41. VNA, "Nguyen Huu Tho Meets with Superior Bonze Thich Tin Thu," in English, May 20, 1980, FBIS, *YB*, p. K10. See also Radio Hanoi, DS, Apr. 10, 1980, FBIS, *YB*, Apr. 11, p. K8.
42. *Le Monde*, Feb. 6, 1981, FBIS, *YB*, Feb. 13, p. K4.
43. Chanda, "Vietnam's Parish of Resistance," p. 12.
44. "Military Unit Works with the Hoa Hao Sect," Radio Hanoi, DS, Sept. 21, 1976, FBIS, *YB*, Sept. 21, p. K12.
45. *Duoc Tu Bi*, new edition no. 1 [n.d.]: 2–3, 8–11; and no. 2 (June 15, 1981): 21–22.
46. *Duoc Tu Bi*, no. 1 (n.d.): 9.
47. Author's interview, Aug. 1980, with Huynh An, a refugee from Vietnam who came to the United States that year, in Los Angeles.
48. Radvanyi, *Delusion and Reality*, p. 22.

Chapter 9

1. *Saigon Giai Phong*, "Pull Husbands, Children and Younger Brothers Back onto the Right Path," Today's Topic Column, June 13, 1975, FBIS, *YB*, June 16, pp. L4–L5.
2. Radio Saigon, DS, May 3, 1975, FBIS, *YB*, May 5, p. L10.
3. Ibid., May 7, 1975, FBIS, *YB*, May 8, p. L13.
4. Ibid., FBIS, *YB*, May 9, pp. L3–L4.
5. Radio Saigon, DS, May 23, 1975, FBIS, *YB*, May 27, p. L2.
6. Ibid.
7. Radio Saigon, DS, June 10, 1975, FBIS, *YB*, June 11, p. L1.
8. Ibid., p. L2.
9. Radio Saigon, DS, June 11, 1975, FBIS, *YB*, June 16, p. L3.

10. Ibid., June 20, 1975, FBIS, *YB*, June 23, pp. L2–L4.
11. Ibid., pp. L4, L5. A communiqué was later issued exempting President Duong Van Minh and Prime Minister Vu Van Mau from undergoing thought reform in a re-education camp. Instead, they were allowed to join leading educators and intellectuals at a fourteen-month Marxist study class in Saigon. Senior officials of the Ministry of Education received the same exemption because the Communists did not want to close down the entire educational system.
12. Ibid., p. L5.
13. Terzani, "Wir sterben und haben keinen Sarg," p. 117.
14. Author's interview, Oct. 1980, with Dr. Tran Xuan Ninh, former professor of Saigon Medical School, in Redwood City, Calif.
15. Nguyen Cong Hoan, "Problems of Imprisonment in Vietnam," p. 32.
16. Ibid.
17. *Saigon Giai Phong*, "Responding to the Policy of the Revolution: What Must Families with Members Undergoing Reform Study Do To Request Permission for Their Return for Family Reunion," Aug. 24, 1975, p. 1, JPRS, no. 66054, *Vietnam*, no. 1725 (Oct. 31, 1975): 155.
18. Le Kim Ngan, "Hoc Tap Cai Tao" [Thought reforms], *NVTD*, JE, Oct. 1977, pp. 24–25.
19. PRG, Policy Statement No. 02/CS/76, May 25, 1976, signed by [PRG] President Huynh Tan Phat, Radio Saigon, DS, June 9, 1976, FBIS, *YB*, June 10, pp. L1–L5.
20. Ibid., pp. L3, L4.
21. Ibid., p. L5.
22. Ibid., pp. L4, L5.
23. Vo Van Sung [Vietnamese ambassador to France], Statement at press conference in Paris, VNA, in English, Feb. 3, 1977, FBIS, *YB*, Feb. 4, p. K1.
24. *Nhan Dan*, "The Barbarous Clique Speaks of Human Rights," Jan. 29, 1977, Radio Hanoi, DS, Jan. 29, FBIS, *YB*, Feb. 2, p. K1.
25. Nguyen Cong Hoan, "Problems of Imprisonment in Vietnam," p. 51.
26. Ibid.
27. Amnesty International, *Report of an Amnesty International Mission to the Socialist Republic of Vietnam, 10–21 December 1979, Including Memoranda Exchanged Between the Government and Amnesty International* (London and New York: Amnesty International Publications, 1981), p. 3 (hereafter cited as Amnesty International, *Report*).
28. Terzani, "Wir sterben und haben keinen Sarg," p. 117.

29. Amnesty International, *Report*, p. 26.
30. Phu Yen [pseud.], "Hien co bao nhieu nguoi Viet Nam bi Cong San giam cam?" [How many Vietnamese are there being detained by the Communists?], *Viet Nam*, Aug. 1981, pp. 17–19 (hereafter cited as Phu Yen).
31. Ibid., p. 18.
32. U.S. Embassy, Bangkok, Airgram, Pol./Ref. Sections to U.S. Department of State, Dec. 21, 1981, unclassified, ref. no. A-152 (hereafter cited as Bangkok A-152), p. 2.
33. Ibid.
34. Bangkok A-152 and U.S. Embassy, Bangkok, Airgram, Pol./Ref. Sections to U.S. Department of State, Jan. 25, 1982, unclassified, ref. no. A-004 (hereafter cited as Bangkok A-004). Uniform reports of two pages each on fourteen camps are enclosed with these two documents as follows. Bangkok A-152: Ben Gia, Gia Rai Z-30, Gia Trung, Ham Tan Z-30D, Nam Ha, Thanh Phong, Xuyen Moc, Nghe Tinh, and Phuoc Long. Bangkok A-004: Tan Hiep (Suoi Mau), Vuon Dao, Con Cat, Vinh Quang, and Cay Cay (Bau Co).
35. Phu Yen, pp. 19, 41.
36. Nguyen Cong Hoan, "Problems of Imprisonment in Vietnam," p. 31.
37. Ibid.
38. Data on camp populations from Bankok A-152 and A-004.
39. Nguyen Cong Hoan, "Problems of Imprisonment in Vietnam," p. 31.
40. See, for instance, Tran Huynh Chau, *Nhung nam Cai Tao o Bac Viet* [Years of thought reform in North Vietnam] (Culver City, Calif.: Kim An Quan, 1981), p. 90.
41. Phu Yen, p. 18.
42. Ibid.
43. Ibid.
44. Ibid.
45. Bangkok A-004, enclosure p. 9.
46. Douglas Pike, "Social Reconstruction in Vietnam" (Washington, D.C.: the author, January 1977).
47. Bangkok A-004, enclosure p. 40.

Chapter 10

1. Terzani, "Wir sterben und haben keinen Sarg," p. 118.
2. Ibid., pp. 117–118.

3. Besides the showcase camp of Ha Tay, the Amnesty International delegation visited Nam Ha and Ham Tan camps and Chi Hoa Prison in Ho Chi Minh City (Amnesty International, *Report*, p. i). John P. Wallach of the *San Francisco Examiner*'s Washington bureau, drawing on Bangkok A-152 and A-004, stated in that newspaper (Mar. 7, 1982, p. A22) that there was "no indication of any visit by the International Red Cross or Amnesty International" to any of the camps, but he appears to have exaggerated. Some of the prisoners at Ham Tan and Nam Ha did at least hear of the visits; so much is clear from the accounts in Bangkok A-152, quoted by Wallach in *San Francisco Examiner*, Mar. 28, 1982, p. B8. Wallach also committed the error, in his Mar. 7 report, of referring to the camps named in Bangkok A-152 and A-004 as "the 14 known camps," although Bangkok A-152 (p. 2) states that refugees from over 100 different camps had been interviewed.
4. Nguyen Cong Hoan, "Problems of Imprisonment in Vietnam," pp. 31, 32.
5. Ibid., p. 51.
6. Ibid., p. 31.
7. Le Kim Ngan, "Hoc Tap Cai Tao" [Thought reform], *NVTD*, JE, Sept. 1977, p. 24. The policy that underlies these practices is expounded in Nguyen Ngoc Giao, "Continue to Manage, Educate, and Reform Well the People Who Were Previously in the Enemy's Military Organization," *Quan Doi Nhan Dan*, no. 6 (June 1975): 49–53, JPRS, no. 65795, *Vietnam*, no. 1709 (Sept. 30, 1975): 39.
8. Nguyen Cong Hoan, "Problems of Imprisonment in Vietnam," p. 31.
9. Ibid.
10. Bangkok A-004, enclosure p. 7.
11. Ibid., enclosure p. 1.
12. Bangkok A-152, enclosure p. 3.
13. Nguyen Cong Hoan, "Problems of Imprisonment in Vietnam," p. 31.
14. Le Kim Ngan, "Thought Reform," p. 25.
15. Ibid., p. 26.
16. Bangkok A-004, enclosure p. 5.
17. Bangkok A-152, enclosure p. 5.
18. Bangkok A-004, enclosure p. 9.
19. Ibid.
20. Bangkok A-152, enclosure p. 3.
21. Ibid., enclosure p. 17.
22. Ibid., enclosure p. 8.

23. Ibid., enclosure p. 14.
24. Bangkok A-004, enclosure p. 3.
25. Author's interview with Hoang Xuan Tuu's son, Sacramento, Calif., Feb. 1981.
26. Author's interview with Tran The Min's daughter, San Jose, Calif., Mar. 1981.
27. Terzani, "Wir sterben und haben keinen Sarg," p. 118.
28. Author's interview with Nguyen Tieu, a former member of Father Quynh's parish in Binh An Thuong, Eighth Precinct, Saigon. Tieu fled Vietnam in 1980 and now lives in Santa Barbara; the interview was held in Hayward, Calif., in Oct. 1981.
29. Information from Mrs. Mai Van An, who fled Vietnam with her three daughters in 1979 and now lives in San Francisco.
30. Thich Tam Quan, "The Bird Has Flown Away," *Phat Giao Viet Nam Monthly Magazine*, Dec. 1979, p. 23.
31. Ibid., p. 21.
32. Che Viet Tan, "Population Growth, Labor Deployment and Population Redistribution," *Vietnam Courier*, Mar. 1977, p. 10.
33. Pham Anh Hai, "Nhan Dan Mien Nam o cac Vung Kinh Te Moi" [The South Vietnamese people in the New Economic Zones], *NVTD*, JE, Sept. 1977, p. 31.
34. Nguyen Cong Hoan, "Human Rights Problems in Vietnam," p. 16.
35. Pham Anh Hai, "The South Vietnamese People in the New Economic Zones," p. 30.
36. Ibid., p. 31.
37. Terzani, "Wir sterben und haben keinen Sarg," p. 122.
38. Author's interview with Vu Van An, financial expert (see Chapter 1, Note 12).
39. Ibid.
40. See Note 3, this chapter.
41. Amnesty International, *Report*, pp. 17–19.
42. Ibid., pp. 36–37.
43. Ibid., p. 17.
44. Ibid., p. 23.
45. Nguyen Chi Thien, "From Ape to Man," in English, from *Muoi Bai Nguc Ca* [Ten prison songs], broadsheet on reverse of "Tien Vong Tu-Day Vuc" [A cry from the abyss], program for "an evening of poetry and songs" held by the Vietnamese Student Association, University of

California at Berkeley, May 1, 1981. See also *Tieng Vong Tu Day Vuc*, a 160-page collection of Thien's poems, in Vietnamese, that identifies him only as "a northern writer," and was published jointly in 1980 by the Committee of Struggle for Political Prisoners in Vietnam, the International Committee for the Protection of Intellectuals' Integrity, and *Thoi Tap Magazine*, at 7706 Random Run Lane, Falls Church, Va.

Chapter 11

1. Leo Goodstadt, "Viet-Soviet Ties," *FEER*, Nov. 21, 1975, p. 40.
2. Derek Davies, "Carter's Neglect, Moscow's Victories," *FEER*, Feb. 2, 1979, p. 17.
3. Ibid.
4. Ibid.
5. Nayan Chanda, "A Prophecy Self-Fulfilled," *FEER*, June 1, 1979, p. 20.
6. Miles Hanley, "Moscow Terms to Asia," *FEER*, May 25, 1979, p. 10.
7. CBS TV News, Nov. 12, 1980.
8. Chanda, "A Prophecy Self-Fulfilled," p. 19.
9. Quoted in Frank Cranston [defense and aviation correspondent], "West's Military Aircraft Being Caught," *Canberra Times*, Nov. 7, 1980, p. 9.
10. James Laurie [ABC correspondent], Interview with Premier Pham Van Dong, April 4, 1979, *FEER*, May 18, 1979, p. 13.
11. Quoted in P. J. Honey, "A New Light on Vietnam: Hoang Van Hoan's Revelations," *CNA*, Oct. 26, 1979, p. 4.
12. Ibid.
13. Vo Van Sung [Vietnamese ambassador to France] (Press Conference in Paris, Feb. 2, 1977), VNA, in English, Feb. 4, FBIS, *YB*, Feb. 4, p. K1.
14. *Vietnam Courier, Those Who Leave: The "Problem of Vietnamese Refugees,"* in English (Hanoi: *Vietnam Courier*, 1979), p. 28.
15. Nayan Chanda, "Laying the MIA Issue to Rest," *FEER*, Mar. 11, 1977, p. 11.
16. Stephen Barber, "The Team for Hanoi," *FEER*, Mar. 18, 1977, p. 28.
17. Edith Lenart, "Hanoi's Terms for Détente," *FEER*, May 20, 1977, p. 16; Stephen Barber, "Negotiations, Slowly, Slowly," *FEER*, Jan. 6, 1978, p. 16; Derek Davies, "Caught in History's Vice," *FEER*, Dec. 25, 1981, p. 19.
18. "Japanese Businessmen on SRV Leaders' Attitude Toward U.S.,"

KYDO Tokyo, May 29, 1978, JPRS, no. 71345, *Vietnam*, no. 2039 (June 23, 1978): 20.

19. *FEER*, Intelligence Column, May 19, 1978, p. 5.
20. Lenart, "Hanoi's Terms for Détente," p. 17 (s.v. "Stephen Barber Adds from Washington").
21. Seymour Hersh, "Nguyen Co Thach: Normalization Agreed to Last Year, but U.S. Backed Out," *Southeast Asia Record*, via Reuters, Aug. 3, 1979, p. 7.
22. James Laurie, Interview with Premier Pham Van Dong, April 14, 1979, *FEER*, May 18, p. 13.
23. See, for instance, Don Luce, "Boat People: U.S. Can Best Help by Recognizing Complicity," *Southeast Asia Record*, week of Aug. 31–Sept. 6, 1979, pp. 11–12; and Michael Morrow, "Vietnam's Embargoed Economy: In the U.S. Interest?" *Southeast Asia Record*, week of Sept. 7–13, 1979, p. 11.
24. Luce, "Boat People . . . ," p. 11.
25. *Vietnam Courier, Those Who Leave*, pp. 28–29.
26. François Nivolon, "Vietnam on the Aid Trail," *FEER*, Dec. 9, 1977, p. 39.
27. Ibid.
28. François Nivolon, "Paris Goes Its Own Way," *FEER*, Jan. 22, 1981, p. 16.
29. Patrice de Beer, "New Port in a Storm," *FEER*, Apr. 23, 1982, p. 44.
30. Nayan Chanda, "Vietnam Looks to Trade Prospects," *FEER*, Jan. 6, 1978, p. 67.
31. Turner, *Vietnamese Communism*, p. 35.
32. Ibid., p. 76.
33. Quoted in P. J. Honey, "Frontier War with Cambodia," *CNA*, Mar. 17, 1978, p. 2.
34. Honey, "Duoc Lam Vua," p. 261.
35. Honey, "Frontier War with Cambodia," p. 4.
36. Nayan Chanda, "A Secret of Former Friends," *FEER*, June 15, 1979, p. 38.
37. David Bonevia, "China Decides to Sit This One Out," *FEER*, May 25, 1979, p. 10; Nayan Chanda, "A Prophecy Self-Fulfilled," *FEER*, June 1, 1979, p. 19.
38. Nayan Chanda, "Protestations of Peace, Undertones of War," *FEER*, May 4, 1979, p. 8.

39. Ibid.
40. Nayan Chanda, "Last Chance for the Khmer Rouge," Interview with Vice-Minister Han Nianlong, *FEER*, Apr. 18, 1980, p. 12.

Chapter 12

1. Le Duan, *Outline*, p. 24.
2. Nayan Chanda, "Hanoi Blows Cooler," *FEER*, Mar. 5, 1976, p. 13.
3. Ibid.
4. P. J. Honey, "Vietnam's Dispute with China: Its Causes and Effects," *CNA*, Sept. 15, 1978, p. 6. See also Nayan Chanda, "Vietnam's Dove Flies Home," *FEER*, July 30, 1976, p. 12.
5. SRV Vice-Premier and Foreign Minister Nguyen Duy Trinh, quoted in Nayan Chanda, "Asia Puzzles over the Faceless Men," *FEER*, Jan. 14, 1977, p. 17.
6. John Everingham, "The Best of Neighbors," *FEER*, Feb. 27, 1976, p. 13.
7. Quoted in Nayan Chanda, "Hanoi: Turning Words into Deeds," *FEER*, Aug. 6, 1976, p. 28.
8. Rodney Tasker, "A Courteous Rebuff for Dong's Diplomacy," *FEER*, Sept. 29, 1978.
9. The refugee, a teacher, now lives in San Jose, Calif. While escaping from Vietnam by sea in December 1979, he landed on the Thai coast, at night. A few hours later, another boat came in at the same place; it was full of Vietnamese men, who landed. Early next morning the teacher went around to look for them, but they had all disappeared. After being admitted to a camp in Thailand, he talked with other refugees about the incident. They told him the men must have been VCP agents. Infiltration of such agents into Thailand has been attested to by Nguyen Van Thiep, a PAVN soldier captured by the Khmer Rouge (*Southeast Asia Record*, Sept. 1979, p. 6). For official Thai fears on the subject, see John McBeth, "A Perilously Short Fuse," *FEER*, June 15, 1979, p. 26.
10. Richard Nations, "The Makings of Friendships," *FEER*, Sept. 28, 1978, p. 28.
11. VOA, in Vietnamese, June 13, 1980.
12. John McBeth, "Waving a Mailed Fist at ASEAN," *FEER*, July 4, 1980, pp. 14–16.
13. VOA, in Vietnamese, Mar. 19, 1981.

14. Nayan Chanda, "New Shots in the Refugee War," *FEER*, July 4, 1980, p. 15.
15. Anthony Goodman, "General Assembly Vote on Indochina Encouraging for ASEAN," *Southeast Asia Record*, Nov. 16, 1979, p. 2.
16. *Vietnam Hai Ngoai*, Special News Page, Dec. 1, 1981, p. 4.
17. David Jenkins, "Second Thoughts on Kuantan," *FEER*, Oct. 20, 1980, p. 27.
18. Rodney Tasker, "Behind the Friendly Shadow," (Interview with Sinna Thanby Rajaratnam), *FEER*, Sept. 15, 1976, p. 21.
19. Ibid.
20. Information from Singapore Trade Office, Los Angeles World Trade Center, Oct. 18, 1982.
21. *U.S. News & World Report*, "Interview: Lee Kuan Yew of Singapore," reprinted in *San Francisco Chronicle*, Feb. 10, 1982, p. F3.
22. Nayan Chanda, "Hanoi's Show of Friendship," *FEER*, Jan. 21, 1977, p. 14.
23. K. Das, "Hanoi's New War of Words," *FEER*, Feb. 4, 1977, p. 10.
24. Jusuf Wanandi, "An Indonesian View," *FEER*, May 15, 1981, p. 20.
25. Derek Davies, "Time to Encourage the Vietnamese Titoists," *FEER*, July 17, 1981, p. 31.
26. Rodney Tasker, "Zone of Peace: Vietnam's Variation on Theme," *FEER*, Aug. 4, 1978, p. 9.
27. K. Das, "Slowly Settling Differences," *FEER*, Aug. 4, 1978, p. 9.
28. Nayan Chanda, "Putting the Heat on ASEAN," *FEER*, Jan. 18, 1980, p. 14.
29. Ibid.
30. Susumu Awanohara, "Opening for Business in South Vietnam," *FEER*, Jan. 2, 1976, p. 36.
31. Susumu Awanohara, "The Rush for Vietnam's Oil," *FEER*, Feb. 20, 1976, pp. 36–37.
32. Ibid., p. 37.
33. "Japan Witholds Economic Aid, Fears Appearing to Side with Vietnam," *Southeast Asia Record*, via Reuters, Oct. 12, 1978, p. 7.
34. James Laurie [ABC correspondent], "Seeking the West's Goodwill," *FEER*, May 18, 1979, p. 14.
35. P. J. Honey, "Vietnam's New Policies in Perspective," *CNA*, Dec. 15, 1978, p. 7.

Glossary

Vietnamese-English

bep	cook; kitchen
Biet Kich	members of special forces
cai tao	thought reform or re-education
cai tao tu tuong	thought; thought reform
Can Lao Nhan Vi Dang	Personalist Labor Party
Chien Dich Dong Khoi	Concerted Uprising Campaign
Chieu Hoi	Open Arms [Program]
Dai Viet Quoc Dan Dang	Greater Vietnam Nationalist Party
Dan Chu	Democracy [Party]
Dang Lao Dong Vietnam	Vietnam Workers Party
Dan Xa Dang	Social Democratic Party
di ban chinh thuc	leaving in a semiofficial way
di chui	escape
di dang ky chinh thuc	leaving by means of official registration
Doan Thieu Nhi Quang Khan Do	Red Scarf Children's Group
doi tuong doan	target of the Youth League

dong	piaster (French colonial and RVN usage)
hoc tap	education; study
hoi chanh	rallier; defector
khu vuc	area; sector
luong	tael
Kim Thanh	a trademark of Vietnamese gold
mua bai	purchase of a loading place (escape with permission of local authorities after payment of a certain amount of U.S. dollars or gold)
piaster	*see* dong
Quoc Dan Dang Vietnam	Vietnam Nationalist Party
thanh phan tap trung	blacklisted persons; former re-education camp detainees
thich	religious title similar to "reverend"
tieu to	subcell
to dan pho	neighborhood solidarity cell
tong trai	general camp
Viet Cong	Vietnamese Communist(s)
Vietnam Cong San	Vietnamese communism
xa hoi chu nghia	socialism
xao het cho noi	lying too much to tell the difference

English-Vietnamese

district	quan; huyen
front organization	to chuc ngoai vi
golden music	nhac vang
manager system	che do thu truong
party caucus	bo phan dang
party cell	to dang
people's committee	uy ban hanh chanh

people's council	hoi dong nhan dan
people's organs of control	uy ban kiem tra nhan dan
precinct	quan
procurator	cong to uy vien
production team	toan san xuat
re-education camp	trai hoc tap; trai cai tao
sector	khu vuc
self-criticism	tu kiem
three revolutions, doctrine of	ba cuoc hay dong thac cach mang; ly thuyet
ward	phuong
work points	diem; can cu tren ngay lam viec
Youth League	Doan Thanh Nien

Bibliography

A. Principal Works Cited

Amnesty International. *Report of an Amnesty International Mission to the Socialist Republic of Vietnam, 10–21 December, 1979, Including Memoranda Exchanged Between the Government and Amnesty International.* London and New York: Amnesty International Publications, 1981.

Anh Phong, "Catholicism in Vietnam and Reintegration into the National Community." *Vietnam Courier*, November 1977.

Barrin, Jacques de. "Vietnam: Le socialisme à pas lents." *Le Monde*, March 17, 1981, p. 5.

Cameron, W. Allan. *Indochina: Prospects After the End.* Washington, D.C.: American Enterprise Institute for Public Policy Research, 1976.

Canh, Nguyen Van, *see* Nguyen Van Canh

Chanda, Nayan. "Speeding Towards Reunification." *Far Eastern Economic Review*, December 5, 1975, p. 12.

———. "Vietnam's Parish of Resistance." *Far Eastern Economic Review*, February 27, 1976, p. 12.

———. "Hanoi Blows Cooler." *Far Eastern Economic Review*, March 5, 1976, p. 13.

———. "Towards Socialism—on the Double." *Far Eastern Economic Review*, July 9, 1976, p. 10.

———. "A Prophecy Self-Fulfilled." *Far Eastern Economic Review*, June 1, 1977, p. 20.

———. "Protestations of Peace, Undertones of War." *Far Eastern Economic Review*, May 4, 1979, p. 9.

———. "Putting the Heat on ASEAN." *Far Eastern Economic Review*, January 18, 1980, p. 14.

———. "Asia Puzzles over the Faceless Men." *Far Eastern Economic Review*, January 14, 1981, p. 16.

Chi, Hoang Van, *see* Hoang Van Chi

Davies, Derek. "Cartėr's Neglect, Moscow's Victories." *Far Eastern Economic Review*, February 2, 1979, p. 17.

Dien, Tran, *see* Tran Dien

Duan, Le, *see* Le Duan

Dung, Van Tien, *see* Van Tien Dung

Hai, Pham Anh, *see* Pham Anh Hai

Hanley, Miles. "Moscow Turns to Asia." *Far Eastern Economic Review*, May 25, 1979, p. 10.

Hoan, Nguyen Cong, *see* Nguyen Cong Hoan

Hoang Van Chi. *Tu Thuc Dan Den Cong San* [From colonialism to communism]. Translated from English into Vietnamese by Mac Dinh. San Jose, Calif.: Nguoi Viet Tu Do, 1980.

Honey, P. J. "Frontier War with Cambodia." *China News Analysis*, March 17, 1978, pp. 2, 4.

———. "Duoc Lam Vua" [Winner will be king]. *Asian Affairs* 3, pt. 3 (October 1978): 264.

———. "A New Light on Vietnam: Hoang Van Hoan's Revelations." *China News Analysis*, October 26, 1979, p. 4.

Hung, Nguyen Tien, *see* Nguyen Tien Hung

Huu, To, *see* To Huu

Khoa, Vu Van, *see* Tran Dien and Vu Van Khoa

Laurie, James. "Interview with Premier Pham Van Dong, April 4, 1979." *Far Eastern Economic Review*, May 18, 1979, p. 13.

Le Duan. *On the Socialist Revolution in Vietnam*. Hanoi: Foreign Language Publishing House, 1965.

———. "Outline of the Draft Political Report of the Central Committee of the Vietnam Workers Party to the Fourth Party Congress." *Vietnam Courier*, December 1976.

Le Duc Tho. "Report Summarizing Party Building Work and the Amended

Party Charter." Read at Fourth Party Congress, Hanoi, December 1976. *Nhan Dan*, December 20–23, pp. 2–6, FBIS, *YB*, January 31, 1977, vol. 4, supp. 5, and ibid., February 3, 1977, vol. 4, supp. 6.

Le Kim Ngan. "Hoc Tap Cai Tao" [Thought reform]. *Nguoi Viet Tu Do*, Japanese Edition, September 1977, p. 24.

———. "Toi Ac Huy Diet Quyen Lam Nguoi cua Cong San Viet Nam" [Crimes of destruction of human rights by the Vietnamese Communist Party]. *Nguoi Viet Tu Do*, American Edition, January 1980, pp. 24–25.

Lenart, Edith. "Hanoi's Terms for Détente." *Far Eastern Economic Review*, May 20, 1977, p. 16.

Linh, Nguyen Van, *see* Nguyen Van Linh

Lu Phuong. "Concerning the Sale and Circulation of Cultural Items Printed and Produced in Saigon Prior to April 30, 1975." *Saigon Giai Phong*, January 21, 1976, JPRS, no. 66918, *Vietnam*, no. 1778 (March 8, 1976): 39–41.

Luce, Don. "Boat People: U.S. Can Best Help by Recognizing Complicity." *Southeast Asia Record*, week of August 31–September 6, 1979, pp. 11–12.

Nash, H. George. "The Dissolution of the Paris Peace Accords." In Anthony T. Bouscaren, ed., *All Quiet on the Eastern Front: The Death of South Vietnam*. Old Greenwich, Conn.: Devin-Adair Company, 1979.

New Straits Times. "Religious Groups Plan Resistance Movement." Kuala Lumpur: *New Straits Times*, July 14, 1979, p. 4.

Ngan, Le Kim, *see* Le Kim Ngan

Nguoi Viet Tu Do. "Cong Giao o Viet Nam" [Catholicism in Vietnam]. *Nguoi Viet Tu Do*, Japanese Edition, December 1976, p. 33.

[Nguyen Chi Thien]. *Tieng Vong Tu Day Vuc* [A cry from the abyss]. Falls Church, Va.: Committee of Struggle for Political Prisoners in Vietnam, International Committee for the Protection of Intellectuals' Integrity, and *Thoi Tap Magazine*, 1980.

Nguyen Cong Hoan. "Van De Lao Tu tai Viet Nam" [Problems of imprisonment in Vietnam]. *Nguoi Viet Tu Do*, Japanese Edition, June 1977, pp. 30–31.

———. "Van De Nhan Quyen tai Viet Nam" [Human rights problems in Vietnam]. Statement at the U.S. House Subcommittee on International Organizations, July 26, 1977. *Nguoi Viet Tu Do*, American Edition, August 1977, p. 18.

Nguyen Tien Hung. *Economic Development of Socialist Vietnam, 1955–1980*. New York: Praeger, 1977.

Nguyen Van Canh. *Chien Tranh Chinh Tri Cua Cong San* [The communist political warfare]. Saigon: Saigon University Law Faculty, 1974.

Nguyen Van Linh. Interview in *Dai Doan Ket*, November 5, 1977, JPRS, no. 70463, *Vietnam*, no. 2003 (January 11, 1978): 21.

Nhan Dan. "A General Revolution." Editorial. *Nhan Dan*, June 30, 1976, Radio Hanoi, domestic service, July 29, FBIS, *YB*, July 1, p. K8.

———. "Election of Members of People's Councils at the District, Village and Equivalent Levels." *Nhan Dan*, February 3, 1979, JPRS, no. 73106, *Vietnam*, no. 2109 (March 29, 1979): 6–7.

Nivolon, François. "Vietnam on the Aid Trail." *Far Eastern Economic Review*, December 9, 1977, p. 39.

———. "Correcting Past Mistakes" [interview with Nguyen Khac Vien]. *Far Eastern Economic Review*, May 16, 1980, p. 61.

Pham Anh Hai. "Nhan Dan Mien Nam o cac Vung Kinh Te Moi" [The South Vietnamese people in the New Economic Zones]. *Nguoi Viet Tu Do*, Japanese Edition, September 1977, p. 31.

Pham Quang Phuoc. "Participate in the Discussions of Young and Old: The First Step. Young Catholic Priests Urged to Keep Up With Times." *Chinh Nghia*, November 6, 1975, p. 3, JPRS, no. 66613, *Vietnam*, no. 1758 (January 19, 1976): 7.

Phu Yen [pseud.]. "Hien co bao nhieu nguoi Viet Nam bi Cong San giam cam" [How many Vietnamese are there being detained by the Communists?]. *Vietnam Magazine*, August 1981, pp. 17–19, 41.

Phuoc, Pham Quang, *see* Pham Quang Phuoc

Phuong, Lu, *see* Lu Phuong

Pike, Douglas. *History of Vietnamese Communism, 1925–1976*. Stanford: Hoover Institution Press, 1978.

———. "Social Reconstruction in Vietnam." Washington, D.C.: the author, January 1977.

Provisional Revolutionary Government, *see* South Vietnam, Provisional Revolutionary Government of

Quan, Thich Tam, *see* Tam Quan, Thich

Radvanyi, Janos. *Delusion and Reality*. South Bend, Ind.: Gateway Editions, 1978.

South Vietnam, Provisional Revolutionary Government of. Policy Statement No. 02/CS/76, May 25, 1976. Signed by [PRG] President Huynh Tan Phat. Radio Saigon, domestic service, June 9, 1976, FBIS, *YB*, June 10, pp. L1–L5.

Sung, Vo Van, *see* Vo Van Sung

Su That. "Giao Hoi Mien Bac" [Catholicism in North Vietnam]. *Su That*, no. 2, *Nguoi Viet Tu Do*, Japanese Edition, December 1976.

Tam Quan, Thich. "The Bird Has Flown Away." *Phat Giao Viet Nam Monthly Magazine*, December 1979, pp. 21, 23.

Terzani, Tiziano. "Wir sterben und haben keinen Sarg" [We are dying and have no coffin]. *Der Spiegel*, August 24, 1981, pp. 110–18.

Thu, Thich Tri, *see* Tri Thu, Thich

To Huu. "Completely Eradicate Exploitation and Unite the Laboring Peasants to Vigorously and Steadily Advance the Agricultural Cooperativization Movement." Speech at Conference on Agricultural Transformation in the South, November 21–23, 1978. Radio Hanoi, domestic service, broadcast in segments on January 3, 4, 5, 8, and 9, 1979, JPRS, no. 72678, *Vietnam*, no. 2094 (January 1979): 19.

Todd, Olivier. "Comment Hanoi nous a trahis: Une interview de Truong Nhu Tang, ancien ministre du G. r. p. [How Hanoi has betrayed us: An interview with Truong Nhu Tang, former minister of the Provisional Revolutionary Government]. *L'Express*, June 14, 1980, pp. 88–94.

Tran Dien and Vu Van Khoa. Interview in February 1980 with Hoang Huu Quynh. *Viet Nam Hai Ngoai*, March 16, 1980, p. 51.

Tri Thu, Thich. Open letter to chairmen of PRG, Presidium of NLF Central Committee, and Ho Chi Minh City Military Management Committee, November 28, 1975. Distributed November 29 by Executive Council, UBCVN, Ho Chi Minh City. English translation distributed by Vietnamese Buddhist Peace Delegation, 68 boulevard Desgranges, 92330 Sceaux, France.

Turner, Robert. *Vietnamese Communism: Its Origins and Development.* Stanford: Hoover Institution Press, 1975.

United States Embassy, Bangkok, Thailand. Airgram, Pol./Ref. Sections to U.S. Department of State, December 21, 1981. Unclassified; reference no. A-152.

———. Airgram, Pol./Ref. Sections to U.S. Department of State, January 25, 1982. Unclassified; reference no. A-004.

Van Tien Dung. *Dai Thang Mua Xuan* [Great spring victory]. San Diego, Calif.: *Hon Viet Magazine*, 1976.

Vietnam, Socialist Republic of. "'Full Translation' of New SRV Constitution." VNA, in English, December 19, 1980, FBIS, *YB*, December 22, pp. K1–K28.

———, Council of Ministers. Resolution No. 297, November 11, 1977, "On Some Policies Concerning Religion." *Chinh Nghia*, December 20, 1977, p. 6, JPRS, no. 70656, *Vietnam*, no. 2012 (February 17, 1978): 6.

Vietnam Courier. Those Who Leave: The "Problem of Vietnamese Refugees." Hanoi: *Vietnam Courier*, 1979.

Vietnamese Communist Party, Politburo. "Full Text of Resolution on Educational Reform Made Public." Resolution No. 14-NQ/TW, January 11, 1979. *Nhan Dan*, August 25, 1979, JPRS, no. 74380, *Vietnam*, no. 2145 (October 16, 1979): 27–51.

Vo Van Sung. Statement at press conference in Paris. VNA, in English, February 3, 1977, FBIS, *YB*, February 4, p. K1.

V. Q. V. [author's initials]. "National Unification of Legislation." *Vietnam Courier*, June 1977.

Vu Van Khoa, *see* Tran Dien and Vu Van Khoa

Weiss, Peter. *Notes on the Cultural Life of the Democratic Republic of Vietnam.* New York: Delta Books, 1970.

Wilson, Paul. "How Vietnam Profits from Human Traffic." *Far Eastern Economic Review*, January 12, 1979, p. 10.

Yen, Phu, *see* Phu Yen

B. Suggested Reading

Asian Relations Center, Sophia University, Tokyo. *Refugees: The Cry of the Indochinese.* Tokyo: Asian Relations Center, 1980.

Alderman, Jonathan R. *Communist Armies in Politics.* Boulder, Colo.: Westview Press, 1982.

Blakey, Scott. *Prisoner at War: The Survival of Commander Richard A. Stratton.* Garden City, New York: Doubleday, 1978.

Blaufarb, Douglas. *The Counter-Insurgency Era: U.S. Doctrine and Performance.* New York: The Free Press, 1977.

Braestrup, Peter. *Big Story: How the American Press and Television Reported and Interpreted the Crisis of Tet 1968 in Vietnam and Washington.* Boulder, Colo.: Westview Press, 1978.

Brown, Weldon A. *The Last Chopper: The Denouement of the American Role in Vietnam, 1963–1975.* Port Washington, N.Y.: Kennikat Press, 1976.

Buttinger, Joseph L. *Vietnam: The Unforgettable Tragedy.* New York: Horizon Press, 1977.

Chandler, Robert W. *War of Ideas.* Boulder, Colo.: Westview Press, 1981.

Dawson, Alan. *55 Days: The Fall of South Vietnam.* Englewood Cliffs, N.J.: Prentice-Hall, 1977.

Duiker, William J. *The Communist Road to Power in Vietnam.* Boulder, Colo.: Westview Press, 1981.

———. *Vietnam Since the Fall of Saigon.* Athens, Ohio: Ohio University Center for International Studies, 1980.

———. *The Rise of Nationalism in Vietnam, 1900–1941.* Ithaca, N.Y.: Cornell University Press, 1976.

———. *The Comintern and Vietnamese Communism.* Athens, Ohio: Ohio University Center for International Studies, 1975.

Emerson, Gloria. *Winners and Losers.* New York: Random House, 1976.

Gallucci, Robert. *Neither Peace Nor Honor: The Politics of American Military Policy in Vietnam.* Baltimore. Md.: Johns Hopkins University Press, 1975.

Gelb, Leslie, and Betts, Richard. *The Irony of Vietnam: The System Worked.* Washington, D.C.: Brookings Institution, 1978.

Goodman, Allan E. *The Lost Peace: America's Search for a Negotiated Settlement of the Vietnam War.* Stanford: Hoover Institution Press, 1978.

Grant, Zabin. *Survivors.* New York: Norton, 1975.

Hinton, Harold C. *Three and a Half Powers: The New Balance in Asia.* Bloomington, Ind.: Indiana University Press, 1975.

Holsti, Ole R., and Rosenau, James M. *Vietnam, Consensus, and the Belief Systems of American Leaders.* Los Angeles, Calif.: Institution for Transnational Studies, University of Southern California, 1978.

Hooper, Edwin B.; Allard, Dean C.; and Fitzgerald, Oscar P. *The United States Navy and the Vietnam Confrontation*, vol. 1, *The Setting of the Stage to 1959.* Washington, D.C.: U.S. Government Printing Office, 1976.

Hosmer, Stephen T. *The Fall of South Vietnam: Statements Made by Vietnamese Military and Civilian Leaders.* Santa Monica, Calif.: RAND Corp., 1978.

Hubbell, John G., et al. *P.O.W.: A Definitive History of the American Prisoner of War Experience in Vietnam, 1964–1973.* New York: Reader's Digest Press, 1976.

Huynh Kim Khanh. *Vietnamese Communism, 1925–1945.* Ithaca, N.Y.: Cornell University Press, 1982.

Kearns, Doris. *Lyndon Johnson and the American Dream.* New York: Harper & Row, 1976.

Kinnard, Douglas. *The War Managers.* Hanover, N.H.: University Press of New England, 1977.

Kissinger, Henry A. *White House Years.* Boston: Little, Brown & Co., 1979.

Lacouture, Jean. *Vietnam: Voyage à travers une victoire.* Paris: Éditions du Seuil, 1976.

Lake, Anthony, ed. *The Legacy of Vietnam: The War, American Society and the*

Future of American Foreign Policy. New York: New York University Press, 1976.

Lamb, Helen B. *Studies on India and Vietnam*. New York and London: Monthly Review Press, 1976.

Le Duan. *This Nation and Socialism Are One*. Chicago: Vanguard Books, 1976.

Lewy, Guenter. *America in Vietnam*. New York: Oxford University Press, 1978.

MacLear, Michael. *The Ten Thousand Day War: Vietnam, 1945–1975*. New York: St. Martin's Press, 1981.

Millett, Allan R. *A Short History of the Vietnam War*. Bloomington, Ind.: Indiana University Press, 1978.

Nixon, Richard. *RN: The Memoirs of Richard Nixon*. New York: Grosset & Dunlap, 1978.

Nguyen Cao Ky. *Twenty Years and Twenty Days*. New York: Stein and Day, 1976.

Palmer, Dave Richard. *Summons of the Trumpet: U.S.–Vietnam Interspective*. San Rafael, Calif.: Presidio Press, 1978.

Pauker, Guy J.; Golay, Frank H.; and Enloe, Cynthia H. *Diversity and Development in Southeast Asia: The Coming Decade*. New York: McGraw-Hill, 1977.

Porter, Gareth. *A Peace Denied: The United States, Viet Nam and the Paris Agreement*. Bloomington, Ind.: Indiana University Press, 1975.

Provencher, Roland. *Mainland Southeast Asia: An Anthropological Perspective*. Pacific Palisades, Calif.: Goodyear Publishing Co., 1975.

Rees, David. *Vietnam Since Liberation: Hanoi's Revolutionary Strategy*. London: Institution for the Study of Conflict, 1977.

Richer, Philippe. *L'Asie du Sud-Est: Indépendances et Communismes*. Paris. Imprimerie Nationale, 1981.

Salzburg, Joseph S. *Vietnam: Beyond the War*. New York: Exposition Press, 1976.

Santoli, Al, ed. *Everything We Had: An Oral History of the Vietnam War, By 33 American Soldiers Who Fought It*. New York: Random House, 1981.

Sardesai, D. R. *Southeast Asia, Past and Present*. New Delhi: Vikas Publishing House, 1981.

Scalapino, Robert A. *Asia and the Road Ahead: Issues for the Major Powers*. Berkeley: University of California Press, 1975.

Schandler, Herbert Y. *The Unmaking of a President: Lyndon Johnson and Vietnam*. Princeton, N.J.: Princeton University Press, 1977.

Seagrave, Sterling. *Yellow Rain.* New York: M. Evans and Co., 1981.

Simon, Sheldon W. *War and Politics in Cambodia: A Communications Analysis.* Durham, N.C.: Duke University Press, 1976.

Sharp, Grant. *Strategy for Defeat–Vietnam in Retrospect.* San Rafael, Calif.: Presidio Press, 1978.

Snepp, Frank. *Decent Interval: An Insider's Account of Saigon's Indecent End.* New York: Random House, 1977.

Tepper, Elliot L., ed. *Southeast Asian Exodus: From Tradition to Resettlement.* Chicago: University of Chicago Press, 1982.

Terzani, Tiziano. *Giai Phong.* Translated by John Shepley. New York: St. Martin's Press, 1976.

Thompson, Scott W., and Frizzell, Donaldson D. *The Lesson of Vietnam.* New York: Crane, Russak & Co., 1977.

Tran Huynh Chau. *Nhung Nam Cai Tao o Bac Viet* [Years of thought reform in North Vietnam]. Culver City, Calif.: Kim An Quan, 1981.

Trooboff, Peter D., ed. *Law and Responsibility in Warfare: The Vietnam Experience.* Chapel Hill: University of North Carolina Press, 1975.

Trullinger, James Walker. *Village at War: An Account of Revolution in Vietnam.* New York: Longman, 1980.

Van der Kroef, Justus M. *Communism in Southeast Asia.* London: Macmillan, 1981.

Westmoreland, William C. *A Soldier's Report.* New York: Doubleday, 1976.

Wilson, Dick. *The Neutralization of Southeast Asia.* New York: Praeger, 1975.

Woodside, Alexander B. *Community and Revolution in Modern Vietnam.* Boston: Houghton Mifflin, 1976.

Zasloff, Joseph, and MacAlister, Brown. *Communist Indochina and U.S. Foreign Policy.* Boulder, Colo.: Westview Press, 1978.

Index